ROCKIN' DOWN THE HIGHWAY

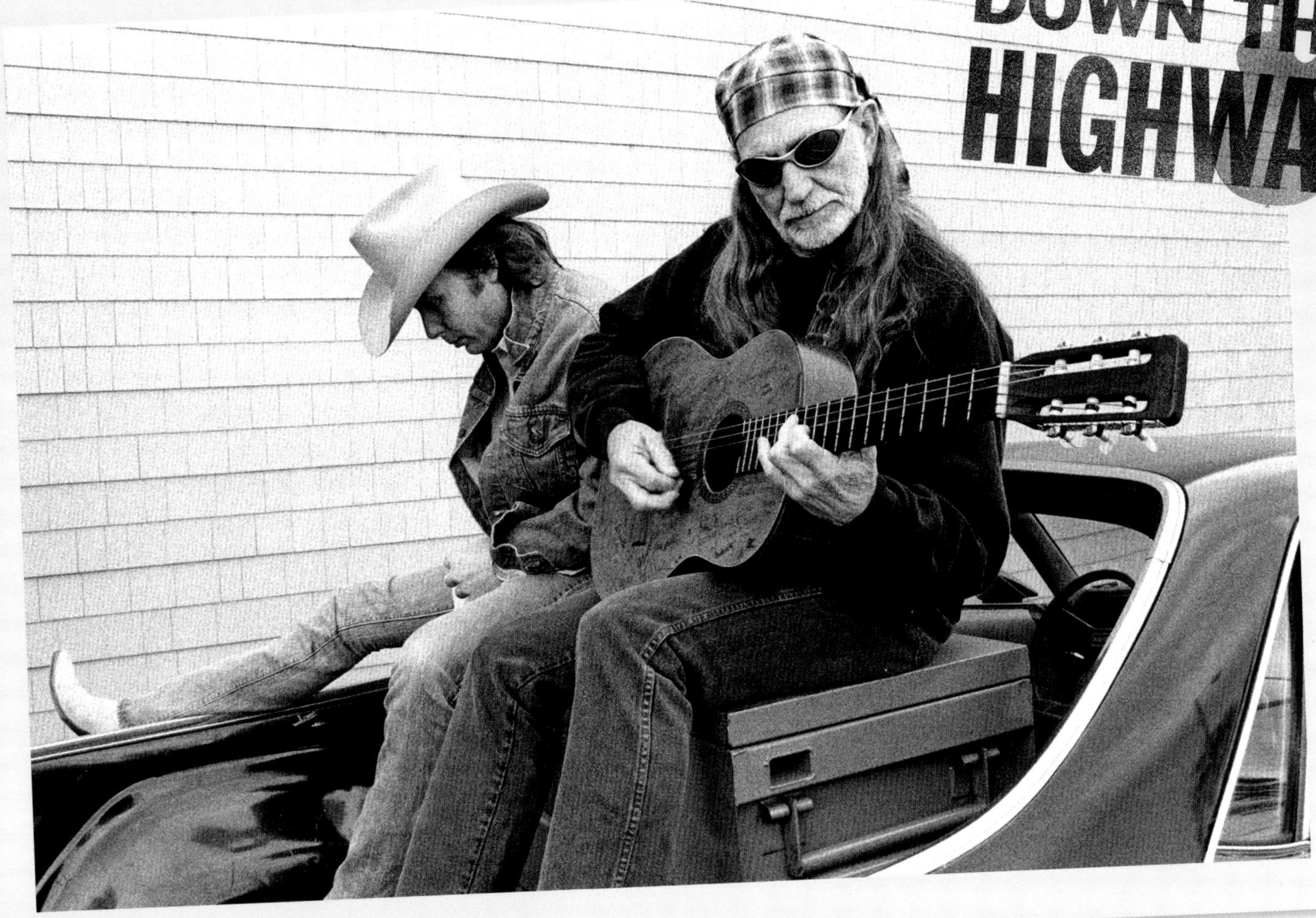

JAY BLAKESBERG

Dwight Yoakam and Willie Nelson

A FAST CAR MAKES YOU WANT TO GET OUT AND DO THINGS IN THE U.S. OF A.

GUIDED BY VOICES,

DRIVING IN THE U.S. OF A.

ROBERT E. POLLARD JR./NEEDMORE SONGS (BMI)

First published in 2006 by Voyageur Press, an imprint of MBI Publishing
Company, Galtier Plaza, Suite 200, 380 Jackson Street, St. Paul, MN
55101-3885 USA

MBI Publishing Company titles are also available at discounts in bulk
quantity for industrial or sales-promotional use. For details write to
Special Sales Manager at MBI Publishing Company, Galtier Plaza,
Suite 200, 380 Jackson Street, St. Paul, MN 55101-3885 USA

MBI Publishing Company titles are also available at discounts in bulk
quantity for industrial or sales-promotional use. For details write to
Special Sales Manager at MBI Publishing Company, Galtier Plaza,
Suite 200, 380 Jackson Street, St. Paul, MN 55101-3885 USA

Library of Congress Cataloging-in-Publication Data

Grushkin, Paul.
Rockin' down the highway: the cars and people that made rock roll/
by Paul Grushkin.
p. cm.
ISBN-13: 978-0-7603-2292-5 (hardback)
  ISBN-10: 0-7603-2292-9
1. Rock music–History and criticism. 2. Rock musicians. 3. Motor
vehicles. I. Title. ML3534.G8 2006
781.660973–dc22

2006004848

Title-page illustration by Coop

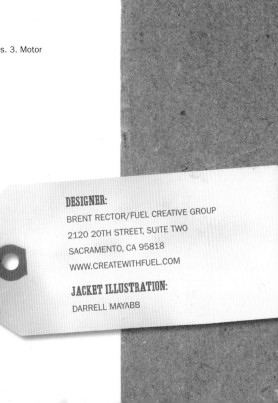

DESIGNER:
BRENT RECTOR/FUEL CREATIVE GROUP
2120 20TH STREET, SUITE TWO
SACRAMENTO, CA 95818
WWW.CREATEWITHFUEL.COM

JACKET ILLUSTRATION:
DARRELL MAYABB

Printed in China

TO MY WIFE, JANE;
MY DAD, PHILIP;
MY MOM, JEAN;
AND REMEMBERING THE
GRUSHKINS' 1963
COUNTRY SQUIRE.

CONTENTS

STEVE COONAN/THE RODDER'S JOURNAL

CHRISTINE MAR

FOREWORD

Growing up in Southern California you can't help but feel all the influences — the beach scene, Hispanic culture, motorcycle culture—and want to create your own riff on it. My uncles were low riders out of Bellflower, and some of my earliest memories are of Impalas and Harley trikes with the real big slicks parked out in front of my grandma's house. They're the same uncles who got me into rock & roll.

I was raised on American roots music, the right stuff: Woody Guthrie, Harry Smith's *Smithsonian Anthology of American Folk Music*, early, early Rolling Stones, Johnny Cash, and Buck Owens. I related to the beat and to the subject matter. By the time I got to high school, the music of the '70s was so self-indulgent that I had to turn to punk rock. I was a pretty angry guy and punk rock was just like early rock & roll: working class, meaningful, short, sweet, and from the heart. It's like when I cruise in my blue Cadillac; I can't help but think of "Maybelline"—it's pure and it's right.

Likewise, for me, customizing cars is all about finding the pure line, refining a shape to get to its essence. It's all about taking something Detroit started and making the necessary adjustments. Trim it down, stretch it out,

and get rid of the unnecessary stuff. It's the same thing I'm searching for in my own music. Whittle it down, *find the line*.

The Hootenanny Festival that we produce in Southern California says a lot about the merging of car culture and the music scene. I mean, they go hand in hand, right? There's a new hands-on appreciation these days for cars from the '40s—rebuilding flatheads, primer paint, exposed welds—but also the really beautiful work, too. From my perspective, it's got the right *punk attitude*. And the best thing is, you can learn from the older people. I know I do—every chance I get.

It's funny, though . . . when someone is playing music on the tour bus, I can listen to it. But when I'm alone in my own car, the '54 Chevy or one of the Cadillacs, whether I'm just running errands or taking a drive up the coast, I don't play music. I think while I drive. Always have. I listen to the engine and I listen to my thoughts. I try to take in the essence of the open road. Tooling down a highway, your mind just drifting all over the place—that's really the greatest feeling in the world.

— *Mike Ness*

SAM SARGENT

Paul Grushkin

FROM THE AUTHOR

They say the first hot rod was the second car sold—to the guy who wanted *his* car to go faster than the first guy's. It doesn't seem unreasonable to imagine, then, that the first car song was written by a guy up the street, about the second guy's hot rod. It wasn't exactly rock & roll yet—for rock did not yet exist—but it *was* the antecedent to what has become one of the most infamous and pervasive aspects of American pop culture: the combination of fast cars and rock music.

Exactly when the hottest popular music evolved into rock & roll is as much up for debate as when the first factory-built iron was chopped, channeled, stroked, and bored into the first "gow job," an early term for hot rod. But certainly by the 1930s, people knew a souped-up car when they saw one. Rock & roll was no different: You knew it when you saw it.

No one had to tell you what rock & roll was. It was obvious when it arrived in your life. Most important, each one of us—even Elvis—has discovered it for our self, like a personal epiphany. *That's All Right Mama.* Memphis. Sun Studios. July 1954.

The kind of rock & roll you discovered depended completely on when and where you grew up. Ohio? Denver? New Jersey? In due course, most people took a position on one very essential matter: What *really* rocked was what really rocked *your* particular socks. Not unlike one's personal apprecia-

tion for a smokin', super-cherry GTO. If you instinctively like it when you first see it, then you as a person—that is, you as a person of *taste*—are in part newly defined, and, congrats, you've just joined the club.

Long before car radio evolved into car stereo, it also was clear to people of taste that any car—hot rodded, customized, or bone stock—drove a lot better with rock & roll swirling around the front seat, and, just as surely, that same rock sounded even better in a bitchin' custom, rod, or stocker moving proudly down the avenue, heading for the highway.

When America's early love affair with the automobile finally melded with the coming of rock & roll by the early 1950s to form the rebellious American lifestyle we embrace today, it defined Car Culture, or as it was later interpreted by Robert Williams, Ed "Big Daddy" Roth, and others, *Kustom* Culture. Rock music was the missing link. Rock was the first completely "hopped up" sound made by and for white, black, Latino, and Asian American teens and hip adults, that pivotal segment of society which for generations since has determined and defined "cool".

In the case of the automobile, "hopping something up" is the instinctual response to "the need for speed." It dates back to the turn of the twentieth century when Henry Ford developed two race cars whose performance attracted the financing to kick-start Ford Motor Company. It continued in the 1920s when the first no-name gearheads modified their cars by extracting weight (usually by removing some combination of the roof, hood, bumpers, windshield, and fenders), lowering the profile, tuning the engine, and substituting tires and wheels for added traction. All of this combined to achieve an amalgamation of mysterious good looks at first most apparent to the builder and his friends. That is, the vehicle now looked *personalized*, if not downright racy and hip.

Before long, it was not hard for the general public to distinguish a go-fast ride from a purely factory-built one. The byproduct was a culture with its own clothes, language, and icons that achieved its notoriety post–World War II, when much of the country was just beginning to discover what was going on in heretofore isolated California. But whether you caught it in its infancy (prewar) or its teenage years (postwar), the establishment generally frowned upon it. The rebels loved it. "It" sounded like *Vrrrrroooooomm.* "It" smelled like danger to society. "It" looked pure and simply *outlaw.* "It" was getting ready for rock & roll.

The essence—and paradox—of cool is to look and sound *different,* but in a thoroughly appealing way. Hot rodding, as one example of cool, speaks to the American penchant for promoting individuality and finding freedom, in this case speed and the open road. With the advent of hot rodding, as with the soon-to-be advent of rock & roll, *anyone* could modify *anything* and in fact create something altogether incomparable, one-off, and supremely unique (i.e., cool) out there in the garage, hidden away from Mom, Dad, and the Preacher Man. Same thing went for making rock music, out in that same garage.

What's curious is that rock & roll took so much longer— decades longer—than hot rodding to evolve into its own and finally enable a point of view that instinctively *rocked* (we now know this is due in part to the racial divide obstructing white America from recognizing its soul brothers).

Once rock arrived—possibly in 1951, likely by 1954, almost assuredly by 1955, and most definitely by 1956—it emulated qualities already inherent in the hopped-up automotive world, particularly in regard to "sound" and "attitude." Once melded, the two were inseparable. The point of view was identical: It was about the stance, about the pose. That's one *rockin'* rod. That sound? It *rocks.*

Cars and the music it attracted were all about the appeal to the individual's libido, that unfettered, creative, sexual energy that defines personality and individuality—which in essence is the desire to *git sum.* In rock & roll, it's why people instinctively want to rush the stage when the music's on fire. In car culture, it's about the ever-hopeful longing one has for a particularly fine machine of a special vintage.

But neither rock nor car culture nor the adventure behind *gittin' sum* comes with a road map. Rather, all involve the discovery of the basic concepts (cars, sex, rock) and their application (rodding, getting laid, rockin' out). Turning on to previously unheard new sounds or stepping back to admire something with inexplicably good looks involves speaking in tongues to the faithful about basic lust, getting to third base, and then finally (yes!) scoring. The passion for rock and cars is about hitting the chord, getting the keys, making the score. It's always been about firing up the ride and mashing

down the accelerator. And, as Bruce Springsteen tells us, kickin' back on those crushed velvet seats. So cool.

The cars came first. We generally think of mainstream hot rodding as beginning after World War II. The years 1945 through 1950 were the first to show a greater sophistication in style and purpose, fueled by the emergence of the first speed equipment shops and the abundance of vintage tin from the 1930s. Particularly, but not exclusively, Southern California provided attractive flat spaces—broad streets and endless boulevards, not to mention the first-era highways leading out of Burbank and central L.A. to dry lakes like Muroc and El Mirage—for people to open up the throttle, drag with other cars, and establish performance standards. And just as important, to meet, provocatively, at the drive-ins and car hops, to cruise up and down the avenues and sneer at the straights, and above all else, to wow others, particularly of the opposite sex.

Like The Who later sang, it was all about "Going Mobile." From the very beginning, the idea was that you had your ride, you had your honey by your side, and the car radio (soon to be car stereo) was singing to you and everybody around you (well, at least to those who know to tune in).

As Tower of Power would later assess the tally-ho, young America, naïve but eager, was on the first leg of the great hip trip, where the grandest adventures awaited the hipper than hip. So if this evolution started, in the words of Chuck Berry, "Riding along in my automobile," just as steel would beget fiberglass and 8-track would beget MP3, the full spectrum of cars in rock came to encompass everything from rockabilly to classic British blues to snarly-ass punk. Yet, it was all good. As in five thousand very different rods and customs at a state fairgrounds show, as in a hundred very different rock & roll concerts. All unique in concept, yet all imbued with the same rebellious, questing, scoring spirit. Thereby the phrase (thank you, Talking Heads), *Same as it ever was.*

One of the great unanswered questions has been "What were the first hot rodders listening to?" Not rock & roll, but certainly its predecessors. It depended on who and where you were in those years. The first breakaway tunes might have ID'd themselves by the words "rock" or "rock & roll" in their titles (e.g., Bill Haley's "Rock Around the Clock"). What became rock might have been in the first antitheses to the jitterbugging wartime big bands now heard in the eager squawk of smaller, sax- or piano-led boogie-woogie combos and the rumble of "jump blues" bands like Wynonie Harris and His All Stars, road-testing songs like "Good Rockin' Tonight."

Or, the first rock might have been made—if you heard it that way—by black vocal groups, urban doo-woppers like the funky Medallions out of Los Angeles. Possibly it was in the music of Hank Williams, who by 1951 was one of the first to push country beyond hillbilly and give it a more worldly sensibility. But almost certainly rock evolved out of rhythm-and-blues, the by-then-constantly-evolving black sound that white America—including Elvis—at first discovered, then craved, and then emulated, contorting it into something even newer and more explosive.

Billy Vera, writing in the foreword to *What Was the First Rock 'N' Roll Record?*, put it this way: "[Did we wait] to call it rock when the lyric content finally dealt with dumb white teenage concerns, like cars, school, and milkshakes? When did R&B wake up one morning and find it had devolved into another genre of another color? It's perhaps the most subjective question in the history of (popular) music—and the answer might depend upon any number of things. *When* was one growing up? *Where* did one grow up? Did one have access to radio stations that played this music?"

Rock met "the roll" when the high school quarterback picked up his date in Pop's '57, toe-tapping to Pat Boone's cracker-honky version of Little Richard emanating from the AM frequency through two tinny below-dash speakers. It was the same "moment" when perhaps some fine R&B was playing in the SO-CAL push truck as Alex Xydias hurtled down the salt flats on another record-setting run. Rock met "the roll" in the same first-generation tune heard in a London-bound cab when Gene Vincent raced with the Devil, Eddie Cochran at his side, as the slippery black pavement rolled up and vanished in a sudden, awful crash.

The confluence of the rock & roll and the car worlds is served best by what appear first as apocryphal tales: The night so-and-so dropped a 327 into his '54 Chevy, or the night the Yardbirds became Led Zeppelin at a small club in Denmark. One such tale I find telling was recently remembered by Richard Harrington of the *Washington Post*, writing about the simultaneous discovery of fuzztone, feedback, distortion, the power chord, and "the notion of the electric guitar as a dangerous weapon." All this in the innocence of Link Wray introducing "Rumble," a hot rod tune if ever there was one.

"When Wray went into U.S. Recording Studios at Vermont Avenue and L Street NW in Washington, D.C., in 1958," wrote Harrington, "he had trouble replicating a song originally improvised a few months earlier at a Fredericksburg, Va., sock hop. Link and his Waymen were backing the Diamonds, who had a dance hit with 'The Stroll.' Wray didn't know the song, but when he was asked to play it, he followed a strong, stroll-like beat laid down by drummer and brother Doug Wray and bassist and cousin Shorty Horton. What slowly unfurled was a menacing guitar sound so dangerously cool the crowd demanded it three more times.

"'Onstage,' Wray further explained in a 1997 interview, 'I'd been playing it real loud through these small 6-watt Sears and Roebuck amplifiers, and the kids were hollering and screaming for it. But, in the studio, the sound was too clean, too country. So I started experimenting, and I punched holes in the speakers with a pencil, trying to re-create that dirty, fuzzy sound I was getting onstage. And, on the third take, there it was, just like *magic*.'"

Wray had just hot-rodded his equipment. He'd just *scored*.

Wray's inventive—and extremely cool—sound influenced rockers as diverse as Pete Townshend, Paul McCartney and John Lennon, Bob Dylan, the Sex Pistols, and Bruce Springsteen. Not unlike the influence Bob Hirohata's cool, Barris-customized 1951 Mercury had on hot rodders and customizers of his and future generations.

Certainly that same rock & roll parable is in the evolution of the American custom car, a side-by-side invention with the hot rod. Custom cars sometimes had hot rod aspects in the engine and drivetrain, but the focus was on eye-popping, low-riding modifications and the cars' potential as practical daily drivers. The custom was a purely American vision of the highway-mobile as conveying truly personal style. That same vision was imbued in the music which accompanied the ride. Reflect, perhaps, on the almost singular sound of Golden Earring's "Radar Love," nearly unanimously selected on most people's lists as one of the great driving songs because of the grandeur imagined. Or, reflect upon the pure highway look imagined-up in ZZ Top's CadZZilla.

Customizing. Just as the custom car is a reflection of the highly personal, nearly everyone has his or her own feeling for the "best car music" or its corollary, the "best driving music." The choices appear instinctive and deeply felt, personally customized, as it were. Arguments on the topic have been wrangled over for generations—as in, "What station do we listen to?" or "What CD do ya wanna hear?" all the way to online blogs about appropriate MP3s for a road trip.

But there's always this unwavering rule: Rock and custom culture, and indeed the auto industry, must evolve to stay ahead (again, Tower of Power: *What's hip today may soon become passé.*). The comfortable is invariably met head-on by the uncomfortable. *Chhhhh-changes*, as David Bowie would tell you. We see this currently in the resurgence of so-called "rat rods" as an understandable reaction to new-millennium $100K jobs that were putting rodding out of reach. Kind of how punk rock was the reaction to corporate rock in the '70s and '80s. This constant evolution reminds me of Robert Hunter and Jerry Garcia's great driving song, "The Wheel," as played by the Grateful Dead, *The wheel is turning, and you can't slow down. You can't let go and you can't hold on. You can't go back and you can't stand still.*

After absorbing all this and settling in behind the wheel, the side mirror tells us a grand parade has formed. The entourage that's to take us *Rockin' Down the Highway* (thank you, Doobie Brothers) includes Ike Turner and cousin Jackie Brenston's Rocket 88, the Catallo family's *Little Deuce Coupe*, Springsteen's Pink Cadillac, the Merry Pranksters' "Further" bus, Joni Mitchell's phantom '57 Biscayne, Mustang Sally in her "1965," the Big Three's muscle cars with all the gearhead punks aboard, and the ringmaster, Funkmaster Flex, and all the rappers' latest whips taking point. All the rides and musical points of view are quite different, all are different hues and flavors, yet all are linked in spirit through the passage of time.

This history, then, is all about a nexus, when people who'd discovered "The Look" first heard "The Sound," or vice versa. Best of all, since the story has no end, the reader will find that, as Paul Simon once put it, "Every generation throws a hero up the pop charts." What's next? *Who's* next?

Ride on Josephine, Ride On. We're On the Road to Find Out.

— Paul Grushkin

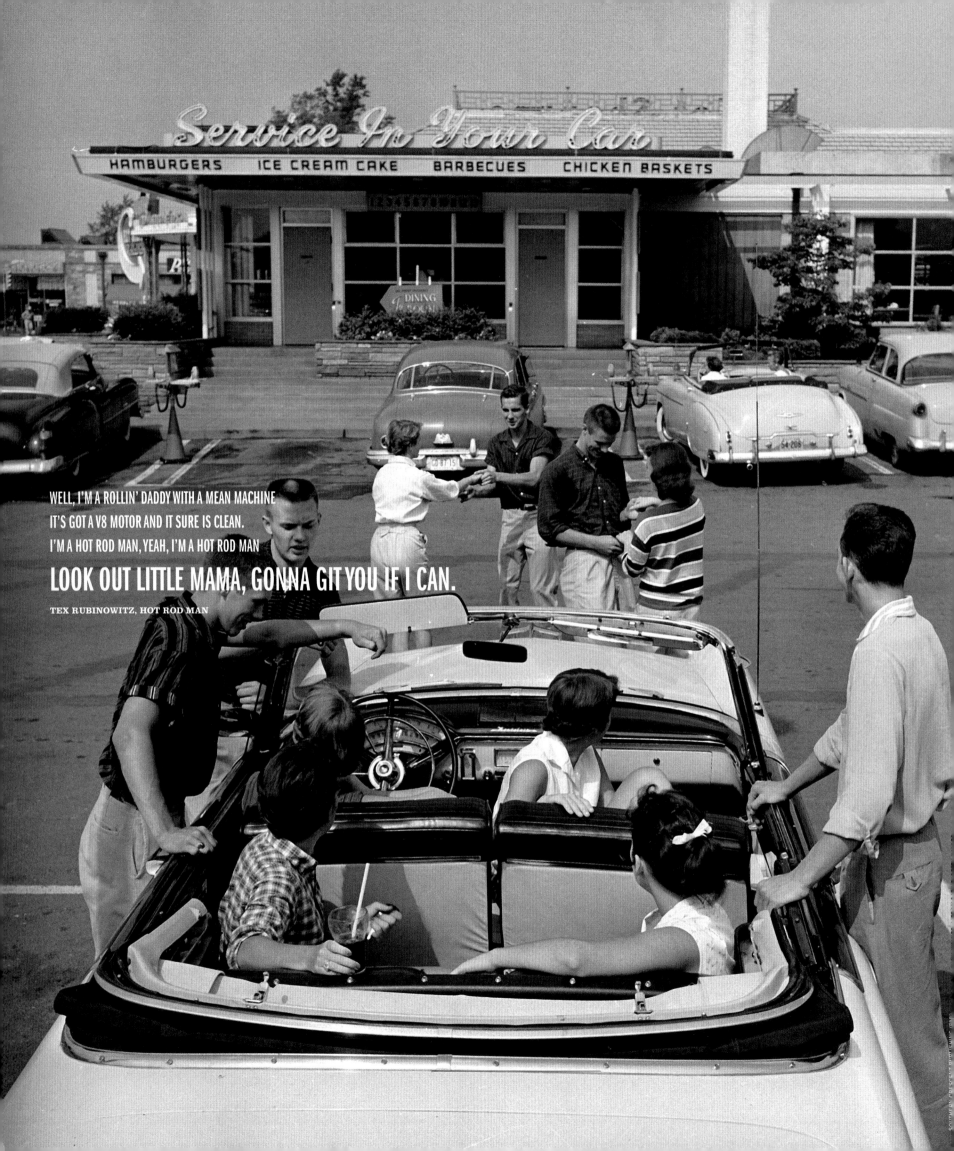

WELL, I'M A ROLLIN' DADDY WITH A MEAN MACHINE
IT'S GOT A V8 MOTOR AND IT SURE IS CLEAN.
I'M A HOT ROD MAN, YEAH, I'M A HOT ROD MAN

LOOK OUT LITTLE MAMA, GONNA GIT YOU IF I CAN.

TEX RUBINOWITZ, HOT ROD MAN

ROCKET 88
The First Generation

The car hop was the first "place" actually defined by the combination of cars and rock & roll (as well as young people and fast food).

Following World War II, once rationing ended and factories began producing new goods for a vast, clamoring public, just about everyone in America who had dreamed about replacing their old car had purchased one. It was the New Age of the automobile, the *American* car made in Detroit. Lots of chrome, more horsepower, and, shortly, a sleek, modern look. The idea was, in the words of the Chevrolet commercial, "See the USA," but the general concept was, "Get out of the house and be seen in your new ride."

Postwar Americans loved their vehicles so much they did everything possible in them. More babies were probably conceived in automobiles than at any time previous. People watched movies while comfortably seated at outdoor drive-in theaters. And they ate out on Fridays and Saturdays at drive-in restaurants soon to be dubbed "car hops." They did not purchase a carry-out meal and drive to a picnic area—they drove to a drive-in restaurant where they were served a meal, quite comfortably, on their car's mohair bench seats, with the radio on. Their servers were young men and women (also known as "car hops"), and popular music often played on loudspeakers in the parking lot.

There had been drive-in restaurants before World War II started. On the Jersey Shore a small chain of drive-ins, Celia Brown's, was operating as early as 1936. But the true popularity of drive-in dining came in the late 1940s, lasting well into the mid-1960s, precisely mirroring the rise of rock & roll.

While some independent drive-ins served local fare, such as fried clams if near a seashore, or hush puppies in the Deep South, most were of the type made popular by two chain restaurants: White Castle and A&W Root Beer. The food here seemed newly conceived, almost like the fine new hopped-up music that accompanied the scene   it was all about cheeseburgers, French fries, milkshakes, brand-name soft drinks, and Wolfman Jack.

While many car hops operated just in the summer months, and at some the servers actually worked on roller skates, all car hops presented a new semi-secret opportunity to *get it on*. It was all about the *pull* of the scene. The car hop was the new gathering point, an asphalt landscape that changed nightly, where popular culture replicated and transformed to the beat.

Car hops were all about showing off the new ride, the new speed equipment, the new boyfriend or girlfriend, and sharing the latest tunes with your friends. Of course it also was, for many, the first opportunity to sneak beer and learn how to make out without going all the way.

Most postwar drive-ins functioned like large parking lots with a highly efficient restaurant in the center. The owner worked inside with a cook in a back room. Car hop servers kept track of each order, carried the tray to the customers, hooked it to the open window of the car, and collected the money. When finished, the driver flashed his lights so the server could remove the tray.

Really big drive-ins had parking slots for the cars, often covered like carports. They also had a pillar in each slot that held a two-way microphone so the driver could order the meal from a menu displayed on the pillar. It was the microphone, sadly, that led to the rise of drive-*thru* restaurants like McDonalds.

The car hop was a constant, unspoken, modern-day invitation to teenagers and young singles to break out of their home or work environment and gather independently of Mom, Dad, and the boss. It was a step beyond structured high school entertainment. It was a place to go to get more than just good eats—it was where young people tasted some of their first serious lip action. And in due course, the car hop became a place to go instead of the movies and before "parking somewhere"—which, like all parents know, is the beginning of the "Highway to Hell."

IN BURBANK, CALIFORNIA, NEXT TO THE TOWN OF TOLUCA LAKE AND HARD BY THE FILM STUDIOS OF NBC, DISNEY, AND WARNER BROS., IS **THE ORIGINAL BOB'S BIG BOY RESTAURANT,** WHERE UNDER AN ENORMOUS NEON SIGN THE CAR HOP IS ALIVE AND WELL TODAY. THERE YOU CAN STILL GET THEIR FAMOUS DOUBLE-DECKER HAMBURGER, FRIES, AND A CHERRY COKE FOR UNDER $10. YOU ALSO GET AUTHENTIC CAR HOP SERVICE UNDER THE AWNINGS.

BOB'S WAS FOUNDED IN 1949 BY SCOTT MACDONALD AND WARD ALBERT. THE BUILDING IN BURBANK WAS DESIGNED BY ARCHITECT WAYNE MCALLISTER, WHO WENT WITH A STREAMLINE MODERNE DESIGN THAT ANTICIPATED THE MORE ROCK & ROLL '50S COFFEE SHOP FEEL TO COME—AN EXTRAORDINARY ACHIEVEMENT, ACTUALLY.

TODAY THE SCENE IS "RETRO," BUT NEVERTHELESS QUITE REAL. ON WEEKEND NIGHTS YOU CAN TAKE IN THE GATHERINGS OF THE CLASSIC CARS AND SOMETIMES EVEN DO SIDE-BY-SIDE CHOCOLATE CONES WITH SOME OF THE GREAT LOS ANGELES DEUCE COUPE PERSONALITIES, SUCH AS ARTIST ROBERT WILLIAMS. IT'S ALSO JUST BLOCKS DOWN THE STREET FROM GEORGE BARRIS' KUSTOM CITY HEADQUARTERS.

WELL YOU GASSED HER UP, BEHIND THE WHEEL
WITH YOUR ARM AROUND YOUR SWEET ONE

IN YOUR OLDSMOBILE
BARRELIN' DOWN THE BOULEVARD

YOU'RE LOOKING FOR THE HEART OF SATURDAY NIGHT

TOM WAITS, LOOKING FOR THE HEART OF SATURDAY NIGHT

FIFTH FLOOR MUSIC INC. (ASCAP); RALPH CRANE, BLACK STAR, LIFE MAGAZINE/GETTY IMAGES

LET'S GO TO THE HOP

A major rite of passage for every rock & roller is the drive to the first rock show, to see the bands play live. The concert poster is the invitation. *Let's go!* But the music itself first must be the enticement, and by 1948, the big band sound was becoming stale and dated.

Rock appeared at a time when centuries of racial tensions in the United States finally came to the surface. Following the lead of the landmark 1954 Supreme Court decision overturning "separate but equal," African Americans began to protest, at first timorously and then very vigorously, the rampant segregation in the schools and public facilities, as well as discrimination in the armed services and the workplace. Their music—the urban blues and its cousin, rhythm & blues—gave them both succor and pleasure, and, surprisingly, a leadership position. Now young white people, including those who'd survived the killing fields of Europe and the Pacific, began to hear black popular music not as "race records" or "New Orleans–style jazz," but as a modern attraction with a whole new sound.

In early 1951, Cleveland disc jockey Alan Freed visited Alan Mintz's downtown record store and learned that white teenagers were snapping up R&B records. Immediately sensing the making of *something big,* Freed changed the name of his music show on station WJW from the lame "Record Rendezvous" to "Moondog's Rock & Roll House Party," and began broadcasting black music to his white audience. It's said Freed, a.k.a. "Moondog," first used the term "rock & roll" to describe the music because he thought the racial connotation of "rhythm & blues" might limit its appeal.

On March 21, 1952, Freed organized the first rock & roll concert, advertised as "The Moondog Coronation Ball." The audience and performers were drawn from places well outside Cleveland, and were mixed in race. This was a *huge* development. With the excitement building and then climaxing, the night ended just as soon as it began, after just one song, as a riot broke out when thousands of fans tried to get into the sold-out concert hall. But all was not a loss—now the world could see the attraction was no longer Frank Sinatra, Bing Crosby, the Andrews Sisters, and the Dorsey bands. To borrow from Nirvana, many years later, "it smelled like teen spirit."

A culture industry began to form around teen entertainment. Social and racial barriers slowly began to crumble against the forces of good old American capitalism. Before long, cars themselves were being marketed to the emergent youth market. Now young people could drive any distance to hear the sound they loved.

Did high school and college really look this way back then? Did everyone have a so-carefully, so-cleanly constructed hot rod as the ones depicted on the covers of the November 1951, May 1952, and February 1954 issues of *Hot Rod* magazine? Probably … not. Furthermore, as the 1950s began, were all the white kids dancing to rock & roll? Definitely not (rock & roll was still a few years away). But myth-making is part of the American hot rod and rock & roll fantasies.

More likely, the soon-to-be rockers were listening to R&B, country, and what remained of the late swing era as a precursor to cool jazz. Perhaps they were even jiving. But segregation was the order of the day, and there was no fundamental and lasting black-white crossover yet. That would come with Elvis Presley and Little Richard in 1955. Something was about to launch nationwide, but it had not yet done so, despite the popular myths we often look back at.

Further, high school kids were likely driving not-yet-customized postwar sedans (Mom and Dad's cars), and only the hippest were piloting junkers and beaters daily. Automotive artist Kent Bash remembers those staid but inexorably changing times this way: "Like many young impressionable boys in the early '50s, my imagination raced with the burgeoning images of America's emerging pop revolution. Comics, science-fiction magazines (now dealing with rockets, jets, and nuclear arms), and pulp paperbacks—now including Henry Felsen's juvenile novels (the first, *Hot Rod*, coming in 1951)—were all required reading. So I watched with envy as my brothers built their first hot rod and listened to Hank Williams and early rockabilly on the one country music station in the rural west San Fernando Valley.

"There are mysteries both real and imagined waiting to be discovered by those who reach driving age. I got to share in many of the first adventures, discovering the joys of leaf springs and dirt roads. It was just about the time for Jack Kerouac (*On the Road*, written a few years earlier, was finally published in 1957), the beatniks and the beat generation, and the frenetic building of model racers and kits. It was not a full-blown change-in-the-weather … yet … but it was all part of the backdrop of my youth."

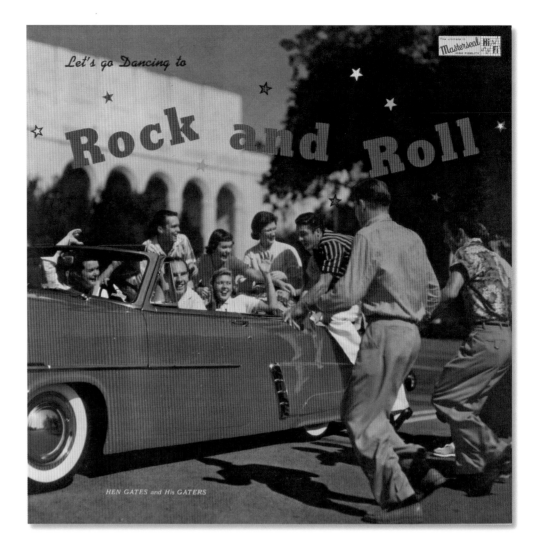

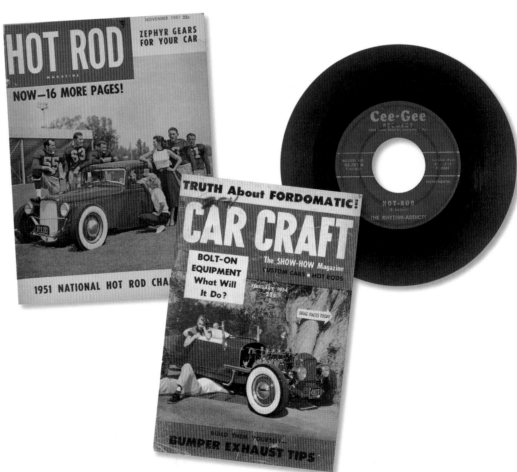

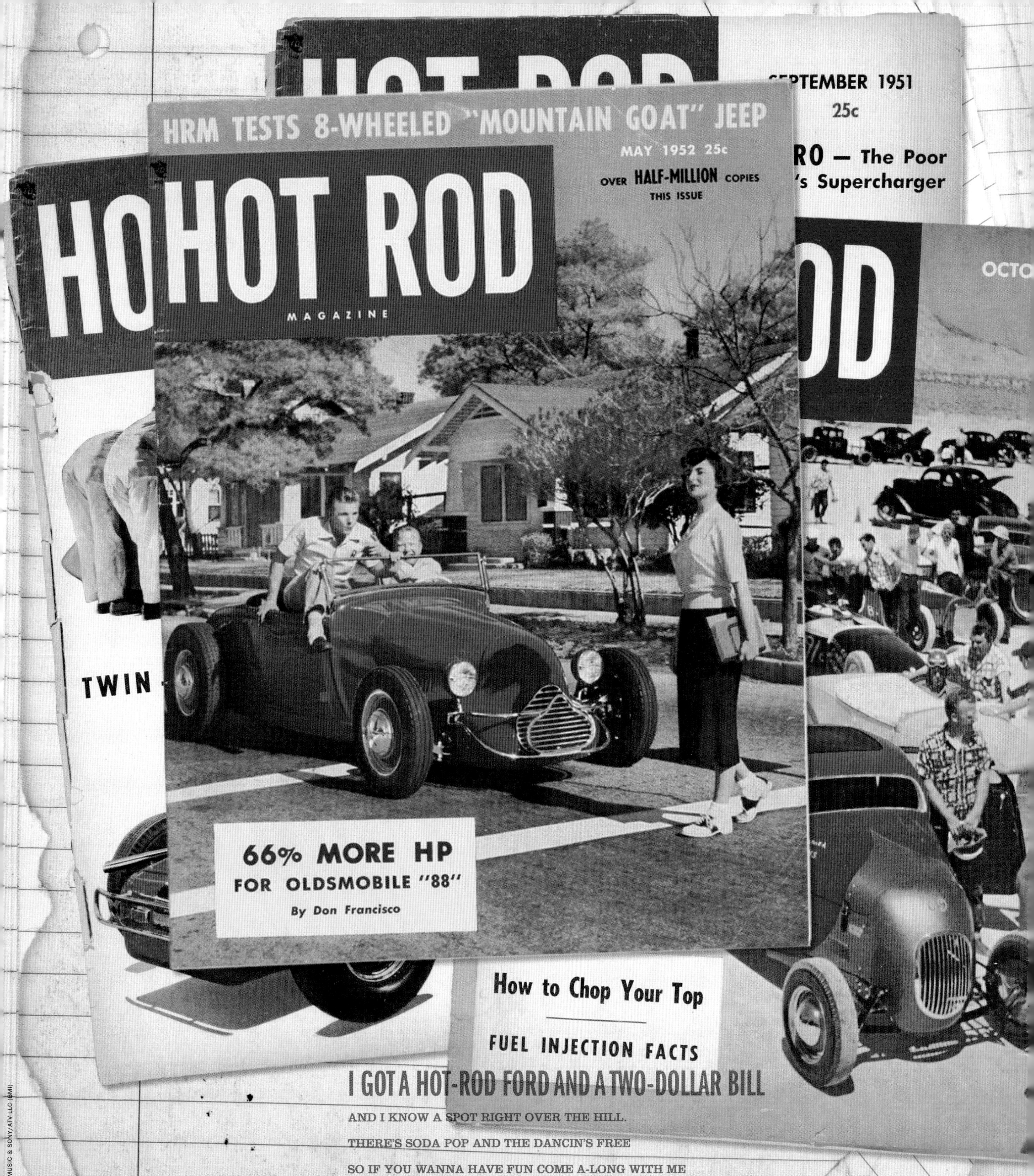

SEPTEMBER 1951

25c

RO — The Poor
's Supercharger

HRM TESTS 8-WHEELED "MOUNTAIN GOAT" JEEP

MAY 1952 25c

OVER **HALF-MILLION** COPIES
THIS ISSUE

HOHOT ROD
MAGAZINE

OCTO

OD

TWIN

66% MORE HP
FOR OLDSMOBILE "88"

By Don Francisco

How to Chop Your Top

———

FUEL INJECTION FACTS

I GOT A HOT-ROD FORD AND A TWO-DOLLAR BILL

AND I KNOW A SPOT RIGHT OVER THE HILL.

THERE'S SODA POP AND THE DANCIN'S FREE

SO IF YOU WANNA HAVE FUN COME A-LONG WITH ME

HANK WILLIAMS, HEY, GOOD LOOKIN'

DISCHARGED

WRENCHING

The hot rod movement (as with its counterpart, rock & roll) has always been a grassroots groundswell, an underground, highly personalized art form inspiring awe in race-eager young people and—most important—instilling fear in their elders … their newly *suburban* elders. It's always been about swapping ideas, tearing old cars apart, rebuilding, and—ultimately—racing on the streets, two-lane highways, and dry lakes. Not unlike the concept of garage rock and trying out the music in the clubs.

How did the word get out? In the beginning—immediately post World War II—it was about timing associations (the most famous being the Southern California Timing Association), even before the proliferation of car clubs. Then came the first national magazines, beginning with Robert E. Petersen's *Hot Rod*, first published in January 1948. Others followed, including *Honk!*, *Throttle*, *Hop Up*, *Car Craft*, and *Rod & Custom*. These publications brought on early specialized how-to handbooks. Dog-eared, oil-stained copies circulated among the cognoscenti, disseminating tips and technique, customizing trends, lip-smacking photos, and the latest track records.

The demand for speed and power equipment resulted in the inevitable: the advent of the speed shop. The fact is, most of the pioneers did a little bit of everything but over time the men who essentially invented the automotive aftermarket would come to be remembered for more specific achievements: manufacturers such as Vic Edelbrock, Ed Iskenderian, Kong Jackson, and Eddie Meyer; dealers such as Alex Xydias (So-Cal Speed Shop); engine builders such as Ed Pink and Bobby Meeks; customizers such as Sam and George Barris, Gene Winfield, and Darryl Starbird; innovative car owners and builders such as Doane Spencer; and racers such as Ak Miller, Mickey Thompson, Ray Brown, and Don Garlits, all combined to popularize custom aftermarket product. Motorama events on both the West and East Coasts solidified the appeal, and Wally Parks first proposed, then formed, the National Hot Rod Association to sanction drag strips. Heroes all, just like the early rockers who were about to ascend their own stage.

HOT ROD
The Automotive "HOW-TO-DO-IT" Magazine

SPECIAL
SOUP THAT CHEV!
HYDRAULIC LIFTERS
Operation and Care

MAY 1955 25c

SPEED MECHANICS

AUTO RACES

JANUARY 25c

SO YOU WANT TO BUILD A HOT ROD!!

HOW TO SOUP ON A BUDGET

THE NORTHWEST'S WILDEST ROD

LAKES PLUGS FOR..... $1.50

EIGHT CARB LOG MANIFOLD $28

EXPERTS PLAN YOUR BEST $150 SOUP-UP

GEAR FOR GO WITH Q-C COGS

1951 WYOMING
18 316

How To Build HOT RODS

FAWCETT 75c BOOK 156

SPEED DIRECTORY

OFFICIAL PROGRAM OF THE 1950 HOT ROD AND MOTOR SPORTS SHOW

Sponsored by
RUSSETTA TIMING ASSOCIATION

25¢ AT THE SHOW 50c ELSEWHERE

LAURIE
LAURIE RECORDS INC. NEW YORK

RECORD NO. LR 3219
Schwartz Music Co., Inc.
ASCAP

Time: 2:14
PK4M 4627-2

HOT ROD CITY (Vocal)
(E. Maresca–T. Bogdany)
THE HUBCAPS

POPULAR MECHANICS

75c
IN UNITED STATES AND CANADA

HOT ROD Handbook
and Directory of America's Finest Speed Shops

How to...
HOP UP AN ENGINE
GET 25% MORE HP.
DESIGN A CHASSIS
FORM A HOT-ROD CLUB
QUALIFY FOR RACING
Plus complete listings
OF MANUFACTURERS...
SPEED SHOPS...HOT-ROD
AND SPORTS-CAR
ASSOCIATIONS

By GEORGE HILL
Charter Member, 200 MPH Club

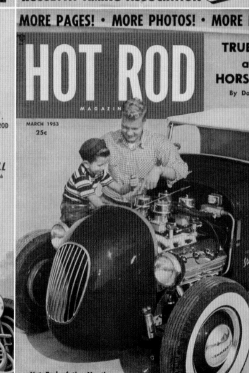

MORE PAGES! • MORE PHOTOS! • MORE

HOT ROD
MAGAZINE

TRUE
a
HORS
By Do

MARCH 1953
25c

Hot Rod of the Month—
FIREPOWER Street Roadster

HOT ROD RECORDS

In 1948, Robert E. Petersen began publishing *Hot Rod* magazine, the first national publication for a small, but growing group of enthusiasts. Arguably the first hot rod cartoonist, Tom Medley created the "Stroker McGurk" cartoon character while he was also the ad salesman for *Hot Rod*. Subsequently, he became publisher of *Rod & Custom* magazine and helped create the first-ever hot rod swap meet, in the early '50s at the L.A. Roadsters' Father's Day get-together, and the first Street Rod Nationals in 1970. A top photographer (page 89) and enthusiastic automotive entrepreneur, Medley also had the idea for Colossal Hot Rod Records in the early '50s (although the music was the work of Kid Ory's Dixieland jazz band, fronted by Scatman Crothers). Colossal's "big hit" was the double-sided "Saturday Night Drag Race," which received an unexpected plaudit in *Time* magazine and paralleled Arkie Shibley's "Hot Rod Race" (page 54).

RHINO RECORDS' *HOT RODS & CUSTOM CLASSICS* BOXED SET, SPORTING COVER ART BY VON FRANCO, WAS RELEASED IN 1999. IT CAME WITH AN AUTHORITATIVE 66-PAGE BOOKLET, WINDOW DECALS, A MOONEYES BOTTLE OPENER, AND A SET OF FUZZY DICE.

THE DUKE LABEL

A decade before the ascendance of Motown, Houston's Duke Records flourished as an African American-owned company. The crest employed on the paper label was an homage to Cadillac.

ROBERT WILLIAMS IS A FAMED PAINTER, WAS A FOUNDING MEMBER OF THE LATE-1960S UNDERGROUND ZAP COMIX COLLECTIVE, WORKED AS ART DIRECTOR FOR ED "BIG DADDY" ROTH STUDIO, AND MORE RECENTLY FOUNDED LOWBROW ART MAGAZINE *JUXTAPOZ*. HIS FOUR-PICTURE-DISC *CHROME, SMOKE & FIRE* CAR SONG LP COMPILATION WAS RELEASED IN 1987.

THE LONG-DEFUNCT HOT ROD RECORDS, OUT OF SAN ANTONIO, TEXAS, HAD ONLY CAJUN BANDS ON ITS SMALL, LATE-1940S ROSTER, DESPITE COMPELLING HOT ROD LABEL ART.

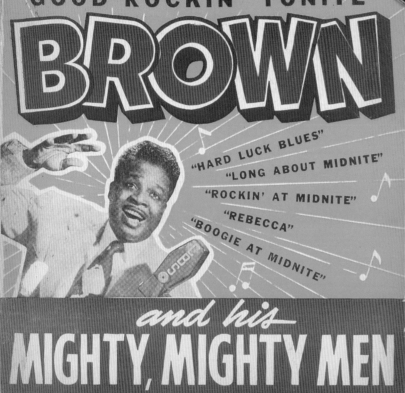

HOW THAT WOMAN LOVES TO RIDE

YES, CADILLAC BABY

YES, CRAZY 'BOUT THAT HYDROMATIC

GIVES HER SUCH AN EASY RIDE

SHE LOVES HER ROLLIN'

HOW SHE LOVES TO BALL THE JACK

YES, CRAZY 'BOUT HER ROLLIN'

HOW SHE LOVES TO BALL THE JACK

YES, CRAZY 'BOUT THAT EASY RIDIN'

CRAZY 'BOUT THAT CADILLAC

ROY BROWN, CADILLAC BABY

ROY BROWN

On any short list of the R&B pioneers who were primary influences on the development of rock & roll, Roy Brown's name is near the top. He entered show business as a professional boxer who sang on the side at talent shows and in neighborhood juke joints, but his 1947 DeLuxe Records waxing of "Good Rockin' Tonight" (the first of many pivotal Brown compositions) was immediately ridden to the peak of the Billboard R&B chart by shouter Wynonie Harris, and subsequently covered by Elvis Presley, Ricky Nelson, Jerry Lee Lewis, Robert Plant, and others—even Pat Boone.

Brown's gospel-steeped delivery impacted the vocal styles of B. B. King, Bobby "Blue" Bland, Little Junior Parker, Clyde McPhatter, Little Richard, and fellow pugilist Jackie Wilson. He was an early pre–rock & roll crossover act. Brown, considered a Louisiana product (and a contemporary of Fats Domino and Professor Longhair), conjured up "Good Rockin' Tonight" while fronting a band in Galveston, Texas. Brown then scored 15 hits from mid-1948 to late 1951 for DeLuxe, ranging from "Hard Luck Blues" (his biggest seller of all, in 1950) to "Cadillac Baby."

Prior to 1954 (the year Elvis Presley recorded his first song at Sun Studios in Memphis), hip hot rodders listened to Hank Williams, cool jazz, and—most importantly—the hottest R&B. Little Richard, along with rock & roll, was about to burst upon the scene.

THE STANDARD OF THE WORLD

Cadillac, during the first decades of its existence in the early twentieth century, had as its advertising slogan "The Standard of the World." Up through the gas crisis of the '70s, that statement was the unalloyed truth. The Cadillac has been seen as a status symbol, representing for all races a showcase of wealth and success, proof of the ability to move beyond your own neighborhood. A gleaming new Cadillac in the driveway is a display of manhood and a rite of passage. And then there are the famous tailfins, first incorporated into Cadillacs in 1948, and the "dagmar" bumpers, so-called for their likeness to the exuberant breasts of '50s television personality Virginia Ruth "Dagmar" Egnor, a likeness heightened in 1957 when the bumpers received black rubber "nipple" tips.

In 1949, Cadillac released the two-door Coupe DeVille, their first pillarless hardtop with the first modern high-compression overhead-valve V8. The Coupe DeVille is simply preeminent among '50s and '60s cars referenced in American popular music, whether rap, country, rock, or blues (see Neil Young, Steve Earle, OutKast, Meat Loaf, Ludacris, Chuck Berry, Ice Cube, Beastie Boys, Fabulous Thunderbirds, and so many others).

In 1953, the company unleashed its lush top-of-the-line Eldorado, a styling leader notable for its wraparound windshield and cut-down beltline. In 1957 the fabled and virtually hand-assembled Eldorado Brougham was created, then costing more than a Rolls-Royce Silver Cloud. Then came "the last of the big ones," the early '70s ultra-luxurious Fleetwood Broughams and Eldorado convertibles desired by many rappers today.

In 1955, Sun Records owner Sam Phillips presented Carl Perkins with a Cadillac (see below), recognizing the success of Perkins' hit "Blue Suede Shoes," the first record to hit the top of all three Billboard charts: pop, country, and R&B. What Phillips didn't tell Perkins as he handed him the keys was that the car had just been deducted from his royalties.

Carl Perkins and Sam Phillips, Sun Studios.

BOO YA TRIBE

HENRY DILTZ

JUICY BAR-B-QUED MEATS

HOODOO Rhythm DEVILS

BIG T'S PIT BAR B QUE
To Go

Aretha

Freeway Of Love

RY COODER   MANUEL GALBÁN

MAMBO SINUENDO

ON THE BEACH

BILLY BOY ARNOLD
Eldorado Cadillac

BRUCE SPRINGSTEEN

NEW KIDS ON THE BLOCK

PAMELA SPRINGSTEEN

LYNN GOLDSMITH

ELVIS PRESLEY, LAMAR STREET HOME, MEMPHIS

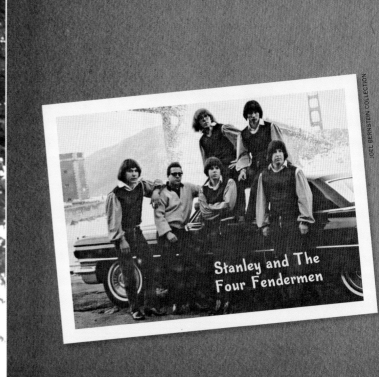

Stanley and The Four Fendermen

BOB MARLEY.

DOGHOUSE BASS

AROUND THE TIME RONNIE HAWKINS FORMED A GROUP
CALLED THE HAWKS (WHICH LATER BECAME THE BAND), I WAS
IN HIGH SCHOOL IN HELENA, ARKANSAS, BUT TRYING TO GET
OUT OF HIGH SCHOOL, IF YOU KNOW WHAT I MEAN! THE ONLY
THING SLOWING ME UP WAS GRADES [LAUGHS]. I REALLY HAD
RAMBLING ON MY MIND, I WANTED OUT. EVEN THOUGH I WAS A
DRUMMER, ONE OF THE PRETTIEST SIGHTS IN THE WORLD WAS A
BIG-ASS CADILLAC ROLLING DOWN THE ROAD WITH A DOGHOUSE
BASS TIED TO THE TOP OF IT. THAT LOOKED LIKE THE CAR I
WANTED TO BE IN.

— LEVON HELM
INTERVIEWED BY DALE INMAN

JERRY GARCIA, OUTSIDE CLUB FRONT RECORDING STUDIO, SAN RAFAEL, CALIFORNIA

Above: NASCAR's Bill Schade, 1949;
Ike Turner's Kings of Rhythm, 1951.

ROCKET 88

Though less heralded than Thomas Edison, GM research director Charles Kettering is responsible for inventions that changed the way we live. In addition to the electric self-starter (1912), Kettering also developed the storage battery–powered electrical ignition still used in every gasoline-powered vehicle today. In 1949, just after his retirement, Kettering's "Rocket" V8 engine was introduced at GM's Oldsmobile Division. He reasoned that if an engine used a higher than normal compression ratio, more power would result. But he also recognized higher compression engines would knock themselves to death on the low-octane gasoline then available. To make his 7.25:1 compression ratio engine practical, Kettering perfected a higher-octane fuel (with tetraethyl lead). The Rocket V8, with its overhead valves and lightweight pistons, set the standard for every American V8 engine for at least three decades.

Immediately after World War II, Oldsmobile featured two models: the near-luxury 98 and the mid-range 76. At first the Rocket engine seemed destined for just the 98, but better thinking prevailed and it was offered in a much lighter chassis as the 1949 Model 88. A legend was born. It was the fastest car on the street at that time (sold only with a Hydra-Matic transmission because the Oldsmobile manual transmission of the time could not handle the load) and can be considered a precursor to the muscle cars of the late 1960s. The 135-horsepower 88 also was a huge hit on the NASCAR circuit, winning 6 of 9 races in 1949, 10 of 19 in 1950, and 20 of 41 in 1952 (before being eclipsed by the Hudson Hornet).

The Rocket 88 inspired the song of the same name. Released on the just-founded Chess label, "Rocket 88" was a Billboard #1 R&B hit in 1951 and the #2 best-selling record that year (there were no rock charts at the time). The song's pioneer producer, Sam Phillips, claimed "Rocket 88" was the first rock & roll song and many scholars have subsequently agreed. Phillips would found Sun Records in 1954, the same year he discovered Elvis Presley "fooling around" with an R&B sound in his studio (Arthur Crudup's "That's All Right").

"Rocket 88" was credited to Jackie Brenston and His Delta Cats, a band that did not actually exist, *per se*. The song was written by legendary guitarist-producer Ike Turner (born Izear Luther Turner in 1931) and recorded by him and his band from high school, the Kings of Rhythm. St. Louis–based Turner was a great talent scout (later discovering a young Annie Mae Bullock, marrying and renaming her Tina Turner) who also played on some of the earliest recordings of Howlin' Wolf, Elmore James, Junior Parker, B. B. King, Otis Rush, and Buddy Guy.

Turner and his band were playing black clubs in the American South when King set up a March 3 recording session for them in Memphis at Phillips' Sun Studios. Turner wrote "Rocket 88" on the way to the session. Brenston (born in 1930), who was also Turner's cousin, played baritone alto saxophone in the Kings of Rhythm but only sang the vocal on "Rocket 88" (ironically, he was a last-minute replacement for another Turner singer, Johnny O'Neal). Working from the raw material of post–big band jump blues, Turner had cooked up a mellow, cruising boogie with a steady-as-she-goes back beat now married to Brenston's enthusiastic, sexually suggestive vocals that spoke of opportunity, discovery, and conquest. This all combined to create (as one reviewer later put it) "THE mother of all R&B songs for an evolutionary white audience."

"Rocket 88" is the prototype for all rock—and automotive—records, in style, sound, and attitude. The recording featured one of the first examples of distorted or "fuzz" guitar. As the story goes, on the early-March drive from Mississippi to Memphis, on Highway 61 (an especially harrowing trip, Turner later recalled: "We got arrested for speeding three times, we had the bass on top of the car, it blew off. It was raining, we got to Memphis late,

YOU MAY HAVE HEARD OF JALOPIES
YOU HEARD THE NOISE THEY MAKE
WELL, LET ME INTRODUCE YOU TO MY ROCKET 88
YES IT'S GREAT, JUST WON'T WAIT

**EVERYBODY LIKES MY ROCKET 88
GALS WILL RIDE IN STYLE
MOVIN' AND GROOVIN' ALONG**

V-8 MOTOR AND THIS MODERN DESIGN
MY CONVERTIBLE TOP AND THE GALS DON'T MIND
SPORTIN' WITH ME, RIDIN' ALL AROUND TOWN FOR JOY

JACKIE BRENSTON, ROCKET 88

so we didn't record on the day we were supposed to."), one of the band's guitar amplifiers came loose from its moorings as they parked their car and took a few hard bounces on the asphalt, breaking the speaker cone. Inside the studio Turner stuffed it with paper in an attempt to salvage it. The result that Phillips heard was a new, distinct sound and a legendary "effect" was born. "We had no way of getting it fixed," Turner later recalled, in an interview with historian Robert Palmer. "So, we started playing around with the damn thing, stuffed a little more paper in there, and it started sounding good." Authors Jim Dawson and Steve Propes, writing in *What Was the First Rock 'N' Roll Record?,* added, "Any other engineer would have sunk the amp's distortion low in the balance, or mix, but not Phillips. He over-amped the fuzzy guitar instead, in hopes it would enhance the boogie riff that guitarist Willie Kizart played against Turner's reckless piano and Raymond Hill's careening, tire-skidding tenor saxophone ('Blow the horn, Raymond!' Brenston tells him at one point, and he does)." One critic later wrote, "It was like the guitar was being played through the Sunday supplement of the *Memphis Commercial Appeal,* yet, no question, it rocked."

General Motors gave Brenston a Rocket 88 to thank him for the publicity generated for the car. Brenston later admitted he and Turner stole the idea for "Rocket 88" from Jimmy Liggins' 1947 song "Cadillac Boogie," which in turn was a pull from Robert Johnson's "Terraplane Blues," recorded in 1936. "Rocket 88" also was covered by Bill Haley and the Saddlemen (before they were the Comets), just before "Rock Around the Clock" made Haley a star. Turner's piano intro on "Rocket 88" also was echoed by Little Richard on "Lucille" and "Good Golly Miss Molly."

"Rocket 88" was Turner's first bona-fide smash hit (as well as the first #1 R&B hit for Chess and the first #1 hit recorded at Sun Studios); yet, reportedly, it was a last-minute decision to record the song in the first place. As Turner later explained, "Man, we were just puttin' something together to get some gas to get back home." To make matters even more confusing, Chess, at the time the record was pressed, changed the name on the label of "Rocket 88" to Jackie Brenston with His Delta Cats, with Turner's name nowhere in sight. Not surprisingly, Turner and Brenston had an immediate falling out. Brenston toured the country for two years straight on the strength of "Rocket 88," but his follow-up record, "My Real Gone Rocket" tanked. He later rejoined Turner's band, receiving minimum-scale wages and little attention, just as Ike and Tina Turner's career took off … like a rocket.

STANDIN' AT THE CROSSROADS

"Bluesman Robert Johnson," according to a version of the hoary tale spun by raconteur Henry Goodman, "been playing down in Yazoo City, Mississippi, trying to get back up to Beulah. Ride left him out on a road next to the levee. Been walking up the highway, guitar propped up on his shoulder. October, cool night, near midnight, full moon filling up the dark sky. Johnson thinking about Son House preaching to him, 'Put that guitar down, boy, you drivin' people nuts.' Johnson needing as always a woman and some whiskey.

"A crazed brindle dog howling and moaning in a ditch nearby, electrified chills go up and down Johnson's spine. Then, coming up on a crossroads just south of Rosedale. Knows people past that point in Gunnison. Can get a drink of whiskey and more up there. Suddenly, come upon a man sitting on a log. Man says, 'The dog ain't for sale, Robert Johnson … but that sound can be yours.'"

And there the legend begins of Johnson selling his soul to the devil in return for legendary guitar skills. What also began was the endless hunt for that exact crossroads, a singular triangulation in automotive and rock & roll roots history. Where was it? The confluence of Highways 61 and 49 is most often cited, in the city of Clarksdale, or just outside. Others say it was at the south end of Rosedale, the intersection where Dockery Farms Road (now Highway 1) crosses old Highway 8.

Johnson's "Crossroads" (recorded November 1936 and later covered by Cream and separately by Eric Clapton) and Big Bill Broonzy's 1941 "Key to the Highway" (Derek and the Dominoes, and again Clapton solo, earlier by Jazz Gillum and John Lee Hooker) are two cornerstones of automotive folk blues. In rhythm & blues standards, the salient points are more superstition than what's sung about cars directly, but the haunting quality of the real Delta blues has affected bands like The Rolling Stones and Led Zeppelin ever since.

"Terraplane Blues," referencing one of the fastest American cars of the 1930s, the Hudson Terraplane, was Johnson's biggest hit when he was alive, selling 5,000 copies in the Deep South. He never owned or drove an automobile, despite recording as far away as San Antonio and Dallas.

Howlin' Wolf, raised in Mississippi, settled in 1952 at age thirty-eight in Chicago, where two labels, Chess and RPM, released his records. Of all the urban bluesmen, his automotive 78s are the most memorable, including "Mr. Highway Man" and "I Asked for Water, She Gave Me Gasoline." Wolf had a commanding stage presence; according to one early fan, "His voice was born in the bottom of a gravel pit. He whooped and hollered over his band's fully electrified wail. He could bring down the house while at the same time scaring the patrons out of their wits."

KENDALL MESSICK

JOHN HAMMOND

SLICK CROWN VIC

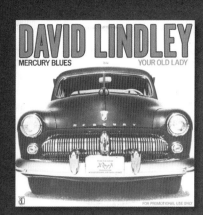

WELL, IF I HAD MONEY
TELL YOU WHAT I'D DO
I'D GO DOWNTOWN AND BUY
A MERCURY OR TWO
CRAZY 'BOUT A MERCURY
LORD I'M CRAZY 'BOUT A MERCURY
I'M GONNA BUY ME A MERCURY
AND CRUISE IT UP AND DOWN THE ROAD

WELL THE GIRL I LOVE
I STOLE HER FROM A FRIEND
HE GOT LUCKY, STOLE HER BACK AGAIN
SHE HEARD HE HAD A MERCURY
LORD SHE'S CRAZY 'BOUT A MERCURY
I'M GONNA BUY ME A MERCURY
AND CRUISE IT UP AND DOWN THE ROAD

MERCURY BLUES

"MERCURY BOOGIE" IS BAY AREA BLUESMAN
K. C. DOUGLAS' MOST FAMOUS COMPOSITION,
RECORDED IN 1949 WHILE HE WAS WORKING
AT THE VALLEJO, CALIFORNIA, NAVAL SHIPYARDS.
THE SLEEK, FAST MERCS WERE THE COOL CARS
OF THEIR TIME. DAVID LINDLEY COVERED IT AS
"MERCURY BLUES," AS DID STEVE MILLER,
AND ALAN JACKSON HAD A #1 COUNTRY HIT
WITH THE TUNE IN 1992.

K.C. DOUGLAS AND ROBERT L. GEDDINS (B-FLAT PUBLISHING CO. & TRADITION MUSIC CO.(BMI)

DAVID JENSEN

DJ and concert promoter Alan Freed and bandleader
Bill Haley were renowned in the early and mid-1950s
for promoting and playing African American–based
R&B on the radio and on stage under the name rock
& roll. While neither is specifically renowned for his
association with car songs, the impetus they gave to a
burgeoning art form led to the first countrywide, bus-
driven rock & roll tours of black and white musicians,
playing together for the first time on nonsegregated
stages.

Freed pioneered racial integration among youth
at a time when most adults were still promoting racial
divide. While working as a disc jockey at Cleveland's
WJW, he organized the first rock & roll concert,
called "The Moondog Coronation Ball," held March
21, 1952. The event, attended mainly by young
black couples, was oversold and cancelled due to
overcrowding.

Freed moved to New York City where he turned
WINS into a pioneering rock & roll station. In 1956
and 1957, he organized the first tours under his name
and appeared in key motion pictures (*Rock Around the
Clock* with Bill Haley; *Rock, Rock, Rock* with Chuck
Berry; and *Don't Knock the Rock* with Little Richard).
The early-'60s payola scandal (accepting bribe money
to play records in favorable rotation) effectively ruined
his career.

Haley led his band, the Comets, to initial chart success with the pre-rock prototype "Crazy, Man, Crazy" in
1953. Like Pat Boone subsequently, they covered black
music hits in a somewhat knee-jerk reaction, such as
their version of Ike Turner and Jackie Brenston's "Rocket
88." But what Haley did successfully was bring the first
fully realized concept of rock & roll to the American
public before Elvis Presley. His career never came close
to that of Elvis, but he's widely regarded as the "Father
of Rock & Roll" on the basis of "(We're Gonna) Rock
Around the Clock," recorded in April 1954 (which
predated Elvis' July recording of his first song, "That's
All Right"). Oddly, upon its first release, "Rock Around
the Clock" was not even as successful as Haley's next
single, a cover version of Joe Turner's "Shake, Rattle
and Roll," which made Haley a true national star on
the airwaves.

The following year, "Rock Around the Clock" was
heard under the opening credits of the world's first
rock-era movie, the controversial *Blackboard Jungle*,
starring Glenn Ford as a high school teacher confronted
by violent students. Haley's "Rock Around the Clock"
was re-released and shot to #1 that July. Rock & roll was
here to stay.

Paramount Theater, Brooklyn, New York

BILL HALEY AND HIS COMETS

A COUNTRY ACT, BILL HALEY AND THE SADDLEMEN HAD THEIR FIRST HIT IN 1951 WITH A TONED-DOWN COVER OF JACKIE BRENSTON'S R&B CHART-TOPPING "ROCKET 88." IN 1952, THE RE-NAMED BILL HALEY WITH HALEY'S COMETS HIT WITH "ROCK THIS JOINT," AND IN 1953 THEY PUT OUT "CRAZY, MAN, CRAZY," BOTH GENUINE ROCK & ROLL PRECURSORS. FINALLY, IN 1954, AS THE GROUP'S FINAL ITERATION, BILL HALEY AND HIS COMETS, THEY RECORDED "DIM, DIM THE LIGHTS," "ROCK AROUND THE CLOCK," AND THEN "SHAKE, RATTLE AND ROLL." ROCK & ROLL WAS OFFICIALLY BORN, ALTHOUGH IT WOULD TAKE ELVIS' FIRST RECORDINGS IN THE SUMMER OF 1954 AND THE RIOTOUS HIP-SHAKING PERFORMANCES THAT FOLLOWED TO GIVE THE NEW ART FORM ITS TRUE NOTORIETY.

HALEY AND HIS BAND FIRST DROVE TO THEIR GIGS IN CARS, THE MUSICIANS SANDWICHED IN BETWEEN THE EQUIPMENT. LATE IN 1954, FLUSH WITH THEIR FIRST MAJOR SUCCESS, THEY BOUGHT A CHEVY PANEL TRUCK TO HAUL THE GUITARS, DRUM KIT, AMPS, AND SUITCASES. IN 1955, WITH THE MONEY TRULY ROLLING IN, THE BANDMEMBERS EACH BOUGHT CADILLACS. FINALLY, IN 1956 THE BAND BOUGHT ITS OWN BUS, ALTHOUGH OVER THE NEXT SEVERAL YEARS HALEY STILL PREFERRED TO TRAVEL IN HIS OWN PASTEL-PINK CADILLAC (NO APOLOGIES TO ELVIS).

Little Richard's stage technique, wrote one observer, was that of "a bisexual Lucifer running amok, carrying on in preacher-in-the-pulpit gospel fashion, pounding his piano to matchsticks." One newspaper called it "voodoo speaking in tongues, a riot with a six-inch pomp and a face covered in Pancake 31."

Born Richard Penniman in 1932, Little Richard was washing dishes in the Greyhound bus station in Macon, Georgia, in 1954 when, at the suggestion of singer Lloyd Price, he sent Specialty Records owner Art Rupe a demo of a song he'd written. "Tutti Frutti" hit the R&B chart in November 1955, zooming all the way to #2, five months before Elvis charted nationally with "Heartbreak Hotel." Little Richard waxed 11 best-sellers for Specialty over the next three years, all cut at Cosmo, the studio in New Orleans where Fats Domino did virtually all of his recording.

Arnold Shaw, writing in *Honkers and Shouters: The Golden Years of Rhythm and Blues*, noted, "Fats had a friendly baritone; Little Richard was strident and slam-bam. Fats' Cajun inflections had a seasoned appeal; Little Richard was a beater and a shouter. For Fats, the band played New Orleans jazz with an afterbeat; with Little Richard's crashing piano triplets, the same band picked up drive and went *'awopbopaloobopawop-*

bamboom.' In person he was a cauldron of sweat, an electric-arcing dynamo, banging the keys with his heels and rear end, and resorting to all the gambits Jerry Lee Lewis later imitated." His music was the first *car music*.

In his 1984 biography of Little Richard, Charles White notes the performer's gift was to "free people from their inhibitions, unleash their spirit, enable them to do exactly what they felt like doing—scream, shout, dance, jump up and down, or do even more unusual things. At one of his 1956 shows, in Baltimore, Maryland, he changed concert history forever. According to newspaper accounts, people had to be restrained from jumping off the balcony. Police removed more than two dozen hysterical girls who rushed the stage. Suddenly, something flew through the air and landed on the drummer's high-hat—a pair of panties. Seconds later, the air was filled with flying undergarments as the other girls in the front rows followed suit."

"Rip It Up," like Ike Turner and Jackie Brenston's 1951 hit "Rocket 88," referenced the still-hot Oldsmobile 88. It reached #17 on the Billboard pop chart in 1956. Bill Haley and His Comets quickly covered it (as did Elvis, somewhat later), but his version peaked only at #30. Critic Dave Marsh suggests no one really could cover Little Richard. "'Rip It Up' was a hillbilly tune sung by a bouffant Negro against a vividly sensual rhythmic backdrop. Give in to it, and you'll not only have a great time but a standard of exhilaration to measure the rest of your life against."

MIKE GUASTELLA/STARFIRE

GOT ME A DATE AND I WON'T BE LATE
PICKED HER UP IN MY 88

WELL, IT'S SATURDAY NIGHT AND I JUST GOT PAID
FOOL ABOUT MY MONEY, DON'T TRY TO SAVE
MY HEART SAYS GO GO, HAVE A TIME
SATURDAY NIGHT AND I'M FEELIN' FINE
GONNA ROCK IT UP, GONNA RIP IT UP
GONNA SHAKE IT UP, GONNA BALL IT UP
I'M GONNA ROCK IT UP, AND BALL TONIGHT
GOT ME A DATE AND I WON'T BE LATE
PICKED HER UP IN MY 88
SHAG ON DOWN BY THE UNION HALL
WHEN THE JOINT STARTS TO JUMP I'LL HAVE A BALL

LITTLE RICHARD, RIP IT UP

MY LOVE IS BIGGER THAN A CADILLAC

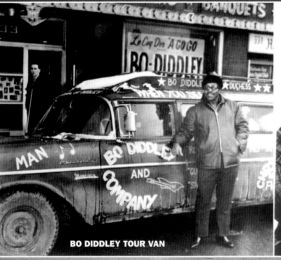

BO DIDDLEY TOUR VAN

BO DIDDLEY

NOT FADE AWAY
THE ROLLING STONES

LONDON
45-9657

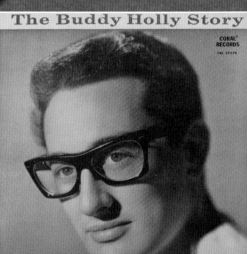

The Buddy Holly Story

CORAL RECORDS
CRL 57279

THE BO DIDDLEY BEAT

THINK "SHAVE AND A HAIRCUT … TWO BITS," AND YOU CAN BANG IT OUT YOURSELF. THE "BO DIDDLEY BEAT" IS A SIGNATURE OF BLUES AND EARLY-ROCK LEGEND BO DIDDLEY (BORN ELLAS MCDANIEL), WHO HAS USED IT TO DRIVE MANY—EVEN MOST—OF HIS SONGS. OTHER ARTISTS HAVE HAD SUCCESS WITH THIS GROOVE, TOO, INCLUDING BUDDY HOLLY AND THE CRICKETS ("NOT FADE AWAY"), JOHNNY OTIS AND ERIC CLAPTON ("WILLIE & THE HAND JIVE"), THE WHO ("MAGIC BUS"), THE GRATEFUL DEAD ("WOMEN ARE SMARTER"), BOW WOW WOW ("I WANT CANDY"), AND U2 ("DESIRE").

DIDDLEY IS GIVEN CREDIT FOR POPULARIZING THE RHYTHM, WHICH STEMS FROM EARLY FORMS OF LATIN AND AFRO-CUBAN SYNCOPATION DERIVED FROM AFRICAN AND CARIBBEAN HOMELANDS.

BUDDY HOLLY'S AND CO-WRITER NORMAN PETTY'S "NOT FADE AWAY" AND ITS IMMORTAL LINE, "MY LOVE IS BIGGER THAN A CADIL-LAC" WAS A MEMORABLE THIRD SINGLE, IN 1964, FOR THE NASCENT ROLLING STONES, AND FOR NEARLY THREE DECADES A SECOND-SET PINNACLE IN THE DEAD'S LIVE REPERTOIRE.

Brunswick
RECORDS

Brunswick

Your
NEW POP LABEL

IT'S
BETTER ON
BRUNSWICK!

ELVIS PRESLEY'S EARLY AUTOMOTIVE MILESTONES

Elvis and Yvonne Lime, 1957

AUGUST 1954 ONE MONTH AFTER RECORDING HIS FIRST SINGLE, "THAT'S ALL RIGHT MAMA," ELVIS AND BLUE MOON BOYS BANDMATES SCOTTY MOORE AND BILL BLACK BEGIN TO USE SCOTTY'S WIFE BOBBIE'S 1954 CHEVROLET BEL AIR AS THE BAND'S OFFICIAL CONVEYANCE.

OCTOBER 15, 1954 SUN RECORDS PRESIDENT SAM PHILLIPS, ELVIS, SCOTTY, AND BILL DRIVE SEVEN HOURS TO SHREVEPORT, LOUISIANA, WHERE SAM HAS ARRANGED A TRYOUT ON THE LOUISIANA HAYRIDE (A COUSIN OF THE GRAND OLE OPRY). A MONTH LATER, ELVIS IS STOPPED FOR SPEEDING ON HIS WAY HOME FROM A HAYRIDE CONCERT.

DECEMBER 1954 ELVIS, WITH THE HELP OF THEN-MANAGER BOB NEAL, PURCHASES A USED, TAN-COLORED 1951 LINCOLN COSMOPOLITAN WITH A RACK ON TOP FOR THE BASS AND "ELVIS PRESLEY—SUN RECORDS" PAINTED ON THE SIDE.

MARCH 1955 BILL BLACK WRECKS THE LINCOLN UNDER A HAY TRUCK IN ARKANSAS.

APRIL 3, 1955 ELVIS IS STOPPED FOR SPEEDING OUTSIDE OF SHREVEPORT IN THE 1954 FOUR-DOOR PINK-AND-WHITE CADILLAC HE BOUGHT AFTER BILL WRECKED THE LINCOLN.

APRIL 13, 1955 IN THE MORNING, ELVIS LEAVES BRECKENRIDGE, TEXAS, WHERE HE PLAYED IN THE HIGH SCHOOL GYM THE NIGHT BEFORE, BEHIND THE WHEEL OF THE 1954 CADILLAC, AND SPORTING PINK SLACKS AND AN ORCHID-COLORED SHIRT.

APRIL 26, 1955 ELVIS RIDES ATOP A CADILLAC IN A NOONTIME PARADE FOR JIMMIE RODGERS DAY IN MERIDIAN, MISSISSIPPI.

JUNE 3, 1955 ELVIS PLAYS THE JOHNSON-CONNELLY PONTIAC SHOWROOM IN LUBBOCK, TEXAS.

JUNE 5, 1955 AFTER A SHOW IN HOPE, ARKANSAS, ELVIS, SCOTTY, AND BILL SET OFF FOR TEXARKANA IN HIS 1954 CADILLAC. HALFWAY THERE, IN FULTON, ARKANSAS, THE CAR DRAGS A PIECE OF METAL, CATCHES FIRE, AND BURNS. PEOPLE RECALL ELVIS SITTING BY THE SIDE OF THE ROAD, LOOKING DESOLATE. SCOTTY RETURNS TO HOPE TO GET THE NEW PINK-AND-WHITE 1955 FORD CROWN VICTORIA THAT ELVIS RECENTLY PURCHASED FOR HIS PARENTS.

JUNE 23, 1955 ELVIS AND BAND ARRIVE FOR SHOWS IN LAWTON, OKLAHOMA, IN THE CROWN VICTORIA, BILL'S BASS STRAPPED TO THE ROOF.

JULY 7, 1955 ELVIS BUYS A BLUE 1955 CADILLAC FLEETWOOD SIXTY WITH A BLACK TOP TO REPLACE THE BURNED 1954 CADILLAC. A REMOVABLE WOODEN ROOF RACK IS USED FOR THE BAND'S INSTRUMENTS. THIS IS THE CAR ELVIS IS SEEN WAXING (PAGE 25) AT HIS 2414 LAMAR STREET, MEMPHIS HOME. HE LATER HAS THE CAR REPAINTED PINK AND WHITE BY HIS NEIGHBOR, ART, WHO CREATED A FORMULA CALLED "ELVIS ROSE."

SEPTEMBER 2, 1955 FIFTEEN MILES SOUTH OF TEXARKANA, ARKANSAS, SCOTTY MOORE DRIVES THE 1955 CADILLAC INTO AN ONCOMING VEHICLE THAT'S IN THE PROCESS OF PASSING A PICKUP TRUCK. REPAIRS TOTAL $1,000.

SEPTEMBER 6, 1955 FIRST REPORTED SIGHTING OF ELVIS' YELLOW 1954 CADILLAC ELDORADO CONVERTIBLE, NEAR BONO, ARKANSAS.

APRIL 13, 1955 ELVIS REPLACES THE UPHOLSTERY IN THE 1955 CADILLAC AND HAS ITS ORIGINAL BLACK ROOF REPAINTED WHITE. NOT LONG AFTER, ELVIS PRESENTS THE REFURBISHED CAR TO HIS MOTHER, GLADYS, WHO WILL ALWAYS PROUDLY POINT TO IT AS "HER" CAR, THOUGH SHE DOESN'T DRIVE. (THIS CAR NOW IS SHOWCASED AT THE ELVIS CAR MUSEUM ACROSS THE STREET FROM GRACELAND IN MEMPHIS.)

APRIL 10, 1956 ON AN INSURANCE FORM, ELVIS' FATHER, VERNON, LISTS A 1954 CADILLAC CONVERTIBLE AND A 1955 CADILLAC FLEETWOOD AS OWNED BY ELVIS. THE FORM ESTIMATES THE TWO CADILLACS WILL BE DRIVEN 100,000 MILES IN THE NEXT YEAR, MUCH BY ELVIS HIMSELF.

APRIL 17, 1956 IN WACO, TEXAS, ELVIS DRIVES OUT ON THE FIELD AND UP TO THE STAGE IN HIS 1954 CADILLAC.

JUNE 12, 1956 ELVIS ORDERS A 1956 IVORY-COLORED CADILLAC ELDORADO BIARRITZ CONVERTIBLE. ALLEGEDLY, HE SQUASHES A HANDFUL OF GRAPES ON THE FENDER AND TELLS CUSTOMIZER JIMMY SANDERS THAT THAT'S THE COLOR HE WANTS.

APRIL 10, 1956 BY SUMMER, PHOTOS SHOW THE BAND WITH A YELLOW 1954 CADILLAC LIMOUSINE THAT THEY WILL USE FOR JUST A FEW MONTHS BEFORE GRADUATING TO A BLACK 1956 CADILLAC LIMOUSINE.

JULY 12, 1956 ELVIS TRADES IN HIS YELLOW 1954 CADILLAC FOR A LAVENDER 1956 LINCOLN PREMIERE.

JULY 25, 1956 ELVIS TRADES IN THE LINCOLN, ALREADY DEFACED BY FANS' MESSAGES SCRAWLED IN LIPSTICK, FOR AN EVEN MORE UPSCALE WHITE 1956 LINCOLN CONTINENTAL MARK II. HE'S ALLOWED $3,515 FOR THE OLD CAR AGAINST THE $10,588 PRICE OF THE NEW ONE.

OCTOBER 11, 1956 ELVIS ENTERS THE COTTON BOWL IN DALLAS, TEXAS, IN AN OPEN CONVERTIBLE THAT TAKES HIM TO THE STAGE SET UP AT THE 50-YARD LINE BEFORE A CROWD OF 26,500.

DECEMBER 3, 1956 ELVIS BUYS A NEW 1957 TWO-DOOR CADILLAC ELDORADO SEVILLE FOR $8,400. A WEEK LATER HE RUNS OUT OF GAS IN DOWNTOWN MEMPHIS AND IS MOBBED BY FANS.

JANUARY 4, 1957 ELVIS DRIVES HIS SEVILLE TO THE KENNEDY VETERANS HOSPITAL IN MEMPHIS FOR A PRE-INDUCTION ARMY PHYSICAL.

JANUARY 16, 1957 VERNON SHIPS ELVIS THE SEVILLE WHILE ELVIS IS IN LOS ANGELES SHOOTING HIS SECOND FILM, *LOVING YOU.*

FEBRUARY 1957 ELVIS ARRANGES TO PURCHASE A 1957 CADILLAC ELDORADO BROUGHAM NO. 274, A LUXURY CAR WAY AHEAD OF ITS TIME, WITH CUSTOM FEATURES INCLUDING MEMORY SEATS, SUICIDE DOORS, AND DUAL-ZONE AIR CONDITIONING.

FEBRAURY 25, 1957 LOUIS ARMSTRONG IS QUOTED IN A NEW ORLEANS NEWSPAPER AS SAYING, "YOU ASK ME IF I THINK ELVIS IS ANY GOOD. HOW MANY CADILLACS WAS IT HE BOUGHT? THAT BOY'S NO FOOL."

BILOXI, MISS.

June Juanico of Biloxi, Mississippi, was Elvis' first sweetheart (and the only girl his mother, Gladys, ever approved of). They met June 26, 1955, and dated for three years. In July 1956 Elvis and his cousins spontaneously drove the pink Cadillac and the newly purchased Lincoln Mark II down to Biloxi in pursuit of June.

EPE, INC. ARCHIVE

ELVIS SPEEDING TICKET

THE BIG SHINY CAR HAS LONG BEEN THE QUINTESSENTIAL AMERICAN STATUS SYMBOL, AND ELVIS WAS THE ULTIMATE CON-SUMER. WHEN ON HIS FIRST TELEVISION INTERVIEW WINK MARTINDALE ASKED WHY HE HAD SO MANY CARS, ELVIS GOT PLAIN BASHFUL AND REPLIED, "YOU MIGHT SAY CARS ARE MY HOBBY." HE LOVED TO OWN CARS, AND HE LOVED TO DRIVE CARS. HE DROVE HIS FRIENDS AND GIRLFRIENDS ALL OVER MEMPHIS AND GOT HIS FAIR SHARE OF SPEEDING TICKETS (PHOTO ABOVE).

ELVIS "ELVIP" CAR

THE "ELVIP" CADILLAC-LIKE TINPLATE CAR SURFACED AT PAUL AND CHRIS SCHARFMAN'S CHIC-A-BOOM MEMORABILIA STORE IN LOS ANGELES. NO ONE KNOWS ITS EXACT ORIGIN, AS THIS IS POSSIBLY THE ONLY EXAMPLE EXISTING, BUT IT IS THOUGHT TO HAVE BEEN MANUFACTURED IN INDIA IN 1958. THE FRONT AND SIDE PORTRAITS ARE EXQUISITE, BUT IN UNMISTAKABLY INDIAN GARB.

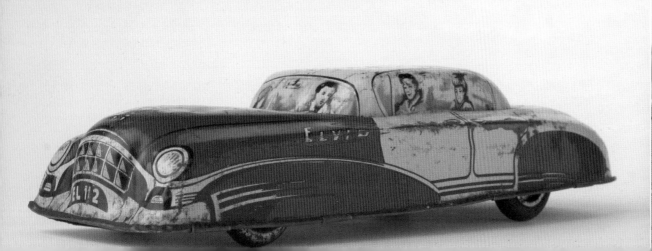

SAM SARGENT

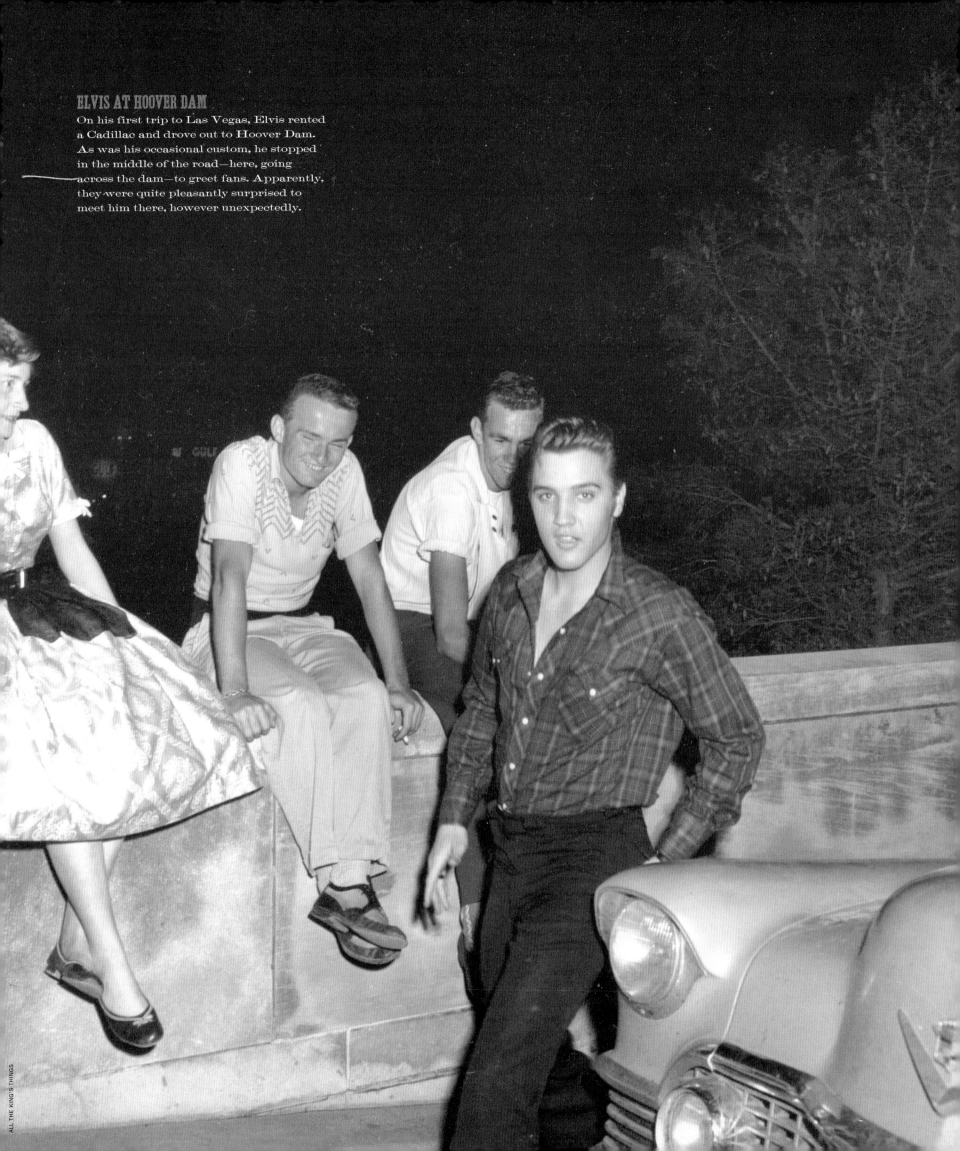

ELVIS AT HOOVER DAM

On his first trip to Las Vegas, Elvis rented
a Cadillac and drove out to Hoover Dam.
As was his occasional custom, he stopped
in the middle of the road—here, going
across the dam—to greet fans. Apparently,
they were quite pleasantly surprised to
meet him there, however unexpectedly.

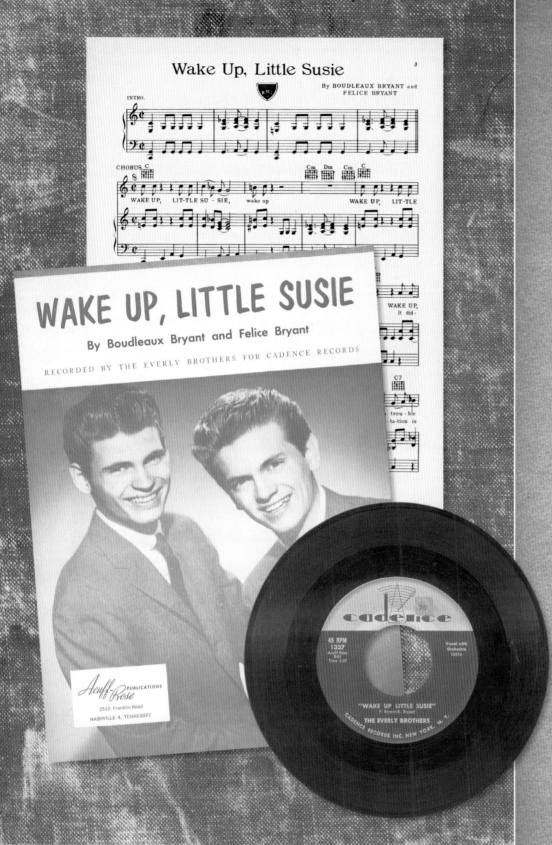

UNFORGETTABLE

THE EVERLY BROTHERS WERE RAISED ON COUNTRY MUSIC BUT QUICKLY ADAPTED TO ROCK & ROLL. "WAKE UP, LITTLE SUSIE," THEIR #1 SINGLE IN 1957 (AND THE FIRST OF FOUR #1 U.S. CHART-TOPPERS FOR DON AND PHIL EVERLY), WAS WRITTEN BY THE HUSBAND-AND-WIFE TEAM OF BOUDLEAUX AND FELICE BRYANT, WHO WROTE MANY OF THE EVERLY BROTHERS' HITS IN THE 1950S. THE BRYANT TECHNIQUE WAS TO APPLY AN R&B SHUFFLE TO EASY-ON-THE-EARS TIN PAN ALLEY, VIA NASHVILLE. INFLUENCED BY OLD-TIME COUNTRY BROTHER ACTS LIKE BILL AND CHARLIE MONROE, IRA AND CHARLIE LOUVIN, AND ALTON AND RABON DELMORE, THE EVERLY BROTHERS HAD THE DISCIPLINED HARMONIES TO MAKE THE BRYANT SONGS INSTANTLY MEMORABLE, HUMMABLE, AND UNFORGETTABLE—A POTENT COMBINATION THAT WAS TO HAVE GREAT EFFECT FIRST ON BUDDY HOLLY AND THEN ON THE BEATLES SIX YEARS LATER.

"WAKE UP, LITTLE SUSIE" WAS THE EVERLYS' ONLY TRUE CAR-RELATED SONG. SEVERAL BOSTON RADIO STATIONS BANNED IT BECAUSE OF THE LYRICS, WHICH RELATE THE STORY OF A YOUNG COUPLE WHO FALL ASLEEP AT A DRIVE-IN THEATER, REALIZE TO THEIR DISMAY THEY'RE OUT WAY PAST CURFEW, AND MAKE UP A STORY TO TELL SUSIE'S PARENTS. THOSE BOSTONIANS WERE CONVINCED THE TWO KIDS WERE ACTUALLY DOING THE DEED IN THE BACKSEAT (*WHAT ARE WE GOING TO TELL OUR MAMA?*), ALTHOUGH THE LYRICS ARE SUFFICIENTLY AMBIGUOUS ON THAT POINT.

EDDIE COCHRAN'S "SUMMERTIME BLUES" PEAKED AT #8 IN AUGUST 1958. IT WAS A MEMORABLE CAR SONG BECAUSE OF THE LINES "SON, YOU GOTTA MAKE SOME MONEY/IF YOU WANNA USE THE CAR TO GO RIDIN' NEXT SUNDAY" AND "YOU CAN'T USE THE CAR 'CAUSE YOU DIDN'T WORK A LICK." COCHRAN WAS NINETEEN WHEN HE RECORDED HIS BREAKTHROUGH HIT; HE WAS IMMEDIATELY TAGGED WITH THE IMAGE OF A REBEL WITH A GUITAR AND COMPARED TO MOVIE STAR JAMES DEAN (WHO WAS TWENTY-FOUR WHEN HE DIED ON THE HIGHWAY, CRASHING HIS 1955 PORSCHE SPYDER NICKNAMED "LITTLE BASTARD").

THE WHO ARE OFTEN FIRST ASSOCIATED WITH "SUMMERTIME BLUES," DUE TO ITS INCLUSION ON *LIVE AT LEEDS* (1970) AND *WOODSTOCK*, THE FILM DOCUMENTARY. AMONG THE MUSICIANS WHO'VE PAID HOMAGE TO THIS CLASSIC ARE GEORGE THOROGOOD, THE STRAY CATS, RUSH, BRUCE SPRINGSTEEN, THE FLAMING LIPS, GUITAR WOLF, JOAN JETT, LEVON HELM, MOTORHEAD, THE ROLLING STONES, T-REX, AND VAN HALEN. BLUE CHEER'S VERSION REACHED THE TOP FIFTEEN IN 1968, AND IS CONSIDERED ONE OF THE FIRST HEAVY METAL SONGS. COCHRAN'S ORIGINAL SONG ALSO IS A PRECURSOR TO TEEN-ANGST ANTHEMS LIKE ALICE COOPER'S "I'M EIGHTEEN," NIRVANA'S "SMELLS LIKE TEEN SPIRIT," AND GREEN DAY'S "BOULEVARD OF BROKEN DREAMS."

MY BABY BESIDE ME AT THE WHEEL

OH MAYBELLENE

Chuck Berry's "No Particular Place to Go" reached #10 on Billboard's pop chart in 1964. His first hit, "Maybellene," had reached #5 (pop) and #1 (rhythm & blues) simultaneously in 1955 and put him on the map forever. Berry's irresistible teen anthems were immediately successful in part because of his "raceless" enunciation, meaning radio stations that refused to broadcast rhythm & blues of the period did not immediately realize he was black, kind of a reverse crossover to Elvis Presley (a white man who "sang black").

"When I wrote 'Maybellene,'" explained Berry in *Chuck Berry: The Autobiography* (Random House, 1989), "I'd never been in a funeral or parade, which would have been the only opportunity I could have had to ride in a Cadillac. The body of the song was composed from memories of high school and trying to get girls to ride in my 1934 V8 Ford. I was inspired by a country song, 'Ida Red'… . I originally titled it 'Ida May,' which has the same swing in the three syllables.

"We struggled through the song, taking maybe thirty-five tries before completing a track satisfactory to Leonard Chess, the producer… I was surprised when days and weeks passed with no word from anyone about the recording. I wondered if all the effort now was in some trash can.

"Suddenly, people started telling me they'd heard 'Maybellene' on the radio. I first heard it driving home from my dad's house in my station wagon. There is no way to explain how you feel when you first hear your first recording for the first time in your first new car."

Berry is considered the most influential single black contributor to the evolution of white rock. He was the first all-around player—an intuitive writer, performer, and lead instrumentalist. Yet, as a sign of the times, Chess gave disc jockey Alan Freed a composer credit on "Maybellene" (and also some cash), in exchange for playing it on the radio. Deals like this led to Freed's later downfall in the payola scandals.

"Maybellene" is significant because it's prototypical rock & roll. It has all the essential elements of rock: women, cars racing on a highway, the protagonist breaking the rules, not to mention a voluble, ringing guitar. It also coined the term "motorvating."

Chuck Berry, circa 1955.

Pin Stripe Sweeps Country

Car gets final touch by Darrell Mayabb pin striping enthusiasts.

The popularity of pin striping doesn't need to be mentioned, for in the last couple of years this trade has become as standard as lowering blocks to hot rod and custom car enthusiasts.

Ever since the day of the horseless carriage, the pin stripe has been a characteristic of vehicles of distinction. This has been true for custom cars as well as for royal limousines. Yet the possibilities of the stripe becoming a customizing touch remained doubtful. By 1955 it was very popular in the West, and by 1956 it began to catch on slowly in the East.

Now things have changed. A crop of young artists has developed, and a rise in popularity is greatly noticeable.

One such artist is a student here at Belmont. Junior Darrell Mayabb has been in the business striping for the last six months. Darrell, shown above working with the brush.

Darrell commented, "The most current product produced by the brush is a wild scallop sported by several customs in this area."

"I don't feel that pin striping should be something that is looked at and then forgotten. It is really to be considered an art."

Darrell Mayabb, circa 1958.

RED HEADED FLEA

My high school days in Ohio were spent dreaming about cars. I had three hot rods in four years. We named our cars in those days. We took titles from songs, names of girlfriends, or whatever struck our fancy. I even lettered the names on the cars (I also pinstriped and did Stanley Mouse–like "weirdo" shirts, but that's another story).

My first car was a '39 Chevy sedan ("Lil' Honey Pot"). My second hot rod was a '34 Ford sedan; it went in and out of my life quickly because I turned a profit on it, so I didn't have time to name it. But my favorite was my third, a '55 Chevy two-door. I named it after the 1958 instrumental song, "Red Headed Flea," or so I believed.

I've been in love with two women in my life. This was the time of my first love, Nancy Stewart (if you look closely at the glove compartment door, there I lettered her name and mine). The second lady I fell in love with and to whom I have been happily married for 38 years—Sharon Carpenter Mayabb—has always gently accused me of naming my '55 after a song that "sounded like" Nancy. But I could never remember the sound of what turns out to be one of rock & roll's most incredibly obscure songs (which gave the car its name), and I could never find a record of that name to prove it.

It haunted me for nearly 40 years: Why did I name that car the "Red Headed Flea"? I think after awhile I began to believe the whole episode was a figment of my imagination, despite the name obviously having been written on the side of the car. Year after year I asked every disc jockey I ever met, "Have you ever come across the song 'Red Headed Flea'?" and the answer always was, "No, never heard of it."

I was working in my studio one day some time back and there was a new radio station in town playing old rock & roll and this song came on and it sounded like what my memory was of "Red Headed Flea." I immediately got in touch with the DJ and told him he just played a song that I'd been hunting for decades. He said, "Hey, that's great. It's 'Green Mosquito' by the Tune Rockers."

An awful moment. I got off the phone completely dejected. He too had never heard of the song "Red Headed Flea." I began to think I must have been crazy back then. I mean, could I have painted the wrong song on the side of my car?

Then, in 2005, I was asked to meet the public at a car show held in Milwaukee. When I got there, the promoters asked if I was okay doing an interview on the local radio station. It was Mark Dietrich's The Gearhead Show. He turned out to be a real motorhead and versed in old rock & roll. We talked about my art and my hot rods. He said he'd found something very interesting, looking into my past. "You had a Chevy in high school and you named it the "Red Headed Flea," did you not?" I jumped right on the comment and told him of my recent realization that the car was named after the "Green Mosquito," despite the paint job.

Ah, but then Mark proceeded to blow my mind. He said, "Darrell, do I have a surprise for you," and he played a very hot instrumental by The Caps, an early Ohio band, and it all came flooding back. I did name my hot rod "Red Headed Flea."

— Darrell Mayabb
Arvada, Colorado

ROY ORBISON'S "CLAUDETTE"

THE EVERLY BROTHERS COVERED ROY ORBISON'S "CLAUDETTE" AS THE B-SIDE OF "ALL I HAVE TO DO IS DREAM" AND AS A SINGLE ON ITS OWN. IT CHARTED WITH BOTH RELEASES, RISING TO #1 ON BILLBOARD'S POP SINGLES CHART IN APRIL 1958 AND STAYING FOR FIVE WEEKS.

"CLAUDETTE" WAS WRITTEN IN 1955 AND NAMED FOR ORBISON'S FIRST WIFE, CLAUDETTE FRADY (PICTURED ABOVE). THE FIRST THING ORBISON DID WITH HIS ROYALTY EARNINGS FROM THE EVERLY BROTH-ERS' RELEASES WAS PURCHASE A NEW 1958 THUNDERBIRD, WHICH HE BROUGHT HOME TO HIS THRILLED YOUNG FAMILY.

ON THE BASIS OF "CLAUDETTE," ORBISON BOUGHT OUT HIS CONTRACT WITH SUN RECORDS AND EVENTUALLY LANDED AT MONUMENT RECORDS, WHERE HIS INIMITABLE, OPERATIC STYLE—USING A CRESCEN-DOING FALSETTO—FULLY DEVELOPED AND YIELDED #1 HITS SUCH AS "RUNNING SCARED" AND "OH, PRETTY WOMAN."

SADLY, IN THE MIDST OF RECONCILING WITH CLAUDETTE, SHE DIED IN A MOTORCYCLE ACCIDENT IN 1966. TWO OF THEIR THREE SONS DIED TWO YEARS LATER IN A FIRE AT THEIR HENDERSONVILLE, TENNESSEE, HOME. ORBISON LATER MARRIED BARBARA WELLHONEN-JAKOBS IN 1969, HIS WIDOW SINCE 1988, WHO GRACIOUSLY PROVIDED THESE PHOTOS.

Martin

RACE WITH THE DEVIL
The Temptation of Speed

STEVE WALTERS

Go fast, then faster, and hit the finish line first. That's always been the idea. The Dictators (in "(I Live for) Cars and Girls") put it very well: *The fastest car and a movie star are my only goals in life/It's the hippest scene, the American dream, and for that I'll always fight.* Even punk's Angry Samoans raved about the passion and the mania, in "Hot Cars."

Nothing makes a statement like owning and driving a fast car. Larry Erickson, designer of Billy F Gibbons' CadZZilla (pages 124–129), lectures on this very point at colleges and universities. "You can't drive your house, you can't drive your stock portfolio," Erickson pointed out in an interview with the author. "But you can build and race a really fast car. You can even race it on the street if you're not afraid of The Man. A hot car is one of those visual things that clarifies everything, is understood by everyone. 'Wow—check *that* out. Betcha *that's* bad-ass.'

"Cars change who you are and where you came from—it puts all that stuff behind you, lays out everything in front of you. A fast car—even a cool car—tells us it's still the land of promise and that you're in the driver's seat. You make your own myth with a car, and it doesn't matter what culture you're from—black, white, Latino, Asian. It's just … how fast will that thing run?"

The myth of the American gunslinger is very much alive in car culture. It's about being the baddest man in the whole damn town, to cop a line off Jim Croce. The quickest on the draw wins. Line up, stomp on the gas, hope you can stop in time. "In a world where people feel like, 'I got no control, I got no influence,' they can strap on the black leather, climb into a hot machine, pull their hat down tighter, and they're a force to be reckoned with," Erickson continues. "It's always been about two people figuring which one stands taller. What else besides a very mean car, or a gun, says—legally, you have to hope—'I'm here, now *get out of my way.*'"

A fast car signifies so many things. It means you can fight back. It means you can protect your own. It means you can risk everything. Lay it on the line, bet against the come. Roll dem bones. But there's always risk involved. You could lose, you could be injured, you could die. Racing with the devil means taking chances and admitting you're doing it impulsively. It's one of several dramas played out in George Lucas' *American Graffiti.* Milner against Balfa. The five-window versus the Chevy. Win? Or lose? Who can say? But everyone in the theater seats knows neither will leave anything behind.

That experience of challenging and winning is a theme echoed in many a rockin' car song. Rush's "Red Barchetta" celebrates a Mille Miglia–like encounter between three vehicles on the open road (*I spin around with shrieking tires/To run the deadly race/Go screaming through the valley/As another joins the chase*). The Beach Boys' "Shut Down" has "two cool shorts," a Sting Ray and a Superstock Dodge, in each other's face on the quarter-mile strip (*Tach it up, tach it up, buddy gonna shut you down*). Then there's Public Enemy's street-racy Oldsmobile 98 in "You're Gonna Get Yours" (*My 98-0 blows 'em all away*) side by side with country-rock singer Kathy Mattea's take on the Dave Rawlings/Gillian Welch–penned "455 Rocket."

Musicians will tell you there are similarities between operating a fast car, with all its risks and rewards, and making rock & roll. When you're onstage you're expected to turn it up, to turn it loose, to hold nothing back. You risk your reputation if you can't reinvent yourself one more time. The crowd demands you get it up. So, big boy, are you gonna win or lose?

Perhaps Rawlings and Welch put it best: *Well, whose junkpile piece of Chevelle is this?/You boys come here to race, or just kiss?*

THE PLAYMATES' "BEEP BEEP" WAS A PERVERSE NOVELTY HIT ACROSS AMERICA. ONE OF THE FIRST ROCK & ROLL GROUPS SIGNED TO NEW YORK'S ROULETTE RECORDS, THE BAND WAS ORIGINALLY KNOWN AS THE NITWITS AND PERFORMED MOSTLY AROUND WATERBURY, CONNECTICUT.

"BEEP BEEP" WAS ONE OF THOSE TOO-OFTEN-PLAYED SINGLES THAT DROVE PEOPLE CRAZY, WITH ITS *BEEP BEEP. BEEP! BEEP! BEEP BEEP. BEEP! BEEP!/HIS HORN WENT BEEP BEEP BEEP* CHORUS. DESPITE THE IMPOSSIBLE STORYLINE IN WHICH A NASH RAMBLER OUTPERFORMS A CADDY WHILE STUCK IN SECOND GEAR, THE SONG CLIMBED TO #4 ON BILLBOARD'S POP CHART IN DECEMBER 1958.

"BEEP BEEP" STARTED ITS OWN TRADITION OF BEEP SONGS, INCLUDING "BEEP A FREAK," "LITTLE BO BEEP," "BONGO BEEP," "ZIP-SQUAT-BEEP," "JEEP BEEP SUITE," "LISTEN FOR MY BEEP," AND ABOUT FIFTY OTHERS, SOME OF WHICH ARE ABOUT BEEP-TONES, OTHERS ABOUT—*MOVE IT, SISTER!*—HASSLING FELLOW MOTORISTS ON THE MEAN STREETS. THERE'VE EVEN BEEN SURF (THE IMPACTS) AND HIP-HOP (69 BOYZ) SONGS WITH "BEEP BEEP" AS THE TITLE.

THE ORIGINAL "BEEP BEEP" HAS TAKEN ON A NOTORIETY SIMILAR TO OTHER NOVELTY TUNES SUCH AS LONNIE DONEGAN'S "DOES YOUR CHEWING GUM LOSE ITS FLAVOR (ON THE BEDPOST OVERNIGHT)."

IN 2006, FORD RELEASED THE VERY POP "BEEP! BEEP!" COMMERCIAL, STARRING THE BAND 13 STORIES. THE TRACK WAS TAKEN FROM THE GROUP'S *FUNKYPOPSEXY-HOUSERAP* ALBUM, AND INSPIRED HUNDREDS OF ANNOYED COMMENTS ON DOZENS OF BLOGS. EVEN MORE RECENTLY, THERE'S COME TO LIFE NOISE-ROCK FROM AN OUTFIT CALLED, YES, BEEP BEEP.

GENE VINCENT, CIRCA 1958

I'LL OUTRUN THE DEVIL ON JUDGEMENT DAY

A HIGH FIDELITY RECORDING

RCA VICTOR 45 Extended Play EPA 535-

THE WILD ONE

ON THE COLUMBIA PICTURE "THE WILD ONE"

BLUES FOR BRANDO
CHINO
THE WILD ONE

SHORTY ROGERS and his orchestra

HELLS ANGELS

Legendary photographer Jim Marshall took this shot of the Hells Angels in front of the Winterland dance arena in San Francisco on October 31, 1967, the night of the "Trip or Freak" concert with the Grateful Dead, Big Brother and the Holding Company (with Janis Joplin), and Quicksilver Messenger Service.

ANTISOCIAL CELLULOID GEARHEADS

The Wild One (1953), starring Marlon Brando as the surly leader of the Black Rebel Motorcycle Club (clad in leather jackets sporting a skull above two crossed pistons), was groundbreaking stuff in its day. It glamorized/exploited an early "antisocial" subculture and helped spawn such classics as the James Dean epic *Rebel Without a Cause* (1955), *Hot Rod Girl* (1956), *Hot Rod Rumble* (1957), and *Thunder Road* (1958), among others.

The Wild One was very loosely based on the 1947 Fourth of July weekend in Hollister, California, when several thousand motorcyclists roared into town for the Gypsy Tour and Races. These motorcycle enthusiasts overwhelmed the tiny burg's facilities and were afterwards remembered (somewhat unfairly) as "having ransacked the town." Brando's classic line in the film was his answer to the question "Hey Johnny, what are you rebelling against?" to which Brando's character replied, "What've you got?"

Thunder Road and *Hot Rod Rumble* took moviegoers deeper into the mainstream's confrontations with postwar automotive subculture. *Thunder Road*, starring Robert Mitchum in his '50 Ford, running moonshine through the mountains, set the tone for internally modified, late-model car culture in the southeastern United States for nearly a decade, and in the process underscored NASCAR's growing appeal. Mitchum also sang the hit song of the same name.

Hot Rod Rumble was the first prototypic look at the culture of hot rod car clubs. The plot, outlined on the back jacket of the movie's score, is particularly instructive as to the dynamics:

Big Arny Crawford has been asked to join the Road Devils even though he has a way of clobbering guys who look twice at Terry, his girl. Terry likes to flirt a bit and has come to the Jamboree with Hank. Arny shows up, and not able to keep his temper, starts a rumble with some of the Road Devils.

Terry leaves with Hank, but not before Ray, a weak type who wants to be like Arny, has asked Terry for a date and is rejected. Furious, Ray follows Terry and Hank and after a chase through the dark, runs their car off the road. In the crash, Hank is killed instantly and Terry is knocked unconscious.

The next day the Road Devils gang up on Arny, believing he ran the car off the road. At a drag race soon after, the leader of the Road Devils, Jim, ruins the motor of Arny's car and the gang beats up Arny badly. Now having lost his job, Arny is depending on winning the Sweepstakes Race and its $1,500 check.

With his motor rebuilt from scratch, Arny gets to the starting line in the nick of time and wins the race by a hair. Arriving at the track with Ray, Terry finds the earring she lost the night of the accident under Ray's seat, proving Ray's guilt. After the race, the gang tells Arny the truth, and he almost kills them all. Instead, he relents and takes a tearful Terry from the scene, riding into the smog in his rod.

The order of the songs on the original score sheds further light on the growing relationship between hot rod culture and the new jump sounds of the period:

SIDE ONE (SELECTIONS)

MAIN TITLE 3:03: BIG ARNY ARRIVES AT THE JAMBOREE.

ROCKIN' WITH ARNY 2:10: KIDS DANCING AT THE JAMBOREE.

DENTED FENDER 1:28: RAY REPAIRS HIS CAR.

ARNY'S BLUES 3:30: ARNY LEAVES THE JAMBOREE.

CHICKEN RACE 3:52: KIDS DRIVE TOWARD EACH OTHER FAST TO SEE WHO GIVES WAY.

RACY DRAG 1:23: HOT INSTRUMENTAL.

SIDE TWO (SELECTIONS)

HOT ROD ROCK 3:05: KIDS DANCING.

NIGHT CHASE 4:14: RAY FOLLOWS HANK AND TERRY AND RUNS THEM OFF THE ROAD.

JAZZ DIRGE 2:25: HANK IS DEAD.

THE RACE 4:35: RODS RACE THROUGH THE HILLS.

END TITLE 1:04: ARNY WINS THE RACE, RAY CONFESSES, AND TERRY WINS BACK ARNY.

Gene Vincent easily could have passed for a Road Devil. Although Virginia-born, he personified the wild, social misfit generally associated with early rock & roll music—a music also widely considered to be of Southern California origins. As a kid, when Vincent wasn't listening to the Grand Ole Opry on the radio or hearing the gospel music of the local black churches, he could often be found on the porch of his parents' general store, jamming with black musicians from the neighborhood.

Vincent joined the Navy at the age of seventeen and just after signing up for a second six-year stint was involved in a motorcycle accident that shattered his left shinbone. While in the Veterans Hospital in Portsmouth, Virginia, Vincent passed time by playing guitar. While at the hospital, he paid a fellow patient, Don Graves, $25 for a song Graves had written about a local stripper. "Be-Bop-A-Lula" was recorded in Nashville in April 1956 and went on to become one of the first rockabilly hits. At that same session, Vincent and his band, later billed as His Blue Caps, waxed "Race with the Devil," which today is thought of as "classic Gene Vincent," although radio stations of the time rejected it because of its subject matter.

Vincent also starred in *Hot Rod Gang* (1958), a cheesy flick if ever there was one, but also a rare opportunity to catch a genuine rock legend—a true rival of Elvis—in his prime, in action, on film.

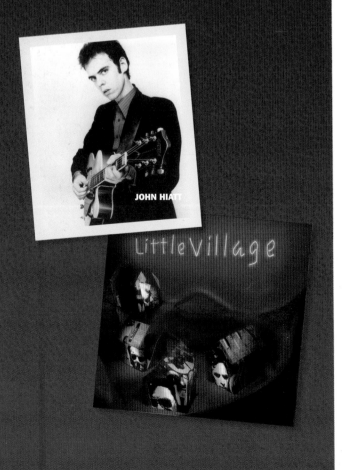

JOHN HIATT

LittleVillage

AT THE DRAGS

The first sanctioned drag strip opened on a Santa Ana, California, airfield in
1950, but the songs about the culture of the strip and the nomenclature involved
(blowers, burnouts, "Christmas tree," nitromethane fuel, slicks, traps, etc.) did
not come in earnest for several years.

Drag racing songs have always been a niche unto themselves, best enjoyed by
purists, although they did evolve from street racing and hot rod music. Many 45s
and LPs even mixed in the sounds of the drags—unmuffled pipes, tire shrieks,
announcers' calls of new records set, and roars of appreciative crowds.

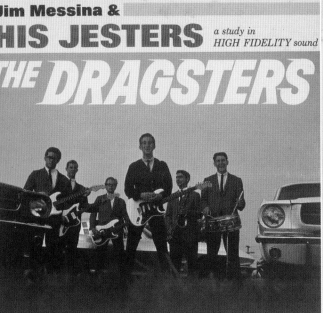

STEREOPHONIC AF AUDIO FIDELITY STEREODISC DFS 7037

Jim Messina &
HIS JESTERS *a study in HIGH FIDELITY sound*
THE DRAGSTERS

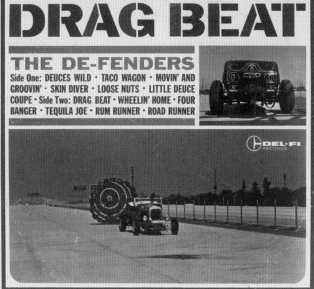

DRAG BEAT
THE DE-FENDERS
Side One: DEUCES WILD • TACO WAGON • MOVIN' AND GROOVIN' • SKIN DIVER • LOOSE NUTS • LITTLE DEUCE COUPE • Side Two: DRAG BEAT • WHEELIN' HOME • FOUR BANGER • TEQUILA JOE • RUM RUNNER • ROAD RUNNER
DEL-FI RECORDS
A BOB KEENE PRODUCTION
DFLP-1242

DRAG KINGS
DEUCE OF DEUCES • FENDER BENDERS • SATANS ANGELS
ROAD KINGS • DEMONS • REBELS • DUSTERS • BANSHEES
BEARING BURNERS • WAILERS • JOKERS • ROAD ANGELS
SONNY AND THE DEMONS UNITED ARTISTS
DRAG KINGS • SONNY AND THE DEMONS • UNITED ARTISTS UAL 3315 MONAURAL

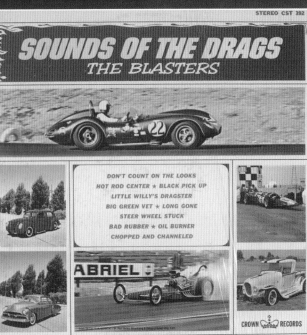

STEREO CST 392
SOUNDS OF THE DRAGS
THE BLASTERS
DON'T COUNT ON THE LOOKS
HOT ROD CENTER ★ BLACK PICK UP
LITTLE WILLY'S DRAGSTER
BIG GREEN VET ★ LONG GONE
STEER WHEEL STUCK
BAD RUBBER ★ OIL BURNER
CHOPPED AND CHANNELED
ABRIEL
CROWN RECORDS

SCHOOL IS A DRAG THE SUPER STOCKS FEATURING GARY USHER
SATURDAY'S HERO • LITTLE HONDA • A GUY WITHOUT WHEELS • SCHOOL IS A DRAG • GRIDIRON GOODIE
READIN', RIDIN' AND RACING • LET FREEDOM RING • CLASS DAY • HOT ROD HIGH • SCHOOL BUS BLUES
Capitol Record

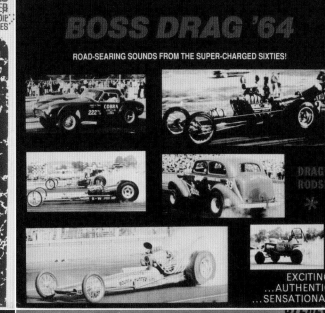

Hot Rod HIGH FIDELITY
MONO
BOSS DRAG '64
ROAD-SEARING SOUNDS FROM THE SUPER-CHARGED SIXTIES!
DRAG RODS
EXCITING
...AUTHENTIC
...SENSATIONAL

HP
Hayden Proffitt
presents Jim Head
and his DEL RAY'S

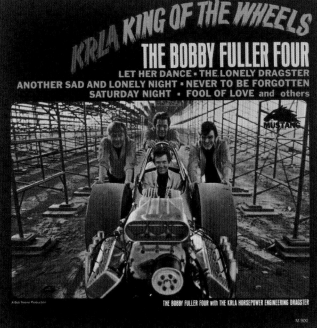

KRLA KING OF THE WHEELS
THE BOBBY FULLER FOUR
LET HER DANCE • THE LONELY DRAGSTER
ANOTHER SAD AND LONELY NIGHT • NEVER TO BE FORGOTTEN
SATURDAY NIGHT • FOOL OF LOVE and others
MUSTANG
THE BOBBY FULLER FOUR WITH THE KRLA HORSEPOWER ENGINEERING DRAGSTER
M-900

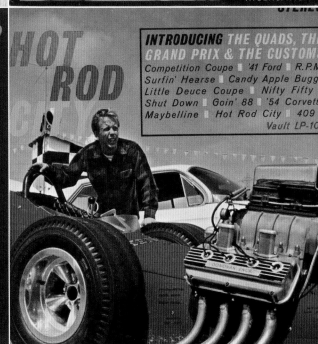

INTRODUCING THE QUADS, THE
GRAND PRIX & THE CUSTOMS
Competition Coupe ☐ '41 Ford ☐ R.P.M.
Surfin' Hearse ☐ Candy Apple Buggy
Little Deuce Coupe ☐ Nifty Fifty
Shut Down ☐ Goin' 88 ☐ '54 Corvette
Maybelline ☐ Hot Rod City ☐ 409
Vault LP-10
HOT ROD CITY

SHIRLEY

DRAG RACING IS THE STUFF OF LEGENDS ("DYNO DON" NICHOLSON, TOM "MONGOOSE" MCEWEN, ARNIE "THE FARMER" BESWICK, "BIG DADDY" DON GARLITS, "TV TOMMY" IVO, "JUNGLE" JIM LIEBERMAN,
AND SO ON). HOWEVER, POSSIBLY ONLY ONE SONG (SEE OPPOSITE PAGE), "SHIRLEY," FROM L7'S *HUNGRY FOR STINK* ALBUM (1994), PAID HOMAGE TO A SPECIFIC DRAGSTER DRIVER, IN THIS CASE SHIRLEY
MULDOWNEY, THE NHRA'S WINSTON TOP FUEL CHAMPION IN 1977, 1980, AND 1982. L7, LED BY DONITA SPARKS, WAS AT THE FOREFRONT OF GRUNGE-PUNK'S RIOT GRRRL CONTINGENT. *HUNGRY FOR
STINK'S* ALBUM ART FEATURED A KNIFE-WIELDING, STRANGELY MASKED LUNATIC, POISED TO STRIKE, IN A CAR.

STAINBOY

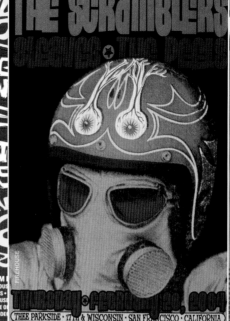

FIREHOUSE

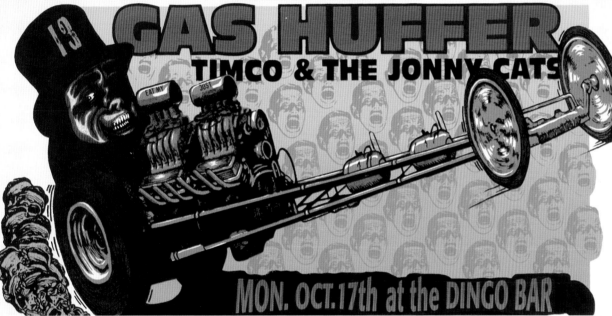

ANOTHER KILLPEOPLEPRODUCTION

GAS HUFFER
TIMCO & THE JONNY CATS

MON. OCT.17th at the DINGO BAR

FIREHOUSE

NEBULA
BLACK MOUNTAIN CREEPER
AMPS II ELEVEN

september 18.2004

HIGH FIVE BAR AND GRI

1227 N. HIGH CO. COLUMBUS OH

MIKE MARTIN/ENGINEHOUSE 13

JENNIFER FINCH/DROP TROU (BMI)

JOSEPH MOMAN

SUGGEST YOU FIND A SEAT IN THE GRANDSTANDS

'CAUSE YOU DON'T WANT TO MISS THIS!

"I WONDER IF SHIRLEY'S GOT IT IN HER TO HOLD

THAT THROTTLE DOWN"

KILLS YOUR JOKE

AS SHE'S BURNING SMOKE

"SHIRLEY MULDOWNEY IS PULLING AHEAD …

AND SHE TAKES THE RED LIGHT"

AND YOU FIND

CROSSING THE FINISH LINE

SHIRLEY MULDOWNEY HAS JUST SET

A NEW TRACK RECORD!

SATISFACTION!

WHAT'S A BEAUTIFUL GIRL LIKE YOU DOING RACING

IN A PLACE LIKE THIS?

WINNING.

WINNING. WINNING. WINNING. WINNING.

WHAT'S DRAG RACING COMING TO?

THERE'S NOWHERE THAT WE DON'T GO

L7, SHIRLEY

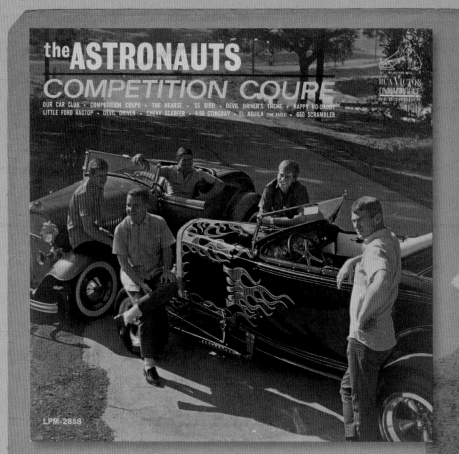

AMERICAN VERSION

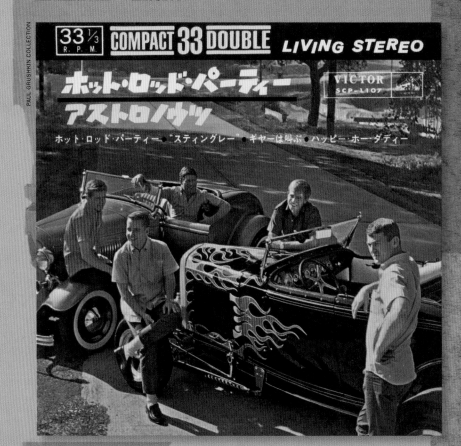

JAPANESE VERSION

THE ASTRONAUTS

SOME PEOPLE SAY THE ASTRONAUTS, FROM BOULDER, COLORADO, HEWED MUCH CLOSER TO THE TRUE SPIRIT OF SURF AND DRAG MUSIC THAN MANY OF THE BETTER-KNOWN CALIFORNIA GROUPS. THEY WERE INSTRUMENTALISTS WHO OCCASIONALLY TRIED OUT VOCALS, INCREASINGLY SO AFTER THE BEACH BOYS HIT IT BIG WITH "409" AND "LITTLE DEUCE COUPE." THE ASTRONAUTS' COMPETITION COUPE EP RELEASED IN JAPAN WAS CONTEMPORARY WITH ITS U.S. COUNTERPART, MEANING THE FLAMED ROADSTER PICTURED ON THE SLEEVE WAS ONE OF THE FIRST HOT RODS THAT JAPAN CAME TO ASSOCIATE WITH THE NEWEST AMERICAN SOUND. THE TITLE COMPETITION COUPE WAS TRANSLATED ONTO THE JAPANESE EP AS HOT ROD PARTY.

Rev **H** HORTON Heat

MERRITTVILLE SPEEDWAY

8PM TUES
29
OCTOBER

Higher Ground
One Main St Winooski VT

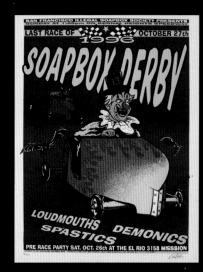

YOU WANT TO RACE? IF YOU INSIST AT THAT PRICE, I CAN'T RESIST.

ZZ TOP, MANIC MECHANIC

Checkered Flag — Dick Dale and His Del-Tones — Capitol Records — ST 2002

Dick Dale's new album, "Checkered Flag," presents the "King Of The Surfers Stomp" performing an entire set of the new hot-rod music. In "Checkered Flag," Dick's raunchy-guitar talent clearly shows through on such numbers as "The Scavenger," which is already a hit on the West Coast, and "The Wedge." Dale has included four instrumentals which he wrote himself: "Surf Buggy," "Night Rider," "Ho-Dad Machine" and "Motion." His vocal numbers fail in several spots, especially on "It Will Grow On You" and "Hot Rod Racer." Nevertheless, these do not keep the disc from having that big, rockin' sound that has made Dick Dale a surfin' music star. The fantastic, "reeved-up" sounds on this L.P. come from a guitar and amplifier especially built by Leo Fender of the Fender Guitar Company. It seems that this is the only guitar that has been able to withstand the tremendous beating it gets from Dick. No offense to this great artist, but if he'd stick more to his instrumentals, which are all great, and forget the singing, his album would be even better than it is. ■

DICK DALE

Dick Dale was the gen-u-wine article, a surfer, hot rodder, and guitar picker combined. He liked everything loud—the roaring waves down at his favorite break, his Fender Stratocaster and amp turned up to 10 and the throaty exhaust notes from his own stable of cars, which, as pictured in *Life* magazine in 1964, included a custom-built MG racer, an early Econoline-style van to haul his gear, and a '59 Cadillac convertible.

His hot rod hits included "Mr. Eliminator," "Grudge Run," "Nitro," and "Taco Wagon." With his backing band, the Del-Tones, Dale's live performances were legendary (especially those at Balboa's Rendezvous Ballroom) and he came to be known as "King of the Surf Guitar."

Dale, born Richard Mansour in 1937, is primarily recognized for introducing guitar reverb, now a staple of the surf sound. His other trademark is his fast staccato picking. Since Dale is left-handed—and few guitar shops cater to left-handed players—he initially was forced to play a right-handed model. However, he did so without restringing it, leading him to, in effect, play the guitar upside-down, much like Jimi Hendrix would later do.

In 2005, the Black Eyed Peas' song "Pump It" (also one of the best car-focused videos ever filmed) heavily sampled from Dale's Middle Eastern–inflected surf hit "Misirlou."

CHEVROLET 409

GIDDY UP, 409

Some say the muscle car was born with the introduction of the Chrysler 300 in 1955. Still others say that the optional LeMans package that a young GM engineer named John DeLorean conceived for the Pontiac Tempest in 1964 marked the start of the muscle car era.

Still others say the muscle car was launched in 1961, with Chevy's Impala SS and its big-block 409. An extension of the 348 truck engine, the 409-ci engine was Chevrolet's top regular production engine from 1961 to 1964, with a choice of single- or dual-four-barrel carburetors. Output reached 409 horsepower—one horse per cubic inch—in 1962, when the Impala was the preferred street tire-squealer, and its cousin, the Bel Air Sport Coupe, became *the* item for drag racers such as "Dyno" Don Nicholson, who won "Mr. Stock Eliminator" at the 1962 Pomona Winternationals. That same

year, equipped with the "four-speed, dual-quad, Positraction" equipment prescribed by songwriters Gary Usher and Brian Wilson, a Bel Air recorded a heady 12.22-second quarter-mile at 115 miles per hour. Now, zero to 60 miles per hour could be achieved in four seconds flat.

Today, the '61–'63 Bel Air and Impala two-door models enjoy a cult-like following, as they were among the finest-looking cars on the market in their day—due particularly to the crisply drawn side panels—and are avidly sought-after by lowriders and hip-hop aficionados.

The Usher/Wilson tune, "409," was the B-side to The Beach Boys' "Surfin' Safari." Sadly, the graphics on the single's packaging never reflected the car's street or drag racing heritage.

HOT ROD RACE

NOW ME AND MY WIFE AND MY BROTHER JOE,
TOOK OFF IN MY FORD FROM SAN PEDRO.
WE HADN'T MUCH GAS AND THE TIRES WAS LOW,
BUT THE DOGGONE FORD COULD REALLY GO.
NOW ALONG ABOUT THE MIDDLE OF THE NIGHT,
WE WERE RIPPIN' ALONG LIKE WHITE FOLKS MIGHT,
WHEN A MERCURY BEHIND, HE BLINKED HIS LIGHTS,
AND HE HONKED HIS HORN AND HE FLEW OUTSIDE.
WE HAD TWIN PIPES AND A COLUMBIA BUTT,
YOU PEOPLE MAY THINK THAT I'M IN A RUT,
BUT TO YOU FOLKS WHO DON'T DIG THE JIVE,
THAT'S TWO CARBURETORS AND AN OVERDRIVE.
WE MADE GREASE SPOTS OUTTA MANY GOOD TOWNS,
AND LEFT THE COPS' HEADS SPINNIN' ROUND 'N ROUND.
THEY WOULDN'T CHASE, THEY'D RUN AND HIDE,
BUT ME AND THAT MERCURY STAYED SIDE BY SIDE.
NOW WE WERE FORD MEN AND WE LIKELY KNEW,
THAT WE WOULD RACE UNTIL SOMETHIN' BLEW.
AND WE THOUGHT IT OVER,
NOW, WOULDN'T YOU?
I LOOKED DOWN AT MY LOVELY BRIDE,
HER FACE WAS BLUE, I THOUGHT SHE'D DIED.
WE LEFT STREAKS THROUGH TOWNS ABOUT FORTY FEET WIDE,
BUT ME AND THAT MERCURY STAYED SIDE BY SIDE.
MY BROTHER WAS PALE, HE SAID HE WAS SICK,
HE SAID HE WAS JUST A NERVOUS WRECK.
BUT WHY SHOULD I WORRY, FOR WHAT THE HECK,
ME AND THAT MERCURY WAS STILL NECK-AND-NECK.
NOW ON THROUGH THE DESERTS WE DID GLIDE,
A-FLYIN' LOW, AND A-FLYIN' WIDE.
ME AND THAT MERCURY WAS A-TAKIN' A RIDE,
AND WE STAYED EXACTLY SIDE BY SIDE.
NOW I LOOKED IN MY MIRROR AND I SAW SOMETHIN' COMIN',
I THOUGHT IT WAS A PLANE BY THE WAY IT WAS A-RUNNIN',
IT WAS A-HUMMIN' ALONG AT A TERRIBLE PACE,
AND I KNEW RIGHT THEN IT WAS THE END OF THE RACE.
WHEN IT FLEW BY US, I TURNED THE OTHER WAY,
THE GUY IN THE MERCURY HAD NOTHIN' TO SAY.
FOR IT WAS A KID, IN A HOPPED UP MODEL A.

ARKIE SHIBLEY, HOT ROD RACE

HOT ROD RACE/HOT ROD LINCOLN

In 1905 a singer named Billy Murray recorded "In My Merry Oldsmobile," the first known homage to a car—his own car, apparently. Fifty years later, Charlie Ryan recorded "Hot Rod Lincoln" as a tribute to his own rod, a customized '41 Lincoln Zephyr.

Ryan was a true-blue hot rodder. On his King label LP, *Hot Rod* (1961), Ryan launched his explanation of the contents thusly: "This album has a 3/4 cam, two four-barrel carbs, a hot ignition, a 270 block, 456 rear end, and twin straight stacks. It's not music 'to relax to;' [this is] music that will have you hanging onto your chair at every screeching two wheel turn." Obviously, Ryan was *the* man to narrate a hot rod race of epic proportions.

But Ryan's song (written in 1955 and first released as a single by Souvenir in 1957, before becoming a hit in 1960 after having been slightly rewritten by Ryan and W. S. Stevenson of 4-Star Records) actually was a modernized takeoff on Arkie Shibley's release, "Hot Rod Race." Shibley, about which little is known, possibly was the "George Wilson," to whom the song's writing is credited ("Arkie" likely was slang for the Arkansas immigrants who flooded into California during the 1930s Dust Bowl).

Shibley's 1950 tune about a legendary highway race commencing in the Los Angeles port city of San Pedro between a Ford and a Mercury, was a homegrown product released on Shibley's Mountain Dew label before 4-Star Records picked it up and it became a hit on their Gilt-Edge label, peaking at #5 on the country charts.

Jim Dawson and Steve Propes, in their *What Was the First Rock 'N' Roll Record?*, noted that Shibley never really benefited from the song. "Though it accelerated onto the country charts in the last weeks of 1950," they wrote, "three cover versions on major labels overtook him and, like the kid in the Model A, eventually blew him off the road. Ramblin' Jimmy Dolan (on Capitol) and Tiny Hill (on Mercury) hit the country charts in early February 1951, with Hill's version swerving over onto the pop strip. Two weeks later, Red Foley, Decca's all-purpose hillbilly cover-record man, entered the running.

"One thing that might have slowed Shibley down on the stretch," Dawson and Propes continued, "was his bragging about 'rippin' along like white folks might.' Smug references to livin' like a white man might have gone over in Southern California in 1951, but stations back East considered

HOT ROD LINCOLN

WELL YOU'VE HEARD THE STORY OF THE HOT ROD RACE THAT FATAL DAY,

WHEN THE FORD AND THE MERCURY WENT OUT TO PLAY.

THIS IS THE INSIDE STORY I'M HERE TO SAY,

I WAS THE KID THAT WAS A-DRIVIN' THAT MODEL-A.

IT'S GOT A LINCOLN MOTOR AND IT'S REALLY SOUPED UP,

AND THAT MODEL A BODY MAKES IT LOOK LIKE A PUP.

IT'S GOT TWELVE CYLINDERS, AND USES THEM ALL,

WITH AN OVERDRIVE THAT JUST WON'T STALL.

IT'S GOT A FOUR-BARREL CARB AND DUAL EXHAUST,

4-11 GEARS, SHE CAN REALLY GET LOST.

GOT SAFETY TUBES AND I'M NOT SCARED,

THE BRAKES ARE GOOD AND THE TIRES ARE FAIR.

WE LEFT SAN PEDRO LATE ONE NIGHT,

THE MOON AND THE STARS WERE SHINING BRIGHT,

EVERYTHING WENT FINE UP THE GRAPEVINE HILL,

WE WAS PASSIN' CARS LIKE THEY WAS STANDIN' STILL.

THEN ALL OF A SUDDEN, LIKE A FLICK OF AN EYE,

A CADILLAC SEDAN HAD PASSED US BY.

THE REMARK WAS MADE, "THERE'S THE CAR FOR ME,"

BUT BY THEN THE TAILLIGHTS WERE ALL YOU COULD SEE.

WELL THE FELLERS RIBBED ME FOR BEIN' BEHIND,

SO I STARTED TO MAKE THE LINCOLN UNWIND.

I TOOK MY FOOT OFF THE GAS, AND MAN ALIVE,

I SHOVED IT DOWN INTO OVERDRIVE.

WELL I WOUND IT UP TO A HUNDRED AND TEN,

TWISTED THE SPEEDOMETER CABLE OFF THE END.

I HAD MY FOOT KEYED CLEAR TO THE FLOOR,

SAID, "THAT'S ALL THERE IS, THERE AIN'T NO MORE."

I WENT AROUND A CORNER AND I PASSED A TRUCK,

I WHISPERED A PRAYER, JUST FOR LUCK,

THE FENDERS WAS CLICKIN' A GUARDRAIL POST,

THE GUYS BESIDE ME WERE WHITE AS A GHOST.

I GUESS THEY'D THOUGHT I'D LOST MY SENSE,

THE TELEPHONE POLES LOOKED LIKE A PICKET FENCE.

THEY SAID, "SLOW DOWN, I SEE SPOTS,"

THE LINES ON THE ROAD JUST LOOKED LIKE DOTS.

SMOKE WAS ROLLIN' OUTTA THE BACK,

WHEN I STARTED TO GAIN ON THAT CADILLAC.

I KNEW I COULD CATCH HIM, AND HOPED I COULD PASS,

BUT WHEN I DID, I'D BE SHORT ON GAS.

WE WENT AROUND A CORNER WITH THE TIRES ON THE SIDE,

YOU COULD FEEL THE TENSION, MAN, WHAT A RIDE!

I SAID, "HOLD ON, I GOT A LICENSE TO FLY,"

AND THE CADILLAC PULLED OVER AND LET ME GO BY.

THEN ALL OF A SUDDEN, THE RODS STARTED KNOCKIN',

WHEN DOWN IN THE DIP, SHE STARTED A-ROCKIN'.

I LOOKED IN MY MIRROR AND RED LIGHTS WAS BLINKIN',

THE COPS WAS AFTER MY HOT ROD LINCOLN.

WELL, THEY ARRESTED ME, AND PUT ME IN JAIL

I CALLED MY POP TO GO MY BAIL.

HE SAID, "SON, YOU'RE GONNA DRIVE ME TO DRINKIN'

IF YOU DON'T STOP DRIVIN' THAT HOT ROD LINCOLN."

CHARLIE RYAN, HOT ROD LINCOLN

CHARLIE RYAN & W. S. STEVENSON/ACUFF-ROSE MUSIC & SONY/ATV LLC (BMI)

themselves too progressive to play such intimations of racism on the air. So, the other artists altered the offensive line. Dolan made it 'plain folks,' Foley 'poor folks,' and Hill 'rich folks;' later on, Ryan changed it to 'nice folks.'"

Shibley, seeing a window of opportunity, began to record a series of followup records, all in 1951, beginning with "Hot Rod Race #2" and ending with "#4," each extending the basic story. None cracked the country or pop charts.

On his own Hot Rod Lincoln, Ryan replaced the 1941 Zephyr body with a '30 Model A Ford five-window coupe body and substituted a '48 Lincoln V12 with a high-torque overdrive transmission. It was painted black with red wheels. Another racy aspect was that Ryan cut 2 feet off the frame to shorten the wheelbase, making for a compact, very efficient highboy-style unit.

Ryan later said it was while he was wrenching on his car in 1955 that he remembered Shibley's hillbilly-influenced composition and determined to give it an aggressive country update with Los Angeles–area landmarks such as the Grapevine Hill, a dangerous stretch of mountain highway linking the L.A. Basin with the San Joaquin Valley. He also specifically referenced his

12-cylinder rod: "Got a Lincoln motor, and it's really souped up/That Model A body makes it look like a pup." His band, the Timberline Riders, cleverly played out the dramatic highlights, including engine knocking, horns squawking, fenders clicking against guardrail posts, and, most important, the culminating police siren. The last stanza, with his pop coming to "throw" his bail, and the refrain, *Son, you're gonna drive me to drinkin'/If you don't stop drivin' that Hot Rod Lincoln*, was forevermore a classic summing-up that also set the stage for Commander Cody's inimitable 1971 growl of the same line, with His Lost Planet Airmen doing the sound effects honors.

When his own song hit, Ryan and his wife, Ruthie, often took the car out with them on tour, displaying it in the parking lot of the clubs he played. In 1960, when country singer Johnny Bond recorded yet another "new" version, this time with an 8-cylinder Lincoln motor, Ryan was pulled back into the studio to answer, also dropping in the new engine. That year, both artists competed furiously, Ryan on the East Coast, Bond on the West, in an attempt to gain on-air advantage and the most bookings. Ironically, also in 1960, Ryan himself installed a new V12 pulled from a 1939 Lincoln into his own hot rod and had the car repainted bright red for maximum attention.

Commander Cody

Asleep at the Wheel

LOST IN THE OZONE

ONE OF ROCK'S GREAT PLEASURES OF THE EARLY 1970S WAS HEARING BACK-TO-BACK SETS BY THE YOUNG COMMANDER CODY AND HIS LOST PLANET AIRMEN (FORMED IN 1968) AND ASLEEP AT THE WHEEL, LED BY RAY BENSON. ALTHOUGH CODY AND BAND HAILED FROM ANN ARBOR, MICHIGAN, AND "THE WHEEL" CAME FROM PAW-PAW, WEST VIRGINIA, THEIR WORK CAME TO REAL FRUITION IN NORTHERN CALIFORNIA CLUBS SUCH AS HOMER'S WAREHOUSE IN EAST PALO ALTO AND MANDRAKES AND THE KEYSTONE IN BERKELEY. THERE, YOU COULD HEAR THE FIRST STOMPING-GOOD VERSIONS OF "TOO MUCH FUN," "LOST IN THE OZONE," "MAMA HATED DIESELS," "TAKE ME BACK TO TULSA," "I'VE BEEN EVERYWHERE." EACH BAND ALSO PROUDLY TROTTED OUT ITS OWN VERSION OF "HOT ROD LINCOLN." BOTH BANDS THEN RELOCATED TO TEXAS AND BECAME MAINSTAYS AT HISTORIC VENUES SUCH AS THE ARMADILLO IN AUSTIN.

THE CODY BAND, WHICH TRAVELED IN AN OLD DOUBLE-DECKER GREYHOUND BUS, AND THE WHEEL INTRODUCED WESTERN SWING, ROCKABILLY, AND HONKY-TONK C&W TO LEGIONS OF POT-SMOKING LONGHAIRS. DUE TO "HOT ROD LINCOLN'S" POPULARITY ON FREE-FORM ROCK RADIO, CODY'S MONOLOGUE-LIKE VOCAL (THAT OF BANDLEADER GEORGE FRAYNE) WAS HEARD BY MORE PEOPLE IN ONE YEAR THAN ALL THE OTHER VERSIONS (SHIBLEY, RYAN, DOLAN, BOND, HILL, ETC.) COMBINED OVER THE YEARS. IT EVEN REACHED THE POP TOP 10 IN 1972.

LATER, AFTER LEAVING THE CODY BAND, LEAD GUNSLINGER BILL KIRCHEN BECAME RENOWNED FOR *HIS* VERSION THAT INCLUDES A SHOW-STOPPING SEGMENT IN WHICH HE RECOUNTS, PLAYED THROUGH HIS VIRTUOSO TELECASTER GUITAR, ALL THE GREATS WHO "PULLED OVER AND LET ME BY," INCLUDING JOHNNY CASH, DUANE EDDY, ROY ORBISON, JOHNNY RIVERS, MARTY ROBBINS, BUCK OWENS, MERLE TRAVIS, MERLE HAGGARD, LESTER FLATT, EARL SCRUGGS, BO DIDDLEY, CHUCK BERRY, LINK WRAY, ELMORE JAMES, JIMMY REED, MUDDY WATERS, B. B. KING, FREDDIE KING, ALBERT KING, BEN E. KING, STEVIE RAY VAUGHAN, ELVIS PRESLEY, DEEP PURPLE, THE ROLL-ING STONES, THE BEATLES, THE SEX PISTOLS, AND JIMI HENDRIX.

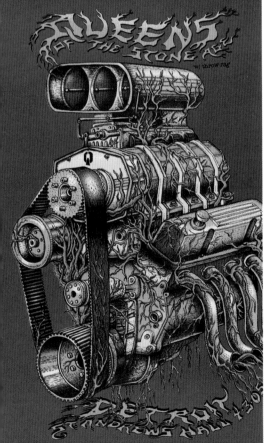

HEAVY HORSES

In 1939, Chrysler began design work on the first Hemi engine (designed with hemispherical combustion chambers), a V16 for fighter aircraft. In 1951, the company stunned the automotive world with its 180-horsepower Hemi V8 engine. Shortly thereafter, engines were being stripped from Chryslers, Dodges, and DeSotos to power dragsters, salt lakes racers, and street-driven hot rods. By the early 1960s, and before the muscle car era collided with the 1973–1974 gas crisis, and officially ended with the 1979 worldwide energy crisis, rock & roll songs celebrated both the Hemi engine and the concept of Ram (resonant manifold tuning for additional horsepower and torque).

Thanks to the Hemi and Ram, Mopar (Chrysler) milestones came fast and furious, and were major elements in popular and automotive culture:

- 1952: A special Hemi is tested in a Kurtis-Kraft Indy roadster; it's banned by officials as too powerful.
- 1953: A Dodge Hemi breaks 196 stock-vehicle records at the Bonneville Salt Flats.
- 1954: Lee Petty (father of Richard) wins the NASCAR Grand National championship running Chrysler and Dodge Hemis.
- 1955: A Chrysler 300 with a dual four-barrel 331-ci Hemi is the first production car to make 300 horsepower.
- 1956: Don "Big Daddy" Garlits begins his 46-year winning association with Chrysler Hemis.
- 1958: Garlits breaks the 170-mile-per-hour barrier in his *Swamp Rat* dragster.
- 1959: The original Ramchargers racing team of

Chrysler engineers debut *High & Mighty*, a Hemi-powered C/A class '49 Plymouth to win NHRA Nationals.

- 1964: Richard Petty debuts the 426-ci Hemi and laps the field while winning the Daytona 500. He captures the first of seven NASCAR driving championships.
- 1964: Garlits breaks the 200-mile-per-hour quarter-mile barrier in his Hemi dragster (201.34 miles per hour in 7.78 seconds). Chrysler builds a small number of Dodges and Plymouths with the new 426 Hemi for sanctioned drag racing, shortly to be termed "Funny Cars," based on radical wheelbase alterations, and to run in the A/FX class.
- 1965: NASCAR outlaws the Hemi by setting minimum production levels for street use.
- 1966: Chrysler releases the "Street Hemi" to meet minimum production levels and returns to NASCAR.
- 1967: Richard Petty wins an incredible 27 Grand National races in his Hemi Plymouth, including ten in a row.
- 1968: Plymouth introduces the Road Runner as the first budget muscle car, with a 426 Hemi option.
- 1970: In the second installment of the two-season epoch known as the "Aero Wars," the winged Plymouth Super Bird is Chrysler's answer to Ford's 1969 dominance of NASCAR. The spiraling speeds brought about by the period's aerodynamics and dueling 426 and Ford 429 Boss mills cause a driver boycott of the 1969 Talladega 500 and the introduction of restrictor plates in 1970.
- 1970: Sox & Martin Hemi Plymouths win seventeen major drag-racing championships and are runners-up in all the other major events entered.

PAUL GRUSHKIN

BLOWER ART

ED "BIG DADDY" ROTH AND STANLEY MOUSE (SEE PAGES 60–63) WERE MASTERS OF HOT ROD "BLOWER ART," AS DEFINED BY THEIR ILLUSTRATIONS FOR T-SHIRTS AND DECALS PROMINENTLY FEATURING BLOWER SCOOPS, THOSE DEVICES THAT FORCE AIR INTO AN ENGINE'S CARBURETION SETUP. SCOOPS CAN MERELY FUNCTION TO IMPART A RACE-WORTHY LOOK TO A STREET MACHINE, OR THEY CAN BE FULLY FUNCTIONAL FOR THE DRAG STRIP. MICHAEL LEDERMAN'S BLOWN 1937 DESOTO, PICTURED HERE, HOWLS AT EVERY OPPORTUNITY (LEDERMAN RUNS THE CRYSTAL GROUP, ROCK'S LEADING MERCHANDISE SALES COMPANY; THE CAR APPEARS AT MANY ROCK AND CAR EVENTS). MANY TOP ROCK & ROLL ARTISTS, HERE INCLUDING EMEK (QUEENS OF THE STONE AGE) AND DAN QUARNSTROM (JOHNNY RENO), AS WELL AS MIKE MARTIN (PAGE 42) AND JOHNNY CRAP (PAGE 200), HAVE TAKEN "BLOWER ART" TO GREAT ARTISTIC HEIGHTS.

EMEK

FINKS AND MOUSES

Over some forty years Ed "Big Daddy" Roth built a career loosely based on the ubiquitous monster-car T-shirt. Along with Stanley Mouse, he's considered a father of the movement. But long after Roth's death in 2001, it remains in dispute as to whether he or Mouse should be credited as *the* father. We do know this: both were there at the beginning (the late '50s); both were skilled at the improvisation necessary to create on-the-spot, airbrushed commissions; and both had tremendous visual memory banks that could call up makes and models of cars over which they cartooned the monsters.

When Roth got out of the Air Force in 1955 he teamed up with a hot rodding friend, Tom Kelly. Kelly's grandfather, "The Baron," was a pinstriper, and by 1957–1958 the three had established a shop in Bellflower, California, where hot rodders could obtain a Baron pinstripe, a Kelly scallop, or a Roth "flake" (an exterior paint formula in which crushed substances like shells or metal dust create a glittery finish).

According to longtime fan David Burge, "During slow times, Roth would amuse his customers by painting wild monster cartoons onto T-shirts using the shop's spray-paint equipment. This proved to be an early bonanza. Some of Roth's first magazine ads from that period featured 'individually styled Weird-O Shirts' for $5. Then, after a falling out with Kelly and Baron, he began traveling to car shows, where he perfected his technique and sold monster shirts to a hungry market of adolescent boys."

Mouse (see following pages) says he already had established himself airbrushing car-cum-monster designs on the East Coast Autorama car circuit when Roth started showing up. At a Pittsburgh show where Mouse had the exclusive, Roth hustled the promoter for an exception. According to Mouse, he was called over to listen to Roth boast, "Lemme show you how the big boys do it." Over the next six hours, Mouse sold $300 worth of airbrushed creations—a tidy sum then—and Roth $100. But in due course and with industrial-capacity silkscreening, Roth became the more aggressive promoter of the art form, especially after he brought out Rat Fink.

Mouse is quite clear on this subject: Roth appropriated Mouse's Freddy Flypogger to create Rat Fink. In fact, Mouse has a particularly telling relic from that period (see opposite page). Mouse laid down his Freddy, Roth added his Rat Fink features, then Mouse whited out the Rat Fink, although the resulting piece definitively shows both artists' work. On the back of the drawing Roth wrote, "Rat Finks eat mouses and their gutses" and signed it.

A Detroit native (early on, he established the Mouse House, where his mother and father helped run the silkscreening operation), Mouse would move to San Francisco in 1965, where he partnered with fellow adventurer Alton Kelley to create psychedelic posters for concerts at Bill Graham's Fillmore Auditorium and the Family Dog's Avalon Ballroom—including the skull and roses art for FD26, soon to be the Grateful Dead's trademark.

Roth, again according to David Burge, "became determined to push the creative envelope in car customization. With limited metalworking skills, he was at a disadvantage against customizing masters like Sam and George Barris, Darryl Starbird, and Dean Jeffries. Until he discovered fiberglass.

"There has seldom been such a natural click between artist and medium. Roth would buy the gooey stuff by the barrel, pouring it into plaster molds that he had created by hand—literally. Without benefit of tools, plans, or even a tape measure, Big Daddy would knead the concoction into the desired shape, letting the car happen, like a gearhead Jackson Pollock. And when the molds were cast off, they revealed some of the most stunning sculptural statements ever to sprout four wheels."

And so were born the *Outlaw*, *Beatnik Bandit*, *Orbitron*, *Rotar*, *Road Agent*, and *Mysterion*, among others. The Revell Company manufactured millions of replica scale models (Mouse had only two brought to life). In his heyday, Roth produced millions of mail-order monster shirts and decals, employing artists and art directors that would include Ed Newton and Robert Williams.

Roth, otherwise known as "Mr. Gasser," also hooked up with songwriter/producer Gary Usher in 1963 and co-created several Weirdos LPs, "featuring the voice of Mr. Gasser" (Roth). Roth also did the cover art for The Birthday Party's *Junkyard* LP, a project of rock musician Nick Cave. Roth, though flattered by the invite, was said to be subsequently utterly appalled by the near-incomprehensible music.

When the hot rod boom petered out in the early '70s, coinciding with the gas crunch, Roth found himself adrift for some ten years until collectors embraced the new "lowbrow" movement and rediscovered Roth's marvelous eccentricities. By this time Mouse and Kelley were regarded as *the* pioneering San Francisco rock artists (along with Rick Griffin, Victor Moscoso, Wes Wilson, and David Singer), and were painting for the Dead, Journey, and other bands, as well as matching wits with the Zap Comix creators.

RAT FINKS
EAT
MOUSE'S AND
THEIR GUTSES!
ED "BIG DADDY"
ROTH

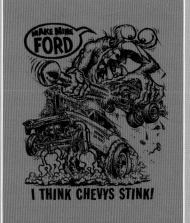

MOUSE SPEAKS

When I was sixteen, in tenth grade, I got kicked out of my first high school for painting graffiti all over the local hang out. And, I was in a band, and we did a little too much rockin' out at one of the high school dances. So, I went to art school for a year, then I got into an Ivy League–like high school where I was on the honor roll—and became the school cartoonist. I was in twelfth grade when the T-shirt thing started happening.

Are artists popular in high school? For me, on Saturdays, there'd be an actual lineup in my driveway where I'd be pinstriping dashboards and painting names on cars. I did lots of flames and skeletons. And my own car—my first was a '51 Ford—would be a different color every week. I'd test my spray gun on the car! I liked the motion of the spray gun; it was like dancing 'cause you always had to keep it moving. Then I found my first airbrush when I was looking in hot rod magazines and I saw the first ads for T-shirts by Dean Jeffries and Roth … and I was impressed. That must have been around '57–'58.

My dad showed me how to sign-paint. He'd worked in California for Disney, but it was slave labor in the '30s. After the war he decided to return to Detroit with the family. He couldn't support a family being an artist, which was frustrating. But he always promoted my work, supported me in the arts, and he was the one who showed me how to handle a brush.

When I got my airbrush, all the kids in the neighborhood came up to our house saying, "Paint my T-shirt." They'd bring me a T-shirt and I'd paint it up, right there in the garage. I knew a hot rod shop down the street, and I realized I could paint ten to twenty shirts a week, sell them for $5 each. That was good money back then. And the shirts sold! And the store wanted more!

Then I got a table at my first indoor car show. There are real early pictures of me with a pinstriping brush doing sunglasses, wallets, belts. I said to myself, "Y'know, I've always liked the state fair. I should be doing the state fair." I kept bugging and bugging my parents. Finally, they said yeah, okay. I got my uncles to help me and we built a giant booth. It was 1959 and I was a big hit at the state fair. They say you don't dream in color? By the last few days of the run, I was dreaming in *fluorescent*. And I started signing my name as Mouse, and it was m-o-n-e-y. It was the funniest thing I'd ever done.

I came up with Fred Flypogger when I was fourteen or fifteen. One of the first paintings of him was on a tonneau cover, based on the Ray Charles song "What'd I Say." All these drunk monsters sittin' around wearing zoot suits. Fred was my guy. He was my monster. He's the root of it all.

The strange thing about doing the cars shows was there was no competition. Roth wasn't doing it regularly yet. So it was totally freeform. I was able to just draw, just go crazy. Someone would ask me to do a monster-car piece, and I'd go wild with the airbrush and flo colors. People didn't know what an airbrush was—only book jacket illustrators and retouchers were using it. It was like having a magic trick. I remember one kid said to me, "Hey man, you didn't paint that, the machine did."

After that first state fair, there was a buzz. So I talked to the people doing the Autorama circuit. They'd only been using guys who colored in pre-printed designs. Nobody was doing it freeform, on the spot, like I was. But now I had to learn about cars—people wanted specific makes and models on their monsterized shirts. And as soon as I got the hang of that, my parents both quit their jobs and started managing me on the road and the studio

we'd created. My mom did the mail order; we issued catalogs. We started getting $100 a day in our mailbox; that's like $1,000 or more a day now. Just coming in like crazy.

I went off to Washington, D.C., Baltimore, Rhode Island, New York. In Chicago I saw my first gangsters. This one gangster bought like $200 worth of stuff from me. Last year I got a call from a guy who said, "I'm the son of a man you did a bunch of shirts for. He bought me all this stuff, years ago, when I was a kid." It was the same guy, that gangster.

The show I did in Madison Square Garden turned me on in other ways. I bought a Bob Dylan record, the one with "Blowin' in the Wind." With my portable record player, I sat in the back of my truck playing Dylan over and over and over again. And then we got into the show and heard Kennedy was assassinated. The teamsters cut my airbrush hoses—they thought I was some kind of Midwest wise-ass.

At one state fair, I'm pretty sure it was 1964, my booth was next to the music shell, the primo spot. All day long the bands from the Motown Revue were playing, and I was painting T-shirts. I was in heaven. Smokey's band came up, and I painted them some shirts. I'd take a break while the Temptations were singing, walk out into the crowd, and the top of my head would just rise up 6 feet. I'll always remember hearing "I'll Be There," walking through all those people—everybody singing along—thinking how lucky I was to be part of that scene. The half-black, half-white love-for-music thing has always affected me greatly, coming from Detroit.

Finally I did get to California. Late in the summer of '64. A bunch of friends and I were out on Catalina Island, at a Dairy Queen. There was a group of guys a few tables away, talking about shirt painting. I went, "Shirt painting? I'm a shirt painter." And they said, "So, who are you? What's your name?" I said "Mouse." They just about fell off their chairs. They said they had a shirt-painting booth on the island and they were drawing out of my catalog.

In the spring of 1965 I drove out to a show in Orange County. I'd been planning to move to California. What a life—I was sitting there eating some of my first peyote buttons and painting shirts. And this kid walks up and says, "Can you do 'Murph the Surf?" I had no idea what he was talking about. Of course, Murphy was Rick Griffin's character from *Surfer* magazine. They brought me a copy and I painted it the next day.

While I was in L.A. all these people said, "Stanley, you've got to go up to San Francisco. It's all artists and they're painting and it's a completely juicy scene. It happened pretty soon after that. I went from being a Bermuda shorts and tennis shoes kind of car guy to painting in a windmill in Berkeley. Then, I met up with (Alton) Kelley, and beginning in 1966 we spent hours and hours in the library starting to apply all this historic stuff to psychedelic concert posters. I couldn't have been happier. Painting T-shirts all those years made my hand strong. I don't mean to come off with a big ego here, but I felt like a virtuoso.

— Stanley Mouse
from an interview with the author

Coop, as Chris Cooper is known throughout the world, came west (out of Bixby, Oklahoma) to Los Angeles in the late '80s. Within ten years he'd made his bones as an "underground" artist, a contemporary of Robert Williams and Frank Kozik, and influenced by R. Crumb, Ed "Big Daddy" Roth, and "a host of other degenerates." He became renowned for his provocative rock concert posters, and along with his other exercises in vulgarity and fantasy-tease (porcelain sculptures, stickers, tattoo flash), Coop took pop culture's fascination with the devil to the nth degree (one of his self-published art books is titled *The Devil's Advocate*). He's now actively painting, with his most recent exhibition being oversize depictions of automotive pieces (manifolds, lifters, etc.) and titled *Parts with Appeal*.

"All artists' work—even what they become known for, early on—eventually turns into a dead end," Coop told this author. "You have to find the next intellectual pursuit to stay alive. I'm into painting aspects of cars at the moment, but in fact car culture's been a consistent interest of mine. I've worked on cars my whole life. Whenever I do a drawing of a car or any sort of mechanical element, I always sweat the details, 'cause if you don't do it right, you'll get called on it. I've the highest regard for car builders, metalworkers, pinstripers. The thing is—in fact, it's how I've judged my own art—it's about the application of technical expertise, and also knowing when *not* to rely on the newest technology. I'm impressed with people who learn how to do shit properly. It's about the appreciation for traditional styles, about respecting history. At the same time, the best car artists—fine artists or metalworkers—aren't afraid to step past history and add their own thing to it.

"Plus, I believe the process is innate. The best guys, the guys with their own forte, are not obsessed with learning about theory. What they create comes out of them because "it wants to" and because they've developed the chops. Truth is always intuitive that way. That's why some cars have that "correct look," why some rock posters work and others never will. Technique, history, and the willingness to take it further: those are the elements—but there's no blueprint to make it so. Which means, you can never stop working at it.

"My mom has drawings of mine from when I was four years old, and it was all cars, like Corvettes with crazy side pipes. I've always built model kits. My whole life! When I was a kid in the '70s, custom vans were the big thing. In the '80s, when I was, say, 14, I built all the muscle car kits. Hot Wheels came out the same year I was born, 1968, and if you look at the '29 Model A I'm driving now, it looks like a Hot Wheels car. It's got five-spoke mags, black Rustoleum paint (painted with a brush!), big tires in back, little tires in front, so it has all the right Hot Wheels aspects.

"I've a huge new fondness for chrome. While I was painting the mag wheel panel for my room-size installation, I found it gave me something unexpected, an abstraction. The chrome surface itself is wonderfully fluid; you look at it and you fall into it because the horizon line is in constant motion. You forget about the object itself—the wheel—and instead you start to see a fantasy landscape, almost mandala-like. And the wheel, of course, takes us across the literal landscape.

"The (installation's) first three panels are takes on a '55 Chevy gasser; the last four panels deconstruct a blown Hemi dragster motor. The rather gigantic scale I'm working in has power just by itself. All the technical elements are fascinating to me, as are the parallels to music. The car is such an essential part of the American dream; and ever since its inception, the popular music of the time—'50s, '60s, punk, Untamed Youth, Beach Boys, whatever—has provided the necessary social commentary, just like hip-hop is the commentary on the modern car scene.

"I recently traded my Model T for a phaeton that's under construction. I think about it a lot. I tend to analyze the elements that will make it right. One of the first things you do when you're building a rod is set the rails and then the body up on blocks. You set the grille up on 2x4s. Because the most important thing is to get the stance correct. It has to look right. It has to look … *intuitive*. Everything flows from that. Once it's at its zero-point, you can begin your work. I think my best creations have come from establishing that moment, the place where it's okay to begin your work."

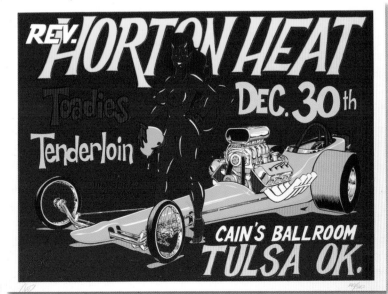

COOP'S STUDIO

JERSEY TURNPIKE, RIDIN' ON A WET NIGHT 'NEATH THE REFINERY'S GLOW, OUT WHERE THE GREAT BLACK RIVERS FLOW. LICENSE, REGISTRATION: I AIN'T GOT NONE, BUT I GOT A CLEAR CONSCIENCE 'BOUT THE THINGS THAT I DONE. MISTER STATE TROOPER, PLEASE DON'T STOP ME. BRUCE SPRINGSTEEN, STATE TROOPER

THE LAW

The story of famed middleweight boxer Rubin Carter's arrest in Paterson, New Jersey, as told in Bob Dylan's "Hurricane" (*Desire*, 1976), is just one of the many classic, ominous confrontations between citizens—many not exactly law abiding—and The Man to be played out in rock and rap for as long as there have been a black-and-white with cherries on the roof.

43 FROM WHERE I WAS SITTIN', 30 MILES AN HOUR IS THE LAW OF OUR LAND PLEASE PRODUCE YOUR LICENSE, FIND YOUR REGISTRATION, AND WHAT IS THE NAME OF YOUR INSURANCE MAN?

ME AND MY PARTNER GO PATROL CAR CRUISING
IN THE PARKING LOTS AT THE SHOPPING MALLS
SCANNING THOSE DASHES, THOSE MIRRORS AND VISORS,
THE LITTLE DETECTORS THAT RUIN IT ALL.
JOHNNY GOT ONE ON AN '86 T-BIRD,
PULL UP SLOW JUST AS CLOSE AS I CAN
MILI-WATT SECONDS ON MAXIMUM OUTPUT,
WE'LL DUST THAT PUPPY WITH ONE SMALL BLAST FROM MY
RADAR GUN, RADAR GUN
I'M MAKIN' MONEY AND I'M HAVIN' FUN WITH MY
RADAR GUN, RADAR GUN
WITH MY BRAND NEW RADAR GUN

BOTTLE ROCKETS, RADAR GUN

TEN RAP SONGS GUARANTEED TO
ROCK YOUR CAR AND DRAW FIRE

WAR 504 BOYZ

STILL FLY BIG TYMERS

BOYZ IN DA HOOD EASY E

GANGSTA (PUT ME DOWN) GETO BOYS

99 PROBLEMS JAY-Z

LAWS PATROLLING MIKE JONES

YA BETTER BRING A GUN KING TEE

THEY WANT MONEY KOOL MOE DEE

RIDE WIT ME NELLY

CADILLAC PIMPIN' YOUNGBLOODZ

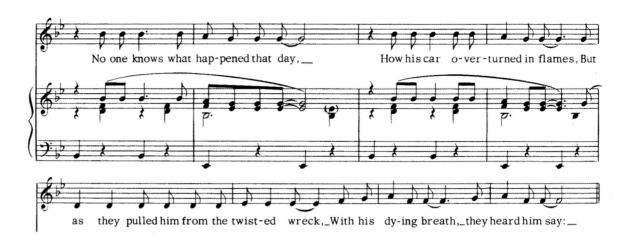

No one knows what hap-pened that day, _ How his car o-ver-turned in flames, But as they pulled him from the twist-ed wreck,_With his dy-ing breath,_they heard him say: _

TEEN MELODRAMA

Among all the teen-tragedy songs (cars, motorcycles, planes, drowning, warring families, etc.), the "car crash" subgenre reigns supreme. The most memorable songs feature themes of young love misunderstood, presided over by hushed, spoken verse and angelic choruses.

The saddest and most morbid, the most operatic and the most embarrassing, got the most attention. The most extreme example probably was Jimmy Cross' "I Want My Baby Back" (1965; #92 on the Billboard pop charts), which took the car crash milieu to its most horrifying extreme—be assured, he *does* get his baby back, one way or another, at the gravesite.

Other cult favorites include the Cadets' "Car Crash," the Avengers' later version of the same-titled tune in 1981, Blondie's "Susie and Jeffrey," the Ramones' "7-11," and "Dead Joe" by the Nick Cave–fronted Birthday Party.

The four melodramas that have vied for the most attention over the decades, however, are "Teen Angel" by Oklahoma's Mark Dinning (1960; #1 in the United States, although radio stations in the United Kingdom deemed the lyrics too morbid for airplay), Ray Petersen's "Tell Laura I Love Her" (1960; #12), Jan & Dean's "Dead Man's Curve" (1964; #8), and Wayne Cochran's

"Last Kiss" (1962), two years later covered by J. Frank Wilson and the Cavaliers (1964; #2).

At a 1963 gig in Texas, Wilson and his band met up with Sonley Roush. Roush was obsessed with a song called "Last Kiss," written and recorded by a blue-eyed Georgia soul singer named Wayne Cochran. It was the tragic tale of a girl who was killed on her first date with her sweetheart. Cochran based the song on a true-life tale of three teenage couples who were killed when their car struck a flatbed logging truck. Unfortunately, the song went nowhere—until Roush brought it to the attention of the Cavaliers.

Wilson's cover of "Last Kiss" was an unexpected triumph against the domination of the British Invasion in 1964. But sudden fame also can bring on tragedy. Wilson's personal excesses were so great the Cavaliers left him behind after just a handful of gigs. Nevertheless, he continued to promote the record with a new group of Cavaliers and with Roush as their manager.

En route to a concert in Canton, Ohio, that fall, Roush fell asleep at the wheel, resulting in a head-on collision. Roush died immediately and Wilson was badly injured; when he performed on *American Bandstand* shortly thereafter, it was on crutches.

THE CRYIN' TIRES, THE BUSTIN' GLASS, THE PAINFUL SCREAM THAT I HEARD LAST

THERE WE WERE — AT DEAD MAN'S CURVE

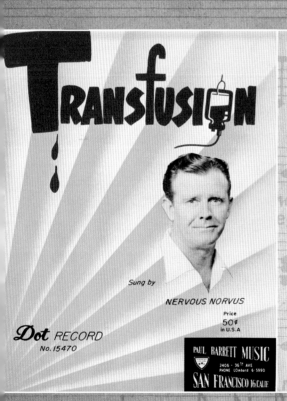

Transfusion

Sung by

NERVOUS NORVUS

Price 50¢ in U.S.A.

Dot RECORD

No. 15470

PAUL BARRETT MUSIC
2406 - 36TH AVE
PHONE LOmbard 6-5990
SAN FRANCISCO 16 CALIF

NERVOUS NORVUS

NERVOUS NORVUS WAS JIMMY DRAKE, A TRUCK DRIVER TURNED SONGWRITER INSPIRED BY CALIFORNIA RADIO LEGEND RED BLANCHARD, WHO CREATED A BEATNIK-LIKE SLANG HE CALLED "ZORCH" REFERENCED IN DRAKE'S 1956 HIT "TRANSFUSION" (#8 ON THE BILLBOARD POP CHART). "NERVOUS" IS A ZORCH WORD FOR "COOL," AND "NORVUS" WAS A MADE-UP HEP-CAT PERSONA THAT RHYMED.

THE GHOULISH "TRANSFUSION" WAS ONE OF THE CREEPIEST RECORDS EVER TO GRACE THE TOP 10. IT BEGAN AS A DEMO SENT BY DRAKE TO BLANCHARD, WHO, UPON HEARING IT, SPONTANEOUSLY PULLED A 78 FROM THE STATION LIBRARY'S *STANDARD SOUND EFFECTS* SERIES, CUED IT TO "AUTO SKIDS AND CRASHES," AND DUBBED IN DISASTER SOUNDS THAT PUNCTUATE THE SONG'S MINI-TALES OF RECKLESS DRIVING. BLANCHARD AIRED THE PASTICHED "TRANSFUSION" ON KPOP (LOS ANGELES) AND IT WAS AN OVERNIGHT SENSATION. DOT RECORDS CALLED WITHIN DAYS TO SEE IF THE RECORDING WAS AVAILABLE FOR RELEASE AND OBTAINED THE SIMPLE DEMO TAPE WITH ITS ADDED EFFECTS.

RELEASED IN MAY 1956, THE SINGLE WAS UNLIKE ANYTHING AMERICA APPARENTLY HAD EVER HEARD. REPORTEDLY, A HALF-MILLION COPIES WERE SOLD WITHIN THE FIRST TWO WEEKS. BLANCHARD'S SMALL SHARE OF THE ROYALTIES WAS POUNCED UPON BY AN UNEXPECTED THIRD PARTY—THE CREATORS OF THE EFFECTS, WHO RECOGNIZED THEIR OWN CRASH SOUNDS.

"TRANSFUSION" REMAINED ON THE POP CHARTS FOR 14 WEEKS AND WAS GORY ENOUGH TO BE BANNED BY BOTH THE ABC AND NBC RADIO NETWORKS. IT WAS DRAKE'S ONLY HIT, AND BEING UNCOMMONLY SHY, HE TURNED DOWN HIS ONE OFFER TO LIP-SYNCH IT ON *THE ED SULLIVAN SHOW*.

Just before sunrise on New Year's Day in 1953, a sleek, powder-blue Cadillac roared up to the rural Oak Hill, West Virginia, hospital in the cold Appalachian darkness. The driver was just 17, exhausted, and scared. The passenger was barely 29 and dead.

At the wheel was Charles Carr, a college freshman on Christmas break from Auburn University. The man in the backseat was singer-songwriter Hank Williams. "I ran in and explained my situation to the two interns who were in the hospital," said Carr, now a 70-year-old Montgomery, Alabama, businessman. "They came out and looked at Hank and said, 'He's dead.' I asked 'em, 'Can't you do something to revive him?' One of them looked at me and said, 'No, son, he's just dead.'"

It was a last ride that would help define American music and pop culture for decades to come.

Long before there was Janis Joplin or Jimi Hendrix or Kurt Cobain — self-destructive stars who flamed out at their zenith—there was Hiram "Hank" Williams, a hard-drinking, rough-around-the-edges, but thoroughly beloved Alabama boy who wrote simple, heart-tugging songs about loneliness, many of which peaked at #1 on the country charts. Only Carr knows the truth about Williams' final hours.

He thinks Williams died—the official cause was heart failure—somewhere between Bristol, Tennessee, and Oak Hill, on the way to a New Year's Day 1953 show in Canton, Ohio. "I'm certainly not an authority on Hank Williams," said Carr, "But I'm the only authority on Hank Williams' death."

Carr maintains Williams was very much alive and wearing white cowboy boots, a stylish blue overcoat, and a white fedora when they left Knoxville, Tennessee, at 10:45 p.m. New Year's Eve en route to a concert 500 blustery miles north. What ensued has been material for considerable speculation ever since.

By the time Carr got behind the wheel of Williams' ragtop Cadillac on December 30, 1952, the troubadour's life was in a full-tilt meltdown. He was recently divorced from his first wife, Audrey. Though remarried, he was staying at his mother's downtown Montgomery boardinghouse, having been demoted from the Grand Ole Opry to the Louisiana Hayride, the farm team of country music. He was taking morphine shots for constant back pain after major surgery the year before, and regularly ingested a dangerous sedative—chloral hydrate—to sleep.

Williams knew Carr's father, who ran a Montgomery taxi service, and the teenager was asked to drive an obviously ailing Williams to gigs in Charleston, West Virginia, and Canton, major concert dates that Williams hoped would be the start of a comeback. It was a journey that seemed doomed from the start.

By the time Carr helped Williams load his guitars and stage suits into the car trunk, the weather across much of the South was deteriorating. Rain was turning to ice and snow. Carr recalls the 6-foot-2 Williams was sick and frail at the time, weighing perhaps 130 pounds, but disputes reports that the singer, long a heavy drinker, was guzzling booze most of the trip. Carr remembers Williams being in good spirits as the trip began. They told jokes, sang songs, and traded tales as they navigated the two-lane highways of the pre-interstate South. "We were just a couple of young guys on a car trip having fun," Carr said.

It was snowing hard by the time they reached Chattanooga, and Williams decided to try to catch a flight from Knoxville to make the Charleston show on time. The flight took off at 3:30 p.m., but was turned back due to the bad weather. So, Carr and Williams found themselves stuck in Knoxville for the night. The Charleston show was a bust, but they still hoped to make Canton. "We talked a while and ordered steaks up in the room," Carr said. "As I remember, Hank didn't eat much." Carr also called a doctor, who came and gave Williams two injections—later determined to be morphine mixed with vitamin B12. "He calmed down after that, but, looking back, maybe it was a combination, along with his bad health, that led to the coronary," Carr said.

Williams dozed off fully clothed, but about 10:30 p.m. Carr got a call from the concert promoter telling him they had to leave right away and drive through the night to make the Canton show. "There was a penalty clause in his contract … so we had to be there for the New Year's Day concert, or else," Carr said.

Carr said there was little traffic as they pulled out of Knoxville. "What traffic you did see was moving at a snail's pace because the roads were so awful," Carr said. "We were trying to push it, but we didn't have much luck."

Carr got a ticket about an hour later in Blaine, Tennessee, when he almost ran into a patrolman while trying to pass another car. He paid a fine and got back behind the wheel, with Williams asleep in the back. It was after midnight by this time—already New Year's Day—and Carr had been behind the wheel since early that morning.

The teenager stopped in a small town to gas up and get a quick bite to eat. Carr said it could have been Bristol, Tennessee, about 120 miles northeast of Knoxville, or it could have been Bluefield, a town in West Virginia. It was pitch dark and he was bone-tired in unfamiliar territory. He specifically remembers a service station on one side of the highway and a diner and a cab stand on the other. "I remember Hank got out to stretch his legs and I asked him if he wanted a sandwich or something," Carr said. "He said, 'No, I just want to get some sleep.'

"I don't know if that's the last thing he ever said. But it's the last thing I remember him telling me."

At the cab stand, Carr picked up a relief driver who helped him drive for a few hours before getting out somewhere in rural West Virginia. Carr drove on, but became increasingly concerned about the eerie silence in the backseat. He pulled off the road to check on Williams, who was lying with his head toward the passenger seat and had his left hand across his chest. "He had his blue overcoat on and had a blanket over him that had fallen off," Carr said. "I reached back to put the blanket back over him, and then I felt a little unnatural resistance from his right arm. It was ice cold."

Carr pulled into the next service station he saw and told the owner he needed to get to a hospital fast. The man pointed the way, and Carr remembers seeing a road sign for Oak Hill, 6 miles away. He was terribly frightened, anticipating the frenzy of concern that would surely follow.

Fifty years later, on a bright late-December day in 2003, Carr strolled through the Hank Williams Museum in downtown Montgomery. He sat for a few minutes in the driver's seat of the Cadillac he drove that night. The overcoat that Williams was wearing was in a glass case nearby. At his own home, Carr has a framed poster for the concert that he and Williams never arrived at, and he keeps a pair of cowhide gloves the singer gave him for that final trip.

— Jim Tharpe
Milwaukee Journal Sentinel

ELEANOR GROSCH "LONG WHITE CADILLAC" (HOMAGE TO DAVE AND PHIL ALVIN, THE BLASTERS)

JESSE BELVIN, WHO WROTE "EARTH ANGEL" AND "GOODNIGHT, MY LOVE," BOTH MAJOR HITS IN THE MID-1950S FOR THE PENGUINS, WAS KILLED IN AN AUTO ACCIDENT ON FEBRUARY 6, 1960, OUTSIDE HOPE, ARKANSAS.

HIS WIFE AND THE CAR'S DRIVER ALSO DIED OF THEIR INJURIES.

THE THREE WERE TRYING TO MAKE A FAST GETAWAY FROM THE FIRST-EVER MIXED-RACE-AUDIENCE POP CONCERT IN THE CITY OF LITTLE ROCK. THAT NIGHT, MORE THAN SIX THREATS HAD BEEN MADE AGAINST BELVIN'S LIFE. THE SHOW WAS INTERRUPTED TWICE BY WHITES IN THE AUDIENCE, SHOUTING RACIAL EPITHETS AND URGING THE WHITE TEENAGERS IN ATTENDANCE TO LEAVE AT ONCE.

THERE WAS SPECULATION BELVIN'S CAR HAD BEEN TAMPERED WITH PRIOR TO THE ACCIDENT, BUT FOUL PLAY WAS NEVER PROVED.

MARC BOLAN WAS ONE OF ENGLAND'S ORIGINAL GLAM ROCK HEADLINERS.

HE HAD A BRIEF CAREER AS A SUPERSTAR WITH HIS BAND T-REX BUT WAS EVENTUALLY REDUCED TO HOSTING A CHILDREN'S TELEVISION SERIES.

ON THE NIGHT OF SEPTEMBER 16, 1977, BOLAN HAD DINNER WITH HIS LOVE, GLORIA JONES, WITH WHOM HE HAD A 2-YEAR-OLD SON, ROLAN. AFTER MUCH MERRIMENT, GLORIA GOT BEHIND THE WHEEL OF HER PURPLE MINI GT TO DRIVE THE TWO OF THEM HOME. THIS WAS AT ABOUT 4 A.M.

SHORTLY THEREAFTER, THE MINI WAS TRAVELING AT A HIGH RATE OF SPEED ON QUEENS RIDE IN SOUTH LONDON. IT LEFT THE ROAD AS IT CROSSED A HUMPBACKED BRIDGE, SHOT THROUGH A FENCE, AND SMASHED INTO A SYCAMORE TREE. MARC WAS KILLED INSTANTLY.

BOLAN WAS A LIFELONG FAN OF CARS, ESPECIALLY AMERICAN ONES, AND WROTE SONGS THAT FEATURED THEM IN THE LYRICS. CADILLACS WERE AMONG HIS FAVORITES. STILL, HE NEVER ACTUALLY LEARNED HOW TO DRIVE A CAR. THE REASON HE WAS THE PASSENGER IN THE CAR WAS BECAUSE GLORIA WAS THE ONLY ONE OF THEM WHO COULD DRIVE.

BLEW HIS MIND OUT IN A CAR

EDDIE COCHRAN, BORN IN ALBERT LEA, MINNESOTA, DIED IN WILTSHIRE, ENGLAND, AT THE AGE OF 21 ON APRIL 17, 1960. SADLY, TIME HAS NOT ACCORDED HIM QUITE THE SAME RESPECT AS IT HAS OTHER EARLY ROCKABILLY LEGENDS LIKE BUDDY HOLLY, RICKY NELSON, AND GENE VINCENT. THIS IS PARTIALLY ATTRIBUTABLE TO HIS VERY BRIEF LIFESPAN, BUT COCHRAN HAD A FAT, BRASH GUITAR SOUND AND HIS SONGS ALL HAD *ATTITUDE*—AMONG THEM, "SITTIN' IN THE BALCONY" (1957; #18 ON THE BILLBOARD POP CHART), "SUMMERTIME BLUES" (1958; #8), AND "C'MON EVERYBODY" (1958; #35), WITH SEVERAL LATER COVERED BY THE BEATLES, THE ROLLING STONES, THE SEX PISTOLS, AND THE WHO.

COCHRAN IS MORE REVERED TODAY IN BRITAIN THAN IN THE UNITED STATES, DUE IN PART TO THE TRAGIC CIRCUMSTANCES OF HIS DEATH.

IN EARLY 1960, HE TOURED THE UNITED KINGDOM WITH HIS GIRLFRIEND, SONGWRITER SHARON SHEELEY, AND FELLOW PERFORMER GENE VINCENT. THE TOUR WAS A RESOUNDING SUCCESS, AS MANY FANS HAD NEVER SEEN AMERICAN ROCK & ROLL STARS ON STAGE. AFTER THEIR FINAL ENCORE, COCHRAN AND VINCENT WERE TRIUMPHANT, ARMS AROUND EACH OTHER'S SHOULDERS. THERE WAS A LONG-AWAITED BREAK JUST AHEAD, FOR VINCENT, A WEEK PLAYING IN PARIS, WHERE HE WAS REVERED NEARLY AS FERVENTLY AS ELVIS, AND FOR COCHRAN, THE COMFORTS OF FAMILY AND HOME, TALK OF AN APPEARANCE ON *THE ED SULLIVAN SHOW*, AND MORE PIONEERING STUDIO EXPERIMENTATIONS WITH REVERB.

THE TWO STARS WANTED TO LEAVE IMMEDIATELY AFTER THE LAST SHOW IN BRISTOL TO CATCH SOME REST IN LONDON BEFORE GOING TO THE AIRPORT IN THE AFTERNOON. THERE WERE NO LATE-NIGHT TRAINS TO LONDON OVER THE EASTER HOLIDAY, SO A LOCAL CAB COMPANY WAS BOOKED.

GEORGE WILLIAM THOMAS MARTIN OF BRISTOL WAS THE EAGER YOUNG CAB DRIVER HIRED FOR THE JOURNEY. THE THREE AMERICANS SAT IN THE BACK OF THE CREAM-COLORED FORD CONSUL. SHEELEY RECALLED BEING FRIGHTENED BY THE RECKLESS SPEED OF THE CAR AS IT ROARED OUT OF BRISTOL TO JOIN THE A4 ROAD TO LONDON. THEY PASSED THROUGH BATH TO THE OUTSKIRTS OF THE SMALL WILTSHIRE MARKET TOWN OF CHIPPENHAM. IT WAS THEN THE PASSENGERS NOTICED MARTIN HAD TAKEN A WRONG TURN AND APPEARED HEADING BACK TOWARD BATH. TRYING TO TURN OR STOP TOO QUICKLY IN MAKING THE CORRECTION, OR POSSIBLY BECAUSE A TIRE BLEW, THE DRIVER LOST CONTROL AND A DEADLY SKID ENDED WITH THE CAR SLAMMING INTO A LAMPPOST.

VINCENT BROKE HIS COLLARBONE AND RIBS; SHEELEY BROKE HER PELVIS. BOTH SURVIVED. COCHRAN, HOWEVER, WAS THROWN THROUGH THE FRONT WINDSHIELD AND DIED 16 HOURS LATER FROM BRAIN INJURIES. ONE OF THE POLICEMEN ON THE SCENE RETRIEVED COCHRAN'S GUITAR FROM THE TRUNK UNSCATHED, AND WOULD PLAY IT ON AND OFF FOR TWO WEEKS BEFORE IT WAS RETURNED TO COCHRAN'S MOTHER. ONE WITNESS AT THE CRASH SCENE RECALLED THAT THE STREET LIGHTS STAYED ON (THEY SHOULD HAVE GONE OUT AT MIDNIGHT) UNTIL THE AMBULANCE WAS LOADED, AND THEN WERE SLOWLY EXTINGUISHED AS IF IN FINAL TRIBUTE TO THE DYING YOUNG MAN. THE CRASH SEVERELY AGGRAVATED AN EARLIER INJURY TO VINCENT'S LEG, WHO LIMPED IN PAIN, DEPRESSED FOR THE REST OF HIS LIFE.

WHILE AT THE HELM OF AC/DC, BON SCOTT WAS ARGUABLY THE MOST CHARISMATIC FRONT MAN AUSTRALIA HAS EVER SEEN. HE WAS A CHEEKY, MACHO ICON WHO MEN REVELED IN AND GIRLS LOVED. HOWEVER, HE ALSO WAS A NOTORIOUS BINGE DRINKER. AFTER A NIGHT OF CAROUSING IN LONDON'S CAMDEN TOWN ON FEBRUARY 18, 1980, HE PASSED OUT IN A FRIEND'S CAR AND WAS LEFT TO "SLEEP IT OFF." HE WAS FOUND DEAD IN THE EARLY HOURS OF THE NEXT DAY, AGE 33. THE CAUSE OF DEATH WAS LISTED AS ACUTE ALCOHOL POISONING AND "MISADVENTURE."

AC/DC'S LAST LP WITH SCOTT WAS APPROPRIATELY TITLED *HIGHWAY TO HELL*. SCOTT'S LAST KNOWN RECORDING IS A VERSION OF "RIDE ON," SUNG WITH THE FRENCH METAL BAND TRUST.

THE GIRLFRIEND OF 1970S ROCK STAR COZY POWELL (BLACK SABBATH, WHITESNAKE, RAINBOW) LISTENED ON THE PHONE AS HIS CAR SPUN OUT, KILLING HIM INSTANTLY, AN INQUEST HAS HEARD.

POWELL, 50, WAS TALKING TO GIRLFRIEND SHARON REEVE ON HIS MOBILE PHONE WHEN HIS BLACK SAAB 9000 TURBO CRASHED ON THE M4 NEAR BRISTOL ON APRIL 5, 1998. REEVE SAID SHE HEARD A "TERRIBLY LOUD NOISE," THEN POWELL SAID "OH SHIT," FOLLOWED BY SILENCE. SHE PHONED EMERGENCY SERVICES WHEN SHE WAS UNABLE TO RING POWELL BACK. HE WAS PRONOUNCED DEAD ON ARRIVAL AT FRENCHAY HOSPITOL IN BRISTOL.

POWELL, WHO WAS OVER THE DRINK-DRIVE LIMIT AND NOT WEARING A SEAT BELT, HAD COMPLAINED TO REEVE ON THE PHONE THAT HE WAS HAVING TROUBLE FINDING FIFTH GEAR, AND SAID HE HOPED THE ENGINE WOULD NOT SEIZE UP BECAUSE HE WAS DRIVING SO FAST. POLICE CAPTAIN IAN CATER, WHO WAS OFF-DUTY AND TRAVELING IN THE OPPOSITE DIRECTION AT THE TIME OF THE ACCIDENT, SAID HE SAW POWELL'S CAR COME "CARTWHEELING" PAST HIM BEFORE IT LANDED ON ITS ROOF.

POWELL ONCE SAID IN AN INTERVIEW, "I DRIVE LIKE I DRUM—MADLY." HE WAS WELL KNOWN FOR HIS LOVE OF FAST CARS, AND EVEN RACED MAZDA SALOONS FOR A BRIEF PERIOD IN THE MID-SEVENTIES.

— SOURCE: BBC

ROBERT WILLIAMS

I DON'T KNOW, COULD'VE BEEN A LAME JOGGER MAYBE
OR SOMEONE JUST ABOUT TO DO THE FREEWAY STRANGLER BABY
SHOPPING CART PUSHER OR MAYBE SOMEONE GROOVY
ONE THING'S FOR SURE, HE ISN'T STARRING IN THE MOVIES
'CAUSE HE'S WALKIN' IN LA, WALKIN' IN LA

NOBODY WALKS IN LA

MISSING PERSONS, WALKING IN LA

I LOVE L.A.
The Road Goes Through So Cal

Most major cities in America have at least one strong automotive association linked to the automobile, but none more so than Los Angeles. Yes, there's the New York City taxicab. There are the Detroit factories and design studios. Indianapolis has the Brickyard. But in L.A., without a car, you wouldn't survive.

Blessed with good weather and only the occasional earthquake, Los Angeles, the second largest city in the United States, sprawls over 465 square miles in an oftentimes smog-filled basin surrounded by the Santa Monica Mountains to the west, the San Gabriel Mountains and Puente Hills to the north, and the Santa Ana Mountains to the southeast. The irony is that some of America's richest oil fields lie beneath the basin. L.A. has a dozen major crisscrossing freeways (27 total), and in Los Angeles County alone (not including the densely packed outlying valleys) a population of just under 9 million is involved in a daily collective migration of about 100 million miles. Nearly 1 million workers drive to and from their jobs—alone, each day—in a motor vehicle. Gridlock is a daily occurrence. A major selling point for L.A.'s two news radio stations is their minute-by-minute traffic reports.

Nowhere else in the country is the myth of the big car, the cool car, the hot rod car so prominently in play—and it was never just about teenagers. Everybody drives stylishly in L.A., even the grannies (e.g., *They toot around town in their big Grand Prix/Sittin' in their bucket seats, shootin' the breeze,* as sung by Jan & Dean

in "The Anaheim, Azusa, and Cucamonga Sewing Circle, Book Review, and Timing Association"). Celebrated in popular song and captured on film, L.A. is justly famous for its palm-bedecked streets leading to the coast in Santa Monica, Malibu, Venice Beach, and farther to the south in Redondo and Hermosa; the winding mountaintop Mulholland Drive; the sand-abutted stretches of Highway 1; the posh Rodeo Drive through Beverly Hills; Sunset Strip; Hollywood Boulevard; drive-in burger palaces like Bob's Big Boy (page 11) … and car chases, or police pursuits, which can last several hours due to the region's many interconnected freeways and enormous street grid. Some local television stations break into regularly scheduled programming to cover a chase from their news helicopter, the most infamous of which, of course, involved O. J. Simpson on the 405.

Given its heritage as the home of national television, movie, and music entertainment, Los Angeles is understandably stacked with car collections assembled by rock stars (pages 224–227) and hip-hop stars (pages 100–101 and 214–217). The Petersen Automotive Museum is a highly recommended, open-to-the-public showcase, but the most prominent car-collecting personality is Jay Leno, host of *The Tonight Show* since 1992, whose collection occupies three football field–size warehouses near the Burbank Airport (the "Big Dog Garage") and includes the 1955 Buick Roadmaster Leno once slept in as a struggling comedian.

CATCHING THE CURL

WITH THE BABY BOOM OF CHILDREN BORN IMMEDIATELY POST WORLD WAR II PROVIDING MORE TEENAGERS THAN EVER BEFORE IN AMERICAN HISTORY, FOUR THINGS MET UP ON CALIFORNIA'S BEACHES IN THE MID-'60S: THOUSANDS OF YOUNG PEOPLE HUNGRY FOR A NEW, HIP SCENE; SURFBOARDS; CARS; AND SURF MUSIC. SURF-THEMED PLASTIC MODEL KITS FOLLOWED (AS DID ROCK & ROLL–INSPIRED KITS DID A FEW YEARS LATER, WITH THE *MONKEEMOBILE* AND PAUL REVERE AND THE RAIDERS' *RAIDERS COACH*).

"THE MODEL COMPANIES CAUGHT THE CURL AT THE PEAK OF THIS NEW NATIONAL OBSESSION," WROTE ROBERT FLETCHER IN *SCALE AUTO* MAGAZINE. THE FIRST SURF KITS APPEARED IN 1964. REVELL, LOCATED IN VENICE, CALIFORNIA, NATURALLY HAD A JUMP ON THE SCENE. AMT HAD A KEY HOLLYWOOD CONNECTION WITH GEORGE BARRIS, MONOGRAM GOT MANY OF ITS IDEAS BY READING ROBERT PETERSEN'S *HOT ROD* MAGAZINE, AND NEW YORK–BASED AURORA HAD A MANUFACTURING PLANT IN LOS ANGELES. THE BOX ART FOR ALL THE COMPANIES FOCUSED ON BEACH PARTIES, BIKINIS, DANCING TO BANDS, AND RIDING THE WAVES—MUCH LIKE THE SURF MOVIES. JO-HAN'S *HEAVENLY HEARSE* WAS BILLED AS A "WILD SURF PARTY MACHINE."

WOODIES, SYNONYMOUS WITH SURFING AND SURF MUSIC, CAUGHT ON WITH THE MODEL-BUILDING CROWD IMMEDIATELY. HAWK'S *WOODY ON A SURFARI* (1964) AND *WILD WOODY* (1965), REVELL'S *SURFITE* ED ROTH KIT (1965), AND AMT'S *SURF WOODY, WACKIE WOODY,* AND *SURF WAGON* (ALL 1965) WERE A FEW OF THE FIRST TO BE OFFERED. *SURF WOODY* WAS A CREATION OF DESIGNER TOM DANIEL; BARRIS EXECUTED THE PROTOTYPE, AND THE COMPLETED CAR WAS FEATURED ON THE COVER OF *ROD & CUSTOM*.

Norm Grabowski and Kookie Kar.

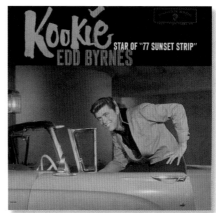

George Maharis and
Martin Milner, Route 66.

SWINGIN'

The advent of both the swingin' detective (e.g., *77 Sunset Strip*, *Bourbon Street Beat*, *Hawaiian Eye*, and *Surfside Six*) and highway-adventure (e.g., *Route 66*) series on television beginning in the late '50s was in sync with America's newly acquired sophisticated palate that now included the L.A. beach scene, cool jazz, and the newest cars out of Detroit. Popular music, however, was in a state of redefinition. Little Richard was no longer cool; The Beach Boys, The Rolling Stones, and The Beatles had yet to surface.

77 Sunset Strip (1958–1964 on ABC) and *Route 66* (1960–1964 on CBS) were the Mack Daddies of the new "Kool TV." The former starred Efrem Zimbalist Jr. and Roger Smith as hip, martini-hoisting private eyes working out of their office at 77 Sunset Boulevard. Their brand-new sports cars shared a driveway with a swinging nightspot called Dino's, a hangout that was an important chick (and trouble) magnet for the boys.

Parking the cars at Dino's was Gerald Lloyd Kookson II (a.k.a. "Kookie"), played by Edd Byrnes, who snapped his fingers in the new beatnik style and spoke in slang. During the first two years of the show, it seemed all the nation's teenagers wanted to be like Kookie. Byrnes and Connie Stevens (herself a star on *Hawaiian Eye*) had a huge hit in 1958 with "Kookie, Kookie, Lend Me Your Comb" (featured on the second episode). Kookie wanted to help the guys solve crimes, but really he was into stylin'.

Kookie drove the *Kookie Kar*, the granddaddy of all T-buckets, built by actor (and later famed woodworking artist) Norm Grabowski. In 1952, after leaving the service, Grabowski purchased a fenderless '31 Model A, then swapped the A body for the front half of a '22 T and added—most

important—a shortened Model A pickup bed. To get the stance and proportions right, Norm and his friends at Valley Customs made further, significant modifications that have had a lasting effect on T-bucket design ever since (including "TV Tommy" Ivo's car, which is nearly as famous). Norm's creative efforts to promote hot rodding led to the car's role (in one of its various guises) on *77 Sunset Strip*. It was also the feature of a pivotal 1957 *Life* magazine spread, shot at Bob's Big Boy drive-in in Toluca Lake, just north of Hollywood (see page 11).

As one critic later succinctly put it, "If *Star Trek* was *Wagon Train* in space, then *Route 66* was *Wagon Train* in a rag top." *Route 66* was filmed on location all over the United States, along the course of the famous (pre-Interstate) Highway 66, "America's Main Street" (and author John Steinbeck's "Mother Road"), stretching from Chicago westward to Southern California. The premise was simple but highly ambitious then and even now. Actors Martin Milner and George Maharis took off in their Corvette to discover America, in search of adventure and enlightenment. There were no other co-stars, just the changing locales and the exotic, conflicted personalities they encountered. It took a traveling crew of fifty, two brand-new, baby-blue (later brown) Corvettes, and two tractor-trailers to produce the series, one of the largest mobile TV operations ever pulled together up to that point. Bobby Troup penned the song "Route 66" in 1946, and subsequently Nat "King" Cole turned it into a signature piece. Later, bandleader and arranger Nelson Riddle recorded the version used as the show's distinctive theme song. Later still, it became one of the earliest recordings by The Rolling Stones.

ANNETTE

ANNETTE FUNICELLO (BORN OCTOBER 22, 1942) WAS DISNEY'S MOST POPULAR MOUSEKETEER. HER FAMILY MOVED FROM NEW YORK STATE TO SOUTHERN CALIFORNIA WHEN SHE WAS FOUR, AND DISNEY DISCOVERED HER WHILE SHE WAS PERFORMING IN A PRODUCTION OF *SWAN LAKE*. AMONG THE ORIGINAL MOUSEKETEERS, ANNETTE WAS THE LAST ONE CAST AND THE ONLY ONE PICKED BY WALT DISNEY HIMSELF.

ANNETTE HAD A NUMBER OF POP RECORD HITS IN 1959 AND 1960, BUT HER LASTING FAME CAME AS A TEEN IDOL, STARRING IN A SERIES OF BEACH PARTY MOVIES WITH FRANKIE AVALON, BEGINNING WITH *BEACH PARTY* IN 1963 AND CONTINUING WITH *MUSCLE BEACH PARTY* AND *BIKINI BEACH* IN 1964, AND *BEACH BLANKET BINGO* AND *HOW TO STUFF A WILD BIKINI* IN 1965.

SHE ALSO STARRED WITH AVALON AND SINGER FABIAN IN THE DARING *FIREBALL 500*, SOMETIMES DUBBED "THE BEACH PARTY GANG ON WHEELS." THE CRUX OF FIREBALL 500 HINGED ON THE TRANSPORTATION OF MOONSHINE WHISKEY, MUCH LIKE THE EARLIER, ROBERT MITCHUM–STARRING *THUNDER ROAD*.

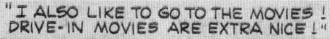

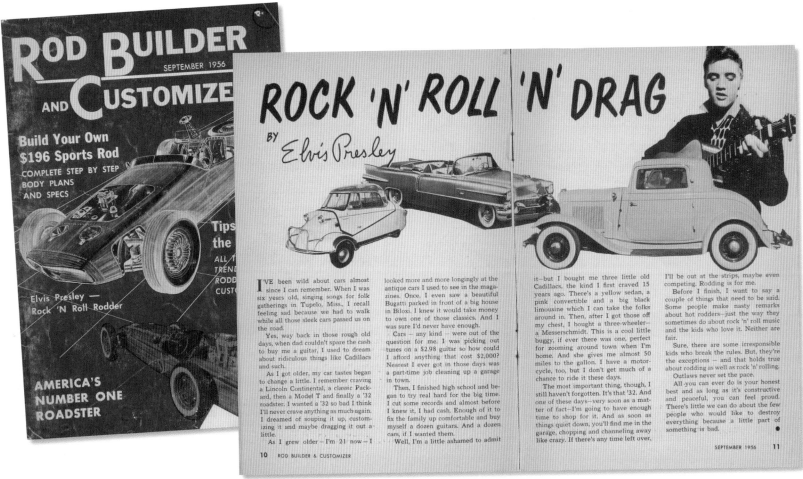

A PLAYFUL MAN

"Elvis was only nine or ten years old when he learned to drive. He was almost seventeen when he went for his driver's license," recalled his mother, Gladys. "He borrowed my brother Travis Smith's car—that was the newest one in our family—to take the test and he had no trouble at all." His father, Vernon, added, "After that, there was no keeping him away from the wheel."

No one knows how many of Elvis' cars there are out there. There could be hundreds. Elvis bought automobiles on a whim. Sometimes he'd go into a dealership and buy a dozen—or more. On a single day he once purchased thirty-two Cadillacs and had given them all away by the afternoon. He never drove the majority of cars he bought—he simply gave them to friends and acquaintances in staggering numbers, although many of these never bore Elvis' name on the registration. Probably one of the earliest occasions Elvis gave a Cadillac away was when he presented a 1954 convertible to Sam Phillips of Sun Records in late 1955.

Elvis fan Rex Fowler made a documentary about Elvis' legendary gift-giving. He called it *200 Cadillacs* after hearing a claim that Presley had given away that many cars. "It's hard to get an actual number," admitted Fowler. "There are people in Elvis' inner circle who say it wasn't anything like 200. But others say it was at least that many, likely more. I don't think we'll ever know."

Joe Esposito, a member of Elvis' inner circle, said, "The first thing that attracted him was the looks of the car. He didn't care if it was a $5,000 car or a $50,000 car, or what brand it was, although he was very partial to American-made cars. He really liked Cadillacs and Lincolns, also some Chryslers. We bought a few foreign cars like the Rolls-Royce because it was very prestigious and looked great, a Mercedes limousine, a Ferrari, but mostly his cars were American-made. He was very patriotic when it came to that.

"If Elvis saw a car he liked in the window, he'd stop and buy it. That was basically it. If the dealership was closed and we knew the owner, we'd call and wake him up. Elvis never carried cash. Someone would write the check and Elvis would sign it, or the bill was simply sent to Graceland and Vernon would take care of it. Elvis never asked for a discount, never even asked the price. He just said, 'OK, I'll take that one.' Of course, one of us would then negotiate. Sometimes he'd buy one for himself, and then he'd say, 'Hey, I think I should buy one for a friend.' That's how he was. He let people share in his enthusiasm for cars."

Myrna Smith, an original member of The Sweet Inspirations, who sang backup for Elvis, recalled, "Elvis was generous to a fault. He rewarded you for singing, or helping him onstage, or if you were a friend, because it made him feel good. It goes back to his humble roots. If he had something, he wanted to share it with you. Black or white, you could eat dinner at his house; it was his pleasure to let you drive with him to the movies.

"Once I was at Graceland and saw all these cars, like, 11, 12, 14 new cars in the driveway. I thought I heard him ask one of the guys, 'Is it all right if I buy her a car?' I didn't think they were referring to me. Then he asked me if I'd go with him to the Cadillac dealer to pick out a car for his dad, because he'd forgotten to thank his dad for something. I said, 'Sure, Elvis, I think that would be very nice.' So we went, and he picked out a big brown Cadillac for his dad. It's nighttime. The place is about to close. We're standing in the lot. Then he takes his flashlight out and goes around looking, asks me what my favorite color was. Around and around the lot he went 'til he found a blue Eldorado. Elvis stands there and tells me, 'Myrna, there's your car.' I mean, how do you respond? You're like What? What? But it was genuine. He wanted to give me a car. And I genuinely appreciated it. He was a playful

man, he had a tender heart, and he loved it when people got new cars, just like him. Of course, it came from all the hard work and the success, but who besides Elvis did what he did?"

In fact, the reports of Elvis' spontaneous, gift-giving whims are endless. One day in 1966 (now living part of the year in Los Angeles), he decided to drive down to dealer row, where he bought a black Cadillac convertible for bodyguard Sonny West as well as a similar convertible for himself because Sonny's looked so nice. Within minutes, he'd also purchased an Eldorado for his other bodyguard, Red West; white convertibles for friends Alan Fortas and Jerry Schilling; and one for Richard Davis, his valet. Larry Geller, Elvis' hair stylist, was the recipient of a black convertible, Graceland friend Marty Lacker a Sedan DeVille, and right-hand man Joe Esposito a maroon convertible.

On July 27, 1975, Elvis spent $140,000 buying 14 Cadillacs for friends, family, and a stranger. Minnie Person, a bank teller, was "just looking," admiring Elvis' new custom-made limousine that was parked in the lot. Elvis suddenly appeared at her side and asked if she liked it. She nodded, and he said, "This one's mine, but let me buy you one." He escorted her to the showroom and said, "Pick one out, dear." She chose a gold-and-white 1975 $11,500 Eldorado. It was another of Elvis' perfectly orchestrated moments.

In Elvis' last years, as his addictions and insecurity grew, his gifts, understandably, could be seen more like empty self-validation, and people who were recipients began to take advantage of him by playing up the resale opportunities. Yet, years after Elvis' death, the cars that survive and are attributable to him retain certain potency. There are Elvis cars scattered throughout America in museums, car showrooms, theme parks, and roadside attractions. There are inevitably more Elvis cars out there than Elvis ever bought.

THE RCA GOLD CAR

ELVIS USED HIS 1960 CADILLAC SERIES 75 FLEETWOOD LIMOUSINE ONLY OCCASIONALLY, BUT HIS MANAGER, COLONEL TOM PARKER, AND HIS RECORD COMPANY, RCA, USED IT VERY SUCCESSFULLY—AND EXTENSIVELY—IN 1966, AS "THE GOLD CAR," TO PROMOTE THE RELEASE OF HIS ENTIRE CATALOG IN 8-TRACK.

FOR ITS TIME, THE CAR WAS THE ULTIMATE IN LUXURY AND OPULENCE. ITS REMODELING, SUPPOSEDLY COSTING OVER $100,000, WAS EXECUTED AT GEORGE BARRIS' KUSTOM CITY IN LATE 1965 WITH GOLD-PLATED INTERIOR FEATURES THAT INCLUDED A PHONE, SHOE BUFFER, VANITY CASE WITH A GOLD ELECTRIC RAZOR, REFRIGERATOR, ENTERTAINMENT CONSOLE WITH A TEN-RECORD AUTOMATIC CHANGER AND REEL-TO-REEL TAPE DECK, AND A SWIVEL TV. IT WAS CLAIMED THAT FORTY COATS OF PAINT MADE WITH PEARL, DIAMOND DUST, AND ORIEN-TAL FISH SCALES WERE HAND-RUBBED ON THE EXTERIOR. THE HUBCAPS, WHEEL COVERS, HEADLIGHT RIMS, AND FRONT GRILLE WERE PLATED IN 24-KARAT GOLD. GOLD LAMÉ DRAPES WERE USED TO COVER THE BACK WINDOWS AND SEPARATE THE DRIVER'S COMPARTMENT FROM THE REAR SEMICIRCULAR LOUNGE. THE GOLD CAR HAD PORTHOLES IN THE REAR SAIL PANELS, À LA THE '57 T-BIRD, AND THE INTERIOR HEADLINER DISPLAYED SOME OF THE KING'S GOLD RECORDS AMID A GOLD FRIEZE IMPORTED FROM FRANCE.

THE GOLD CAR WAS TOURED ACROSS THE UNITED STATES. IN HOUSTON, 40,000 FANS CAME TO TAKE A LOOK AND WERE GIVEN A FREE "ELVIS PRESLEY'S GOLD CAR" POSTCARD. IN ATLANTA, THE CAR WAS THE GUEST OF HONOR AT A DINNER FOR 250 DIGNITARIES. EVEN AS LATE AS 1968, THE CAR WAS GIVEN A RESOUNDING WELCOME IN AUSTRALIA.

KUSTOM CITY U.S.A.
THE KUSTOM KINGS

MONAURAL MGS 27051

THE KUSTOM KINGS IN THE STUDIO

GEORGE BARRIS AND THE KUSTOM KINGS

Chev V8 For '49 – '54 Chev Pickups
CAR CRAFT

CUSTOM UPHOLSTERY for your Street Rod
CAR CRAFT
Now Bonus 16 Page Pictorial Section!
Bigger Than Ever—still only 25¢

CAR CRAFT
Expanded METAL GRILLES
SPECIAL FEATURE
Expanded Metal Techniques
STEP-BY-STEP INSTALLATIONS
Ideas Galore!
EASY-TO-BUILD "Hood Scoops" For All Models

RESTYLING THE '57 FORD
CAR CRAFT
SECRETS—
TOP CHOPPING
by Valley Custom
PRECISION VALVE JOB
by Don Francisco

SEAL THAT HEAD—NEW 'STICK' SHIFT!
CAR CRAFT
MARCH 1960
25¢
GRILLES—THE WILDEST!
TOP '59

CAR CLUB OF THE YEAR
CAR CRAF
THE SECRET'S OUT!
"CANDY" COLORS
Materials Needed
Mixing Formulas
How To Apply

MARVIN GAYE AND GEORGE BARRIS

YOKO ONO, JOHN LENNON, GEORGE BARRIS

THE ELVIS GOLD CAR

GEORGE BARRIS AND THE KUSTOM KINGS

George Barris epitomizes the California car customizer. Just out of high school in Roseville, where he lived with his brother, Sam, and their aunt and uncle, he formed the Kustoms car club (apparently the first such-spelled use of the term). He opened his first shop in Bell, part of metropolitan Los Angeles, in 1944. As the post–World War II hot rod scene began to explode, the Barris brothers were at the forefront; the custom car movement, an offshoot, enjoyed an initial ten-year heyday. Their customization of Bob Hirohata's 1951 Mercury, in 1952, won numerous show accolades, as did their white-pearl custom body for Richard Peters' *Ala Kart*, which won the America's Most Beautiful Roadster (AMBR) trophy at the Oakland Roadster Show in 1958 and 1959, and became the first real rod made into a plastic model, a hugely successful two-in-one AMT kit).

"Around 1948," wrote Pat Ganahl for the Petersen Automotive Museum, "the word 'custom' came to be further popularized with a 'K,' courtesy of George Barris. Some of his first ads in *Hot Rod* magazine read 'Barris' Custom Shop—Kustom Automobiles.' Then, his shop in Lynnwood, California, where he moved to around 1950, was called Barris' Kustom City. Barris liked spelling 'C' words with a 'K.' It got attention. It was, somehow, *more custom.*" Eventually, author Tom Wolfe would take notice, celebrating Barris and other customizers such as Darryl Starbird and Ed "Big Daddy" Roth. Wolfe's first book, a collection of essays that many argue launched New Journalism, took its title from his *Esquire* piece about the custom scene entitled, "The Kandy-Kolored Tangerine-Flake Streamline Baby."

George Barris was a born promoter (Sam, a respected body man, died in 1967), and was not adverse to being called the "King of the Kustomizers." In the early 1950s, their work came to the attention of the movie studios, and they created a hot rod for the low-budget classic *High School Confidential*, then cars for *Hot Rod Girl* and *Hot Rod Gang*. George became the "go-to" guy when it came to movie cars, making the jump to television with such cars as the original *Batmobile* (based on a 1955 Lincoln Futura); Dobie Gillis' wickedly chopped, Eldorado-powered 200-mile-per-hour coupe; *Drag-U-La* and the *Munster Koach*; *The Beverly Hillbillies'* jalopy; and *The Dukes of Hazzard's General Lee*. He also created personal dream cars for hundreds of celebrities, including his close friend, Elvis.

Early in 1964, having moved his operations to North Hollywood, Barris followed the surf/hot rod/drag music trend to create a studio band under the direction of L.A. saxophonist Steve Douglas. They used prominent songs from Bruce Johnston ("In My 40 Ford"), Marshall and Carol Connors ("Hey Little Cobra"), and Roger Christian ("Super Fine 39") to produce the *Kustom City U.S.A.* LP for Mercury Records' Smash Records division (see in-studio photos on these pages).

The album was billed as "the most authentic hot-rod album on the market." Ever the promoter, Barris' press release also noted, "During this session miniature AMT model cars were used to coincide with the original custom and hot rod creations pertaining to the songs and terminology used by the hot rod and custom enthusiasts. [All the musicians on this LP] studied each lyric to get the feel of the powerful hot rod engine sounds and custom styling, to emphasize and bring forth same into this unique rock & roll beat."

Perhaps one of the most famous cars on television was the *Monkeemobile*, which debuted in 1966 from Universal Studios. The cars (there were actually two) transported the rock group The Monkees both on their TV show and at live appearances around the country.

Aided and abetted by Pontiac's key ad agency executive, Jim Wangers, the *Monkeemobiles* were the creation of Los Angeles car customizer Dean Jeffries (also known for the *Mantaray*, used in the 1963 Frankie Avalon/Annette Funicello jiggle-fest *Bikini Beach*, and the Green Hornet's *Black Beauty*). Pontiac supplied Jeffries with two 1966 GTO convertibles as a bases. Each car was equipped with a standard 335-horsepower engine and two-speed automatic transmission, but for a brief period a big-block engine was dropped into the primary car, making it powerful enough (along with its solid-mount rear end and added weights) to pop wheelies. The network, however, was uncomfortable with its actors operating such a dangerous custom (which, admittedly, according to Monkee Mike Nesmith, was fabulous but very difficult to drive), so the stock engine was put back in. A nonfunctional GMC 671 blower was bolted onto the original 389 four-barrel.

Jeffries built the cars in under a month, one for the episodes (see page 81) and another for the custom car circuit. Apparently he took Pontiac somewhat by surprise because they were expecting only minor alterations. His genius was to create a highly striking—even radical—21-foot-long modification.

Jeffries used the stock wheelbase, but opened up the full interior, effectively stretching out the car visually. He tilted the windshield up, and a chrome strip created a split-window illusion. Jeffries then added an old-fashioned permanent touring hardtop, giving the car a near-phaeton-like appearance. Two people could unbolt the top and lift it off the car. Jeffries installed a new floor and trunk pan and altered the rear suspension to accommodate a commodious new rear seat. Four bucket seats added to the fun and frivolity. The hand-formed front and rear metalwork (no fiberglass was used) lengthened the car by nearly 3 feet and afterward thirty coats of candy burgundy-wine paint were laid on and hand-rubbed.

Jeffries exaggerated (but retained) the basic taillight design, and a new center rear compartment was fabricated to house a Dietz drag chute. The shark-like nose was designed to accentuate the GTO-defining grille openings, and the front wheel wells were altered to accept distinctive (but nonfunctional) exhaust trumpets that played off variously used Ansen and Cragar mag wheels. For a short period, a rear hitch was added to pull a customized trailer.

Since Pontiac had picked up the bill for Jeffries' work, they thought it appropriate that the GTO emblems appear on the fenders and on the grille. But the show's producers felt that would make it difficult to attract other carmakers to purchase commercial time, so the GTO grille badge was temporarily removed. Pontiac was irritated, but Jeffries' creation was such an immediate hit with the public that its GTO aspects simply spoke for themselves. The Monkees guitar-script logo appeared on both front doors, although for a time, curiously, the passenger-side logo ran backward.

Today, three *Monkeemobiles* are known to exist. The one used primarily on the TV show is in the hands of a private collector. The other two (one based on a 1966 Pontiac LeMans very similar to the GTO) were modified back to Jeffries' original conception by Dick Dean and are owned and shown worldwide by Barris Kustom Industries.

At the time Jeffries was being considered for the customizing work, he was also under contract to Model Products Corporation, better known as MPC, which also promoted the *GeeTO Tiger* model (see page 175). George Toteff, MPC's CEO, told Wangers about Jeffries, getting him the job. For Toteff's help in the deal-making, MPC was granted exclusive rights to market a model kit of the *Monkeemobile*. More than 7 million MPC *Monkeemobiles* were sold, a number surpassed in overall model kit sales only by *The Dukes of Hazzard General Lee* 1969 Dodge Charger.

Wangers also created "The Kellogg's Rice Krispies and Raisin Bran Screen-Stakes promotion," to coincide with the release of the 1968 GTO and The Monkees' new TV season. Nearly 42 million boxes of cereal were produced for the promotion; since the average box is seen on the breakfast table six times, it was one of the most successful launches in ad history.

DEAN JEFFRIES

Mike Nesmith — Micky Dolenz — David Jones — Peter Tork

"THE MONKEES IN A GHOST TOWN"

EPISODE NO. 7

PRODUCTION NO. 4704 "THE MONKEES IN A GHOST TOWN"

FILMED AT: SCREEN GEMS STUDIOS, HOLLYWOOD, CA

FILMING DATES: JULY 11–15, 1966

ORIGINAL AIR DATE: OCTOBER 24, 1966

SPONSOR THIS WEEK: KELLOGG'S

WRITTEN BY: ROBERT SCHLITT AND PETER MEYERSON

DIRECTED BY: JAMES FRAWLEY

PRODUCED BY: ROBERT RAFELSON AND BERT SCHNIEDER

SYNOPSIS:

The Monkees (David, Peter, Micky, Michael) drive the Monkeemobile from Clarksville to a job out of town. Thanks to a navigational blunder made by Micky, the boys make an unnecessary 150-mile trek through a desert, thus causing the Monkeemobile to run out of gas in a ghost town. The Monkees split up in pairs to search for a gas station and encounter gangsters who are actually bank robbers, who proceed to hold them as prisoners in the town jail. The quartet begins digging escape tunnels (incredibly enough, to a jungle, a railroad track, an Egyptian pyramid, and a baseball diamond), and eventually over come the gangsters' leader, one Bessie Kowalski, all while a variety of shenanigans take place and oddball songs are sung.

PRODUCTION NOTE: VOICEOVER MAESTRO MEL BLANC (BUGS BUNNY) PROVIDED THE SPUTTERING NOISES OF THE SEVERELY GAS-DEPLETED MONKEEMOBILE.

THREE WINDOW COUPE

THREE WINDOW COUPE/THIS LITTLE WOODIE/GAS MONEY/BONNEVILLE BONNIE/HOT ROD U.S.A./SURF CITY
SURFIN' CRAZE/BEACH GIRL/MY BIG GUN BOARD/OLD CAR MADE IN '52/SUMMER U.S.A./BIG WEDNESDAY

THE RIP CHORDS

LSP-2834 STEREO

DEUCES, "T's," ROADSTERS & DRUMS

HAL BLAINE
(THE DRUMMER MAN)
And The Young Cougars

RCA VICTOR
Dynagroove
RECORDING

Challenger II • Green Monster • Nashville Coupé
Big "T" • Mr. Eliminator • Pop the Chute • Deuces, "T's," Roadsters & Drums • Drum Brakes
Gear Change • The Phantom Driver • Gear Stripper • The Traps

STEREO

HIT CITY 64 | THE SURFARIS

DECCA

including: HIAWATHA • SUGAR SHACK • SCATTER SHIELD • WAX, BOARD AND WOODIE
LITTLE DEUCE COUPE • LOUIE, LOUIE • COMIN' HOME BABY • BE TRUE TO YOUR SCHOOL

HIT CITY '65
THE SURFARIS

DECCA

LEADER OF THE LAUNDROMAT • SHE'S A WOMAN
ANYWAY YOU WANT IT • MY BUDDY SEAT
LOVE POTION NUMBER NINE • DANCE, DANCE, DANCE
I'M INTO SOMETHING GOOD • GONE, GONE, GONE
AND OTHERS.

FUN FUN FUN

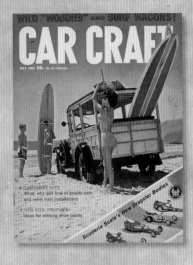

CAR CRAFT

JULY 1962 35¢

WILD "WOODIES" AND SURF WAGONS!

(YOU CAN'T TAKE)
MY BOYFRIEND'S WOODY

AUDITION RECORD

IMPERIAL
66014

THE POWDER PUFFS

BEACH NUTS
PLAY
The Last Ride / Surf Beat '65

Photo: Lee Cain

CORONADO
RECORD CO.

45 RPM

THE LAST RIDE
THE BEACH NUTS

THEY CALL IT A "WOODY"

Nothing looks as much like surfing and the beach as the woody wagon, an easy-on-the-eyes cross between a sedan and a panel truck. Used for grouse hunting on Great Britain's country estates, they were known as "shooting brakes" or "estate wagons" in the United Kingdom.

The earliest woodies were custom-built vehicles. Ford offered an optional woody body on the Model T frame in 1921. The first ever production station wagon was built by Durant Motors in 1923. Exceptionally rare and beautiful woodies were built on '34 and '36 model chassis, but were not the first choice of surfers due to their fragility.

Possibly because in the '20s and '30s East Coast resorts commonly sent big wood-bodied station wagons to meet tourists arriving by train (hence their first moniker, "depot hacks," and the further derivation, "station wagon"), woodies will forever convey an air of being on vacation. But the great woody era—those model years that would be most prized and pervasive among the surfers who rediscovered them—was from 1939 through 1952, when Ford built over 160,000 units, eclipsing Plymouth and Chevrolet in the process (each built less than 30,000 units during that same period). Even DeSoto, Hudson, Oldsmobile, Pontiac, Mercury, and Packard offered woodies in the '40s.

During World War II and for some years after, steel was in short supply and partial wooden-body vehicles were as necessary as they were stylish. So popular were the Fords that the company—always a model of vertical integration—owned its own forest near a coach-crafting plant in Iron Mountain, Michigan, where the wood bodies were made.

By the '50s, wood became less and less practical, subject to rot from exposure to sun and moisture. The original maple, birch, and mahogany constructions were abandoned in favor of molded plywood before laminate and fiberglass veneers were introduced. Ford ended production after 1953 but continued to feature a side-paneled woody look on its Country Squire station wagons through the 1960s, as did a few of its competitors.

In the early '60s, surfers began rediscovering the woody as a hip—even bitchin'—means to transport boards and still have room for buddies and girls, as Jan & Dean pointed out on their 1963 hit, "Surf City." By the late '60s, the beach scene parking lot was taken over by the Volkswagen-engined dune buggy, the Meyers Manx, the ubiquitous first-generation Volkswagen bus, and still later by the all-too-practical Econoline van.

"If ever you should ride in a woody, be sure to roll down the window and rest your arm on the sun-warmed wood door. There's nothing really like it," wrote *Sunset* magazine. Woody car shows—that's nothing but woodies, ma'am—are now hosted everywhere in the western United States, serving as signs of spring (in San Pedro, California), summer (Lake Arrowhead, Santa Cruz, and Santa Barbara—all in California), and fall (Portland, Oregon; Encinitas and San Simeon in California; and, most recently, Phoenix, Arizona).

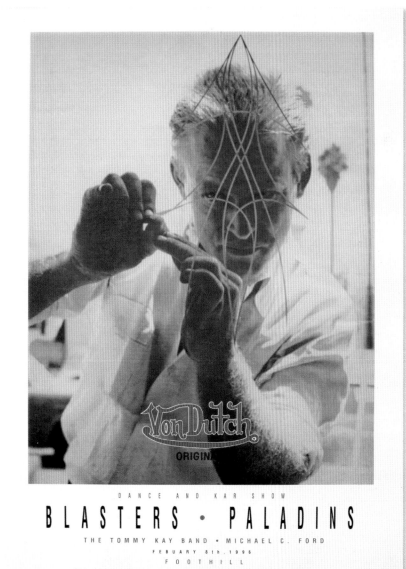

PAUL GRUSHKIN COLLECTION

VonDutch ORIGINAL

DANCE AND KAR SHOW

BLASTERS · PALADINS

THE TOMMY KAY BAND · MICHAEL C. FORD

FEBRUARY 8th, 1996

FOOTHILL

1922 CHERRY BLVD. SIGNAL HILL · $13.00 · HOTLINE 310-984-8349

I'M ONLY FOURTEEN, BUT I'M GOIN' ON FIFTEEN, BUT I WANNA BE SIXTEEN, SO I CAN GET ME A HOT ROD, I WANT A STREAMLINE CHASSIS, MAN IT'S GOTTA BE CLASSY, I'M GONNA GIVE IT THAT CERTAIN TOUCH, WITH A LITTLE BIT OF VON DUTCH.

THE COLLINS KIDS, HOT ROD

BONGOS AND HODADS

Surf music was not always part of the Southern California beach scene. "In 1959 there was not yet any such thing as 'youth/surf' culture," explained Paul Johnson, founder of the Bel Airs surf band, writing in the booklet accompanying *The Bel Airs and the Origins of Surf Music* CD. Surfers were crew-cut collegiate types who had the muscle to haul the heavy boards across the sand. Beatniks mostly patrolled the beaches and their music was cool modern jazz. "Bongo drums fit the surf scene's image more closely than electric guitars," said Johnson. Rock & roll was five years old. The influence of the pioneers (Buddy Holly, Elvis, Little Richard) was waning, and it would be another five years before The Beatles. As yet, no Beach Boys, Rip Chords, or Jan & Dean.

"The cultural hero of 1959 was the hodad," said Johnson. This was a greasy-haired gearhead misfit who listened to what was left of doo-wop and rockabilly. Hodads generally avoided the beach, and soon would be the cultural rivals of the surfers.

Lightweight foam and fiberglass surf boards fashioned by "shapers" made the waves newly accessible to a great many more young people. Also, the advent of the transistor radio freed kids from their cars and allowed them to gather on beaches rather than the streets, without leaving their music behind. And the 1959 surfing movie *Gidget* imagined a bohemian lifestyle that a teenager easily might find tantalizing. Now, as the new decade dawned, surfing was about to discover a music of its own.

"Surf music was about two guitars pushing against each other, energizing each other, propelling each other along," wrote Johnson. "For us, the guitar was a duo rather than a solo instrument, and all of our ideas were born in the context of 'how will my part fit with his part?'" Then Fender brought out their reverb unit, which further refined surf rock's signature tonality.

The Bel Airs were named after bandmember Chaz Stuart's '55 Chevy. By 1961 they'd recorded their signature "Mr. Moto" and began playing "surf stomp" events at venues such as the Rendezvous Ballroom in Newport Beach (where Dick Dale and the Del-Tones reigned), Eagles Hall in Redondo Beach, and the Biltmore Ballroom in Hermosa. A year later, surf bands such as the Challengers and Surfaris came to the forefront, and within another year the scene reached its zenith—largely brought to prominence by The Beach Boys, who, apart from Dennis Wilson, were "gremmies" (not surfers).

Artist Rick Griffin, who illustrated many beach woodies for *Surfer* magazine—and whose Murphy cartoon character came to symbolize the period—also was a close pal of the Bel Airs, illustrating their wave-stoked flyers and business cards. In early 1966 Griffin left his friend John Van Hamersveld, a fellow surfer and art director at *Surfer* (who drew the *Endless Summer* poster for filmmaker Bruce Brown), and headed north to San Francisco, following the beat of a different drummer—psychedelic rock—to make concert posters for the likes of the Grateful Dead, Big Brother and the Holding Company, and Jimi Hendrix.

For two spectacular years—from late 1959 until late 1961—Dick Dale and the Del-Tones were the house band at the legendary Rendezvous Ballroom on Balboa, a tiny island off Newport Beach, south of Los Angeles, where Dale drew nearly 4,000 teenagers every weekend night. At a 1961 gig at the Los Angeles Sports Arena, he drew a crowd of 21,000. When he moved to the Pasadena Civic Auditorium at the beginning of 1962, the "King of the Surf Guitar" was probably the most popular performer in Southern California. Even *Life* magazine took notice.

For a time, Duane Eddy, Jan & Dean, and The Beach Boys all took turns as the second and third billings to Dale, but this was all to change in May 1963, when The Beach Boys' "Surfin' USA" rose to #3 on Billboard's pop singles chart. In June, "Shut Down," their second car song (their first was "409," the B-side of "Surfin' Safari," which debuted in November 1962), hit #23. In July, their *Surfin' USA* LP rose to #2 on the album charts. In September, "Little Deuce Coupe" reached #15. Early the following month, the albums *Surfer Girl* and *Little Deuce Coupe* were released within weeks of each other, the former showcasing surf numbers, the latter all the group's hot rod and car songs. They were also the first Beach Boys LPs produced by Brian Wilson. *Little Deuce Coupe*, sharing songs from the band's three immediately prior LPs, peaked at #4 also that October.

In March 1964, the car song "Fun, Fun, Fun" hit #5, and while the LP *Shut Down Vol. 2* (with the band posing by a Corvette and GTO for the cover) only reached #13, "I Get Around," yet another memorable car song, became the group's first #1 hit in the United States on July 4, selling over a million copies. Pretty heady stuff for 18 months.

Why the Beach Boys? Though they came from the south L.A. (but not beachfront) working-class town of Hawthorne, they were not a surf band, nor was their sound rooted in instrumental surf rock. Their success—serendipitously aided by Brian Wilson's songwriting partnership with friends Gary Usher and DJ Roger Christian—was based on an uncannily visionary interpretation of the Los Angeles and Orange County surf scene of girls, waves, early muscle cars, and woodies. Their formula combined lush multipart harmonies with poetic lyrics. Their sound was undeniably pretty and catchy—perfect beach pop for the nationwide mass market.

"Help Me Rhonda" hit #1 in May 1965, but the band's heyday was all but over. Despite Brian Wilson's talent and ambition, as later showcased on the LPs *Pet Sounds* (1966) and the "lost album" *Smile* (1967), The Beach Boys ultimately were eclipsed by geography—the Southern California beach scene never translated completely to the shores of New England, New Jersey, the Carolinas, and Florida—and the British Invasion, led by the rampaging Beatles, who unleashed an entirely new, Mod sound upon the world.

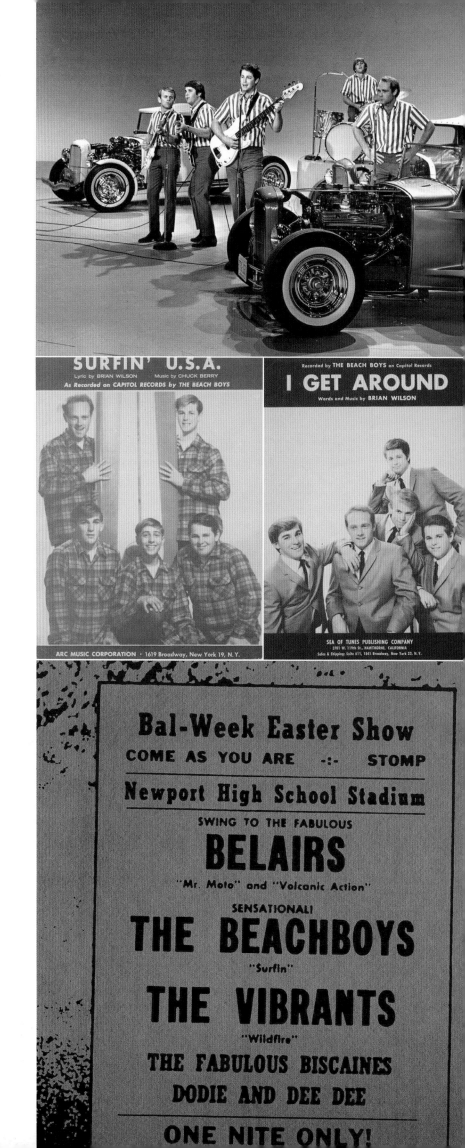

SURFIN' SAFARI...
LOADIN' UP OUR WOODY

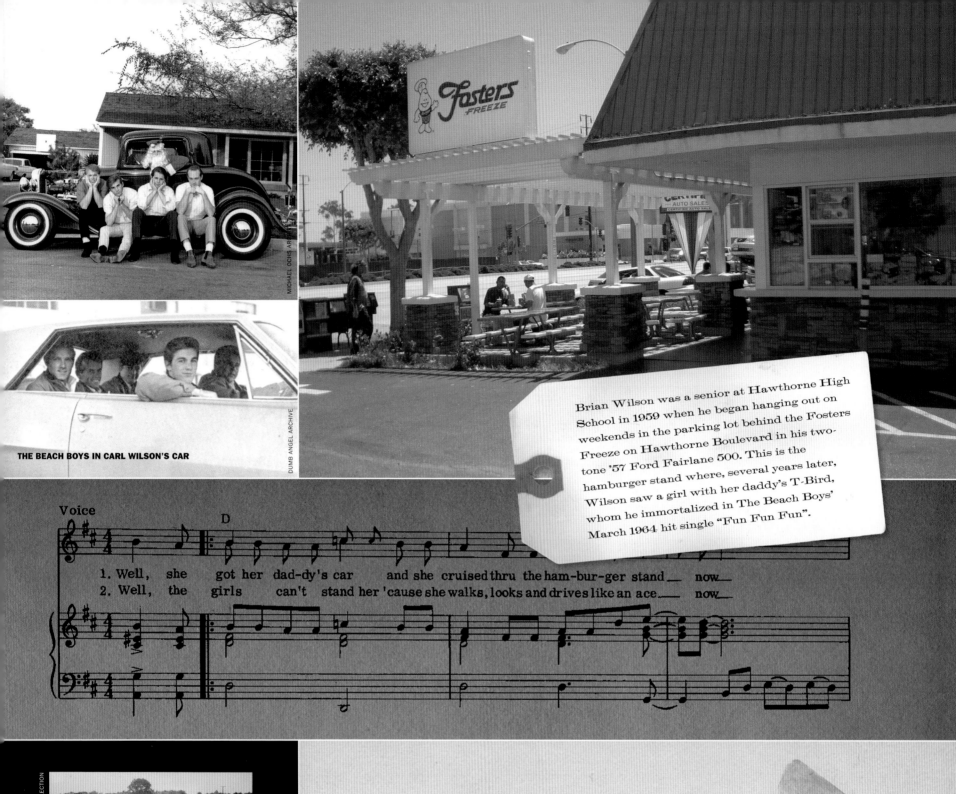

THE BEACH BOYS IN CARL WILSON'S CAR

Brian Wilson was a senior at Hawthorne High School in 1959 when he began hanging out on weekends in the parking lot behind the Fosters Freeze on Hawthorne Boulevard in his two-tone '57 Ford Fairlane 500. This is the hamburger stand where, several years later, Wilson saw a girl with her daddy's T-Bird, whom he immortalized in The Beach Boys' March 1964 hit single "Fun Fun Fun".

Voice

1. Well, she got her dad-dy's car and she cruised thru the ham-bur-ger stand now
2. Well, the girls can't stand her 'cause she walks, looks and drives like an ace now

JAMES TAYLOR IS THE DRIVER
WARREN OATES IS GTO
LAURIE BIRD IS THE GIRL
DENNIS WILSON IS THE MECHANIC

TWO-LANE BLACKTOP IS THE PICTURE

TWO-LANE BLACK-TOP   PAUL GRUSHKIN COLLECTION
JAMES TAYLOR · WARREN OATES · LAURIE BIRD · DENNIS WILSON

Dennis Wilson is the Big Beat of the Beach Boys. His driving rhythms are the solid foundation of the Beach Boys' rock. As are the others, Dennis is a self-taught musician, and is as much at home at the piano or vibes as he is at the drums. In the beginning, Dennis devoted his talents to singing, but it was quickly obvious that his sense of beat made him the number one choice for drummer.

Denny is the middle Wilson brother. He is 5'10" of blond good looks. A rock-hard natural athlete, he is proficient in every sporting activity he has ever tried. He is, in addition to being champion surfer of the group, a top water-skier, skin and scuba-diver, sailor, auto racer and motor biker. He is an excellent shot with rifle or shotgun. He recently set a track record in the quarter mile drags, for double-A sports, speeding his Cobra at more than 118 mph over the short straight-away. His current kick is scuba-diving for lobsters at 3:00 A.M.

He is a complete extrovert, and can usually be found out among the crowds. He loves people in general, with emphasis on the adorable female variety, but avoids pushy people like the plague. He is quick-tempered, but responds to reason and calms down as quickly as he flares up.

The Beach Boys at the Capitol Records building.

Brian Wilson   Al Jardine   Carl Wilson   Dennis Wilson   Mike Love

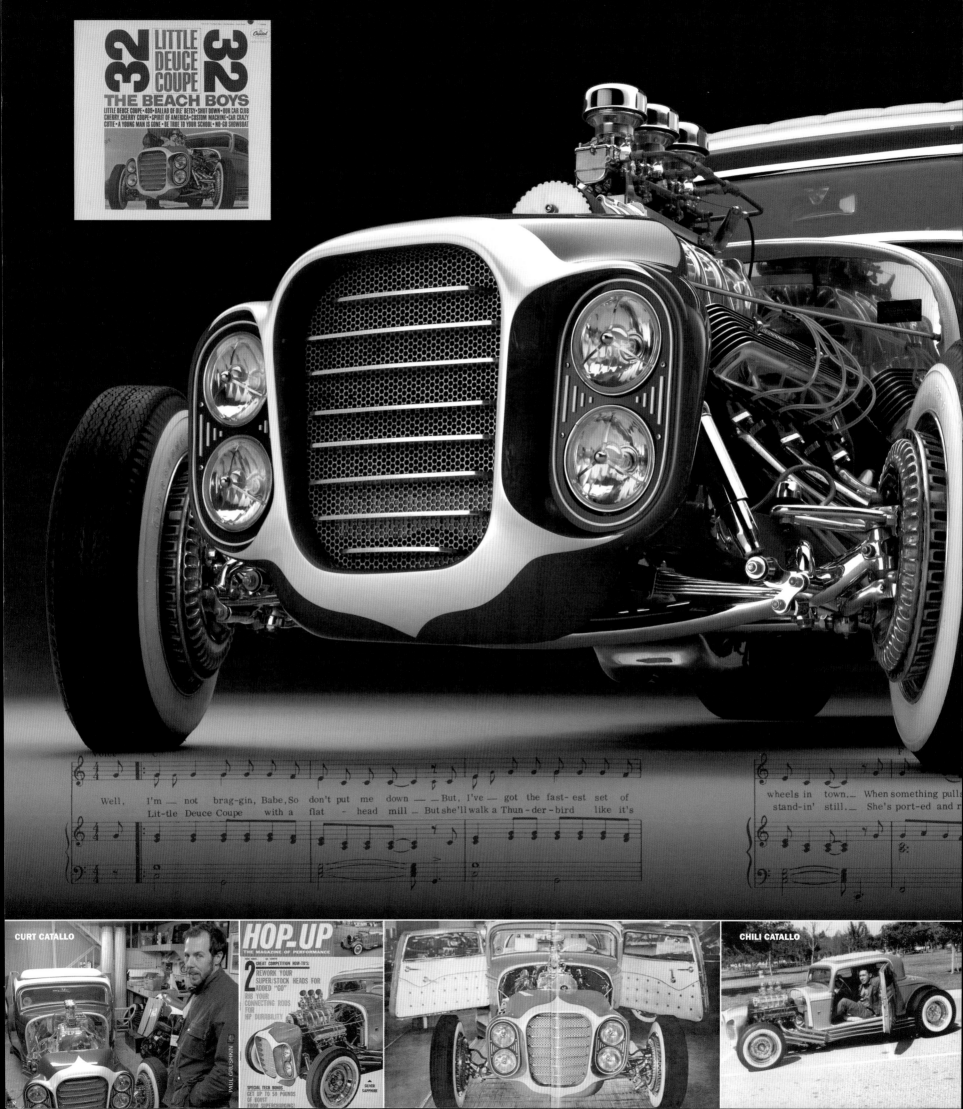

LITTLE DEUCE COUPE

Imagine a late-'50s homegrown hot rod that makes the cover of *Hot Rod*, becomes the double-page centerspread in *Sports Illustrated*'s most famous piece on custom culture and drag racing, and winds up as the album art for one of the world's top rock bands. That would be Clarence "Chili" Catallo's *Silver Sapphire*, better known to the world as the *Little Deuce Coupe*.

Yes, it *is* a deuce coupe. But it doesn't necessarily *look* like a deuce coupe. And it certainly didn't start out as *the* deuce coupe either. And therein hangs the tale.

Catallo, a Michigan native, first brought to Detroit's Larry and Mike Alexander (the revered Alexander Brothers) a rough, channeled '32 Ford three-window he purchased for $75 in 1956. "The bottoms of the doors were rotten, so we cut the bottoms off and made those distinctive aluminum fins to replace the rockers," Mike told *Custom Rodder*. He continued, modestly, "We also thought up the quad-headlight hinged front end (grille, radiator, and shell)." History will show that their inspired, distinctive nose is, visually speaking, one of hot rodding's all-time signature creations.

"We tried to talk Clarence into chopping the car," Mike Alexander continued, "but he just wouldn't go for it." Catallo, aboard the *Silver Sapphire*, took off for college after convincing his dubious parents that Long Beach, California, was *the* place to earn a degree. No fool he, Catallo began hanging around the Barris Brothers' shop, where he swept floors and generally associated. Barris' painter extraordinaire, Junior Conway, finally talked Catallo into chopping the car and painting it the lighter blue and white closely associated with it today. That's when it came to the notice of all the car mags.

"He had the car over at Barris'," recalled Mike Alexander, "and one day George got a call from Capitol Records, from an art director looking for a rod to put on the cover of a new Beach Boys album. George was quick to say, 'Hey, have I got the car for you.'" In fact, Barris has always maintained that Catallo had the coolest coupe in town, the most photogenic, the one that *belonged* on an album cover—although in fairness, not even George Barris knew it would become *the* quintessential hot rod album cover.

The LP photo is a bastardized version of the July 1961 *Hot Rod* cover shot by Eric Rickman—notice Catallo is chopped off at the shoulders, in a bold but unfortunate stroke of art direction. What's not widely known is that Catallo, by then a close friend of Ed Roth, is wearing Roth's personal red jacket, with *Beatnik Bandit* on the back. Curt Catallo, Chili's son, who has maintained the car in top condition, has been searching for the jacket ever since.

GARY USHER AND ROGER CHRISTIAN

Roger Christian, a Los Angeles disc jockey (KRLA, 1960; KFWB, 1961–1964; KHJ, 1965; and KFWB, 1966), was dubbed "Poet of the Strip" (meaning, of course, Sunset Strip). He helped surfer bands, in particular The Beach Boys, write songs about hot rods and dragsters, even though diehard surfers considered rodders (sometimes lumped in with non-surfing, so-called "hodads") to be rivals.

Brian Wilson and Christian first collaborated on "Shut Down," which became a Top 20 hit in 1963. They continued their partnership with "Little Deuce Coupe" and even collaborated on "Spirit of America," a paean to racer Craig Breedlove's three-wheeled 7,800-pound jet car.

Christian also composed songs for Jan & Dean. In 1963, at Jan's request, he and Wilson wrote "Drag City" for the duo, which reached the Top 10. He also wrote most of the other songs on that same-named album, including "Dead Man's Curve," and subsequently co-wrote "Little Old Lady from Pasadena."

•   •   •

Writing in the foreword to compilers John Blair and Stephen McPartland's *The Illustrated Discography of Hot Rod Music 1961–1965*, Gary Usher briefly summed up his celebrated career. "Throughout the years," he wrote, "I've been asked countless times how I became involved with hot rod music and I usually respond by explaining how I wrote the song '409' with Brian Wilson. However, the beginning really goes back to 1960–61 when, as a Titan Records recording artist, I performed with Carol Connors (who later co-wrote "Hey Little Cobra") and Ginger Blake (later of the Honeys) at the Orange Show Fairgrounds in San Bernardino. The host disc jockey was Roger Christian from KFWB.

"After the show, Roger and I struck up a friendship that centered around his car, a customized 1955 Corvette," Usher continued. "Ginger drove my car home, and I 'flew' home with Roger at an average speed of 90 miles per hour! Roger was equally fascinated with my 348 c.i. Chevy. When he discovered I spent my weekends drag racing with Paul Peterson at the San Fernando Airport dragstrip, we became inseparable—and this was before I had the good fortune of meeting and working with the Beach Boys.

"I recall many times driving to Hollywood and meeting Roger after he got off the air at midnight. There was a coffee shop below KFWB where we would sit and talk about cars until dawn.

"The height of the hot rod fad climaxed during a one-month period when Roger and I actually wrote over 50 car songs. By that time, I'd purchased a new 426 Plymouth Hemi Superbird. It's interesting I never did own a 409 Chevy. I won many events at the San Fernando dragstrip with my 426 and a young, exuberant Dennis Wilson by my side."

•   •   •

Gary Usher sketched out a song called "409" (about a Chevy he wanted at the time) on his way to an auto-parts store with Brian Wilson, an indication of how much he was involved in the beach and street scenes that he depicted. He also was insanely successful in his role. During the period from October 1962 to November 1965, thirty record albums featured Usher as songwriter-producer-arranger-vocalist. An additional dozen bore his name as songwriter. Then there are his 45-rpm releases: sixty-nine in sixty-nine months (March 1961 through December 1966).

SOME OF USHER'S 1960–1964 CAR SONG ACHIEVEMENTS INCLUDE:

"Driven Insane" March 1960
GARY USHER

"Surfin Safari" June 1962
BEACH BOYS

"409" June 1962
BEACH BOYS

"R.P.M." February 1963
THE FOUR SPEEDS

"Cheater Slicks" June 1963
THE FOUR SPEEDS

"'41 Ford" August 1963
THE GRAND PRIX

"Little Surfin' Woody" September 1963
THE SUNSETS

"Surfin' Hearse" October 1963
THE QUADS

"Little Stick Nomad" October 1963
THE COMPETITORS

"No Go Showboat" November 1963
THE TIMERS

"Mag Rims" November 1963
THE ROADSTERS

"Hot Rod Hootenanny" November 1963
MR. GASSER & THE WEIRDOS

"Custom City" March 1964
ANNETTE FUNICELLO

"Mr. Eliminator" March 1964
DICK DALE

"Thunder Road" March 1964
THE SUPER STOCKS

"Super Torque 427" May 1964
THE ROAD RUNNERS

"Little Honda" September 1964
THE HONDELLS

"Hot Rod High" October 1964
THE KNIGHTS

"School is A/Gas" October 1964
THE WHEEL MEN

DANCE and SHOW

IN PERSON .... From HOLLYWOOD

The... ★ ★ ★ ★ ★

FOUR SPEEDS

Featuring Their
New Recording Hit

"R.P.M."

FRI. Night AUG. 16th

Eight O'clock to Midnight

CORTE MADERA REC. CENTER

Admission $2.00   Sport Dress

Sponsored By E. S. M. Enterprises - Ph. 453-8046

◆ TILGHMAN PRESS, 1217 - 32nd ST., OAK.—OL 3-4388

SURF ROUTE 101

THE SUPER STOCKS FEATURING GARY USHER · SURF ROUTE 101 · MUSCLE BEACH PARTY · VENTURA · MALIBU BLUES · REDONDO BEACH
SURFIN' SCENE · BALBOA ISLAND · OCEANSIDE · MY FIRST LOVE · MIDNIGHT RUN · SANTA BARBARA · NEWPORT BEACH

Capitol
HIGH FIDELITY

PLUS THIS FREE BONUS RECORD!

CAPITOL DUOPHONIC · FOR STEREO PHONOGRAPHS ONLY   DT 1918

SHUT DOWN

SHUT DOWN · 409 · THUNDER ROAD · LITTL
STREET MACHINE · WIDE TRACK · CHEATE
SLICKS · BRONTOSAURUS STOMP · FOU
ON THE FLOOR · CAR TROUBLE · HOT RO
RACE · BLACK DENIM TROUSERS · CHICKE

WITH THE BEACH BOYS · ROBERT MITCHUM · THE CHEERS · THE SUPER STOCKS

Capitol
RECORDS
HIGH FIDELITY

DUOPHONIC · STEREO

HOT ROD HIGH

HOT ROD HIGH · DITCH DAY · SKIPPIN' SCHOOL · I GET AROUND · SCHOOL DAYS
BE TRUE TO YOUR SCHOOL · ROCK AROUND THE CLOCK · THEME FOR TEEN LOVE
MIDNIGHT AUTO · HOT ROD U.S.A. · THREE WHEELER · LONELY LITTLE STOCKER

THE KNIGHTS

Capitol
RECORDS
HIGH FIDELIT

IT WAS ASSUMED FOR MANY YEARS THAT THE FOUR SPEEDS WERE ONLY A STUDIO INVENTION
OF USHER'S. BUT RECENTLY A CONCERT POSTER TURNED UP THAT SHOWS THE BAND TOURED
AT LEAST ONCE TO NORTHERN CALIFORNIA.

RIGHT PLACE, RIGHT TIME

Jan Berry (born April 3, 1941) and Dean Torrence (born March 10, 1940) became close friends at University High School in West Los Angeles. Once signed to Liberty Records in 1963, they recorded "Linda," a song written in 1944 about a little girl named Linda Eastman, who would one day grow up and marry Paul McCartney. It was in 1963 that the duo Jan & Dean found their groove, after their friend Brian Wilson gave them "Surf City" to record. They topped the U.S. pop charts that July for two weeks, a year before The Beach Boys had their own first #1 hit with "I Get Around."

Like The Beach Boys, Jan & Dean's focus now prominently referenced cars and the hot rod–beach–woody craze, in particular. Early in 1964 their *Drag City* LP, which included their versions of The Routers' hit "Sting Ray" and The Beach Boys' "Little Deuce Coupe," reached #22 on the album charts.

Their greatest success came with "Dead Man's Curve" in May 1964 (co-written by Berry and DJ Roger Christian), which hit #8 with its car horns and crash effects, and with "Little Old Lady from Pasadena" (also co-written with Christian), which hit #3 that August.

Many an American town has its own "dead man's curve," a stretch of road so treacherous that it has (in legend or in fact) tragically claimed lives. But the most famous of those curves belongs to Los Angeles, as immortalized by Jan & Dean. Exactly where it's located is the subject of some debate, but general consensus says that it's a tight corner of Sunset Boulevard near the Bel-Air Estates, north of UCLA's Drake Stadium. Its most renowned victim was Mel Blanc, famous as the voice of Bugs Bunny, who barely escaped death there in 1961.

However, rather than setting their fictional drag race at that exact site, Berry and Christian placed it more to the east, from Hollywood down to the Strip (the portion of Sunset Boulevard between Hollywood and Beverly Hills), in order to incorporate the names of locations familiar to audiences outside of Southern California. A race running the route described in the song would have covered 4.5 miles; extended to the "real" dead man's curve, it would have been a drag of 8.7 miles.

The song's final verse proved eerily prophetic two years later when on April 12, 1966, Berry crashed his Corvette Sting Ray into the back of a

parked truck in Beverly Hills. Initially thought to be dead, he barely survived and spent several weeks in a coma, suffering severe injuries to his head and brain that impaired his speech for the rest of his life. According to one urban legend, Christian had not intended for the song to culminate in a disaster—he thought it should end in a tie. It was Berry who insisted the song end with the horrible crash.

Medical student Don Altfeld—then Berry's roommate—wrote the basis of "Little Old Lady from Pasadena" while sitting in bacteriology class after allegedly seeing a granny in a '32 Ford coupe cruising down Colorado Boulevard the previous night. Berry thought the song could be a winner and Altfeld called up their friend and lyricist, Christian, for his input. Christian drove his Cobra to the guys' apartment and began collaborating. In about three days they had a complete version.

Ironically, on March 21, 1964, at Western Recorders, the studio musicians (including Leon Russell on keyboards) had only six minutes at the end of a union-mandated three-hour session to record the song … and so they did, on take number two, literally with seconds left.

Around the time the three penned the single, ad man Joe Denker got an idea for a commercial for the Southern California Dodge Dealers. He went to the Kohner Agency in Hollywood, casting for a granny type. The first lady through the door was Kathryn Minner, wearing a red shawl, black gloves, and a pair of Keds. Denker thought she was perfect and dreamed up a series of ten-second commercials. The first one shows Granny peeling out in a red Superstock Dodge. As she came to a screeching halt, she uttered the now memorable line, "Put a Dodge in your garage, H-O-N-E-Y." An instant classic.

Jan & Dean put Granny Kathryn on the cover of their *Little Old Lady* LP, and she became a Southern California celebrity, appearing on *Gunsmoke*, *The Bob Hope Show*, and *The Dating Game*, before making personal appearances for Chrysler on the West Coast, promoting their high-performance engines. A favorite of teens, rodders, and bikers, Minner passed away in 1969.

IT'S A MOD MOD MOD MOD WORLD

From the early to mid-'60s, many young Britons joined one of two youth movements: the Mods or the Rockers. The Mods, mostly from London and Southeast England, were "the smarter" of the two and wore sharp designer suits over polo-necked shirts, and donned U.S. Army–style parkas to ride their mirror- and medallion-bedecked Vespa GS-160s and Lambretta GT200 scooters to clubs that played American soul and Jamaican ska music. The Rockers, largely from working-class cities like Liverpool, extolled their macho biker-gang image and wore tight jeans, steel-topped boots, and black leather jackets with polished studs. They rode—often at high speeds and with no crash helmets—souped-up Triumphs, BSAs, and Nortons, and listened to Elvis and Gene Vincent.

The Mods sparked a nationwide enthusiasm for R&B, which soon surpassed cool jazz as the music of choice for most Britons. Beyond The Beatles, whose roots were in skiffle, and who early on dressed Mod, this led to the formation of bluesy-sounding bands such as The Rolling Stones, Yardbirds, Kinks, Small Faces, and later T-Rex with Marc Bolan. But the most popular—and revolutionary—band that could be labeled Mod were the High Numbers, shortly to be renamed The Who. The Who's onstage violence personified Mod aggression. The television show *Ready Steady Go!* re-created the Mod club scene on a large scale, providing other Britons with the latest fashions, music, dance styles, and slang. In the '80s, the Mod fashion scene was reinvented with ska-based two-tone bands such as The Specials, The Beat, Madness, and UB40.

By the mid-'60s, on most Saturday nights the Mods and Rockers would dress up and, armed with coshes and flick-knives (blackjacks and switchblades, in American parlance), go out on the town looking to openly clash. Major scuffles took place in South Coast seaside-resort towns such as Margate and Brighton. In May 1964, a notable (and media-abetted) incident took place involving running, insult-throwing battles with hundreds of combatants—later dramatized by The Who's 1979 film, *Quadrophenia*, as well as the Stray Cats' 1982 track, "Rumble in Brighton" (see pages 202–203).

In the '60s, most Britons in their late teens and early twenties could not afford a full-blown motorcycle, much less a car. For Mods, scooters were a status symbol, nearly equal to a college-age American's first ride, maybe even a custom or hot rod. In the United States, despite considerable entreaties by manufacturers such as Sears and Harley-Davidson, scooters and lightweight motorcycles never really hit. And by 1967 in the U.K., most Mods had turned their attention to London's fashionable Carnaby Street or the burgeoning, more laid-back hippie culture with its psychedelic music and art.

How the short-lived, contentious, and influential Buffalo Springfield (Stephen Stills, Neil Young, Richie Furay, Bruce Palmer, and Dewey Martin) propitiously met in Hollywood is a rock & roll legend all its own. The gist of the story is that during the second week of April, 1966 Young and Palmer, both riding in a 1953 Pontiac hearse driven down to L.A. from Canada by Young, met Stills, Furay, and their friend Barry Friedman, themselves in a van, while (according to some accounts) waiting at a stoplight. The four decided—almost on the spot—to form a band and proceeded to name it after a historic steamroller company.

The precise details of what transpired have become obscured over the years. Though the five participants in the two vehicles agree on the general facts, each differs on the fine points. Who was first to notice the hearse? Did they pass each other going the opposite way, or was the white van *behind* the hearse when recognition was made? Various retellings were gathered in the 2001 Rhino box set *Buffalo Springfield* (below), compiled, edited, and extensively footnoted by archivist Joel Bernstein. Buffalo Springfield historian John Einarson also notes, only somewhat tongue in cheek, in his *There's Something Happening Here*, "This was no mere chance encounter. Those few minutes have taken on mythic proportions. More than pure luck, coincidence or serendipity, at that very moment the planets aligned, stars crossed, divine intervention interceded, the hand of fate revealed itself—or whatever you subscribe to." The story's rich tapestry is illustrated by the fact that Furay has recounted at least three versions of the same event. Each re-telling is noted by the year in which the interview took place.

Neil (1970): I left Toronto when I was eighteen, with Bruce Palmer. We had a black 1953 Pontiac hearse. We drove to L.A. 'cause that's where the sun was. I never thought of going anywhere else. I had a guitar and a dollar in my pocket. I don't know how I did it … or how I lived.

Richie (1968): For about a month or so [Stephen and I] rehearsed and looked for musicians. Just when all was looking dim, we ran into Neil driving down Sunset Boulevard on his way to San Francisco. We were driving in a white van and I saw a black hearse with Canadian plates going the other way. I remembered Stephen had told me that Neil drove a black hearse. So we chased him down. We persuaded him to at least come and listen to our arrangement of "Clancy."

Neil (1975): Bruce and I were tooling around L.A. in my hearse. [We] were taking in California, the Promised Land. We were heading up to San Francisco. Stephen and Richie, who were in town putting together a band, just happened to be driving around too. Stephen had met me before and remembered I had a hearse. As soon as he saw the Ontario plates, he knew it was me. So they stopped us. I was happy to see anybody I knew. And it seemed very logical for us to form a band.

ITSONLY ROCKNROLL.COM

Bruce (1968): We were driving around in an old hearse. We were having trouble going up little hills. I don't know how we thought we were going to make it to San Francisco. We were headed for the freeway on the way out of town.

Richie (1979): Stephen and I were driving down Sunset Boulevard when we got caught up in a traffic jam. As we sat there, we noticed the car in front was a hearse bearing Ontario plates. Stephen shouted, "That has just got to be Neil!" We rushed out and sure enough there sat Neil and Bruce. Neil had come to L.A. looking for us, and being unable to find us, was just about to go off to San Francisco. I'd taught Stephen "Nowadays Clancy Can't Even Sing," which Neil had taught me in New York a few months earlier. So we all went home and played it for Neil. He liked it. We started a rock & roll band.

Stephen (1968): Richie and I were driving down the street wondering what we were going to do. We passed this old hearse, and turned and said to each other, "Hey, I know him."

Richie (1984): We were in this white van, stuck in traffic on Sunset Boulevard. I turned to brush a fly off my arm, looked over into the other lane, and saw this black hearse with Ontario plates going in the other direction. Then Stephen looked across and said, "I'll bet I know who that is." I did a U-turn and pulled up behind the hearse. "Yeah, that's Neil," said Stephen. We honked and waved our arms, and Neil pulled the hearse into a supermarket parking lot. We drove over to Barry Friedman's house and got ripped. [Note: They actually pulled the vehicles into the parking lot of Ben Frank's restaurant, now Mel's Drive-In.]

Friedman (1997): I nudged Stephen and pointed at the old black Pontiac hearse caught in traffic on the other side of Sunset. "Isn't that your friend Neil?" I said.

Bruce (1997): It's the most remarkable karmic event ever. It's hard even to imagine. We passed parallel to one another, and imagine if they had been looking the other way? You wonder about kismet, fate, and all that when you consider this. Each of us were looking for the same thing: musicians. They needed a guitar player and a bass player, and we needed a band, so it was perfect timing.

"If the doors of perception were cleansed, everything would appear to man as it is, infinite." This quote from poet William Blake, via Aldous Huxley, was an inspiration to Jim Morrison, frontman for The Doors, which debuted in 1965. His dramatic voice powered exceptional compositions that included "Break on Through" and the seven-minute "Light My Fire" (a #1 single in 1967). Yet, the band's success was a problem throughout their career; many expected visionary leadership from Morrison & Co., as true underground heroes, while others tarred them as West Coast piffle.

Their second album, *Strange Days*, showcased the ambitious "When the Music's Over," and subsequent releases attempted a marriage of avant-garde poetry and lengthy rock composition, not always successfully. Nor did the anti-authoritarian Morrison take easily to the role of pop idol. His confrontations with middle America led to his indictment for indecent exposure after a concert in Miami in July 1969. Paradoxically, the furor re-awoke The Doors' creativity. *Morrison Hotel*, a tough R&B-based collection released that year, matched the best of their early releases, particularly the roaring "Roadhouse Blues," celebrated to this day for its timeless automotive propulsion.

•   •   •

Gram Parsons, the L.A.-based "father of country rock," was a troubled figure who influenced countless fellow musicians, from The Byrds (of which he was briefly a member) and The Rolling Stones to Elvis Costello and Uncle Tupelo. In 1972, following a stint with the Flying Burrito Brothers, Parsons met Emmylou Harris, who had been leading a relatively normal existence playing folk music at Washington, D.C., cafés and clubs. The two went on to record some of the tightest harmonies since the heyday of country music's Louvin Brothers. In 1973, they embarked upon a legendary road tour with their backing band, the Fallen Angels.

"I was put on a converted Greyhound bus with 'Gram Parsons' emblazoned across the side, driven by an ex-Marine affectionately called Leadfoot Lance, and surrounded by various musicians and fugitives from love and law and order," Harris later recalled. "We set out to play the better hippie honky tonks across America. They came to see this young man whose voice would break and crack, but rise pure and beautiful, full with his sweetness and his pain."

Reflecting further on her first tour and relating it to a career that has seen her go on solo acclaim and to share harmony duties with other male rock icons like Neil Young and Mark Knopfler, Harris remembers, "Driving through the prairies on the way to Amarillo, Texas, Kyle the bass player expressed his dislike for those flatlands because there was no place to hide. I agreed with him at the time, but sometimes I felt like I'd just swallowed a large piece of Oklahoma and a big ol' moon came rising up out of my throat and right on out the top of my head like some half-remembered melody … and that's the way it's been ever since."

•   •   •

Randy Newman is a lyricist of considerable sophistication who has earned multiple Grammy and Oscar nominations. His 1983 album, *Trouble in Paradise*, received great critical acclaim and included the single "I Love L.A.," the video for which featured the songwriter tooling past local landmarks in a Buick convertible. It's an example of Newman's characteristic ambivalence and classic ironic capture of mood and place. Nevertheless, Newman has genuine affection for his subjects. As he explained in a 2001 interview, "There's some kind of ignorance L.A. has that I'm *proud* of. The open car and the redhead, The Beach Boys … that all sounds *really* good to me."

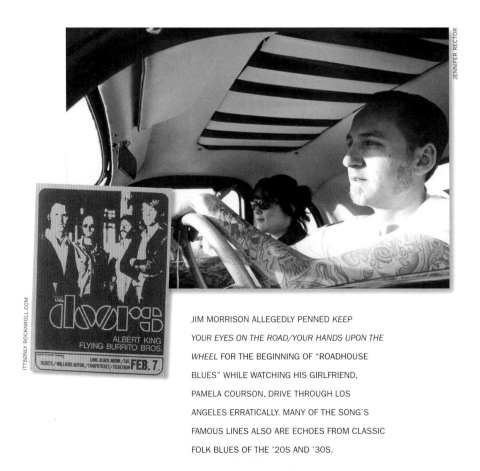

JIM MORRISON ALLEGEDLY PENNED *KEEP YOUR EYES ON THE ROAD/YOUR HANDS UPON THE WHEEL* FOR THE BEGINNING OF "ROADHOUSE BLUES" WHILE WATCHING HIS GIRLFRIEND, PAMELA COURSON, DRIVE THROUGH LOS ANGELES ERRATICALLY. MANY OF THE SONG'S FAMOUS LINES ALSO ARE ECHOES FROM CLASSIC FOLK BLUES OF THE '20S AND '30S.

I LOVE L.A.

RANDY NEWMAN

**JOHN AND MICHELLE PHILLIPS,
THE MAMAS AND THE PAPAS**

WEST COAST WHIPS

Two pioneer West Coast rappers with tremendous affinity for customized cars are Long Beach's Snoop Dogg and Los Angeles' King Tee. Both men have had long associations with premier producer Dr. Dre.

The huge success of Snoop's debut album *Doggystyle* (1993; #1 on the Billboard album chart), created in the hardcore gangsta rap tradition, gave impetus to his career as a rapper, record producer, MC, actor, cultural icon, and trendsetter—and collector of built-to-suit custom vehicles.

King Tee (later known as King T) released a string of historically important albums in the late '80s and early '90s, many in association with rappers Ice Cube and Ice-T, producers DJ Pooh and E-Swift, and rapper/TV

personality (*Pimp My Ride*) Xzibit, among others. All of Tee's albums—many now collectors' items—feature his whips (cars) as the cover art (with esteemed photographer Glen E. Friedman participating in many of the concepts).

Snoop, aided by his friend and car customizer Bigg Slice, set in motion a number of luxury vehicles, with special features such as impressive hydraulics, the most famous of which is the green *Snoop DeVille*. Snoop and Slice have been touring their Los Angeles Lakers–homage car, a re-work of a 1957 Pontiac Parisienne, and *Angel Dust,* a white 1966 Cadillac featured in the music video "P.I.M.P.," starring 50 Cent. "All the ideas come from Snoop," said Slice. "I just make them come to life."

'CAUSE I'M GETTING KINDA TIMID, AT FIRST I WAS WIT IT
TALK ABOUT JACK MOVES, I DID IT
I TOOK CARS, SNATCHED JEWELRY, AND BOY I'D RUN
WITH A COLORED RAG OVER MY GUN
AND THERE WAS TIMES I HAD TO POP FOOLS
BECAUSE THEY DIDN'T BELIEVE THAT THE GLOCK RULES
WHEN I SAY GET OUT, GET OUT! AND I MIGHT NOT SHOOT
THEN I'M OFF TO PUT YOUR DAYTONS ON MY COUPE
BUT NOWADAYS I HAVE TO FIGURE
WHAT GOES AROUND COMES AROUND FOR THE TRIFLIN' NIGGA

KING TEE, TRIFLIN' NIGGA

FRANK C. OCKENFELS. III

TOP FIVE SNOOP DOGG CAR SONGS,
FO' SHIZZLE

"STILL A G THANG" (1998)
"JUST DIPPIN'" (1999)
"SNOOP DOGG" (2000)
"SUITED N BOOTED" (2002)
"STOPLIGHT" (2002)

MARCO ALMERA

YOU KNOW 61 HIGHWAY IS THE LONGEST ROAD I KNOW,
IT RUN FROM CHICAGO DOWN TO THE GULF OF MEXICO

MISSISSIPPI FRED MCDOWELL, 61 HIGHWAY BLUES

JACK CHARLES OF QUARTERFLASH

RADAR LOVE
The Highway Beckons

The highway has been the stuff of inspiration to hundreds of musicians and songwriters. Many times the references are to road trips—journeys without a fixed itinerary or plan. The fun of a road trip, as all rock and car fans know, lies in experiencing freedom simply by being out on the open road, driving, accelerating, escaping, returning. Everyone has a different list of the best road songs and the reasoning behind them—the ones with the best beat, the best story, the best lines. Although rock & roll had barely been invented by the time he became a novelist, Jack Kerouac, one of the key personalities—some say the father—of the Beat Generation, knew those feelings better than anyone.

On the Road, which Kerouac wrote in 1951 but which was not published until 1957, is a semi-autobiographical account of his manic adventures as Sal Paradise, crisscrossing America with friend Dean Moriarty (in real life, Neal Cassady, later a mainstay of the Merry Pranksters). The book had an eye-opening impact on a generation of disaffected college-age young people in the late '50s, and became a backdrop to the early Dick Dale–Rendezvous Ballroom hot rod–beach scene in Southern California.

Though it expressed a new concept in motor-driven freedom—essentially 100-mile-per-hour days of rushing from girl to girl, leaving friends in strange cities, and returning days later to pick them up, all amid an ever-changing cast of shadowy or neon-lit characters— *On the Road* really was all about Kerouac's angst-ridden, fragmented snapshots on the human condition. It also contained some of the finest writings about cool jazz of the period. Years later, Tom Waits and Primus recorded "On the Road (Home I'll Never Be)," mirroring stories Kerouac told about Cassady in another novel, *Vanity of Duluoz.*

"Stories" is the key word here. The common threads among all the great road songs—besides a rockin' beat—are the experiences the songwriters recall, boast about, or otherwise spin. Sometimes it's a fragment from a story that grabs you, as in Marc Bolan of T-Rex singing, inexplicably, *I drive a Rolls-Royce/'Cause it's good for my voice.* Just as often it's the full narrative that transcends and captivates, as in Deep Purple's "Highway Star," KISS' "Detroit Rock City," Bob Seger's "Get Out of Denver," John Hiatt's "Drive South," Joni Mitchell's "All I Want," or any one of a thousand other great road songs.

When it comes to the road, a musician's genius is to make sense of it, to use it as inspiration. Yet, the realities of *being* on the road are sometimes not as exciting as what life is *imagined* to be like on the road. Despite what we may think of a successful rock band's unlimited opportunities for excess, to revel in the freedoms that they sing about in their songs, the truth is—for them—the road has fewer and fewer exits. This is altogether different from what the songs promise, what rock audiences imagine when tripping out upon hearing a great road song. Star musicians' ability to freely adventure can be seriously compromised by the sheer dreariness of the road. When John Lennon famously said about The Beatles' overwhelming success, "Oh, it was a room and a car and a car and a room and a room and a car," it's obvious he knew as much about the dirty lowdown as the sheer inspiration his songs delivered.

REALLY THE BLUES

DURING PROHIBITION, IT WASN'T UNCOMMON FOR POOR SOUTHERNERS TO USE CHEAP CANNED FUEL (A JELLIED ALCOHOL) TO GET HIGH. THEY DUMPED THE JELLY INTO A SOCK AND WRUNG THE LIQUID ALCOHOL FROM IT. THIS LIQUID WAS MIXED WITH ORANGE CRUSH OR COLA, RESULTING IN A POISONOUS ELIXIR THAT COULD PUT THE DRINKER AWAY FOR HOURS. IF YOU HAD TO TURN TO "CANNED HEAT" FOR RELIEF, YOU KNEW THE BLUES.

IN THE SPRING OF 1967, A BAND NAMED CANNED HEAT CAME OUT WITH ITS FIRST ALBUM. THE COVER ART DEPICTED THE BAND AROUND A TABLE LITTERED WITH STERNO CANS, A PARTICULAR BRAND OF JELLIED ALCOHOL. IN JUNE, THE BAND, LED BY SINGER BOB HITE, APPEARED AT THE MONTEREY POP FESTIVAL AND ESTABLISHED THEMSELVES AS L.A.'S ANSWER TO CHICAGO'S PAUL BUTTERFIELD BLUES BAND AND ENGLAND'S JOHN MAYALL AND THE BLUESBREAKERS.

LATER THAT YEAR, CANNED HEAT WERE BUSTED IN A DENVER SETUP THE BAND WAS BOOKED INTO A NEW CLUB THERE BUT THE POLICE WERE DETERMINED TO STOP THE VENUE FROM OPENING. THE COPS SENT A SO-CALLED FRIEND OF THE BAND TO THEIR HOTEL, WHERE HE STASHED SOME WEED UNDER A CHAIR CUSHION. CANNED HEAT WAS LATER ARRESTED.

OVER A GAME OF GIN RUMMY, THE PRESIDENT OF THEIR LABEL, LIBERTY RECORDS, OFFERED TO PAY THE LEGAL FEES TO SPRING THEM, IN EXCHANGE FOR THE THEIR NEXT SONG-PUBLISHING RIGHTS. SO IT WAS THE BANDMEMBERS SOLD A PIECE OF THEIR FUTURES IN EXCHANGE FOR THEIR FREEDOM. SIX MONTHS LATER, THE LP *BOOGIE WITH CANNED HEAT* HIT THE STORES. THE SINGLE "ON THE ROAD AGAIN" BECAME A WORLDWIDE HIT. TO THIS DAY, THE BAND HAS NOT RECEIVED A PENNY OF THE PUBLISHING RIGHTS.

United States
FEATURING
The Interstate Highway System
Esso

Happy Motoring!

DOOBIE BROTHERS

TAKE THE HIGHWAY

AC/DC "Highway to Hell"

Audioslave "I Am the Highway"

Tom Cochrane "Life Is a Highway"

Dire Straits "The Long Highway"

John Fogerty "Rattlesnake Highway"

Billy Idol "Blue Highway"

Elton John "Cold Highway"

Journey "Dixie Highway"

Judas Priest "Heading Out to the Highway"

Kottonmouth Kings "Endless Highway"

Limp Bizkit "My Way or the Highway"

Mazzy Star "Ghost Highway"

Midnight Oil "Gunbarrel Highway"

Van Morrison "Hard Nose the Highway"

Tom Petty "Kings Highway"

Todd Rundgren "Emperor of the Highway"

Sonic Youth "Pacific Coast Highway"

Waterboys "Ahead Down the Highway"

DOOBIE BROTHERS

The Doobie Brothers were the original "roadhouse blues-brothers," founded in San Jose, California, in 1970, and playing many early gigs at the legendary biker bar, Chateau Liberte, an original Wells Fargo stagecoach stop high atop the Santa Cruz Mountains.

Toulouse Street (1972) was the album by which most fans really discovered the band. The LP is close in style and sound to what the Eagles were doing during the same period, except the Doobies threw jazz and R&B into the new three-part-harmony country-rock mix. Tom Johnston's "Rockin' Down the Highway" and "Listen to the Music" also show them capable of Creedence Clearwater Revival–style boogie-rock, but by this time their sound was built on the model laid out by the Allman Brothers' interlocking double lead guitars (Johnston and Pat Simmons) and paired drummers (John Hartman and Michael Hossack).

be removed or defaced.

the kills the sights
the get hustle
monday, march 21, 2005

the casbah

KER . . . CH-U-U-U-KKK

Summer, 1980. My parents' car was a huge, gas-guzzling Chrysler New Yorker, solid white with white leather upholstery. It had an 8-track tape player in the dash. Most of the 8-track tapes I had were secondhand, given to me by friends (people were generally over the 8-track thing by 1980), or bought at garage sales and thrift stores. *Frampton Comes Alive* was big then.

My two Queen 8-tracks were the only ones I ever bought new. Not many stores sold 8-track tapes by that time—I had to go to the specialty music store at Northpark Mall and put my money down. New 8-track tapes had real authority—they were clunky and heavy, real solid, not like those cheapy cassettes. I bought Queen's *Live Killers* album and, of course, Night at the Opera. This was my all-time favorite band, at the time.

That also was the summer I learned to drive. I got a learner's permit and would go out to see my favorite older sister, a 45-minute drive out to Carrollton that could stretch to an hour if you took the long way. Her home was on the edge of nowhere. I would roll down the windows in that big New Yorker and fly down razor-straight two-lane Texas roads past cattle pastures and sleepy Texaco stations, no police, no other drivers in sight for twenty minutes at a clip.

En route, Freddie Mercury would be wailing "Bohemian Rhapsody" and Brian May would be soaring through his extended live guitar solo on "Brighton Rock"—the one where the music runs out midway through and you have to wait for the tape to switch over:

Dadaladalada DOW DOW DAAAHW dahn dahn dookadooka . . .

KER . . . CH-U-U-U-KKK

. . . shookashooka dahn dann dahn . . .

. . . and so forth, but who cared, except for me? It was summer in Texas, too hot to do anything but drive somewhere godforsaken and pretend I was king of the roadways with Queen on full blast.

The car got totaled a few years later (I wasn't driving), my sister and brother-in-law split up, and Carrollton is a bustling community now. The narrow roads through nowhere now squeeze past strip malls, apartment complexes, and office parks. My 8-tracks bit the dust long, long ago.

But I do get a whiff of nostalgia when I listen to May's guitar solo—now on crystal-clear CD—and my mind always still hears that break in the tracks when the tape changed over . . .

KER . . . CH-U-U-U-KKK

— Kellum Johnson

RADAR LOVE

WE'VE GOT A THING THAT'S CALLED RADAR LOVE. OF ALL THE ROAD-DRIVING SONGS EVER COMPOSED, ONE STANDS ABOVE ALL THE REST: THE DUTCH BAND GOLDEN EARRING'S "RADAR LOVE." NO OTHER SONG APPEARS NEARLY AS FREQUENTLY ON ALL THE "BEST ROAD SONGS" LISTS NOW COMMON ON THE INTERNET.

WRITTEN BY GEORGE KOOYMANS AND BARRY HAY, THE SINGLE WAS RELEASED ON AUGUST 25, 1973, AND SUBSEQUENTLY APPEARED ON GOLDEN EARRING'S *MOONTAN* ALBUM. THERE ARE MORE THAN 250 KNOWN COVER VERSIONS OF THE SONG, INCLUDING THOSE BY U2, R.E.M., BRYAN ADAMS, CARLOS SANTANA, THE ALARM, CROWDED HOUSE, DEF LEPPARD. NO DOUBT, THOUSANDS OF OTHER VERSIONS HAVE BEEN PLAYED BY BAR BANDS THE WORLD OVER.

WHILE THE BAND HAD ORIGINS IN 1961 AS THE EARRINGS (MODIFIED TO GOLDEN EARRING IN 1969), IT WAS NOT UNTIL THE MID-'70S THAT IT GAINED INTERNATIONAL RENOWN, IN PART DUE TO TOURS WITH THE WHO.

I'VE BEEN DRIVIN' ALL NIGHT
MY HAND'S WET ON THE WHEEL
THERE'S A VOICE IN MY HEAD
THAT DRIVES MY HEEL
ITS MY BABY CALLIN' SAYS
"I NEED YA HERE"
IT'S HALF PAST FOUR AND
I'M SHIFTING GEAR

GOLDEN EARRING, RADAR LOVE

A rare upside-down, in-car record player.

MOTOROLA SOLID STATE / 8 Track Car Stereo Tape Cartridge Player

ILLUSTRATED CATALOG
RCA STEREO
CARTRIDGE TAPES
OVER 400 SELECTIONS

The Exciting NEW Way to Enjoy the Music You Want
In Your Home...In Your Car ...or Wherever You Roam!

FRANK VACANTI COLLECTION

THE EVOLUTION OF CAR STEREO

1878: THOMAS EDISON BUILDS THE FIRST WORKING TINFOIL-CYLINDER PHONOGRAPH, PREDATING THE FIRST RECORDED DISC.

1898: OVERTAKING CYLINDERS IN POPULARITY, MASS PRODUCTION OF GROOVED SHELLAC DISCS (PLAYED WITH A TONEARM AND RUDIMENTARY STYLUS) BEGINS IN HANOVER, GERMANY. BY 1910, MOST SUCH DISCS WOULD BE RECORDED TO PLAY BACK AT 78 RPM. DISCS WILL DOMINATE THE RECORDED MUSIC MARKET UNTIL 1988.

1906: LEE DEFOREST INVENTS AN AMPLIFICATION DEVICE THAT MAKES RADIO CIRCUITS COMMERCIALLY FEASIBLE.

1918: EDWIN ARMSTRONG INVENTS THE SUPERHETERODYNE CIRCUIT, THE BASIC CIRCUIT OF NEARLY ALL MODERN RADIO RECEIVERS.

1920: FIRST REGULAR LICENSED (AM) RADIO BROADCASTING BEGINS.

1922: FIVE HUNDRED LICENSED RADIO STATIONS OPERATE IN AMERICA, BUT LESS THAN 2 MILLION HOMES ARE EQUIPPED WITH RADIO. THE BEST VACUUM-TUBE RADIOS RECEIVE STATIONS UP TO 500 MILES AWAY.

1924: RADIO NETWORKS ARE CREATED. NBC FORMS IN 1926; CBS FOLLOWS IN 1928.

1926: RADIO IS INTRODUCED TO CARS, BUT AS PORTABLE UNITS: SO-CALLED "TRAVEL RADIOS." WEAK LOUDSPEAKERS, RUDIMENTARY AERIALS, INTERFERENCE FROM THE CAR'S ENGINE, AND THE NEED FOR MULTIPLE, LARGE BATTERIES WORK AGAINST PERMANENT INSTALLATION.

1927: WITH THE INVENTION OF DAMP RESISTANCE, IT BECOMES POSSIBLE TO LISTEN TO A PORTABLE RADIO WHILE A CAR'S MOTOR IS RUNNING.

1929: THE ROAD AND THE RADIO MEET FOR THE FIRST TIME WHEN A YOUNG ENTREPRENEUR, WILLIAM LEAR, INVENTS THE MODERN CAR RADIO. SUPERHETERODYNE TECHNOLOGY PERMITS EASIER TUNING TO SPECIFIC FREQUENCIES, LOUDSPEAKERS ARE IMPROVED, AND POWER IS SUPPLIED BY THE CAR BATTERY. HE SELLS THE IDEA TO PAUL GALVIN (GALVIN MANUFACTURING), WHO COINS THE NAME "MOTOROLA" FOR THE COMPANY'S NEW PRODUCTS, COMBINING THE IDEA OF MOTION AND RADIO. THESE FIRST CAR RADIOS ARE AVAILABLE ONLY AS AFTERMARKET ACCESSORIES.

1930: GALVIN INTRODUCES ITS FIRST COMMERCIALLY SUCCESSFUL CAR RADIO. THE MOTOROLA MODEL 5T71 SOLD FOR $125 AND COULD BE INSTALLED IN MOST AUTOMOBILES.

1930: RCA VICTOR LAUNCHES THE FIRST COMMERCIALLY AVAILABLE VINYL LONG-PLAYING RECORD, DESIGNED FOR PLAYBACK AT 33 1/3 RPM. INITIALLY, IT'S A FAILURE BECAUSE OF THE LACK OF AFFORDABLE, RELIABLE CONSUMER PLAYBACK EQUIPMENT. HOWEVER, VINYL'S LOWER PLAYBACK NOISE LEVEL WAS NOT FORGOTTEN.

1933: IN THE U.S., FORD SELLS CARS WITH THE FIRST IN-DASHBOARD RADIOS.

1936: THE MOTOROLA POLICE CRUISER MOBILE RECEIVER IS OFFERED, A CAR RADIO PRESET TO A SINGLE FREQUENCY TO RECEIVE POLICE BROADCASTS. POLICE CRUISERS WOULD CATCH MANY FAST DRIVERS PLAYING THE RADIO (AND LATER, THE TAPE DECK, CD, AND MP3) AT VOLUME AND NOT PAYING ATTENTION TO THEIR REARVIEW MIRROR.

1937: FORD FIRST USES A STEEL ROD AS AERIAL; A TELESCOPING VERSION IS INTRODUCED THE FOLLOWING YEAR.

1941: FORD ADVERTISES A RADIO THAT CAN BE PRESET FOR FIVE STATIONS AND TUNED TO THE DESIRED STATION BY A FOOT-OPERATED SWITCH.

1945: REEL-TO-REEL AUDIOTAPE IS FIRST MADE AVAILABLE. IN 1953, GEORGE BARRIS WILL ADD A REEL-TO-REEL TAPE PLAYER TO HIS *GOLDEN SAHARA* SHOW CAR.

1948: RESEARCHERS AT BELL LABORATORIES INVENT THE FIRST TRANSISTOR, LEADING TO IMPROVED-PERFORMANCE SOLID-STATE TECHNOLOGY (AND CONVERSION FROM TUBE-BASED RADIOS).

1948: COLUMBIA RECORDS' DR. PETER GOLDMARK DEVELOPS THE 12-INCH LONG PLAY 33 1/3 RPM MICROGROOVE RECORD AS AN ALTERNATIVE TO THE 78. BY THE MID-1950S, ALL RECORD COMPANIES AGREE TO A COMMON RECORDING STANDARD CALLED RIAA EQUALIZATION. THE BRITTLE 78S STILL ARE PRODUCED ALONGSIDE THE NEWER VINYL-BASED FORMAT WELL INTO THE 1950S (THE BEATLES RECORDED SOME OF THE LAST COMMERCIALLY RELEASED 78S).

1950: THE COMMERCIAL RIVALRY BETWEEN RCA VICTOR AND COLUMBIA RECORDS LEADS TO RCA'S INTRODUCTION OF A COMPETING VINYL FORMAT: THE 7-INCH 45 RPM "SINGLE." FROM THE MID-1950S THROUGH THE 1960S, THE COMMON HOME RECORD PLAYER, HI-FI, OR STEREO WOULD TYPICALLY FEATURE A THREE-SPEED TURNTABLE, A CARTRIDGE WITH BOTH 78 AND MICROGROOVE STYLUSES, AND SOME KIND OF ADAPTER FOR PLAYING THE 45S WITH THEIR LARGER CENTER HOLE (WHICH ALLOWED FOR EASIER HANDLING BY DJS AND JUKEBOXES).

1954: PANASONIC STARTS ITS OWN PRODUCTION OF CAR RADIOS.

1955: A GERMANIUM TRANSISTOR INTENDED FOR CAR RADIOS BECOMES MOTOROLA'S FIRST MASS-PRODUCED SEMICONDUCTOR.

1955: CHRYSLER INTRODUCES THE "HIGHWAY HI-FI" AS A FACTORY OPTION FOR 1956: A BUILT-IN, AMPLIFIED HIGH-FIDELITY RECORD PLAYER. DEVELOPED BY COLUMBIA AND MOUNTED UNDER THE DASHBOARD, IT PLAYS STANDARD 7-INCH SINGLES THROUGH THE RADIO SPEAKER. THE COMPANY BROCHURE STATES, "THE PICKUP ARM MOVES ONLY IN A HORIZONTAL PLANE. HENCE, THERE IS NO PROBLEM OF THE ARM ITSELF BOUNCING WHEN THE CAR TRAVELS A ROUGH ROAD. ONLY THE STYLUS CAN MOVE VERTICALLY, AND THIS IS SPRING-LOADED TO HOLD THE POINT AGAINST THE

THE TEST SONG

I FEEL LIKE A RETARDED LITTLE WHITE BOY PLAYING IT, BUT THE TRUE TEST FOR ME TO SEE IF YOU HAVE A *GOOD* IN-CAR SYSTEM OR NOT IS C-MURDER'S "DOWN 4 MY NIGGAS." THERE'S AN INSTRUMENTAL VERSION THAT DOESN'T HAVE THE PROFANITY FOR "SAFE" BUMPING IF YOU LOOK ONLINE . . . BUT IT IS *THE* TEST SONG.

IT HITS SOME LOW PASS NOTES THAT WHEN YOU'VE GOT WELL-INSTALLED AND CAPABLE SUBS, IT WILL *DROP YOUR JAW*. WHEN I WAS DEMONSTRATING THE SINGLE TO A FRIEND OF MINE NEAR THE INSTALL BAY, PLAYING THAT SONG KNOCKED ALMOST AN ENTIRE SHELF OF MERCHANDISE ONTO THE FLOOR AND ATTRACTED NEARLY 100 SHOPPERS TO COME OVER AND SEE THE CAR THAT WAS DOING "THAT." THEY ALL THOUGHT IT WAS SOME DEADLY SET OF SUBS I WAS AIRING OUT, BUT REALLY IT WAS A SINGLE 12-INCH IN THE MOST INSANE PORTED BOX EVER, WHICH I COUPLED TO THAT BAD-ASS TUNE. SHAKE AND BAKE!

— SAM S.

BALTIMORE, MARYLAND

SHOP PRESIDENT RYAN FRIEDLINGHAUS (R) AND "BIG DANE" FLORENCE (L).
GENERAL LEE II AT WEST COAST CUSTOMS, CORONA, CALIFORNIA.

RECORD WITH A PRESSURE OF TWO GRAMS. THE PICKUP ARM IS COUNTERWEIGHTED SO THAT ITS CENTER-OF-MASS IS AT THE PIVOT POINT. THIS OFFSETS THE TENDENCY OF THE ARM TO SWING IN RESPONSE TO FAST ACCELERATION, HEAVY BRAKING, OR HARD-TURNING. IN REPEATED TESTS, IT HAS PROVED EXTREMELY DIFFICULT TO JAR THE ARM OFF THE RECORD OR EVEN MAKE THE STYLUS JUMP A GROOVE. NOW, FOR THE FIRST TIME, YOU CAN HAVE THE MUSIC OF YOUR CHOICE WHEREVER YOU GO!" AN LP VERSION OF THE PLAYER IS AVAILABLE ON THE AFTERMARKET FOR A YEAR, AND RCA INTRODUCES ITS OWN MOUNTED IN-CAR, AUTOMATIC-CHANGING 45 PLAYER IN 1960, INITIALLY FOR PLYMOUTHS AND DESOTOS. DESPITE THE ABILITY TO LOAD AS MANY AS 14 SINGLE RECORDS, THE PUBLIC IS NOT EXACTLY WOWED.

1956: GOLDMARK DEVELOPS A 16 2/3 RPM RECORD PLAYER WITH A 7-INCH ULTRAMICROGROOVE FOR POTENTIAL INSTALLATION IN CHRYSLER'S IMPERIAL MODEL.

1956: THE ENCLOSED-REEL-TO-REEL TAPE MECHANISM IS DEVELOPED, LEADING TO THE INTRODUCTION OF 4-TRACK AND 8-TRACK CARTRIDGES LESS THAN A DECADE LATER.

1958: MOTOROLA INTRODUCES THE MOTRAC RADIO, WITH A FULLY TRANSISTORIZED POWER SUPPLY AND RECEIVER (I.E., NO VACUUM TUBES). ITS LOW POWER CONSUMPTION ALLOWS THE RADIO TO BE USED WITHOUT RUNNING THE AUTOMOBILE ENGINE. PANASONIC FOLLOWS SUIT IN 1959.

1958: THE FIRST STEREO TWO-CHANNEL LPS IN THE U.S. ARE ISSUED BY AUDIO FIDELITY, PROVIDING A LISTENING EXPERIENCE BASED ON THE TRUE LOCATION OF THE SOURCE OF THE SOUND. HI-FI SYSTEM MANUFACTURERS SWIFTLY ADOPT STEREO AND INTRODUCE STEREO HEADPHONES.

1963: PHILIPS DEMONSTRATES THE FIRST COMPACT AUDIO CASSETTE, BUT ITS USE IS CONFINED TO DICTATION MACHINES.

1963: FOLLOWING ON THE SUCCESS OF TUBE-BASED GUITAR AMPLIFIERS WITH SOUND EFFECTS LIKE FENDER'S TREMOLUX, VIBROLUX, AND SUPER REVERB, MOTOROLA OFFERS AN ADD-ON "VIBRASONIC" REVERB SOUND EFFECTS UNIT FOR ALL VEHICLES WITH A MONO OR STEREO RADIO (IT ALSO WORKED WITH 8-TRACKS AND MULTIPLE SPEAKERS). INTENDED TO GIVE CAR RADIO A SOUND LIKE A CONCERT HALL, IT ACCOMPLISHED WHAT EVERYONE WANTED TO DO, BACK IN THE DAY: "MAKE AN IMPRESSION."

1964: PANASONIC INTRODUCES CAR RADIO WITH FM CAPABILITY.

1965: THE 8-TRACK TAPE PLAYER IS CREATED BY BILL LEAR AFTER HE TAKES A RIDE WITH EARL "MADMAN" MUNTZ, WHO'D RIGGED A 4-TRACK TAPE SYSTEM IN HIS CAR AND BEGAN MARKETING IT AS THE "STEREO-PAK." THE NEXT YEAR, FORD INTRODUCES A BUILT-IN 8-TRACK PLAYER AS A CUSTOM OPTION. DESPITE MEDIOCRE AUDIO QUALITY, EASILY BROKEN CARTRIDGES, AND PROBLEMS WITH FITTING AN LP INTO A FOUR-PROGRAM CARTRIDGE, THE FORMAT GAINS GREAT POPULARITY DUE TO ITS CONVENIENCE AND PORTABILITY. EIGHT-TRACK TAPES, THE FIRST SUCCESSFUL NON-DISC, NON-SKIP PRERECORDED PLAYBACK DEVICES, PROVE ESPECIALLY POPULAR AMONG PROFESSIONAL TRUCK DRIVERS.

1967: PANASONIC INTRODUCES CAR STEREO. BEFORE STEREO, THE ONE SPEAKER GENERALLY WAS LOCATED IN THE MIDDLE OF THE DASHBOARD AND AIMED TOWARD THE WINDSHIELD. NOW, SPEAKERS CAN BE POSITIONED IN DOORS AND BEHIND THE REAR SEATS.

1969: DOLBY NOISE REDUCTION IS INTRODUCED FOR PRERECORDED TAPES.

1970: PANASONIC INTRODUCES STEREO COMPACT AUDIO CASSETTE–BASED CAR STEREO, THE CASSETTES BEING HALF THE SIZE OF THE 8-TRACK CARTRIDGE. YET, 8-TRACK PLAYERS REMAIN COMMON IN AUTOMOBILES UNTIL THE EARLY 1980S.

1982: THE FIRST DIGITAL AUDIO 5-INCH COMPACT DISCS (CDS) ARE MARKETED, MERGING THE CONSUMER MUSIC INDUSTRY WITH THE COMPUTER REVOLUTION.

1988: CD SALES SURPASS LP SALES. CDS AND CASSETTES ARE THE TWO DOMINANT CONSUMER FORMATS.

1992: PANASONIC INTRODUCES CD-CAPABLE CAR STEREO.

2000: CAR AUDIO IS NOW AN EVER-IMPROVING SPORT, CONTRIBUTING TO THE GROWTH OF MUSICAL ENTERTAINMENT OVERALL. CARS ARE EQUIPPED WITH HIGH-END EQUALIZED AUDIO SYSTEMS RUN FROM A CD CHANGER AND/OR MP3 PLAYER (STILL OFTEN CALLED THE "DECK," AFTER OLDER TAPE-DECKS) IN THE CONSOLE OR TRUNK. SPEAKER COMPONENTS CONSISTING OF A MATCHED TWEETER, MIDRANGE, AND WOOFER SET IN TWO-SPEAKER AND THREE-SPEAKER COMBINATIONS INCLUDE AN AUDIO CROSSOVER, LIMITING THE FREQUENCY RANGE EACH SPEAKER HANDLES AND INCREASING VOLUME AND TONAL SENSITIVITY. SUBWOOFERS, BUILT INTO SOPHISTICATED ENCLOSURES, PROVIDE LOW-FREQUENCY MUSIC FEEDS. AMPLIFIERS, IN RACKS, ARE HIGHLY REFINED AND CONNECTED BY PRECIOUS-METAL, LARGE-GAUGE CABLE. CAR ALTERNATORS ARE UPGRADED, INCREASING THE CAPABILITY OF THE ELECTRICAL SYSTEM, AND BANKS OF BATTERIES SERVE EXTREME HIGH-VOLUME NEEDS, ALLOWING SYSTEMS TO BE PLAYED FOR LONG PERIODS WITHOUT RUNNING THE ENGINE.

2001: APPLE COMPUTER, INC. INTRODUCES THE IPOD PORTABLE MUSIC PLAYER, AND WITHIN JUST A FEW YEARS, IPOD DOCKS ARE INTRODUCED TO CAR STEREO SYSTEMS.

2004: SATELLITE RADIO IS INTRODUCED, REQUIRING SPECIAL RECEIVERS IN CARS BUT ELIMINATING THE PROBLEM OF STATION SIGNALS BREAKING UP 30 OR 40 MILES FROM THEIR TRANSMISSION POINT. SATELLITE RADIO, WITH ITS GENRE-PROGRAMMED STATIONS, BROADCASTS ITS SIGNAL FROM MORE THAN 22,000 MILES AWAY—IN SPACE.

JOEL BERNSTEIN

LIFE'S BEEN GOOD

It's been said that in 1967 John Lennon loved Procol Harum's "A Whiter Shade of Pale" so much that he would listen to it through headphones over and over during long journeys in the back of his limousine. Upon reaching his destination, he'd remain lying on the backseat, saying he had to hear it a few more times before getting out.

Rock musicians have been riding in limos ever since they started traveling by plane. TV star and pop-rock singer Ricky Nelson's popularity and new wealth—second only to Elvis in the 1950s—both necessitated and provided for his use of limos, especially when he flew to sold-out weekend gigs all over America (he couldn't travel during the week, due to the demands of his television production schedule).

While many emergent stars bought Cadillacs or Lincolns for personal use (and even used them to travel to gigs, as with Elvis and Bill Haley) as early as the late '50s, it really wasn't until The Beatles and The Rolling Stones had to deal with "transport issues," such as how to safely maneuver between the airport and the hotel and the hotel and the concert site (with the streets overflowing and backstage entrances swollen with onlookers), that the limo became a vital conveyance. Many rock fans remember the opening scenes in The Beatles' *A Hard Day's Night*, in which the limo served as the band's refuge and a seeming base of operations to escape the hordes.

Mariah Carey's 1987 music video for "The Roof (Back in Time)" shows Carey in a limousine on a dark and rainy night, recalling an intimate

encounter on a rooftop. Eventually, she gets out of the limo and into the rain to relive her memories. In a national survey, it was subsequently named the eighteenth greatest music video of all time, and its grittiness helped her overcome her bubblegum pop past.

To promote her song "Music" (2000), Madonna created a parody of rap videos, showing her cruising around in the back of a limo, enjoying all the spoils of success. At the 2001 Grammys she opened the evening with "Music" and arrived on stage in a limo "driven" by underage rapper Lil' Bow Wow.

Surprisingly, given its ubiquitous role, relatively few songs have been written about the limo life. There are Bruce Hornsby's "White Wheeled Limousine," Prince's "Blue Limousine," Alice Cooper's "Slick Black Limousine," Paul Simon's "Stranded in a Limousine," The Rolling Stones' "Black Limousine," and of course "Long Black Limousine" (sung by Elvis, Glen Campbell, Hank Williams Jr., and Merle Haggard, among others). Grand Funk Railroad penned "Mr. Limousine Driver," a heavy metal echo of James Taylor's "Limousine Driver."

A few of the odder paeans include Soundgarden's "Limo Wreck," the UK Subs' "Limo Life," and Elvis Costello's "The People's Limousine." Rappers have been more explicit, in particular Ice Cube's "Limos, Demos & Bimbos" and Will Smith's ode to his security guard, "Charlie Mack (1st Out of the Limo)."

LL COOL J

DAVID CASSIDY

HENRY DILTZ/CORBIS

KEITH MOON

SHEPARD SHERBELL/CORBIS

The words "limousine" and "chauffeur" have been in common use since the early twentieth century when the first luxury automobiles required professional drivers to manage them. The word "limousine" originated from the Limousine region of France, where shepherds used a type of hooded raincoat to protect themselves from the weather. Professional automobile drivers later used such garments as they sat in the open cockpits while their masters and their guests rode in splendor in the covered rear seats.

By the early '20s, limousines were a sure symbol of status, oozing wealth, class, and sophistication. By the '30s, the first stretched cars and depot wagons were used to transport famous big band leaders such as Glenn Miller and Benny Goodman and their orchestras, complete with their musical equipment and instruments. By the '40s, "airporter stretch coaches" were produced to transport the rich and famous from airports and ocean liners to hotels. By then, Hollywood actors had also discovered a practical application for the vehicles: conveying them through the streets in a lavishly appointed, secure cocoon, bestowing anonymity while also allowing them to flaunt their celebrity.

Naturally, these advantages would appeal to the rock star in anyone. For decades, limousines have insulated musicians and their guests (and groupies) from admirers and the paparazzi while helping them indulge in noxious habits en route to a gig or home following one. There are a *lot* of inspired nasties one can do in a limo, as the group 112 sang, "Getting freaky in my Bentley limousine/It's even better when it's with ice cream."

With the invention of each new technological marvel (beginning with cocktail cabinets and sliding roofs, then TVs, mirrored ceilings, Jacuzzis, and *whatever*), the stretch became longer, and the vehicle more improbable or exclusive (bulletproof Hummers, customized Suburbans, and modified Lincoln Navigators, Cadillac Excursions, and Maybach 62s have accommodated rockers and hip-hoppers both). Bentley, BMW, Jaguar, Lexus, Porsche, Ferrari, and Rolls-Royce are all marques that have undergone extensive rework at the hands of master coachbuilders to create limousines suiting the whims and eccentricities of clients.

One of the most famous limousine legends belongs to Keith Moon (of course). It supposedly took place in 1967 during The Who's first tour of the United States, then supporting Herman's Hermits. The occasion was Moon's birthday; the scene was the Holiday Inn in Flint, Michigan. After celebrating all day, the debauchery culminated in a massive cake fight around the hotel swimming pool. The police were called. Moon, by then stark naked, sought to escape in the band's hired limousine. Realizing he had no keys, he managed to pop the handbrake, sending the car rolling backward through a fence and into the pool. Moon—the story concluded— narrowly escaped with his life.

WHY DON'T WE DO IT IN THE ROAD?

"Why Don't We Do It In The Road?" is one of the more controversial "screaming" songs on "the White Album," released in 1968. Reportedly, Paul wrote it in India while on a meditation expedition to the Maharishi, having witnessed two monkeys mating in the middle of the road and before a gathering crowd. The actual phrase is said to have come from a comment by Queen Victoria, remembered by McCartney, , in which the legendarily prudish monarch asked about a particular "romantic practice," misunderstood the veiled references to sex, and responded, "It's acceptable, so long as they don't do it in the road and scare the horses."

McCartney later explained, "There's only once incident I can recall of which John publicly mentioned I hurt him. And that was when I went off with Ringo and did 'Why Don't We Do It In The Road?' It wasn't a deliberate thing. John and George were tied up finishing something, and me and Ringo were free, just hanging around, so I said to Ringo, 'Let's go and do this.' I did hear John sometime later singing it. He liked the song—it had the loud, bluesy effect of 'Oh, Darling'—and I suppose he'd have wanted to do it with me. It was a very John sort of song anyway. Anyway, he had his revenge with 'Revolution 9,' having went off and made that one without me."

Years later, a fan commented, "In 1970, when I was 17, I had 'a thing' with a 37-year-old woman. We both felt challenged by 'Why Don't We Do It In The Road?,' so we gave it a try. I regret to report a paved road, no matter how isolated and late at night, is not a good place to 'do it.' Sorry, Paul. Great song, but pragmatically speaking, bad idea."

STEPHEN STILLS, DAVID CROSBY, JONI MITCHELL, AND GRAHAM NASH

RICK SPRINGFIELD

JANIS JOPLIN, NEW YORK CITY

EDDIE VAN HALEN

HENRY DILTZ/CORBIS

PAUL NATKIN/PHOTO RESERVE

LYNN GOLDSMITH

CLARK J. PIERSON

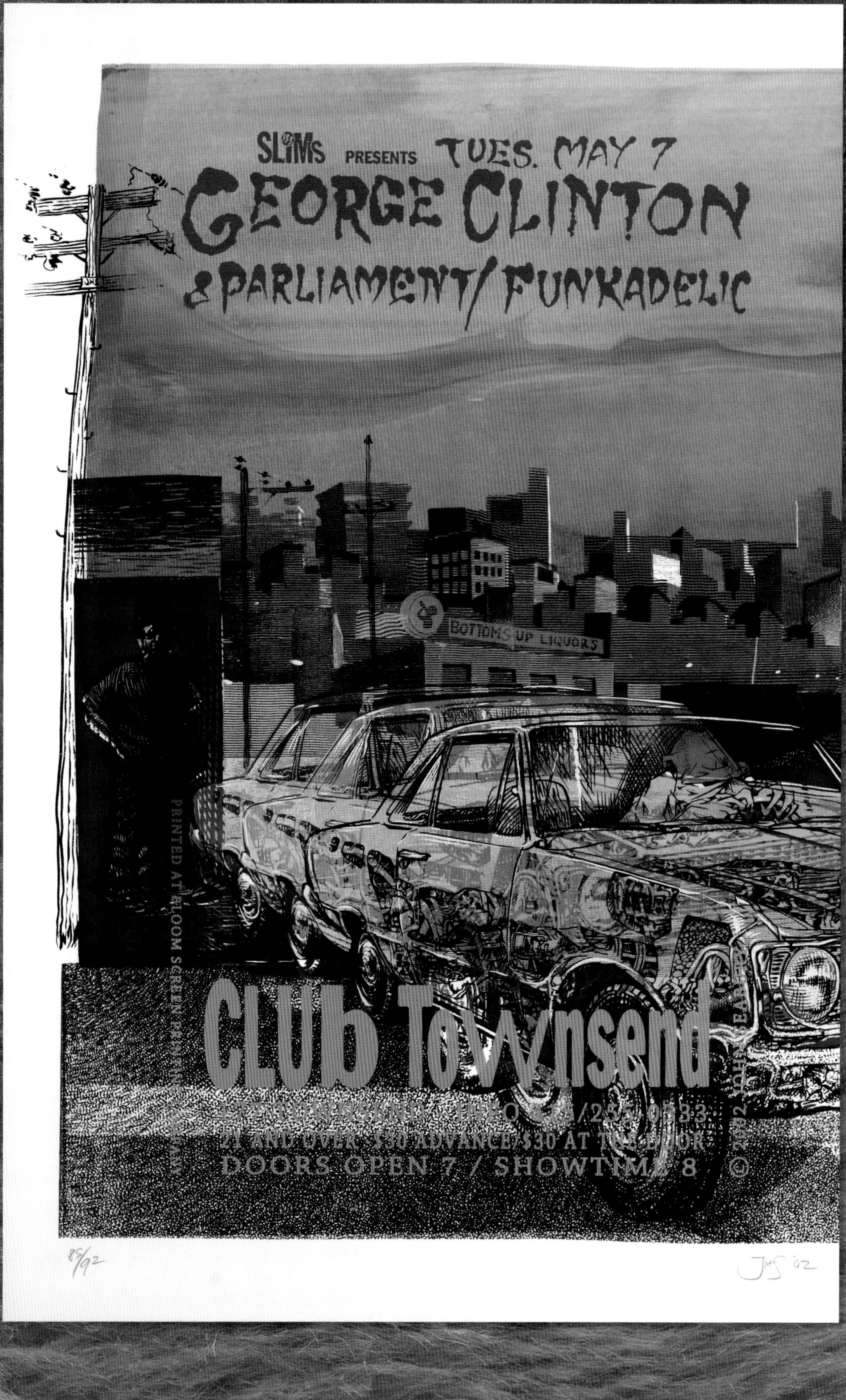

SLiMs PRESENTS TUES. MAY 7
GEORGE CLINTON
& PARLIAMENT/ FUNKADELIC

BOTTOMS UP LIQUORS

CLUb Townsend

21 AND OVER $30 ADVANCE/$30 AT THE DOOR
DOORS OPEN 7 / SHOWTIME 8

85/92   JmS '02

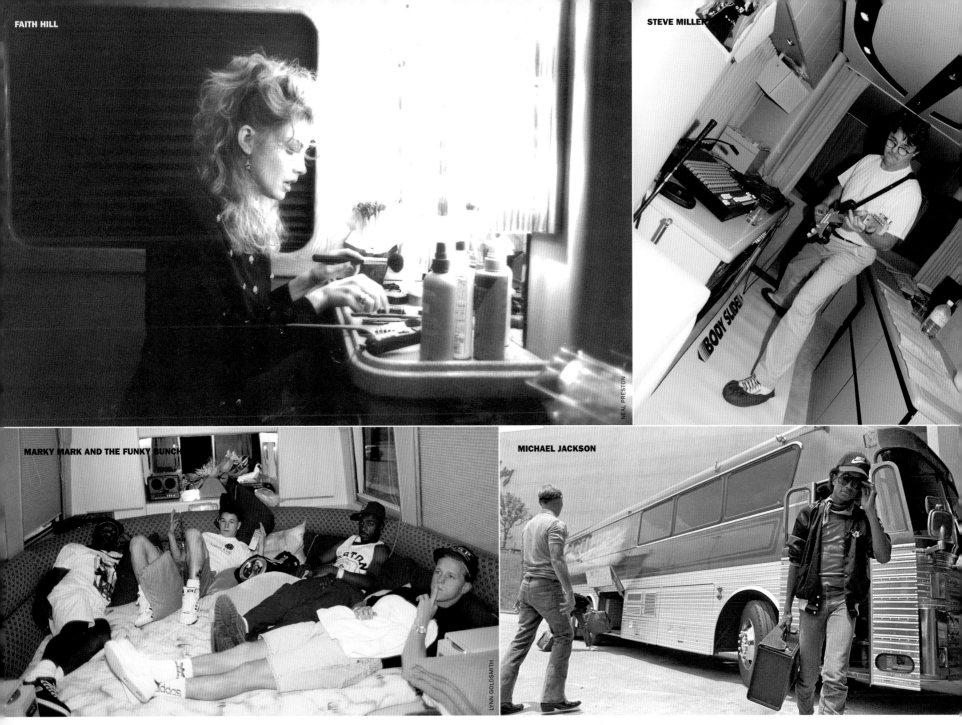

FAITH HILL

STEVE MILLER

NEAL PRESTON

MARKY MARK AND THE FUNKY BUNCH

MICHAEL JACKSON

LYNN GOLDSMITH

SEEMS LIKE I BEEN DOWN THIS WAY BEFORE

There are perks to being a rock star, and they begin with the tour bus. Or, as Kool Keith sang, *Tour bus with the Mötley Crüe/Who gon' stop who?* You get to travel with fellow bandmates who sometimes happen to be your best friends. Girls want to hang with you and more. Reporters come aboard and ask to put your pictures and quotes in newspapers and magazines. But the chasm between the imagined daily diet of "sex, drugs, and rock & roll" and the realities of a grinding tour carried out on the same claustrophobic bus night after night after night and thousands of miles from home is a wide one.

The basic tenet of the road is "a show in a different city every night." The tour bus necessarily becomes the one familiar center in a rock musician's world: the locus for long, boring—albeit quite comfortable—rides between cities, the place to get ready and to escape back into. As much as it can be a place to *par-tay*, the tour bus is also the base of operations for the one guy

who has to be totally serious and together: the road manager, whose best advice to anyone is usually "Don't shit where you sleep."

The reality of touring is that there's little time for exploring new places and making new friends after waking up in the early afternoon on the bus, performing the sound check at the venue, getting fed, putting on the show, taking a shower backstage or at nearby hotel (for some bands that are watching their expenses, a hotel room is booked only once every couple of nights) and . . . getting back on the bus. "Really, I think we're the homeless," said Marty Casey, lead singer of the Lovehammers. "What else do we know about, except living on a tour bus? We used to be Chicagoans, but that's further and further in the past."

Basically the consistent elements of a tour bus come down to lounges, bunks, techno-diversions, a galley, a head, and the driver. The buses can be

opulent: a ten-bunk Prevost Le Mirage XLII can cost upwards of half-a-million dollars, although many bands lease their units. Still, there persists the romantic vagabond notion of life on a tour bus, and, to be fair, it's always a giddy experience as a tour kicks off. For the first couple of hours, there's simply nothing like the camaraderie—it's balls-to-the-walls good times. And for awhile there are new places to explore. In the front, it's a plush lounge with a surprisingly ample kitchen; a big-screen TV with DVD, VCR, satellite tuning, and game controllers; and computers with which to e-mail and blog. Then there's the back, with maybe one master suite and all the "sleeping coffins." Not bad, until the fifth week when the tenth hour becomes the twelfth hour, or a police action up the road grinds everything to an inexplicable halt. Or worse, when bandmates begin complaining about someone else's selfish behavior, or missing their wives and girlfriends, or the flu someone is beginning to spread around.

One of the weirdest documented incidents involving a rock & roll tour bus took place in March 1982. Ozzy Osbourne's new touring band with guitarist Randy Rhoads was in Florida, making its way up the coast during the *Diary of a Madman* tour—a week away from playing New York's Madison Square Garden. A light aircraft carrying Rhoads crashed while performing low passes over the tour bus. The pilot (also the tour bus driver), who was apparently trying to scare his ex-wife (who was also part of the Osbourne entourage), actually clipped the bus and crashed into a nearby house, killing himself, Rhoads, and the band's hairdresser. Osbourne, sleeping on the bus, immediately awoke and managed to save the life of the man living in the house, but those on the plane died on impact. Deeply depressed over the loss of his close friend and bandmate, Osbourne halted the tour for a week—then revved up the bus once again.

NEIL YOUNG'S NOW-RETIRED TOUR BUS

BUFFALO SPRINGFIELD

HENRY DILTZ/CORBIS

JOHNNY FINGERS OF THE BOOMTOWN RATS

GIT

SAXMAN JR. WALKER (BORN AUTRY DEWALT) WAS MOTOWN'S ONLY REAL
INSTRUMENTAL ACT, CRISS-CROSSING AMERICA WITH HIS THREE ALL
STARS, NOW INCLUDING HIS SON, THE CURRENT DRUMMER. HIS HITS
INCLUDE "SHOTGUN," "HOME COOKIN'," AND, OF COURSE, "ROAD RUN-
NER." HE STARTED DOING VOCALS ONLY BY ACCIDENT. HE SMILES OFTEN
AND TRAVELS EASY. ANYTIME, ANYWHERE, THAT'S JR. WALKER. HE ISN'T
COLTRANE; HE'S THE GUY WHO CAN GUARANTEE A PARTY.

"I *AM* THE ROADRUNNER," HE SAYS. "EVER SINCE BERRY GORDY
(MOTOWN'S CHIEF) TOLD ME TO SCARE UP A TRUCK AND GIT—HE HAD
SOME DATES LINED UP FOR ME—I GOT THE TRUCK AND LIT OUT. SAME
NOW. I TRAVEL. I BLOW SOME. PEOPLE DANCE. AND I LIKE IT."

— AS TOLD TO GERRI HIRSHEY
NOWHERE TO RUN: THE STORY OF SOUL MUSIC

ALBERT KING'S TOUR BUS

A KING

17 504 H

DENIS O'REGAN/CORBIS

ARGENTINA

When Queen toured Argentina in the mid-1980s, photographer Neal Preston traveled with them. The band was escorted from their hotel to the concert site by members of the Secret Police. Preston remembers the whole scene as quite unnerving. One can only imagine the plight of the desperate souls—political prisoners of the regime—who were otherwise transported via the same or similar vans, not to a concert but to a much more terrible destination.

INSPIRED CAR-SONG TITLES

B-52'S "DEVIL IN MY CAR"

THE BEAT FARMERS "BUY ME A CAR"

CHUCK BERRY "YOU CAN'T CATCH ME"

BLACK FLAG "DRINKING AND DRIVING"

BOTTLE ROCKETS "HEADED FOR THE DITCH"

JUNIOR BROWN "TOO MANY NIGHTS IN A ROADHOUSE"

ERIC CLAPTON "SLOW DOWN LINDA"

THE COUP "CARS AND SHOES"

DEAD MILKMEN "BITCHIN' CAMARO"

DEATH CAB FOR CUTIE "PASSENGER SEAT"

THE DOORS "CARS HISS BY MY WINDOW"

THE EAGLES "LIFE IN THE FAST LANE"

DAVE EDMUNDS "CRAWLING FROM THE WRECKAGE"

ACE FREHLEY "SPEEDIN' BACK TO MY BABY"

GRATEFUL DEAD "THE GOLDEN ROAD
(TO UNLIMITED DEVOTION)"

GREEN DAY "BOULEVARD OF BROKEN DREAMS"

SAMMY HAGAR "CRUISIN' AND BOOZIN'"

JIMI HENDRIX "HIGHWAY CHILE"

CHRIS HILLMAN "RUNNING THE ROADBLOCKS"

LIGHTNIN' HOPKINS "TOO MANY DRIVERS"

ROBERT EARL KEEN "SWERVIN' IN MY LANE"

AIMEE MANN "DRIVING SIDEWAYS"

PAUL MCCARTNEY "HELEN WHEELS"

MINISTRY "HEY ASSHOLE"

MODEST MOUSE "TRUCKERS ATLAS"

EDDIE MONEY "KEEP MY MOTOR RUNNIN'"

O.A.R. "ABOUT AN HOUR AGO (THE GAS WAS LOW)"

BILLY OCEAN "GET OUT OF MY DREAMS, GET INTO MY CAR"

PEARL JAM "REARVIEWMIRROR"

THE PRETENDERS "MIDDLE OF THE ROAD"

RADIOHEAD "KILLER CARS"

BONNIE RAITT "THE ROAD'S MY MIDDLE NAME"

SNIFF 'N' THE TEARS "DRIVER'S SEAT"

SONIC YOUTH "EXPRESSWAY TO YOUR SKULL"

CAT STEVENS "ON THE ROAD TO FIND OUT"

TALKING HEADS "ROAD TO NOWHERE"

U2 "DADDY'S GONNA PAY FOR YOUR CRASHED CAR"

LOUDON WAINWRIGHT III "DEAD SKUNK
(IN THE MIDDLE OF THE ROAD)"

THE WHO "GOING MOBILE"

LUCINDA WILLIAMS "CAR WHEELS ON A GRAVEL ROAD"

XTC "ROADS GIRDLE THE GLOBE" •

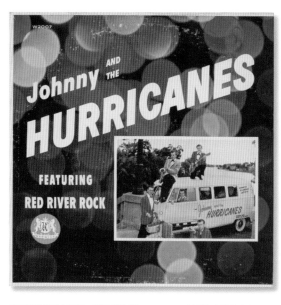

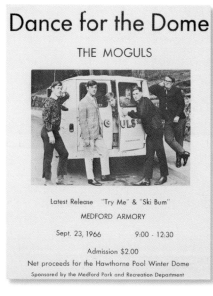

Billy and The Kids   **Wenatchee, Wash.**

"Billy and the Kids," five talented junior high school youngsters from East Wenatchee, Wash., make their professional debut on records with "It's Not The Same," b/w "Say You Love Me." Uniquely, this group is comprised entirely of 12- and 13-year-old boys who write all their own material. The group consists of twins Bill and Bob Burns on the drums and guitar, lead singer Mike Rice, lead guitar man Bob Gourlie, and Ken Laymance on the rhythm guitar. An attractive and vibrant "go-go" girl, Pam Cartwright, joins the group for public appearances. "Billy and the Kids" demonstrated exceptional poise in their first professional recording endeavor. "They play the good hard rock as well as any group I've ever heard," was the appraisal made by veteran Wenatchee disc jockey Don Bernier, who helped launch the professional careers of these teenagers by recording "It's Not The Same" on the Julian label, a Bernier enterprise.

"BILLY AND THE KIDS"
Available For Summer Bookings

OLIVER K. BURNS, Manager
P.O. Box 009, East Wenatchee, Wash.
Phone TUrner 4-7303 or 4-5630

THE NEIN

THE NEIN TOUR NORTH AMERICA

JUST BEFORE I MOVED TO OREGON AT THE END OF 2005, MY BAND, THE NEIN, TOURED MUCH OF THE U.S. AND CANADA IN A '98 FORD ECONOLINE WE BORROWED FROM OUR FRIEND, JAY. THANKS, JAY—IT RAN LIKE A CHAMP.

WE DROVE NEARLY 9,000 MILES. THE TOUR BEGAN IN CHAPEL HILL, NORTH CAROLINA, WENT THROUGH THE MIDWEST, OVER TO SALT LAKE CITY, DOWN TO L.A., UP THE WEST COAST INTO CANADA, ALL THE WAY ACROSS THE WESTERN HALF OF CANADA TO WINNIPEG, DOWN INTO THE U.S. AGAIN, AROUND THE GREAT LAKES, BACK UP INTO CANADA TO HIT ONTARIO, THEN MONTREAL, DOWN TO NEW YORK, BACK HOME FOR A WEEK OR SO, THEN FINALLY UP TO NEW YORK CITY AND BACK AGAIN.

A GRAND TOTAL OF 29 CITIES PLUS OTHER INTERESTING PLACES LIKE JOSHUA TREE AND MOOSE JAW. I THINK I WAS THE ONE WHO DROVE THE LONGEST STRETCH, ABOUT 14 HOURS FROM VANCOUVER TO CALGARY, THROUGH SOME EXTREMELY SERIOUS MOUNTAINS. IT WAS A BEAUTIFUL DRIVE, SO I CAN'T COMPLAIN.

WOULD I DO IT AGAIN? THE MUSIC WE MADE WAS OUR BEST EVER, BUT I'D HAVE TO SAY AT THIS POINT, NO. I'D LIKE TO TRAVEL AROUND THE COUNTRY WITH MY WIFE WAY MORE THAN WITH THREE GUYS (SONGWRITER FINN COHEN ON VOCALS AND GUITARS; ROBERT BIGGERS ON DRUMS AND "NOISE"; AND DALE "TOOTH" FLATTUM ON TAPE DECKS, PEDALS, AND SAMPLERS), EVEN THOUGH WE WERE AND ARE GREAT FRIENDS. FOR ONE THING, A FULL SLEEP-DEPRIVED CONTINENTAL TOUR IS JUST PLAIN EXHAUSTING, NOT TO MENTION NERVE-WRACKING. I'D HAVE LIKED TO TAKE MY TIME REALLY SEEING EVERYTHING I DROVE PAST, INSTEAD OF RACING TO MAKE A LOAD-IN TIME EVERY OTHER DAY. BUT NEVER SAY NEVER. I MEAN, DALE TOURED LIKE A JUGGERNAUT WITH STEEL POLE BATH TUB FOR YEARS, AND I WAS SURE HE'D NEVER WANT TO TOUR AGAIN, EVER. BUT HE HOPPED IN OUR VAN, SET UP HIS CRASH PAD IN THE BACK OVER THE DRUM KIT, AND WE WERE OFF DOWN THE ROAD.

— CASEY BURNS
BASSIST, THE NEIN

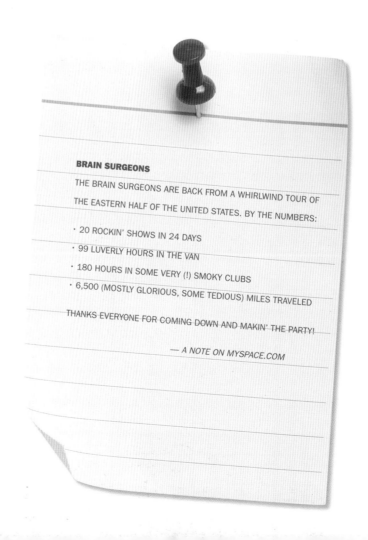

BRAIN SURGEONS

THE BRAIN SURGEONS ARE BACK FROM A WHIRLWIND TOUR OF THE EASTERN HALF OF THE UNITED STATES. BY THE NUMBERS:

· 20 ROCKIN' SHOWS IN 24 DAYS
· 99 LUVERLY HOURS IN THE VAN
· 180 HOURS IN SOME VERY (!) SMOKY CLUBS
· 6,500 (MOSTLY GLORIOUS, SOME TEDIOUS) MILES TRAVELED

THANKS EVERYONE FOR COMING DOWN AND MAKIN' THE PARTY!

— A NOTE ON MYSPACE.COM

THE J5

Berry Gordy, founder of Motown Records and former auto-worker, once was quoted as saying of the Jackson Five, "They were the last big stars to come rolling off my assembly line."

The group rose from humble circumstances in Gary, Indiana, and were the eldest sons in a family of nine children born to steelworker Joe Jackson and his wife, Katherine. They made music-business history when their first four singles shot to #1 in 1970.

When the group formed in 1964, Michael Jackson was all of six years old. By 1967, when they won an amateur-night competition at New York's Apollo Theater, they were a road-tested act, having worked the northern "chitlin' circuit" of black nightclubs from Chicago to Washington, D.C., often traveling by van, catching what shut-eye they could en route.

THE JACKSON FIVE

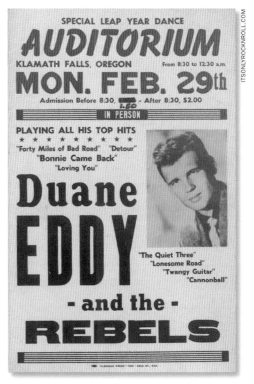

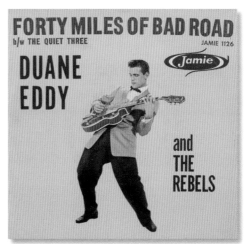

RIFFS FOR CAR RADIO

Born in 1938, Duane Eddy moved to Arizona when he was a teenager. He and Chuck Berry became America's first bona-fide—and most influential—rock & roll guitar heroes. Eddy's energetic, twangy signature sound that defined his trademark instrumentals got more hot rodders boppin' than perhaps any single musician of the period.

Some of Eddy's most famous instrumental singles included "Ramrod" (1957), "Caravan" (1957), "Cannonball" (1958), "Detour" (1959), "Forty Miles of Bad Road" (1959), "Shazam" (1960), and "Peter Gunn" (1960). "Rebel Rouser" reached the Top 10 on Billboard's pop chart in 1958; by 1963, he had fifteen Top 40 hits.

Many of Eddy's recordings got their echo with the assistance of a miked 300-pound, cast-iron water tank in his suburban Phoenix backyard. His producer Lee Hazelwood, a popular Arizona DJ who also wrote songs for Colorado's top band, the Astronauts (page 50), helped Eddy focus his riffs on the bottom end of the fretboard, giving his sound a low-end drive that sounded especially good on the car radio.

Eddy's great rival was Link Wray, master of the power chord, but in their day Eddy was the more popular of the two. He also was a major influence on George Harrison of The Beatles, and similarly upon pioneering surf bands such as the Bel Airs (pages 84–85). In 1994, he was named by Billboard as "The Number-One Rock & Roll Instrumentalist of All Time."

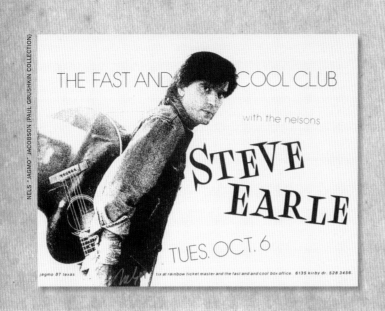
THE FAST AND COOL CLUB

with the nelsons

STEVE EARLE

TUES. OCT. 6

jagmo 87 texas   tix at rainbow ticket master and the fast and cool box office.   6135 kirby dr. 528 3456.

I WORK AT THE FILLIN' STATION ON THE INTERSTATE PUMPIN' GASOLINE AND COUNTIN' OUT-OF-STATE PLATES

THEY ASK ME HOW FAR INTO MEMPHIS SON, AND WHERE'S THE NEAREST BEER AND THEY DON'T EVEN KNOW THAT THERE'S A TOWN AROUND HERE

STEVE EARLE, SOMEDAY

I RUN ON DESPERATION, SHE RUNS ON GASOLINE

Steve Earle writes a well-crafted line better than almost anyone. Couple his songwriting talent with his exceptional eye for scenes along the road of life, and *voila*, you have high-caliber car- and truck-anchored songs such as "Guitar Town," "Breakdown Lane," and "Hillbilly Highway," among others. Throughout his career as a professional musician, Earle, much like Bruce Springsteen, has leaned on the road as a metaphor for larger-than-life issues.

In "Copperhead Road," possibly the finest literary distillation ever of the same postwar South that spawned NASCAR, Earle's narrator recalls his moonshine-running "Daddy" who, in a tasty bit of irony, buys an old Dodge at police auction, shoots it with primer, and overhauls the engine. By most accounts, however, Earle's affinity for internal combustion and the open road comes as much from experience as from an eye for detail and sense of history that have also made him an acclaimed short-story writer. "[Earle] always found moving healing," author Lauren St. John observed in her 2003 Earle biography, *Hardcore Troubadour: The Life and Near Death of Steve Earle.* "It was almost as if the physical act of crossing state lines and borders could erase the grim realities of life and replace them with some new and exotic horizon."

HEY PRETTY BABY ARE YOU READY FOR ME

IT'S YOUR GOOD ROCKIN' DADDY DOWN FROM TENNESSEE

I'M JUST OUT OF AUSTIN BOUND FOR SAN ANTONE

WITH THE RADIO BLASTIN' AND THE BIRD DOG ON

NOTHIN' EVER HAPPENED 'ROUND MY HOMETOWN

AND I AIN'T THE KIND TO JUST HANG AROUND

BUT I HEARD SOMEONE CALLIN' MY NAME ONE DAY

AND I FOLLOWED THAT VOICE DOWN THE LOST HIGHWAY.

STEVE EARLE, GUITAR TOWN

Like Jay Farrar, whom Earle has cited as one of his favorite contemporary songwriters, Earle has translated his own on-the-road experiences into song. Farrar claimed to write much of his band Son Volt's debut album, *Trace*, while motoring along Highway 61 from his home in New Orleans to rehearsals in St. Paul. Similarly, while driving from verdant Tennessee to wide-open Texas one Christmas, "Earle found himself humming songs from Springsteen's *Born in the USA.* Inspired, Earle wrote 'Guitar Town' on the drive home. When 'Down the Road' came to him, he knew it would close the record," St. John reported.

That record, of course, was *Guitar Town*, released in 1986. According to St. John, "Earle had traveled 77,000 miles in 1983 alone, so the freedom of the road as well as its loneliness was bound to seep into his songs."

To further illustrate the point, St. John offered an anecdote. "In 'Someday,' Earle explored his theory that in the USA, interstate highways were like a tunnel running from one end of the country to the other . . . some two years earlier, he and his rockabilly band had stopped at an allegedly open gas station in Jackson, Tennessee. Impatient, they honked the horn three times before a reluctant youth appeared. He'd been out back, working under his car. Driving away, Earle wondered why it was that the kid had taken such an obvious dislike to them. It occurred to him that it was possible he resented them because they were passing through and he was just stuck there."

As much as automobiles have evolved since 1986, the actual realities of car travel have remained relatively unchanged. Earle, in his best moments, has an uncanny ability to re-create the visceral experience of that travel—the actual grind and whine of the road—in his songwriting and composition. That's why lines such as *Hey pretty baby don't you know it ain't my fault/Love to hear the steel belts hummin' on the asphalt* ring as true now as on the day they were first uttered.

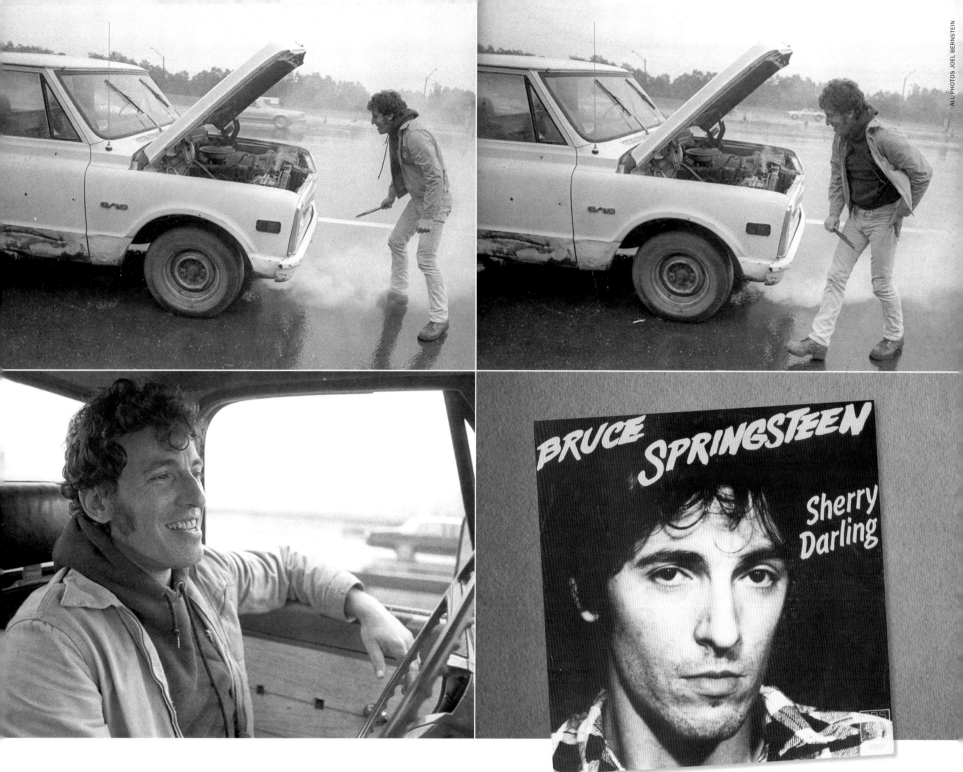

THE TIES THAT BIND

How many Bruce Springsteen songs feature cars? A lot. Springsteen has few rivals in the use of automotive imagery to make a point, define a mood, or characterize a situation. Sometimes the references are autobiographical, as in "My Hometown," where his narrator recalls steering the family Buick from his father's lap. But more than the cars or situations, it's Springsteen's *characters* who resonate. The Magic Rat who drives his sleek machine over the Jersey state line to find a barefoot girl sitting on the hood of a Dodge ("Jungleland"). Or Springsteen's alter ego huddling with the last of the Duke Street Kings ("Backstreets"). There's a highway worker holding a red flag, keeping the traffic back, thinking of a pretty little miss ("Working on the Highway"). Another slaves all day in his daddy's garage ("The Promised Land"). Still another drives a stolen car down on Eldridge Avenue ("Stolen Car").

Springsteen's fans are archivists, too, remembering concerts where they're convinced certain songs were played, where *they* were the first fans introduced to a particularly well-sketched man or woman who then reappeared over a number of years for as long as that composition stayed in setlists. The characters' familiarity remains an essential part of Springsteen's appeal—an everyman's approachability amidst all the stage drama.

So it is that everyone, rock star or fan, at one time or another, sees steam coming out from beneath the hood and pulls over to the side of the road or freeway to deal with it. In this case, it's Springsteen himself, in 1978 with his well-worn GMC pickup on the Garden State Parkway in New Jersey. Photographer and friend Joel Bernstein happened to be riding with Springsteen that misty day. Were you there too? Did you see him? Good thing he had that wrench.

CADZZILLA: BIRTH OF THE BEAST

CadZZilla, that low, menacing Highway Star carved from the body of a '48 Cadillac Sedanette and owned by Billy F Gibbons of ZZ Top, is the inspired result of a long-distance collaboration among several very serious car guys: designer Larry Erickson, Vintage Air president Jack Chisenhall, master metal former Craig Naff, shop owner Boyd Coddington, and naturally . . . BFG himself.

CadZZilla is a new-age custom in a rock & roll style. It's the blurring of defining lines that historically separated customs, hot rods, and street machines. CadZZilla blends a wild, not-seen-this-one-before look based a pivotal model year, with a contemporary drivetrain, suspension, and all the latest accoutrements and interior refinements. Yet, as sinister as it appears, it can function as a street driver, proven when *Hot Rod* magazine staffers Rob Kinnan and Steve Anderson drove it from Los Angeles to the Supernationals in 1990 to underscore the point (the photo of illustrator Darrell Mayabb in CadZZilla on page 129 was taken when the car stopped off at Mayabb's house, en route).

Critical to the success of any such effort are continuous thematic refinements between the owner and designer, and subsequently between the designer and the fabricators. Erickson, now the senior designer at Ford and responsible for the new Mustang unveiled in 2005, is the man credited for seeing CadZZilla through to completion. He'd been talking with Chisenhall at the Street Rod Nationals about certain frustrations Gibbons was then experiencing building another custom. Chisenhall asked Erickson—then General Motors design director—for a dissertation on "what really should be done," and Erickson sent some ideas to Gibbons. That led to a late-night-over-beers Mexican

cantina meeting of the minds and a historic exchange of a napkin drawings (the original is lost to time, but those shown here, which were later passed back and forth between Gibbons and Erickson, show the excitement of the collaboration). Gibbons reveled in the give and take, in which both men added layers of refinement to an inspired concept. With Chisenhall's help, they found their platform car—the first year of the Cadillac's famous tailfin—asleep in a garage near Tucson, Arizona, and packed it off to Coddington's shop in Los Angeles. After nearly $1 million and barely four months, the labor of love was completed, with Gibbons and his compatriots talking on the telephone every Thursday to check on the car's progress, even when ZZ Top was on tour.

"Yes, Billy wanted to do up a Cadillac real good," Erickson said in an interview with the author. "But he also had the opportunity to do more with it than anyone else up to that point. And Billy's just so into these things. You have to love it when you sit with a real car guy and talk about whether the car should be a quarter-inch lower or a quarter-inch higher. I mean, here's somebody that could literally buy most of the cars in the parking lot, and yet he's lost to the new conception.

"Billy knows about the many relationships between mass and line—all the separate visual cues you take in to form your opinion, but really, a car like CadZZilla is the result of an overall gut impression of 'what makes it right.' I recall a radio interview with Brian Wilson where he was talking about one of Phil Spector's wall-of-sound things. He said he first heard it in a car. He pulled over to the side. He said, 'I had to pull over. I couldn't drive anymore.' That's the way it is with Billy too—he was the inspiration because he absolutely knows why he loves something—and CadZZilla was the result."

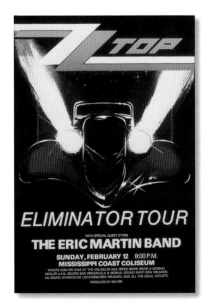

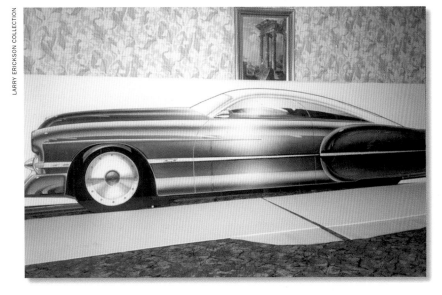

LARRY ERICKSON COLLECTION

THE MOCKUP OF THE FULL-SIZE CADZZILLA, MOUNTED IN A HOTEL ROOM, WAS THE CULMINATION OF ALL THE THINKING INVOLVED AND SENT THE CAR CONCEPT INTO BOYD CODDINGTON'S SHOP FOR FABRICATION.

PAUL GRUSHKIN COLLECTION

WELL I WAS ROLLIN' DOWN THE ROAD
IN SOME COLD BLUE STEEL
I HAD A BLUESMAN IN THE BACK
AND A BEAUTICIAN AT THE WHEEL
'CAUSE I'M BAD, GIRL, I'M NATIONWIDE

ZZ TOP, I'M BAD, I'M NATIONWIDE

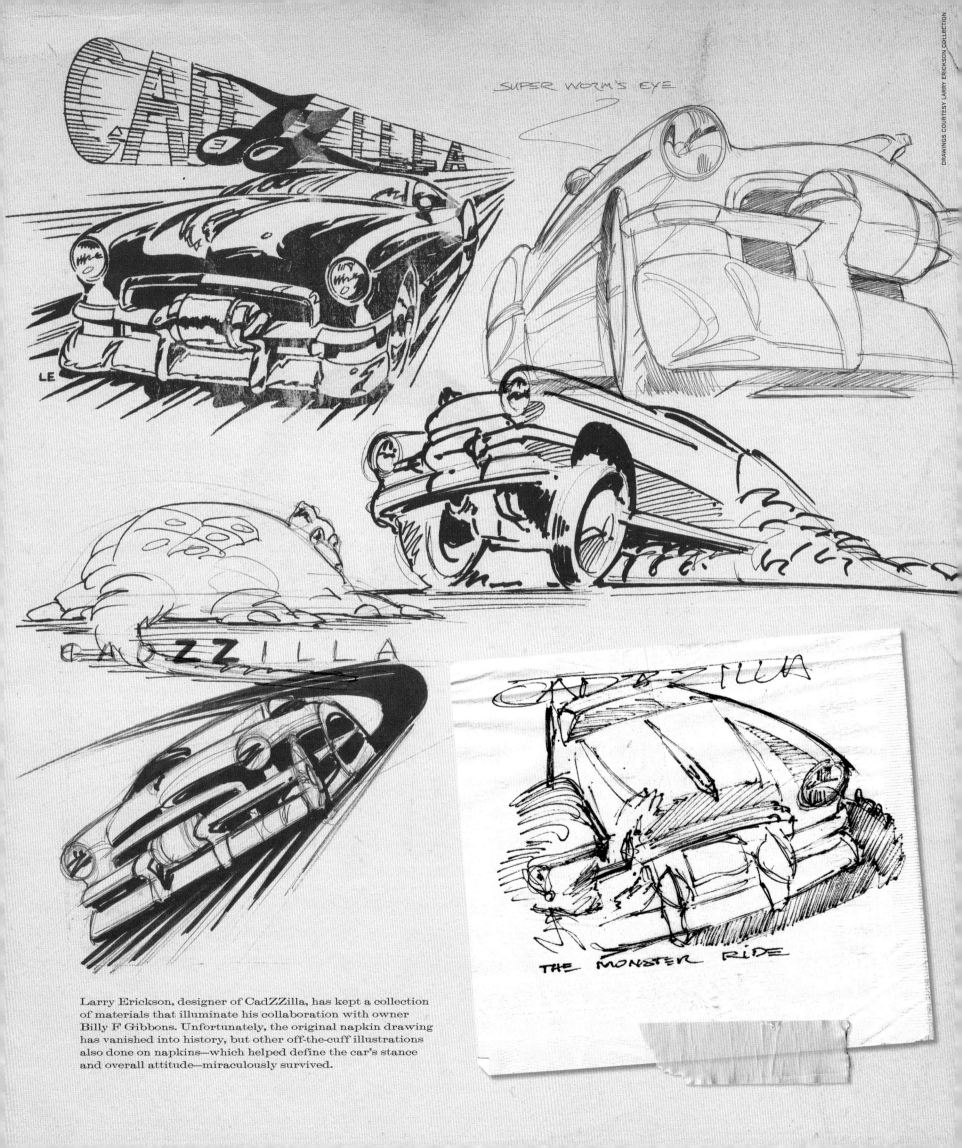

CAD ZZILLA

SUPER WORM'S EYE

LE

CADZZILLA

CADZZILLA

THE MONSTER RIDE

Larry Erickson, designer of CadZZilla, has kept a collection of materials that illuminate his collaboration with owner Billy F Gibbons. Unfortunately, the original napkin drawing has vanished into history, but other off-the-cuff illustrations also done on napkins—which helped define the car's stance and overall attitude—miraculously survived.

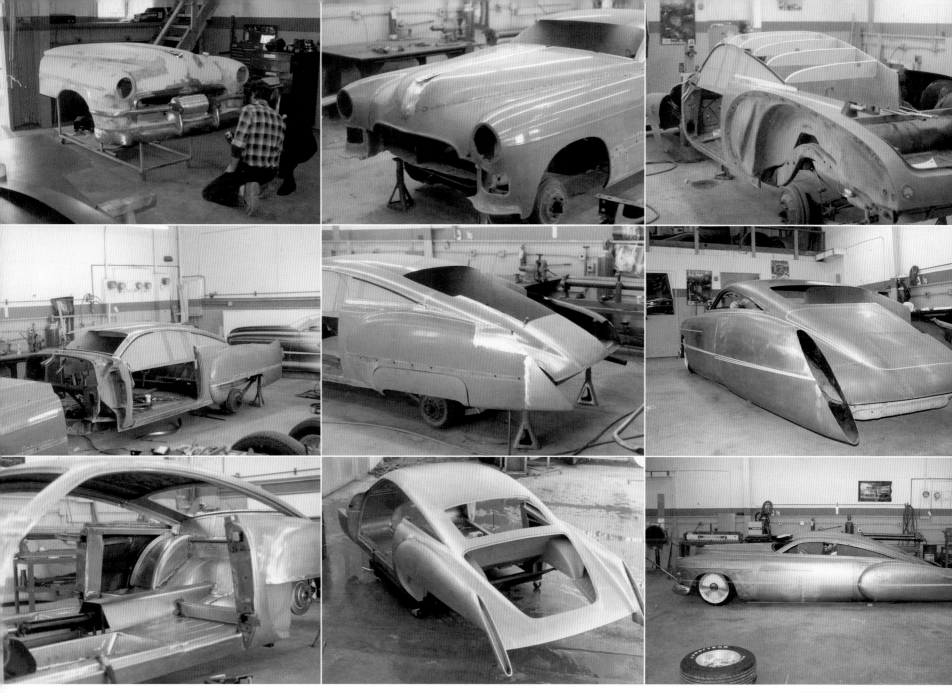

CADZZILLA: WHAT'S IT GONNA TAKE?

There's an old saying in hot rod construction: "Anyone can put one back together, but it takes a real man to cut one up." By the time CadZZilla was done, less than a quarter of the car—Gibbons says 1 square foot—could be perceived as belonging to the original. It was a project only for the thoroughly courageous. For designer Erickson, metal fabricator Naff, shop owner Coddington, and owner Gibbons, the car was an inspired work-in-progress because they necessarily had to "feel" their way into it.

"CadZZilla was an ongoing conversation," Erickson told this author. "It was about the blues. I mean, there was a lot more to it—like its potential pro-street aspect, the black color itself, how low it should be, how the stance should be angled, the amount of chrome to add or retain, should the car appear 'sharp' or 'smooth'—but, in essence, it was about the blues. It was about the pearly gates. It was about a bunch of things that are uniquely 'Billy.' It was a successful project because we all recognized the basic sketch was good, and that gave us the resolve to slice up the car we found and keep on going. But it always was about Billy's vision of the blues.

"We got inspiration from many places. We talked about going to Bonneville to get the proper attitude. We decided to go with the Cadillac motor rather than a big-block Chevrolet because it wasn't the normal thing to do. I mean, we wanted horsepower, we wanted economy, we wanted a nose tank, and we compared it to the nose tank on James Dean's 'Little Bastard.'

"Along the way, we came to the conclusion that Billy wasn't in some kind of contest with another car, or in a race with another builder. He was just doing his own thing. He was pretty much telling us, if you want to get to the basis of the original thought, take off the gloves, open up to 'possibility.' Actually, I think the original intention was a Bonneville-like, lakes-racer-inspired thing. But then it became 'highway,' and a bit later 'screw you.' So I guess it's all of the above, which worked when we started to hear from people, 'Yeah, yeah, yeah, *now* I get it.'"

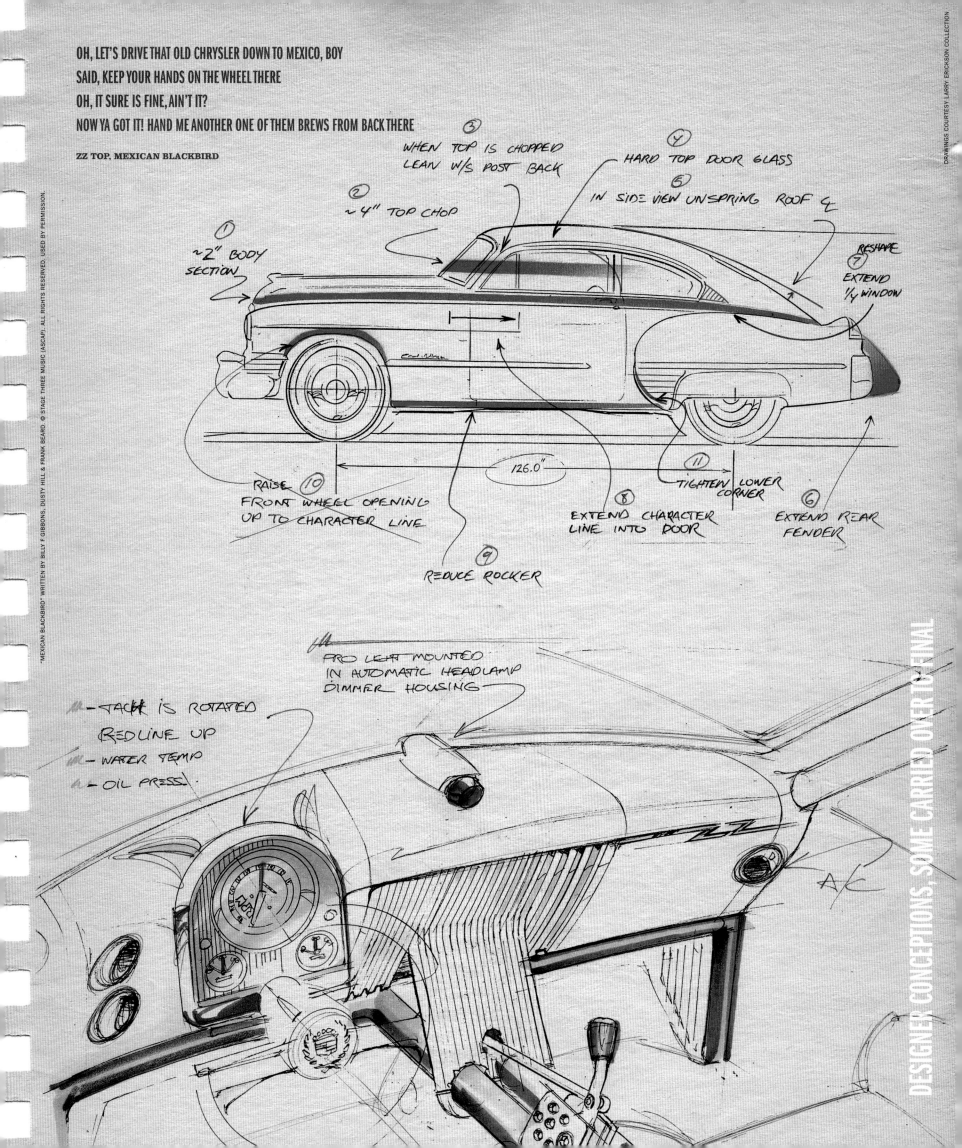

OH, LET'S DRIVE THAT OLD CHRYSLER DOWN TO MEXICO, BOY
SAID, KEEP YOUR HANDS ON THE WHEEL THERE
OH, IT SURE IS FINE, AIN'T IT?
NOW YA GOT IT! HAND ME ANOTHER ONE OF THEM BREWS FROM BACK THERE

ZZ TOP, MEXICAN BLACKBIRD

DESIGNER CONCEPTIONS, SOME CARRIED OVER TO FINAL

CADZZILLA: SLIDE BEHIND THE WHEEL

"Hot rod automobiles have a rather smart-alec element," Billy F Gibbons told a *TopGear.com* interviewer. "There's a sliver of my rebellious personality that leans towards creating something just a tad irritating to the guy beside you." With CadZZilla, Gibbons accomplished what he'd set out to do—irritate some, but also innovate.

CadZZilla came on the heels of Gibbons building what is surely one of the most recognizable custom cars in pop culture: the band's tomato-red '33 Ford coupe known as the Eliminator, which appeared in three memorable music videos ("Gimme All Your Lovin'," "Legs," and "Sharp Dressed Man") in 1983.

With CadZZilla, Gibbons desired something long and organic. To suit his intent for the car to be a classic highway driver, designer Erickson powered it up with a 500-ci Cadillac "torque motor" similar to those used in presidential limousines. The shape and stance has all the attitude of great rock & roll music, and just like ZZ Top, CadZZilla has been seen by millions throughout America. At the 14th annual Yokohama Hot Rod Custom Show in Japan in December 2005, the car was celebrated by more than 100,000 fans in a single day.

NOW JUST THE OTHER NIGHT WITH NOTHIN' TO DO
WE BROKE A CASE OF PROOF 102

AND STARTED ITCHIN'
FOR THAT WONDERFUL FEEL
OF ROLLIN' IN AN AUTOMOBILE

YOU COULD SAY WE WAS OUT OF OUR MIND
AND LET ME TELL YOU WE WERE FLYIN' WHILE BLIND

ZZ TOP, ARRESTED FOR DRIVING WHILE BLIND

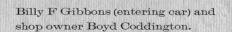

Billy F Gibbons (entering car) and shop owner Boyd Coddington.

Larry Erickson
driving CadZZilla.

Top

Vehicle type: Custom re-built 1948 2-door Cad
Sedanette, Series 62 Coupe

00 cubic inch

Curb weight

Artist Darrell Mayabb inside CadZZilla.

custom leather i
cutom made win

A/OTHER SIDE
MY HEAD'S IN MISSISSIPPI
Taken from the album 'Recycler'
B/THIS SIDE
FOOL FOR YOUR STOCKINGS
Taken from the album 'Deguello'

W0009P · 5439 19343-7

18 TOKYO
TEXAS

Produced by Bill Ham for Lone Wolf Productions

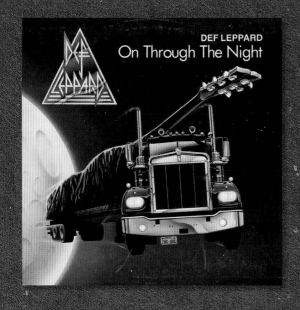

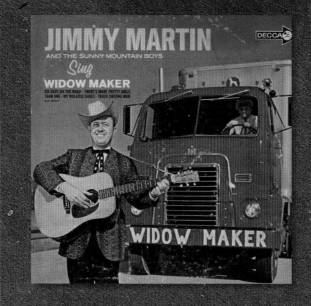

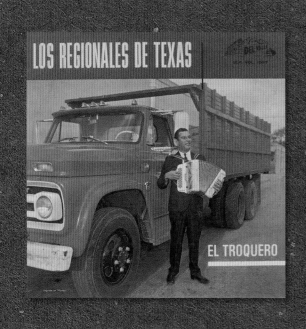

NOW ROLL THEM CASES OUT AND LIFT THEM AMPS, HAUL THEM TRUSSES DOWN AND GET 'EM UP THEM RAMPS,
'CAUSE WHEN IT COMES TO MOVING ME, YOU GUYS ARE THE CHAMPS. JACKSON BROWNE, THE LOAD-OUT

JUST KEEP TRUCKIN' ON

There'd be no rock & roll without techies, 'quippies, roadies, and truck drivers. *Especially* truck drivers. Every band, whether just starting out or a veteran of decades, has had to transport its gear from the studio or warehouse to the club or concert site, whether in a van, a bobtail truck, or as a caravan of semis hauling hundreds of tons.

The roadies' oft-told—and usually off-color—stories are legends in and of themselves. But mostly the antics—and the drudgery—have lived on only inside rock's oral history. Jackson Browne's "The Load Out" is usually cited as the key paean to rock & roll staging. Steve Earle's many lyric references are among truck-driving music's most insightful. And Commander Cody simply cannot be beat for wit. For decades, singers like Red Sovine, Dave Dudley and Buck Owens championed the truck driver as chariot-master. The trucker's mantra might well be—as Johnny Cash sang so often in their honor—*I've been everywhere.*

But there's one song—not exactly about trucking specifically, but rather one band's early-'70s experience on the road—that is the mother of all rock & roll truckin' songs: that song is, of course, the Grateful Dead's "Truckin'."

Issued on their 1970 roots-based *American Beauty* album, "Truckin'" was first played in concert on August 18 of that year, at the Fillmore West in San Francisco. It remained in the Dead's repertoire thereafter, and was played 520 times through the Dead's final show in 1995.

The Grateful Dead were on the road almost continuously for some 30 years, beginning with their first club dates in 1965. They played 2,318 shows and performed 480 different songs (36,504 total), speaking well to their legendary road endurance as chronicled in an apocryphal sense in "Truckin'." The key line from the song (words by Robert Hunter, music by Jerry Garcia, Phil Lesh, and Bob Weir) that has defined the Dead's road experiences ever since, reads, *Lately it occurs to me, what a long, strange trip it's been.* Further, the phrase "long, strange trip" has entered the greater American lexicon to describe a rich but perplexing experience. The word "truckin'" itself has long been linked to a gait usually associated with hipsters and stoners going

back to the 1930s jazz era and recaptured in R. Crumb's late-'60s comic book illustrations.

Weir, who played counterpart guitar to Garcia's lead guitar in the song, spoke about "Truckin'" in the 1997 film *Classic Albums: The Grateful Dead: American Beauty*. "There was a romance about being a young man on the road in America," Weir said, "and you had to do it! It was a rite of passage. And at the same time, it was the material that you drew from to write, sing, and improvise about.

"By 1970, we were starting to become real guys, real traveling musicians, and we were enjoying the hell out of it. We toured more or less six months out of every year. The road was our bread and butter—we weren't selling that many records. And we had a lot of fun out on the road, got into a lot of trouble . . . we left some smoking craters of some Holiday Inns, I'll say that, and there were a lot of places that wouldn't have us back. All this is absolutely autobiographical—all the stuff in 'Truckin'.""

A sidelight to this is the Dead's Wall of Sound, an enormous system built specifically for them in 1971. They sought to create a distortion-free concert ambience by combining 11 separate sound systems, each aiding a specific musician or task. The Wall also served as its own monitor system, so the band could hear exactly what the audience was hearing. It utilized over 90 solid-state and tube amplifiers to produce 26,400 total watts of audio power. It was said to have been the largest portable sound system ever built up to that point (although "portable" might have been a misnomer). Four semi trucks and 21 crew members were required to haul and set up the 75-ton Wall, a record for its time.

Even more sophisticated sound and light systems incorporated into complex rigging and stage decor were subsequently built and hauled for The Rolling Stones, U2, Pink Floyd, ZZ Top, Van Halen, and other stadium-size bands. Then, by the '80s, oftentimes two, even three, versions of the same system would advance in parallel truck-teams to make possible the several-day setup and tear-down in each city.

KC and the Sunshine Band

OOO, SHE'S LIKE A SMOOTH STRETCH OF HIGHWAY
OOO, SHE'S LIKE A COOL SUMMER BREEZE
IF MY MOTOR'S RUNNIN' RIGHT, WE MIGHT LOSE CONTROL TONIGHT

LITTLE FEAT, LET IT ROLL

A DAY IN THE LIFE
Reality and Metaphor

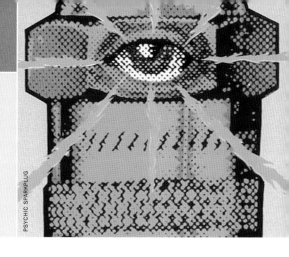

PSYCHIC SPARKPLUG

America is fundamentally a nation of people still searching for means to overcome the wilderness and put down roots. Not surprisingly, Americans have peculiar fascinations with travel and mobility—and getting "there" as fast as possible. As well, they've a long and abiding interest in the tools that offer protection from the outside and comfort on the inside while en route—stagecoaches, Model T Fords, Dodge Daytonas, custom motor homes, rock music on the car stereo (which [outside] keeps the world at bay and [inside] soothes the soul), and now, yes . . . thrill rides.

Case in point: the 1999 debut of the Disney-MGM Studios Rock 'n' Roller Coaster starring Aerosmith. The attraction's actually a metaphor for conquest, combining speed, fame, fortune, and escape—the ultimate rock & roll means of reinforcing our deep-seated notion that cars are our conveyances of freedom and power, that cars allow us to penetrate the as-yet-unknown, the as-yet-to-be-experienced "new territory" still out there. Here, all of America can take in a top rock band, ride in a custom limo, and rock & roll around Southern California as never before—all in 1 minute, 22 seconds, and 3,403 feet.

As with all great American opportunities, the ride comes with options. There are five different cars with different Aerosmith tracks playing in each. Each car also has a unique license plate:

Car 1: "Nine Lives" (1QKLIMO)
Car 2: "Sweet Emotion" (UGOGIRL)
Car 3: "Back in the Saddle" and
"Dude Looks Like a Lady" (BUHBYE)
Car 4: "Love in an Elevator" and
"Walk This Way" (2FAST4U)
Car 5: "Young Lust," "F.I.N.E.," and
"Love in a Roller Coaster" (H8TRFFC)

The ride pulls between 4 and 5 "big, fat, monster G's—and that's more than astronauts feel when they launch," according to Disney. There are three inversions, two rollover loops, and one big-daddy corkscrew. Each limo-car (accommodating 24 passengers) utilizes a 125-speaker, 24-subwoofer, 32,000-watt onboard audio system to create a noise level similar to that of an arena rock concert.

Each car is designed to look like a Cadillac stretch limo, and when launched, does 0–60 miles per hour in 2.8 seconds, creating an experience similar to that of sitting atop a supersonic F-14 Tomcat as it blasts off the deck of an aircraft carrier.

The fantasy is all-inviting. After cueing up under a massive inverted Cadillac, the guests encounter a 40-foot-tall guitar and a vestibule full of vintage guitars, amps, reel-to-reel tape decks, and psychedelic posters—even that famous one done by Rick Griffin for Jimi Hendrix! The official tour begins at the fictional G-Force Records, where guests encounter Aerosmith finishing up a studio recording session. Then the band invites everyone to see them in concert, with backstage passes, transportation—the works! "But, you gotta haul if you're gonna see it," says the attendant. The thrill-seekers then board the "stretch limos," which in fact better resemble chrome-grilled, shark-finned, metallic baby-blue hot rods. Each car's engine revs, and Steven Tyler lets loose with a primal scream: ARE YOU READY TO ROCK??

"The limo blasts off like it was fired out of a cannon," according to one rider. "Guitars howl, drums pound, the limo redlines. Street signs and guardrails whistle by in a blur. We hammer down the straightaway, hitting 60 miles per hour before you can think.

"The car sails up into a double-inverting Cobra Roll, flipping, rising and flat-out charging around L.A. We bottom out, we peel around banked curves, fly past palm trees, some neon thing called Randy's Donuts, interstate markers, through the "O" in the HOLLY-WOOD sign, then finally through a corkscrew loop and we arrive at the arena, where a red carpet awaits us."

Except that everyone's now escorted off and it's back to reality. All this, of course, is available 365 days a year, rain or shine, over and over again. Is this not the modern-day version of "Hot Rod Lincoln"? Outta my way, dude, I'm getting' back on.

RAPTURE

MANY PEOPLE THINK MADONNA WAS REVOLUTIONARY BY RAPPING ON *AMERICAN LIFE*, BUT BLONDIE'S DEBBIE HARRY DID THE WHITE, BLONDE POP-STAR RAPPING *THANG* TWENTY YEARS EARLIER WITH "RAPTURE" (OFF BLONDIE'S FIFTH ALBUM, *AUTOAMERICAN*, RELEASED IN NOVEMBER 1980). THE SONG EXEMPLIFIED A SUDDEN OVERLAPPING OF THE PUNK, NEW WAVE, AND HIP-HOP MUSICS THAT DEFINED NEW YORK CITY'S MANY URBAN CULTURES. THE BIZARRELY AUTOMOTIVE-CENTERED RAP WAS PRIMITIVE BY TODAY'S STANDARDS, EVEN A BIT CORNY, BUT THERE IS LITTLE QUESTION THAT IT WAS GROUNDBREAK-ING (IT WAS THE FIRST RAP SONG TO HIT #1 ON THE BILLBOARD SINGLES CHART, IN EARLY 1981). NEVERTHELESS, GRAND MASTER FLASH, ONE OF RAP'S PIONEERS, SAYS THAT TO THIS DAY HE HAS NO IDEA WHAT THE HELL HARRY WAS TALKING ABOUT.

RAPTURE BLONDIE

Official TUNEDEX

FUN DIAL 124 COLOR RADIO

Sacramento's MOST ACCURATE POPULAR TUNES SURVEY

ROBERT W. MORGAN
6-9

HAP HOPKINS
9-Noon

BUCK HERRING
Noon-4

TONY BIGG
4-8

MARK FORD
8-Midnite

JACK HAMMAR
Midnite-6

THIS WEEK					WEEK OF March 7 to March 13

1. T — WITH THE RECENT UPHEAVAL CREATED BY THE BEATLES IN THE
2. H — RECORD INDUSTRY, IT IS AT THIS MOMENT IMPOSSIBLE TO
3. E — DETERMINE ACCURATELY EXACTLY WHICH RECORD IS NUMBER
ONE. ALSO, KROY CANNOT IN ALL HONESTY PRESENT A LIST OF
4. B — THE "TOP FORTY" RECORDS, WHEN IN TRUTH THERE ARE NOT AT THE
5. E — PRESENT TIME FORTY RECORDS SELLING IN SUFFICIENT QUANTITY
6. A — TO COMPRISE A TOP FORTY LIST.... MEETING THE STANDARD OF
7. T — ACCURACY OF THE KROY TUNEDEX OVER THE PAST YEARS. WHEN
8. L — ONCE AGAIN A RECORD SHOULD CLEARLY EMERGE AS NUMBER ONE,
9. E — IT WILL BE SHOWN ON THE KROY TUNEDEX.
10. S

#	Title	Artist	Label	Last Week
11.	Dead Man's Curve	Jan and Dean	Liberty	17
12.	Fun Fun Fun	The Beach Boys	Capitol	4
13.	My Heart Belongs To Only You	Bobby Vinton	Epic	6
14.	Suspicion	Terry Stafford	Crusader	5
15.	Things You Do	The Temptations	Gordy	7
16.	Baby Don't You Weep	James Brown	King	14
17.	Shoop Shoop Song	Betty Everett	VeeJay	8
18.	Java	Al Hirt	RCA Victor	9
19.	You're A Wonderful One	Marvin Gaye	Tamla	28
20.	We Love You Beatles	The Carefrees	London	23
21.	Nadine	Chuck Berry	Chess	32
22.	Shangri-La	Robert Maxwell	Decca	19
23.	California Sun	The Rivieras	Riviera	10
24.	Stay	The Four Seasons	VeeJay	13
25.	He's A Good Guy	The Marvelettes	Tamla	22
26.	All You Had To Do	Chris & Kathy	Monogram	24
27.	It Ain't No Use	Lou Johnson	Hilltop	20
28.	Hi Heel Sneakers	Tommy Tucker	Checker	33
29.	Dawn	The Four Seasons	Philips	11
30.	Why Me	Paul Bryant	Fantasy	25
31.	Think	Brenda Lee	Decca	39
32.	If You Love Me	Little Johnny Taylor	Galaxy	NW
33.	Shelter Of Your Arms	Sammy Davis Jr.	Reprise	16
34.	Baby Don't You Cry	Ray Charles	ABC/Para	30
35.	It Hurts Me/Kissin' Cousins	Elvis Presley	RCA Victor	15
36.	Competition Coupe	The Astronauts	RCA Victor	21
37.	Easy To Love	The Chiffons	Laurie	40
38.	Hippy Hippy Shake	Swinging Blue Jeans	Imperial	NW
39.	Puppy Love	Barbara Lewis	Atlantic	18
40.	Navy Blue	Diane Renay	20th Fox	27

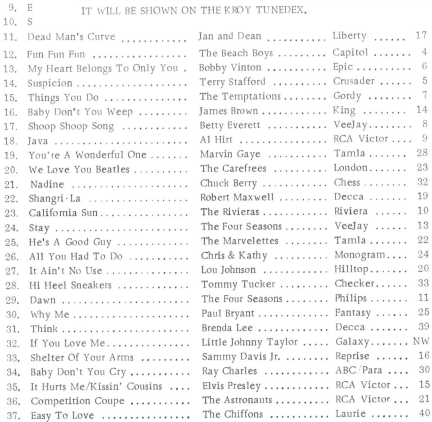

KROY presents the BEATLES and the BEACH BOYS -
together in an exclusive show March 14th and 15th on
the big screen at the Fox Theatre. Advance tickets are
on sale now at the Fox Theatre Box Office ... Better
get yours NOW ... while they're still available.

BABY, YOU CAN DRIVE MY CAR

Even the hottest American car songs could not hold up to the onslaught of The Beatles. The invasion began with "I Want to Hold Your Hand," written by John Lennon and Paul McCartney in October 1963. It was meant to have an American gospel sound, and it was the record manager Brian Epstein hoped would finally break The Beatles in the United States. In December 1963, Carroll Baker James, a DJ at WWDC in Washington, D.C., obtained a British 45—the first Beatles four-track recording in true stereo—from a BOAC airline stewardess and became the first American to broadcast the record. The reaction was instantaneous, and spread quickly to New York, Chicago, and St. Louis, then all over America.

Americans saw The Beatles for the first time a month later, on *The Jack Paar Show*. Within a week of its January 1964 release, "I Want to Hold Your Hand" shot to number one and remained on top of Billboard's Hot 100 singles for seven weeks. Today, it stands as the biggest-selling British single of all time. The importance of "I Want to Hold Your Hand" simply cannot be overestimated. Next to Bill Haley's "Rock Around the Clock," it may be the most significant single of the rock era, having permanently changed the course of popular music.

The Beatles relinquished the number one spot to their own follow-up, "She Loves You," in March 1964, the first time since Elvis Presley's "Love Me Tender" and "Don't Be Cruel" that a single act had supplanted themselves from the top of the Hot 100. The British Invasion had been launched, ushering in the Dave Clark Five, The Rolling Stones, The Kinks, The Hollies, and Herman's Hermits, among others. The first listeners to "She Loves You" remembered the refrain "yeah, yeah, yeah" as much as they did the name of the group itself, leading a Mexican band to rename themselves "Los Ye Ye's" (see die-cast toy car pictured here).

That winter, Beatlemania landed in America with full force. Spurred on by the band's appearances on *The Ed Sullivan Show*, "She Loves You" was joined by four other Beatles songs as the top five on the Billboard pop chart. Regionally, this created huge excitement and controversy. In Sacramento, California, at the city's largest rock station, KROY (see the Tunedex survey on the facing page), "She Loves You" initially toppled The Beach Boys' "Fun, Fun, Fun," in mid-February 1964. Then, scarcely a month later, an inexact amalgamation of Beatles songs (see the station's notes on the chart) knocked "Fun, Fun, Fun" and Jan & Dean's "Dead Man's Curve" down to numbers 11 and 12, respectively. A week later, The Beach Boys' *Shut Down, Volume 2* LP similarly fell victim, along with Chuck Berry's single "Nadine." The great but relatively short-lived dominance of California car songs was effectively over.

The Beatles' most famous car-related song was "A Day in the Life," recorded in 1967 for the album *Sgt. Pepper's Lonely Hearts Club Band*. The song was a merging of two different but ultimately complementary song fragments authored independently by Lennon and McCartney, and is considered one of the most ambitious, influential, and groundbreaking works in pop music history. Lennon started writing the song while reading the *Daily Mail* newspaper. Two stories caught his eye: one was about the death of Tara Browne, the heir to the Guinness brewing fortune, and a friend of The Beatles, who, on December 18, 1966, drove his Lotus Elan into the back of a parked truck in Redcliffe Square, South Kensington, London. The other was about a plan to fill 4,000 potholes in the streets of Blackburn, Lancashire.

Lennon later said, "Tara didn't blow his mind out . . . literally, but it was in my mind when I was writing that verse. The details—not noticing the traffic lights and a crowd gathering at the scene—were part of the fiction."

Unarguably the most iconic roadway-related image of The Beatles—or possibly of any band, for that matter—was the album-sleeve photograph on *Abbey Road*. Originally, the album was to be titled *Everest* and use a cover photo of The Beatles in the Himalayas. But the band decided to use a photo taken on August 8, 1969, outside producer George Martin's Abbey Road recording studio. It's since become one of the most famous and most imitated album covers in recording history and supposedly included clues that contributed to the "Paul Is Dead" phenomenon. In 1970, Booker T. and the M.G.'s covered most of *Abbey Road* on their 1969 album *McLemore Avenue*, named after the street address of the Stax Records studio in Memphis, Tennessee.

A final note in The Beatles' relation to car lore was "The Long and Winding Road," which originally appeared on The Beatles final album, *Let It Be,* and became the group's last American number one pop-charting song on June 13, 1970. McCartney wrote the song at his farm in Scotland, provoked by the growing tension among the bandmembers. The Phil Spector remix of the tune, which McCartney protested but could not stop from being included on the LP, led directly to The Beatles irrevocable breakup.

PAUL MCCARTNEY WENT BAREFOOT ON THE COVER OF THE BEATLES ABBEY ROAD, BUT THE RED HOT CHILI PEPPERS TOOK IT QUITE A BIT FURTHER FOR THEIR INSPIRED EP SPOOF. "COCKS IN SOCKS" WAS REGULAR STAGE ATTIRE FOR THE BAND IN 1988.

BOB DYLAN WITH ROAD MANAGER VICTOR MAYMUDES AND PAINTER-MUSICIAN FRIEND BOB NEUWIRTH (BACK TO CAMERA), SUMMER, 1964, BEARSVILLE, NEW YORK. TWO SUMMERS LATER, DYLAN WOULD CRASH HIS TRIUMPH MOTORCYCLE AND BE HOSPITALIZED WITH NECK AND HEAD INJURIES. HE WENT INTO RECLUSION AND EMERGED IN LATE 1967 WITH THE FIRST OF HIS COUNTRY-ROCK ALBUMS.

IN THE SPRING OF 1964, BOB DYLAN TOURED NEW ENGLAND IN A NAVY BLUE FORD STATION WAGON DRIVEN BY HIS ROAD MANAGER, VICTOR MAYMUDES (L). DYLAN APPARENTLY WAS THE FIRST FOLK ARTIST TO HAVE A ROAD MANAGER. THIS PHOTO WAS TAKEN NEAR THE UNIVERSITY OF MASSACHUSETTS–AMHERST.

THOUSAND-MILE DRUMS

As a drummer, I've always been sort of a Gretsch-Ludwig man myself, particularly back when The Band was playing with Dylan. Those used to be the ones that would hold up well on the road. They were made real heavy and could even carry a Fender amplifier on their backs over a killer road trip in the back of a loaded-down car — for a good thousand miles, even more.

— Levon Helm

HIGHWAY 61 REVISITED

Though 1966's *Blonde on Blonde* is often singled out as Bob Dylan's master-piece, its predecessor, *Highway 61 Revisited* (released in August 1965), marks Dylan's transformation from folk singer to rock poet. It's Dylan's first fully electric album. The lyrics, according to a critic of the time, "Find Dylan finally abandoning conventional linear narrative in favor of poetic abstraction, surreal imagery, and biting sarcasm." Another wrote, "Every song is sung with the pedal to the metal."

As all Dylan fans know, the opening line of the title track was borrowed from the Book of Genesis, but the inspiration—as well as the LP's most famous song, "Like a Rolling Stone"—might have come from a road atlas of classic Americana. Highway 61 is also known as the "Blues Highway" and stretches from the Canadian border through cities in eight states, from Duluth, Minnesota (where Dylan was born and near Hibbing, where he grew up); to Memphis, Tennessee; and all the way down to New Orleans, Louisiana. Famed blues singer Bessie Smith had her fatal car accident on Highway 61. Robert Johnson apocryphally sold his soul to the devil at one of its many crossroads; Muddy Waters and Bo Diddley took the blues to Chicago on that road; and Ike Turner, Jackie Brenston, and their band drove up Highway 61 to Memphis to record "Rocket 88" at Sun Studio. Elvis Presley grew up in a housing project alongside the road and, more recently, Jay Farrar of Son Volt wrote "Afterglow 61" about it.

"A lot of basic American culture came right up that highway," historian Robert Shelton told a BBC interviewer. "As a teenager, Dylan traveled that way via his radio. Highway 61 became to him, I think, a symbol of freedom, movement, and independence and a chance to get away from a life he didn't want in Hibbing."

Dylan's previous LP, the transitional *Bringing It All Back Home*, was released in April 1965. In May, Dylan went on an eight-show U.K. tour that was filmed and became D. A. Pennebaker's acclaimed *Don't Look Back*. In June Dylan began the recording sessions for *Highway 61 Revisited*, interrupted only by his live electric debut on the second day of the Newport Folk Festival (July 25), where he was backed by most of the Paul Butterfield Blues Band (including guitarist Michael Bloomfield and organist Al Kooper, who'd been in the studio creating the basis for the new sound with Dylan). Famously, many in the Newport audience were openly dismayed to hear loud, plugged-in music from Dylan for the first time. Pete Seeger allegedly had to be restrained from chopping through the power cables with an axe.

Highway 61 Revisited was finished in July and released in August to an astonished but increasingly supportive public. Ultimately, most music magazines would list it among the Top Ten rock albums of all time. In September 1965, Dylan went on the road with Robbie Robertson, Levon Helm, Garth Hudson, Rick Danko, and Richard Manuel, thus reuniting 90 percent of the Hawks (later to become The Band). Six months later, in 1966, the third album of Dylan's great trilogy, *Blonde on Blonde*, was released, but that summer Dylan crashed his Triumph motorcycle near Woodstock, New York, and was hospitalized, bringing an end to what had become a physically and emotionally exhausting tour schedule.

"Like a Rolling Stone" became Dylan's signature piece from that period. A young Bruce Springsteen would hear the recording on New York's WMCA while driving in a car with his mother in south Jersey. Springsteen's recollection: "The snare shot which led off the song sounded like somebody'd kicked open the door to your mind."

THE IMMIGRANT SON LEFT THE MINING TOWN
ELECTRIFIED THE TRADITIONAL
AND HAD IT OUT ON HIGHWAY 61

SON VOLT, AFTERGLOW 61

"WHAT DID CHURCHILL SAY ABOUT
RUSSIA? A RIDDLE WRAPPED IN A
MYSTERY INSIDE AN ENIGMA? WELL,
DYLAN IS LIKE THAT. THIS PARTICULAR
PHOTO WAS TAKEN ONE SUNDAY
MORNING IN 1963, WHEN BOBBY,
HIS GIRLFRIEND SUZE ROTOLO, SINGER
DAVE VAN RONK, AND WIFE TERRI
VAN RONK ALL WERE WALKING TO
BREAKFAST IN NEW YORK CITY.
JUST TWO FRAMES WERE SHOT
[OF THE TIRE SEQUENCE]."

— JIM MARSHALL
   NOT FADE AWAY: THE ROCK
   & ROLL PHOTOGRAPHY OF
   JIM MARSHALL

Jackson Browne and family aboard the "Running on Empty" tour bus.

RUNNING ON EMPTY

Conceptually, Jackson Browne's *Running on Empty* (1977) is linked to Neil Young's *Time Fades Away* (1973), R.E.M.'s *New Adventures in Hi-Fi* (1996), and Wilco's *Being There* (1996). All incorporate musical snapshots from the road, most of them recorded on the run, imparting to the totality of each a loose, careening—even desperate—overtone.

Running on Empty sends up a you-could-have-been-there perspective on the milieu of a mid-'70s rock tour, an audio vérité of disillusioned druggy encounters; the constant scoring of sex and companionship; daily-changing friendships forged between the star and the band, the band and the crew; the rigor, grind, and isolation of the road set amid moments of onstage glory; and the bleak tedium of loading up while the band wails on and—*see ya later*—heading out for the next city. The album was recorded while on tour, but is not merely a live album. Of the ten songs, six and a half were recorded onstage (a few at soundchecks); one and a half in motel rooms; one backstage; and one on a Continental Silver Eagle tour bus while passing through New Jersey. None of the tracks had ever appeared previously on a studio album.

Young's painfully honest *Time Fades Away* documents emotionally devastating bad karma while traveling over miles of asphalt. R.E.M.'s *New Adventures* comprises songs largely about travel—as well as being all over the musical map—road-germinated during the band's tour in support of their previous LP, *Monster*. The double-CD *Being There* reflects an eclectic mix of influences relating an equally diverse collection of thoughts and scenarios, real and imagined, from the road. Browne's *Running on Empty* predefined the later MTV-style rockumentary, conceived, as *Rolling Stone* magazine's Paul Nelson pointed out, "with shifting scenes, natural-to-rock & roll settings (motel rooms, tour buses, backstage rehearsal rooms), a cast of supporting characters (roadies, groupies), and a clear narrative arc."

Others opined that *Running on Empty*'s genius was less the informed road diary—as impressive as the new concept was—and more a looming mile marker, as Browne and his fans entered the transitional period of their thirties, leaving their rock & roll excesses behind. Even as he followed up with the #1 charting *Hold Out* (1980), Browne himself went through further personal change, becoming politically active in support of antinuclear causes.

Accessible in Browne's trademark So-Cal style, *Running on Empty* was the most commercially successful of Browne's career, reaching #3 on Billboard's album chart and lasting on the chart for 65 weeks, going on to sell over 7 million copies. The title track was deliberately anthemic, reminiscent of Browne's (and co-writer Glenn Frey's) replete-with-car-references "Take it Easy," which the Eagles drove home to multiplatinum success on *The Eagles* (1972). To augment *Running on Empty*'s ambitious original intent, Rhino's 2005 re-release included a DVD with 300 road-forged photographs taken by Joel Bernstein over the course of the epic 1977 tour.

LOOKING OUT AT THE ROAD RUSHING UNDER MY WHEELS
LOOKING BACK AT THE YEARS GONE BY LIKE SO MANY SUMMER FIELDS
IN SIXTY-FIVE I WAS SEVENTEEN AND RUNNING UP 101
I DON'T KNOW WHERE I'M RUNNING NOW, I'M JUST RUNNING ON
IN SIXTY-NINE I WAS 21 AND I CALLED THE ROAD MY OWN
I DON'T KNOW WHEN THAT ROAD TURNED INTO THE ROAD I'M ON
I LOOK AROUND FOR THE FRIENDS THAT I USED TO TURN TO PULL ME THROUGH
LOOKING INTO THEIR EYES I SEE THEM RUNNING TOO

JACKSON BROWNE, RUNNING ON EMPTY

HENRY DILTZ

HEJIRA

Joni Mitchell's *Hejira* may be rock's ultimate road album. "It has the musing effect of photos from a trip, a weighty scrapbook full of parables and melancholy, wisdom and romance, everything drawn forth from moving steadily down the highways," wrote Jon Popowich, like Mitchell, a Canadian from the province of Alberta. "I can relate to that. Around the time the LP came out, in 1976, I was driving about 1,200km every weekend—from the prairies to the mountains—and this was the unexpected gift: a soundtrack."

The album title refers to Mohammed's journey from persecution in Mecca in 622 A.D. to Medina where his ministry began. More generally, the term conjures a long spate of over-the-road travel complete with symbolic overtones of flight and purpose. Many of the songs on *Hejira* were written sporadically by Mitchell on a car trip from New York to her Los Angeles home.

Hejira is also the third in an almost purposefully linked trilogy of monumental albums, following *Blue* (1971) and *Court and Spark* (1974). Many of the songs became concert staples, especially after being road-tested with the live album *Shadows and Light* (1977).

On songs such as "Amelia" and "Song for Sharon," Mitchell weaves vast word structures over deceptively calm, subtle, and beautifully uplifting musical arrangements. Her bassist at that time, Jaco Pastorius, also one of the founders of the progressive jazz group Weather Report, had great influence on Mitchell's compositions, and many of the songs use the bass

as an insistent source of inspiration, as if to serve as a "traveling undercurrent" linking the vignettes.

The great body of road music includes everything from pounding three-minute rock & roll to half-hour-long jam-band explorations to light opera as in Meat Loaf's "Paradise by the Dashboard Light." With *Hejira,* Mitchell added poetry to the canon. Travel and love, travel because of love, travel to sort out love, and, of course, travel to escape love—Mitchell examines all at length. The road, in Mitchell's parlance, is not merely white-line fever but a refuge for a fertile mind. Sometimes her musings begin with a real moment—"I was traveling across the burning desert, when I spotted six jet planes" ("Amelia")—but her genius is to use that moment only as a touchstone, against which seemingly random thoughts wash over or drift alongside.

"The road runs through every song on *Hejira,*" wrote critic Sam Sutherland. "The old pastoral conventions have been revived in Mitchell's freeways. Like Shakespeare's Forest of Arden or Mark Twain's Mississippi, the highway is—for Joni Mitchell—a source of anonymity and acceptance. There she can masquerade as one in a gang of vagabonds, drink and dance with the locals, or find unencumbered solitude. It's her perfect stage for encounters and revelations, all held together by the motion in the music which is as unceasing and hypnotic as the freeways themselves."

DETROIT
EMERALDS
"YOU WANT IT,
YOU GOT IT"

GONNA TRY 2 TAME YOUR LITTLE RED LOVE MACHINE

Johnny Guitar Watson

I DON'T
WANT TO BE ALONE,
STRANGER

YOU'RE JUST LIKE
CROSSTOWN TRAFFIC

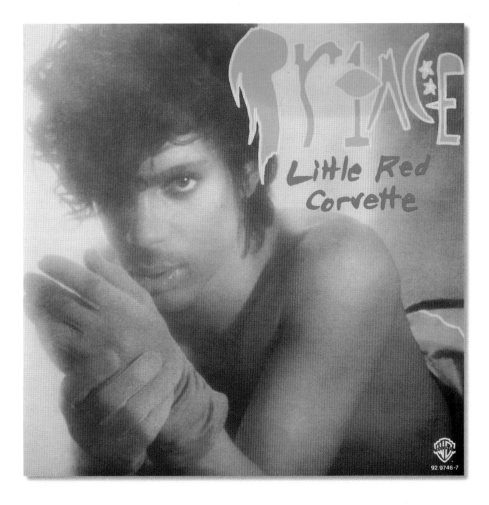

LITTLE RED CORVETTE

According to legend, the idea for "Little Red Corvette" came to Prince as he crashed in backup singer Lisa Coleman's pink Edsel after an all-night recording session. The lyrics, he later reported, came to him piece by piece during this and other slumbers. "It was a skeleton on which to hang wild sexual metaphors, sung with snake-oil charm," wrote critic Dave Marsh.

Michael Jackson had been the first black artist to break the color barrier on MTV, and "Little Red Corvette" came on its heels, reaching as high as #6 on the Billboard pop singles chart and becoming Prince's first pop hit single. Prince's *1999* LP (1983) had been released previous to the single and did not do so well. Re-released on the success of "Little Red Corvette," *1999* rose to #12 on the LP chart. This was Prince's first big hit from *1999*; the single itself would get as high as #6 on the Billboard pop chart. Its title to the contrary, this is not a song about a car, *per se*. It's about sex, but the references are just obscure enough not to be offensive and did not prevent it from receiving major radio airplay.

In 2002, in the tradition of Dinah Shore's mid-'50s "See the USA in Your Chevrolet," Chevrolet's ad agency, Campbell-Ewald, built a successful campaign around "Little Red Corvette." They were not the first to use a

song whose lyrics came off as contrary to the image of the brand being promoted (other examples being The Clash's "London Calling," used to promote Jaguar's new X-Type car; Nick Drake's "Pink Moon" licensed to shill Volkswagens; Iggy Pop's "Lust for Life" promoting Royal Caribbean cruise-ship vacations; and Nike's use of The Beatles' "Revolution" in a 1987 shoe ad). In 1995, Mercedes-Benz received a healthy dose of criticism for using Janis Joplin's "Mercedes Benz," because the sentiment expressed by the singer back in 1968 was not about extolling the brand.

In using "Little Red Corvette" to sell Corvettes, Campbell-Ewald simply chose to ignore the song's sexual innuendos. "People accept the song for the song and they don't get into the background of the artist," said Bill Ludwig, chief creative officer for the agency, in an interview with *AutoWorld*. "Frankly, no other brand has inspired popular culture as Chevy has. The Corvette and rock & roll were both born in America 50 years ago. Coincidence? I think not."

As a coda to the campaign, a billboard in Chevrolet's hometown of Warren, Michigan—placed just in time for the annual Woodward Avenue Dream Cruise—succinctly stated, "They don't write songs about Volvos."

FAITH HILL AND TIM MCGRAW

RHYME PAYS

ARTIST REFLECTS ON TRACY CHAPMAN'S "FAST CAR"

IN MY PAINTING SEEN HERE I SOUGHT TO PORTRAY THE NARRATOR'S ABANDONMENT AND DESPERATION.

AT THE SAME TIME, I FELT STRONGLY THIS PERSON, DESPITE UNFAVORABLE CIRCUMSTANCES, STILL

HOPES IN HER HEART SHE WILL FIND HER WAY OUT AND RISE ABOVE. THE CAR IN THE SONG RECALLS

MOMENTS WHEN THE CHARACTER EXPERIENCED FREEDOM AND REALIZED THINGS DON'T HAVE TO BE

THE WAY THEY ARE. SHE CAN CHOOSE TO CHANGE! IT'S ABOUT INNER STRENGTH, FREEDOM, AND

THE POWER TO START ANEW.

   AS A PAINTER, I WORK IN A NON-LITERAL FASHION, BUT IF YOU FOLLOW ALONG WITH ME,

YOU'LL SEE THAT THERE ARE THESE ASPECTS:

· AN EMPTY CHAIR ON A ROAD, REPRESENTING ABANDONMENT

· RISING WATER INDICATING A SENSE OF URGENCY FOR THE NARRATOR TO CHANGE —

   IF SHE DOESN'T, SHE'LL CEASE TO SURVIVE

· BARE TREES WITH A FEW GREEN LEAVES—A SEEMING FRUITLESS SITUATION

· THE HOUSE IN THE TREE—AN UNSTABLE SITUATION

· WINGS ON THE FIGURE'S HEAD, SURROUNDING THE CITY AND SYMBOLIC OF

   HER DREAMS AND ASPIRATIONS TO FREE HERSELF

· A BIRD IN THE DISTANCE, INDICATIVE OF THAT FREEDOM

· A CLOCK OVER THE FIGURE'S EYE, SHOWING THE NARRATOR'S AWARENESS THAT

   TIME IS PASSING HER BY AND THAT SHE IS AT A CROSSROADS IN HER LIFE

                                                    — ALISON ZAWACKI

WELL I GOT THIS GUITAR, AND I LEARNED HOW TO MAKE IT TALK, AND MY CAR'S OUT BACK, IF YOU'RE READY TO TAKE THAT LONG WALK FROM YOUR FRONT PORCH TO MY FRONT SEAT, THE DOOR'S OPEN BUT THE RIDE IT AIN'T FREE

BRUCE SPRINGSTEEN, THUNDER ROAD

SKIPPIN' THROUGH THE LILY FIELDS, I CAME ACROSS AN EMPTY SPACE
IT TREMBLED AND EXPLODED, LEFT A BUS STOP IN ITS PLACE

THE BUS CAME BY AND I GOT ON, THAT'S WHEN IT ALL BEGAN

THERE WAS COWBOY NEAL AT THE WHEEL, THE BUS TO NEVER-EVER LAND

GRATEFUL DEAD, THAT'S IT FOR THE OTHER ONE

KEN BABBS (L) AND NEAL CASSADY DRIVING THE MERRY
PRANKSTERS' BUS, "FURTHUR" (OR "FURTHER"), 1964

"FURTHUR" (OR "FURTHER"), THE ORIGINAL PRANKSTER BUS, AT REST IN A SWAMP ON KEN KESEY'S FARM IN OREGON.

POSTER FOR THE ACID TEST AT MUIR BEACH, CALIFORNIA, 1965. NOTE DIRECTIONS TO THE EVENT ARE CONSPICUOUSLY MISSING. IN FACT, THIS POSTER, FROM THE COLLECTION OF ALAN TRIST, WHO HEADS THE GRATEFUL DEAD'S SONGWRITING PUBLISHING COMPANY, ICE NINE, IS ONE OF THE VERY FEW TO EVEN STATE *WHERE* THE EVENT WAS.

ROCK SCULLY (GRATEFUL DEAD MANAGER), JERRY GARCIA (GRATEFUL DEAD GUITARIST), AND AUTHOR TOM WOLFE, GATHER BELOW THE FAMOUS HAIGHT/ASHBURY STREET SIGN IN SAN FRANCISCO'S HIPPIE DISTRICT, 1966. WOLFE WROTE BOTH "THE KANDY-KOLORED TANGERINE-FLAKE STREAMLINE BABY" (1965) ABOUT THE SOUTHERN CALIFORNIA CUSTOM CAR SCENE, AND *THE ELECTRIC KOOL-AID ACID TEST* (1968) ABOUT THE MERRY PRANKSTERS AND THE PSYCHEDELIC SCENE INVOLVING THE GRATEFUL DEAD.

NO SIMPLE HIGHWAY

It doesn't matter *when* you got on the bus… it's *that* you got on the bus. That would be a 1939 International Harvester school bus purchased by novelist Ken Kesey to travel cross-country and make merry in the summer of 1964. Named *Furthur* (or *Further*; see below), it became the stuff of late-'60s legend, both a canvas and a stage for Prankster pop art and the changing nature of "awareness" in America. In 1968 it was a focal point in Tom Wolfe's *The Electric Kool-Aid Acid Test*, in which the author unveiled a "new journalism" replete with freely associating thoughts and eccentric punctuation to convey the manic ideas and multiple personalities of Kesey and his followers.

Kesey's bus also was a prototype for The Beatles' own LSD-inspired Magical Mystery bus tour of 1967 that was edited into a much maligned television special and unwieldy album that nonetheless yielded extraordinary songs (John Lennon's "I Am The Walrus" and "Strawberry Fields Forever" and Paul McCartney's "Penny Lane," along with "All You Need Is Love," which capped off the even more psychedelic *Yellow Submarine*, released the following year).

Fresh from the stunning success of his novel, *One Flew Over the Cuckoo's Nest*, Kesey acquired his bus from a San Francisco family that had it fitted out with bunks for use as an oversize motor home. Kesey's plan was to pilot it, with a zany group of friends aboard, to New York City for the World's Fair, and along the way to hold a transcontinental coming-out party for his new book, *Sometimes a Great Notion*.

At Kesey's home in La Honda in the Santa Cruz Mountains south of San Francisco, the Merry Pranksters (as the zany friends now called themselves) installed a sound system and a generator to power extracurricular activities, and went bananas with the paint. Artist Roy Sebern painted the word *Furthur* on the outboard destination placard as a kind of one-word poem and inspirational message to its passengers and a gape-mouthed world at

large. It wasn't until much later that the Pranksters found out he'd misspelled the word, but as the bus was constantly being repainted over by the intrepid travelers, the sign was corrected (contributing to decades of confusion over its proper name).

Kesey recruited Neal Cassady—the speed-talking hero of Jack Kerouac's *On the Road*—and Cassady appointed himself driver. Not surprisingly, the bus was stopped many times by the police, but the Pranksters' short haircuts and preppy clothes were a disguise; no one was ever arrested, even as they carried gallons of orange juice laced with LSD (which was legal at the time). The Pranksters, Kesey, and LSD were quite intertwined. In 1965 and 1966, the Pranksters held legendary "acid tests" that were wild, experimental parties featuring a very young Grateful Dead band. The lightshows and psychedelic music that Bill Graham featured at the Fillmore Auditorium and the Family Dog collective at the Avalon Ballroom over the next several years owed much to the free-form acid tests.

After a wild series of adventures, *Furthur* arrived in New York City with the Pranksters tootling saxophones and blowing soap bubbles from the rooftop dome. Finally they made it to acid-king Timothy Leary's meditation center in upstate New York. Film and audiotape rolled throughout, but by the time they pulled back into their home driveway in La Honda, they found the two media would not synchronize. Nevertheless, the bus's psychedelic paint job impressed many, including Janis Joplin who had her Porsche completely recovered in swirling, vibrant colors (page 149).

Kesey regarded *Furthur* and its occupants as a visual metaphor for a necessary and irresistible—albeit incomprehensible—journey across time and space. He often compared it to *Stagecoach*, but with Cassady in the driver's seat instead of John Wayne. For nearly thirty years the Grateful Dead sang about it in "The Other One," and thus the mythic question was forever planted in the minds of the counterculture: *Are you on the bus… or not?*

YOU CAN'T OVERLOOK THE LACK, JACK, OF ANY OTHER HIGHWAY TO RIDE
IT'S GOT NO SIGNS, NO DIVIDING LINES, AND VERY FEW RULES TO GUIDE

GRATEFUL DEAD, NEW SPEEDWAY BOOGIE

Ken Kesey "sparking up" the ghost of Jerry Garcia at the wheel of the new (replacement) Prankster bus, also named "Further."

Norman Ruth's New Mexico-bound "Terrapin Trailways" bus, 1984. This was a prototypical Deadhead conveyance.

I GOT A RED CAR WITH BLUE TAIL LIGHTS

SHINY RED SEATS WITH LINING IN WHITE

LEOPARD SKIN DASH WITH A LOUVERED HOOD

SHE GOES BA-BA-BA-BA-BA-BA WHEN SHE'S RUNNING GOOD

LET'S GO RIDE INTO THE MOUNTAINS ABOVE

SHE'S LOW

MY BIG RED ROCKET OF LOVE

REV. HORTON HEAT, BIG RED ROCKET OF LOVE

GO WEST, YOUNG MOUSE

In 1965 Stanley Mouse left the Midwest for good, re-establishing himself at the new cornerstone of the world, psychedelic San Francisco. There, he met up with Alton Kelley, a former helicopter mechanic from Connecticut. The two hit it off famously, joyously paging through journals in the public library to find treasures from the French Belle Epoque era that could be re-adapted into the new art form that had just evolved: the psychedelic concert poster.

Kelley and Mouse created dozens of striking pieces for the Family Dog (a hippie production collective), advertising shows at their Avalon Ballroom. One poster's artwork, known as FD 26, became the skull-and-roses trademark for the Grateful Dead. Other Kelley-Mouse posters were produced for Bill Graham's Fillmore Auditorium, Fillmore West, and Winterland dance arena. The duo displayed a sly humor in much of their collaborations, a good example being the piece done for the Pacific Ocean Trading Company, a Haight-Ashbury import shop known to the world as POTCO. Mouse painted a famous portrait of Kelley, used here in a Jefferson Airplane poster.

Rick Griffin came to San Francisco from Orange County in Southern California in 1966. He'd been given a copy of Mouse and Kelley's poster for the Grateful Dead and was shocked to think what he was missing 300 miles to the north. While he mostly moved away from cartooning surf scenes and woodies, his imagination and his inking skills grew at an enormous pace and his pieces came to include the Bill Graham #105 (the "Flying Eyeball" poster for a Jimi Hendrix show), which today may be the most prized piece of all psychedelic-era art. The Flying Eyeball originally was popularized by Von Dutch, the famed So-Cal pinstriper (who claimed to have copped it from an ancient Egyptian symbol), although Griffin—as would others over the decades—made it seem like his own.

In the early '70s, Mouse and Kelley formed Monster Company to create T-shirts showcasing their considerable airbrushing skills (see photo of Mouse airbrushing at a car show). Many car shirts were prominent in the line (including the classic chopped Mercury shown), alongside their own version of the Flying Eyeball and peyote buttons.

RICK GRIFFIN, 1966

Mouse airbrushing at Monster Company booth, circa 1973.

Jefferson Airplane at Edwardian Ball, Fillmore Auditorium, San Francisco; portrait of Alton Kelley by Stanley Mouse.

Alton Kelley and Stanley Mouse, 1967.

Stanley Mouse, 1965, just before leaving for California.

BEAUTIFUL PAINT

On June 3, 1965, John Lennon received a 19-foot-long, 3-ton Mulliner Park-Ward limousine-bodied Rolls-Royce, finished in Valentine black (later repainted to a matte black). That same year he had a radio telephone installed, along with a custom interior/exterior sound system that doubled as a "loud hailer." Along with its rear seat modified to convert to a double bed, Lennon also put in a television and portable refrigerator.

Lennon eventually became bored with the matte black finish and in April 1967, he visited J. P. Fallon Limited, a coachworks company in Surrey, to discuss having the car repainted in a psychedelic fashion. Fallon commissioned "The Fool," a Dutch team of gypsy barge and caravan artists, to do the work, and Lennon took delivery on May 25, 1967. (The Fool also is renowned for having similarly painted Eric Clapton's prized 1964 Gibson SG guitar.)

The Beatles used the psychedelic Rolls for about two years, then loaned it to rock stars, including The Rolling Stones, The Moody Blues, and Bob Dylan. In 1985 it fetched $2.5 million at auction, and today resides at a transportation museum in British Columbia, Canada.

Janis Joplin's Porsche was bought in September 1968 and hand-painted by a friend. She still had it at the time of her death in October 1970. The Who's magic bus was painted in the summer of 1968 when the single "Magic Bus" was released.

One footnote: Paul McCartney's favorite car was his 1965 Aston Martin DB6, the same model as that one driven by James Bond in *Goldfinger*. In 1968 McCartney was on his way to visit John Lennon's wife, Cynthia, and their son, Julian, because the Lennon marriage was breaking up. Paul began composing a song to cheer the boy, repeating the intro "Hey Jules." The story goes that a tape recorder was hung beneath the dash on the Aston's passenger side, with a socket for a microphone. By the end of the drive, the song's title had changed to "Hey Jude," which went on to become The Beatles' best-selling single.

1970 Plymouth Barracuda

Operator's Manual

PAUL GRUSHKIN COLLECTION

Janis Joplin with her psychedelic-painted Porsche.

RICHARD KARL KOCH

HULTON-DEUTSCH/CORBIS

John Lennon and his son, Julian Lennon, with Rolls-Royce painted by The Fool, 1967.

NICK RHODES/MANCHESTER (UK) SCREENPRINTING

TROMPE L'OEIL

Bruce Steinberg, art director for Tower of Power, the famed funkmeisters hailing from Oakland and the East Bay, used automotive imagery for many of the band's well-remembered album covers.

For *Back on the Streets* (1979), Steinberg deftly recreated a '79 Pontiac Trans Am's left front tire, adapting the tire manufacturer's characteristic typeface for the band's name and album title. The shot was taken at the San Francisco–Oakland Bay Bridge toll plaza, and Steinberg was nearly arrested by a cop who thought he was high-jacking the car.

But it was on *Back to Oakland* (1974) that Steinberg's pre-PhotoShop skills went wild. The title suggested a freeway sign, and Steinberg's genius was to place, on the album cover, a totally fictitious sign at the western entrance to the Bay Bridge (on the San Francisco side, heading "back to

Oakland"). He discovered a building immediately adjacent to the bridge from whose roof he could take a photo with the perfect perspective in which to insert the large metal standard topped off by what would be a characteristically California Department of Transportation–approved sign. He then drove freeway after freeway—finally arriving at the intersection of Highways 580 and 680 near Pleasanton, California—to come up with exactly the perfect sign that had the over-the-left-shoulder light, shadow, and size relationships he needed to pull off his *trompe l'oeil*. The resulting album art won Steinberg many graphics-industry awards.

Afterward, Warner Bros. (whose logo Steinberg also readapted into the federal interstate highway format) asked Steinberg to create a 20-by-60–foot billboard resembling the fake sign. This was especially problematic because

it had to look 100 percent like the real thing—as real as an actual freeway on-ramp sign, in exactly the right place above the approach to the bridge, looking east to Oakland.

Steinberg now had to approach CalTrans directly. He was fortunate to find sympathetic souls who revealed to him the secrets of freeway signage, including color and kerning (adjusting the spaces between letters so words can be read at a distance from moving vehicles). And, amazingly, they let him get away with it, a remarkable feat, since it was nearly impossible at first glance to tell the sign was bogus.

Steinberg also art directed Jefferson Airplane violinist Papa John Creach's *Filthy!* (1972) album, taking the shots in a Southern California neighborhood replete with junkers and junkyards. Hot Tuna, a spin-off of the Airplane led by guitarist Jorma Kaukonen and bassist Jack Casady, then needed a cover for their second LP, *Burgers* (1972).

Steinberg and the band met for hours at Stinson Beach, on the ocean just north and west of San Francisco. Steinberg tried shooting the car and band from below a sandy hill, but the proportions never were satisfactory. Then he tried something more prosaic, which eventually became the back cover. Finally, with the sun about to set, Steinberg was down to his very last shot—in fact the last frame on the roll. With the band inside Kaukonen's car—a '34 Buick—the light suddenly and exactly illuminated each band-member. Steinberg squeezed the trigger and . . . *voila*.

The Ramones, promoting the song "Pinhead,"
off their album *Leaving Home* (1977).

Jimi Hendrix relaxing
with dune buggy.

Bonnie, Clyde, and daughter, otherwise known as Kim,
Keith, and Mandy Moon, 1972.

Concert promoter Bill Graham, with Jerry Garcia
aboard sidecar, circa 1985.

The Clash, gracefully arriving backstage, 1975.

Odd scenes along the road. Maybe the
Grateful Dead, who originally wrote these lines
(afterwards covered by Sublime and Jimmy
Buffett), said it best in "Scarlet Begonias":

*Once in a while you get shown the light
In the strangest of places if you look at it right.*

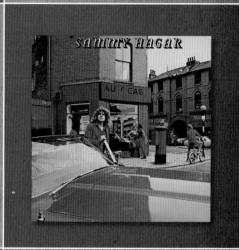

BONZO

Led Zeppelin drummer John "Bonzo" Bonham (1948–1980), an avid collector of antique sports cars and motorcycles, had a famous sequence in the band's 1976 film, *The Song Remains the Same*, in which he:

- drag races
- rides a motorcycle
- rolls around in his Addams Family–esque car
- shows off his cow
- drives a tractor

Bonham kept his collection on his family's farm in England, called The Old Hyde. He also bought a pub in the nearby village of Shenstone and then remodeled it so he could drive his bikes—and cars—right up behind the bar.

On September 24, 1980, Bonham was picked up by one of Led Zeppelin's assistants and driven to band rehearsal for an upcoming tour of the United States—Zeppelin's first since 1977. During the short journey over, Bonham asked to stop for breakfast, where he downed four quadruple vodkas (roughly sixteen shots) along with a bite of ham roll. He continued to drink when he arrived at the studio, and after rehearsals were halted around midnight, he was said to have consumed possibly several dozen more shots. The band drove over to guitarist Jimmy Page's nearby house and Bonham retired for the night. He was found dead the next morning, apparently due to asphyxiation. He was just thirty-two.

STEVE WINWOOD

STING

DAVID BYRNE

STEVE MILLER

ALL PHOTOS BY LYNN GOLDSMITH

SHERYL CROW ON ROAD TRIPS

Road trips for me are not uncommon. In fact, I've driven across the country on several occasions now, by myself and with friends. Some of my favorite "driving music" albums include Pat Metheney's *Offramp*; Neil Young's *Harvest*; The Rolling Stones' *Sticky Fingers*; Joni Mitchell's *Hejira*; James Taylor's *Sweet Baby James*; Emmylou Harris' *Red Dirt Girl*; the Allman Brothers' *Eat a Peach*; Bob Dylan's *Highway 61 Revisited* and *Nashville Skyline*; and Tom Petty's *Damn the Torpedoes*, among others.

I've used the road-trip experience a lot in my creative life as a means of finding inspiration or simply for getting away from the distractions of the day, particularly when I'm trying to write songs. I always come back from driving feeling revitalized and focused. I can't say how many times I've driven up the coast of California with Fleetwood Mac's "Monday Morning" or "World Turning" blasting at obnoxious decibel levels, but that album—Fleetwood Mac— brings me back to my original intent: to write a moving piece of music that's from a place man has spent ages trying to define.

For me, inspiration also can take its cue from memory. My third rock concert experience ever (after Peter Frampton and Ted Nugent) was Lynyrd Skynyrd at the Mid-South Coliseum in Memphis. I was 14 and my best friend's older sister drove us down and promptly told us to get lost while she hung out with her friends. Skynyrd was about as close to southern-outlaw status as anything I'd ever seen, and to this day their music reminds me of what it feels like to be speeding down the freeway in a Z28 with a cop on your tail.

Then, there's *Nebraska*. A few years back, I made a trip to Nashville to see my sister and got caught in one of the worst rainstorms I can remember. I spent close to 30 minutes parked beneath an overpass, unable to drive ahead. I'd been listening to the Boss's *Nebraska* record, but it wasn't until that moment that the title song became visually animated for me. Bruce managed, on that song, to bring understanding to a real-life news story that was so terribly haunting and disturbing. When I hear "Nebraska" I'm always taken back to that afternoon on the road.

— Sheryl Crow
"25 For the Road" *Vanity Fair*, November 2005

MARK LANEGAN

RICHARD E. AARON

MEETING SMOKEY ROBINSON

I WAS WORKING FOR A VIDEO PRODUCTION COMPANY THAT HIRED ME TO SHOOT PRODUCTION SHOTS. IT WAS A THREE-DAY SHOOT AND MOST OF THE GROUPS I'D SHOT WERE NEW, JUST-SIGNED ARTISTS.

THE FIRST ASSISTANT DIRECTOR CALLED LUNCH AND I WENT OUT INTO THE PARKING LOT TO RELAX WHEN IN THE DISTANCE I HEARD A GREAT-SOUNDING AUTOMOBILE COMING TOWARD THE HOUSE WHERE WE WERE SHOOTING. AS THE CAR GOT CLOSER, I REACHED FOR MY CAMERA THAT HAD A LONG LENS TO SEE WHO WAS DRIVING. THROUGH THE LENS I SAW SOMEONE WHOSE MUSIC I REALLY LOVED—IT WAS SMOKEY ROBINSON!

HE CAME TO AN ABRUPT STOP A FEW FEET FROM WHERE I WAS SITTING. HE ASKED ME IF THIS WAS THE RIGHT PLACE. I SAID, YES, BUT I WAS HIRED TO SIT HERE AND SHOOT ANYONE WHO SHOWED UP LATE (OF COURSE I WAS KIDDING). HE LAUGHED, AND SAID THAT WAS VERY FUNNY. HE ASKED ME IF MY PHOTOS WERE AS GOOD AS MY HUMOR. "YES," I SAID, AND INTRODUCED MYSELF. "TO START OFF, LET'S GET SOME SHOTS OF YOU IN THAT GREAT-LOOKING COBRA." HE WAS VERY OPEN TO POSING AND VERY FRIENDLY.

— RICHARD E. AARON

POSTER ARTIST GREG REINEL OF NUTRAJET WITH HIS MUSTANG

155

THE EIGHTS GO EAST AND THE FIVES GO NORTH, AND THE MERGING NEXUS BACK AND FORTH, YOU SEE YOUR SIGN, CROSS THE LINE, SIGNALLING WITH A BLINK

TOM WAITS, DIAMONDS ON MY WINDSHEILD

FIFTH FLOOR MUSIC INC. (ASCAP)

SHOOTING TOM WAITS

February 4, 1999, was the scheduled day for my portrait session with Tom Waits. The location was to be Prairie Sun Recording Studio in Cotati, California. Cotati is 60 miles north of San Francisco in the midst of Sonoma County's miles of bucolic grapevines. Prairie Sun is itself quite rustic. It's set on a 20-acre chicken ranch, where in addition to the studio are old redwood barns with peeling paint, an enormous claw-foot bathtub underneath an oak tree, and more than one old abandoned motorcycle. Visually, you couldn't ask for a better "in character" location to shoot someone like Tom.

On this crisp and clear day, I set up my tripod with a 4x5 view camera behind a tin-walled building that seemed out of another century. For the possible cover photo, I also lit some just-on-the-edge-of-rust wrought-iron furniture I'd spotted and grabbed. I had as my background beautiful late-winter blue sky and rain-soaked green hills. Perfect! I had lots of ambition and a 30-minute window to do the shoot.

Tom arrived. I sat him down on one of the wrought-iron chairs, and shot a test Polaroid. He looked at it, and in his *I just drank a bottle of whiskey and swallowed a box of razor blades voice*, said, "Jay, this looks like my grandmother's furniture. What else you got?" We shot no film.

Next, we went to the claw-foot bathtub. "Nah, don't like it," he said in that raspy voice.

"How about this barn wall with its peeling paint?" I asked.

"Nope, it's not right."

At this point about 10 minutes of my 30 had passed and I'd not taken a single picture. The publicist was just as perplexed as me.

I led Tom to one of the old motorcycles and he proceeded to circle it like a hungry vulture. Feeling a bit nervous about the lack of photos taken, I started snapping pictures of him eyeing the bike. He sat next to it on the ground, in fairly harsh sunlight, looked up at me with squinty eyes, and I blasted off an entire roll of 35mm film. He got up and informed me he "wasn't feeling it."

We walked over to where I had the 4x5 on its tripod, and I asked him to sit. "I prefer to stand," he said. I offered to do a Polaroid of him both sitting and standing, so he could compare. "You know what, Jay, you're right. It's better with me sitting." I shot about six sheets of 4x5 film and about eight frames of 35mm, at which point he stood up and said, "I don't think this is working." Then, out of the blue, he said we should leave the farm immediately.. He had a sudden gleam in his eye, insisting we should drive over to a house just two or three minutes down the road where he'd seen an old, abandoned car earlier that day. Our 30 minutes were pretty much up, but I agreed.

Tom wanted to change out of his jeans and into a black Italian suit that was tailored to fit a man about two sizes smaller... He was moving quickly, so we had to abandon all the lighting and 4x5 camera equipment and just jump into his truck.

I slid into the front bench seat with three cameras around my neck. My assistant and the publicist followed in another car. As we drove down the backcountry roads, Tom and I talked about people we knew in common—mostly musicians—but also about kids and the weird relationship artists have with journalists. After about 20 minutes of steady driving, Tom

informed me he was about to run out of gas. I immediately thought, "How great, pictures of Tom Waits pumping gas. Very cool!" Then he said, much to my dismay, "There are no gas stations on this road." After another 15 minutes, he announced we'd arrived.

About 200 feet up a long, gravel driveway, behind a small house with all its windows covered over by old sheets, and over a barbed-wire cow fence, sat the car he'd scoped out. "Jay, I don't know whose house this is, or who that car belongs to, but you're the captain of this ship, so go knock on the door and ask permission to take some pictures." I started ringing the doorbell that did not seem to be working, then I knocked politely, and then loudly, . No one answered.

I went back to Tom's truck and informed him that no one was home and that we should just do it. He agreed, and the four of us started to work our way up the long driveway toward the car. Halfway there, a little old lady came out from the back. She wore a vintage overcoat and a chiffon scarf tied over her head and below her chin. She yelled at us in what I'd have to describe as a piercing scream, "CAN I HELP YOU?"

I responded that we were wondering if we could hop the fence and take some photos of Tom in front of the car. She responded in an even louder voice, "THAT CAR, IT DOESN'T DRIVE!"

"That's okay," I answered. "We don't want to drive it, just take some pictures," as I held up two of the cameras that were weighing me down like the Dennis Hopper character in *Apocalypse Now*.

Again she hollered, "IT'S GOT NO WHEELS."

I said, with resignation, "We just want to take some photos."

She came up closer and shouted "IT HAS NOT BEEN DRIVEN SINCE MY HUSBAND DIED 30 YEARS AGO!"

Sensing she was deaf, I grabbed a piece of paper and a Sharpie from my assistant and wrote, "All we want to do is shoot some photos. I can pay you $25."

Waving my offer of money away with her hand, she responded in the loudest voice yet, "OK, BUT IT'S GOT NO WHEELS."

She walked back to the house, and we proceeded toward the fence and what was now a setting sun. The car was very funky but in a strange way also very beautiful. When Tom got in front of the car, he went into character as the "sleazy car salesman," furiously waving his hand and adding his famous wide-grin "woodpecker face." He prowled around the car, stopping to inspect the trunk, the weatherbeaten sides, and eventually the front grille where he insisted to me that his face and the grille of the car were much the same. I was shooting as fast as I could, realizing the end could come at any second—even breaking out a fun little plastic toy camera called an "action sampler" in an attempt to capture the surreal moment.

Tom abruptly jumped back over the fence and headed lickety-split down the driveway as I chased him with an old point and shoot 1970's Polaroid camera leaving a trail of developing polaroids scattered down the driveway.. He got to his truck, shook my hand, and headed off driving south, most likely in search of the nearest gas station. I was dazed, confused, and impressed all at once. Was this what Tom's everyday life was really like?

— Jay Blakesberg

BORN TO RUN

ON A STEAMING AUGUST AFTERNOON IN WASHINGTON, D.C., A FEW YEARS
AGO, TWO FRIENDS AND I BUSTED OUT OF CLASS—OOPS, WORK—EARLY, AND
HEADED FOR MARYLAND'S EASTERN SHORE FOR BLUE CRABS AND COLD
BEER. WE WERE BAKING AS WE SAT IN TRAFFIC ON THE BLACK LEATHER SEATS
OF MY CONVERTIBLE. FINALLY, WE GOT TO THE CHESAPEAKE BAY BRIDGE AND
PAID THE TOLL, AND NEIL SLIPPED A DISC INTO MY CD PLAYER. THE FIRST
FAMILIAR PIANO CHORDS SOUNDED: *"THE SCREEN DOOR SLAMS./MARY'S
DRESS WAVES."*

IF YOU STICK TO 61 MILES PER HOUR, IT TAKES EXACTLY 4 MINUTES, 49
SECONDS TO DRIVE OVER THE BAY BRIDGE, THE SAME TIME IT TAKES BRUCE
SPRINGSTEEN TO GET THROUGH "THUNDER ROAD," THE OPENING SONG ON
THE WORLD'S BEST DRIVING ALBUM, *BORN TO RUN.* BRUCE RE-RELEASED
BORN TO RUN THIS WEEK, 30 YEARS AFTER IT FIRST CAME OUT. OVER THE
YEARS, I'VE DRIVEN THOUSANDS OF MILES TO BRUCE, BUT NONE SO SWEET AS
ON THAT DAY WE WENT OVER THE BAY BRIDGE TO "THUNDER ROAD."

HALFWAY ACROSS THE BRIDGE, THE TEMPERATURE DROPPED 10 DEGREES,
TO 88, AND THAT'S WHEN BRUCE GOT HIS GUITAR AND LEARNED HOW TO
MAKE IT TALK. IT WAS THE PERFECT PAUSE IN THE MIDDLE OF AN ANTHEM, A
CHANCE TO LOOK OUT AT THE SAILBOATS DOTTING THE BAY, AT ALL THE OTHER
WASHINGTON ESCAPEES CRUISING IN SEARCH OF TOMORROW. *"MY CAR'S OUT
BACK IF YOU'RE READY TO TAKE THAT LONG WALK/FROM YOUR FRONT PORCH
TO MY FRONT SEAT./THE DOOR'S OPEN BUT THE RIDE IT AIN'T FREE."*

SHAILAGH AND I HAD OUR ARMS UP IN THE AIR—MAYBE CELEBRATING JUST
THE THRILL OF SINGING WITH THE BOSS AS WE BARRELED ACROSS THE LAST
PART OF THE BRIDGE. BRUCE SAID, "I'M PULLING OUT OF HERE TO WIN," AND
WE PLAYED IMAGINARY PIANOS WITH HIM ON THAT LAST TRILL THAT LEADS
INTO CLARENCE CLEMONS' SAXOPHONE PART. WE WERE ON THE EASTERN
SHORE PROPER AND IN A COMPLETELY DIFFERENT PLACE, PSYCHOLOGICALLY,
THAN WHEN WE DROVE PAST THAT TOLLBOOTH.

I GOT THE THIRTIETH-ANNIVERSARY BOX SET ON TUESDAY, THE DAY IT CAME
OUT, AND SPENT THE NEXT THREE HOURS WATCHING THE TWO INCLUDED DVDS
ON A LAPTOP AT WORK (RESEARCH, OF COURSE). BUT MY FAVORITE PART—
LISTENING TO MY BELOVED *BORN TO RUN* CD ALL OVER AGAIN—I COULDN'T
DO IN THE OFFICE. "EVERYBODY ON *BORN TO RUN* IS OUT, OR TRYING TO GET
OUT," BRUCE SAYS ON THE DVD. "THAT'S THE UNDERPINNING." NO KIDDING.
SO I SLID MY NEW CD INTO MY PORTABLE PLAYER AND HEADED OUT, WALKING
THROUGH DOWNTOWN MANHATTAN. BUT I WAS ALSO IN MY CAR ONCE MORE,
CRUISING OVER THE BAY BRIDGE.

— HELENE COOPER

THE *NEW YORK TIMES,* NOVEMBER 18, 2005

I WENT OUT FOR A RIDE

One of the most illuminating exhibitions of rock & roll photography was
the *Springsteen: Troubadour of the Highway* show that traveled cross-country
in 2002–2004. Organized by Colleen Sheehy, director of education at the
Weisman Art Museum at the University of Minnesota, Minneapolis, it
included works by photographers Edie Baskin, Joel Bernstein, David Gahr,
Lynn Goldsmith, David Michael Kennedy, Annie Leibovitz, David Rose,
Pamela Springsteen, Frank Stefanko, and Arnold Levine, director of the
somber "Atlantic City" music video (1982), which was shot from the window
of a moving car driving in and around that New Jersey resort city.

Each artist's photographic document made a visual statement about
Springsteen's life and work at a particular intersection or bend in the road.
One of the highlights of the show was Springsteen's sister Pamela's series of 41
photographs (out of hundreds shot in Los Angeles' barrios and ghettos, along
Route 66, and beside highways in the Mojave Desert) that gave context to
Springsteen's 1995 "The Ghost of Tom Joad" (facing page) and helped shape
the full music video.

In the accompanying booklet's introduction, Sheehy noted that over time
Springsteen's music has followed his changing imagery of the highway. "His
restless characters are on the move, sometimes on the hustle, and often on the
run," Sheehy wrote. "Speeding off to the edge of town, down the New Jersey
Turnpike, or across the desert, their physical movement matches their psychic
and spiritual searches."

All along Springsteen's personal highway—from *Darkness on the Edge of
Town* through *Born to Run, Nebraska, The River,* and *We Shall Overcome: The
Seeger Sessions*—to cite only a few of his many albums—the dotted white
line is a convention central to his craft. Whether cars are the basis for crisply
drawn, take-no-prisoners portraits ("Racing in the Street") or shadows within
a deeper, darker play ("Backstreets"), his listeners sense the cars are real cars,
that he's had them himself, that he mostly knows what he's talking about. To
underscore that point, as Sheehy notes, in the visual record of Springsteen's
career, the number of photographs of him in, on, or next to cars is second
only to images of him on stage with a guitar.

The highway and all the vista points on Springsteen's Jersey and California maps—as well as all the vignettes born of wrenching on, fleeing with,
making out in, or simply hanging out with friends next to their cars—are, in
Springsteen's parlance, basic stuff people can relate to. "Hey," he seems to say,
"we all got cars. Things happen in cars. Cars take us places. We all go down
the highway."

But then something else happens. His language—more poetry, now—*reso-
nates* and thus we remember what Springsteen had to say about something
because where we were at a particular point in time when we first heard what
it was he had to say, and what it meant, really became touchstones about *us.*
Over the years, as with life's changing vistas born of age, maturity, fate, and
circumstance, the specific meaning of the lyrics modulate into another and
another and yet another guise. Or, in the case of, say, "Born to Run," it means
just as much as it did when he wrote it—thank God.

In "Growin' Up," sung in his 1972 audition before legendary Columbia
Records producer John Hammond, Springsteen mused, "I swear I found the
key to the universe in the engine of an old parked car." That introspect was
then and remains now, something to think about, one of hundreds of inspired
lines crafted over the decades by one of America's great songwriters . . . who
just happens to be a gearhead.

BRUCE ON THE HIGHWAY

The photo above was taken in the Mojave Desert at dusk. Here's the story.

One Sunday afternoon Bruce and I decided to drive out to the desert and shoot some pictures for his new record. We got a late start and by the time we reached the desert we didn't have much daylight left. So, instead of driving any farther we just decided to pull over. I got out my 35mm camera and some high-speed film and we started shooting by an old chain-link fence on a dusty road. Those images ended up being used in the album packaging for *The Ghost of Tom Joad.*

Finally, when it looked like all our light was gone, we noticed the two-lane highway up on a nearby hill. We ran up to try and steal a few more shots. The sun had already set and it was getting dark very quickly. I shot as fast as I could as Bruce walked down the highway toward me while cars and trucks flew by.

This shot is one of my favorites, partly because as a professional photographer everything usually is so preplanned, but here nothing was preconceived. It was just something that came from being out on a Sunday drive.

— Pamela Springsteen

WELL, IT WAS BACK IN BLIND RIVER IN 1962
WHEN I LAST SAW YOU ALIVE
BUT WE MISSED THAT SHIFT ON THE LONG DECLINE
LONG MAY YOU RUN

NEIL YOUNG, LONG MAY YOU RUN

HENRY DILTZ

BUY MYSELF A BIG OLD CAR

Many adults who grew up in the '50s owe their infatuation with automobiles to their childhood love of Dinky, Matchbox, Smith-Miller, and Tonka toys. Neil Young's obsession with American cars also developed in the '50s, but one might argue it was due to a childhood brush with polio.

Born in 1945 in Toronto, Young and his mother, Rassie, moved to Winnipeg after his parents split in 1956. Until then, the family lived in Ontario. In 1951, Canada experienced one of the largest polio epidemics in its history. One day late that summer when Young was not yet six years old he went swimming with his father, Canadian broadcaster and sportswriter Scott Young, in the Pigeon River near Omemee. He woke that night with troubling symptoms. Neil survived a hospital stay but his health was permanently affected, so that winter his parents took him to Florida to help him recover in the warmth. There, he saw his first real American cars—a vision, really, because so fewer brands were available in Canada and none seemed as big or new or innovative with their accessories and custom features as what was ubiquitous in the U.S.

What makes Young successful as an endlessly questing musician are his idiosyncrasies and myriad interests—roots music; dense, hardcore rock & roll; vintage cars and toy trains. His ranch in the Santa Cruz Mountains, below San Francisco, has an entire building housing his many museum-

quality Cadillacs, Lincolns, and other vintage marques; others, like the blue Plymouth pictured here, are simply in running order and appear just as attractive to Young. Most are big and friendly in appearance, with wide fenders and toothy grins. Among them is a white '57 Cadillac Eldorado Biarritz which was portrayed on the promo poster for *Trans* (1985). "Neil is a kid at heart," said photographer and friend Joel Bernstein. "He's passionate about cars just like any kid. Cars are still a wonder to him."

Nearly every interview done with Young in Northern California over the past 20 years has had Young meeting the reporter at a mountaintop restaurant parking lot near his home, then driving them for miles out on country roads and down winding rural highways where Young appears most at ease. Wrote Alec Wilkinson in *Rolling Stone* magazine, in one instance: "Young drove us west, toward the ocean, down a road in deep shade; it appeared just wide enough for the car. The descent was steep and the turns were sharp. The steering wheel was very big and Young seemed almost to be wrestling with it. The impression made by the oversize wheel and the car's ample fenders, and by the trees being so tall and gathered in shadow like huge curtains around us, gave one the sense of the unequal scale of childhood. 'You get out here on these old roads in an old car,' Young said, 'You don't know where you are, you don't know what time it is. That's always good.'"

THE SQUIRES WITH "MORTIMER HEARSE."

KIRK HAMMETT (METALLICA) AND LES CLAYPOOL
(PRIMUS) WITH A NEIL YOUNG CAR, BACKSTAGE,
SHORELINE AMPHITHEATER, MOUNTAIN VIEW, CALIFORNIA

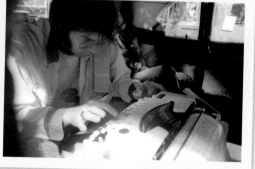

Two of Young's earliest cars stand out in his formative years as a musician. The first is Mortimer Hearseburg, or "Mort" for short, a second-hand 1948 Buick Roadmaster hearse. Later immortalized in Young's "Long May You Run," it was his most prized possession next to his Gretsch guitar, and carried all the equipment for his first band, The Squires. Mort threw its transmission during an impromptu excursion from Fort William, Ontario, to Sudbury, breaking down outside Ironbridge. Mort was towed to Blind River but never would recover, although the circumstance of abandoning the vehicle ironically prompted Young to light out for Toronto where he'd first meet, or hear of, musicians like Stephen Stills.

The second early notable vehicle was the 1953 Pontiac hearse that Young bought after a later band, The Mynah Birds (also featuring a flashy frontman by the name of Rick James), dissolved, and he pawned their equipment so that he and bassist Bruce Palmer could journey west to Los Angeles in the early spring of '66. Young was so nervous on the long trip that when he wasn't driving he was laying in the back listening . . . for knocks in the transmission. How that hearse played a pivotal role in the formation of the Buffalo Springfield is recounted on page 97.

BACKSTAGE TRAILER

WHEN THE CROSBY, STILLS, NASH & YOUNG TOUR WAS JUST A HALF-WEEK AWAY FROM REACHING CLEVELAND MUNICIPAL STADIUM ON AUGUST 31, 1974, NEIL YOUNG FOUND HIMSELF LONESOME FOR ONE OF HIS CADILLACS. HE CALLED A ROADIE AT HIS BROKEN ARROW RANCH IN NORTHERN CALIFORNIA AND HAD HIM DRIVE THE CAR TO CLEVELAND.

PHOTOGRAPHER JOEL BERNSTEIN, ARRIVING EARLY THAT AFTERNOON, SAW THE VINTAGE CAR PARKED NEAR THE STAGE, AND WAS CURIOUS WHY IT WAS THERE. WALKING AROUND IT, AND PEERING INSIDE, HE DISCOVERED YOUNG, NOW QUITE COMFORTABLE IN HIS UNIQUE SELF-PROPELLED BACKSTAGE TRAILER, PECKING AWAY AT AN OLD MANUAL TYPEWRITER, WRITING A NEW SONG.

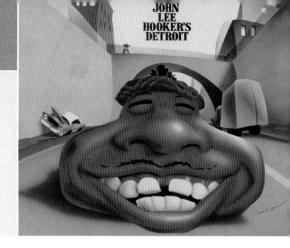
JOHN LEE HOOKER'S DETROIT

DETROIT CITY
Factory Fresh

Turn it up, man! Crank it! Twist it past 11 and let 'er rip! Are we talking cars at the drag strip or rock & roll? Certainly both involve moving metal, literally and figuratively. When it comes to Detroit Rock City, "lettin' 'er rip" was first signified by the mighty cubic inches tradition of the great American V8-powered land yachts of the '40s and '50s, and then by the beat-yer-ass-off-the- line muscle cars of the late '60s and early '70s. In rock & roll, it has to do with a single knob: that marked "VOLUME."

In the early '70s, a Manchester, England, band by the name Black Sabbath took the blues-rock format of Cream and Led Zeppelin, walloped down the bass and right-forwarded the amps past the peg-line to unleash a suitably painful mental anguish of screaming, growling guitars held up by a shirt-shaking bottom end and laced with piercing vocals. The rock audiences were impressed; this was an altogether different concept, say, from the late '60s Grateful Dead jams (which, instrumentally, could be ear-shattering, especially in their second set "space" improvisations).

The Who's live performances were traditionally among the very noisiest. To augment their early-on self-destructive stage antics, they even planted concussion bombs in Keith Moon's drum kit. For most of the early '70s they were listed in the *Guinness Book of World Records* as the loudest rock band in the world, measured at 130 decibels. Deep Purple would go even further, claiming the *Guinness* title initially in 1975 and then over several following years. Serious challenges were subsequently posed by bands such as Blue Cheer, Grand Funk Railroad, Mötörhead, The Ramones, Hüsker Dü,

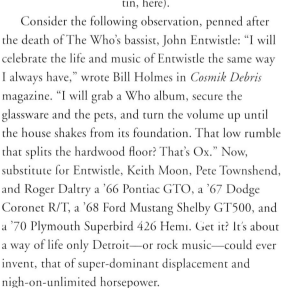
GREAT BIG SHOWS PRESENTS
the Detroit Cobras
WITH THE WOGGLES & THE CLUTTERS EXIT/IN FEBRUARY 4, 2006
ANDREW VASTAGH

Dinosaur Jr., My Bloody Valentine, and countless other notables. In rock & roll, volume is like going for the land-speed record at Bonneville, and in the annals of rock, this commitment to *loud* and its *de facto* tinnitus-engendering ties to meaty American automobiles was perhaps best exemplified by the noisy birth of the MC5 (i.e, "The Motor City Five") in the car factory/drag-strip environs of their hometown (see facing page, *How the MC5 Got Their Sound*, by Detroit's own Mark Arminski).

Rock's classic sonic recipe delivers the biggest bottom end and the loudest high end possible. Non-recording music-heads can (and do) join the fun by playing music through-the-roof at home and by beating back the competition in the street with bass-driven hip-hop insanity (or *hyphy*, as it's now known). There's a parallel as well to America's penchant for good ol' fashioned street racing (and we're not talking about whining, high-revving overseas tin, here).

Consider the following observation, penned after the death of The Who's bassist, John Entwistle: "I will celebrate the life and music of Entwistle the same way I always have," wrote Bill Holmes in *Cosmik Debris* magazine. "I will grab a Who album, secure the glassware and the pets, and turn the volume up until the house shakes from its foundation. That low rumble that splits the hardwood floor? That's Ox." Now, substitute for Entwistle, Keith Moon, Pete Townshend, and Roger Daltry a '66 Pontiac GTO, a '67 Dodge Coronet R/T, a '68 Ford Mustang Shelby GT500, and a '70 Plymouth Superbird 426 Hemi. Get it? It's about a way of life only Detroit—or rock music—could ever invent, that of super-dominant displacement and nigh-on-unlimited horsepower.

PIXAR'S CARS

RANDY NEWMAN (PAGE 99) SCORED MUCH OF THE SOUNDTRACK FOR THE DISNEY/PIXAR ORIGINAL ANIMATED MOTION PICTURE *CARS* (2006), A PRODUCTION FUNDAMENTALLY ROOTED IN DETROIT'S CAR-MAKING HISTORY AND SOMEWHAT IN NASCAR'S RACING HERITAGE, BUT LARGELY IMAGINED AS A JOURNEY DOWN AN APOCRYPHAL ROUTE 66 WITH INSPIRED TONGUE-IN-CHEEK TOUCHES LIKE THE (HOOD) ORNAMENT VALLEY AND THE CADILLAC RANGE OF MOUNTAINS.

AMONG THE CAST OF PERIOD-PIECE VEHICLES ARE A '59 CADILLAC COUPE DEVILLE, A 1957 MOTORAMA SHOW CAR, A '59 CHEVY LOWRIDER, A 1949 MERCURY, A VW HIPPIE BUS, AND A 1951 HUDSON HORNET, VARIOUSLY VOICED BY CHEECH MARIN, PAUL NEWMAN, RICHARD PETTY, GEORGE CARLIN, AND OTHERS.

SHERYL CROW SINGS THE ROCKABILLY-SPICED LEAD SONG, "REAL GONE," AND JOHN MAYER AND CHUCK BERRY SEPARATELY COVER "ROUTE 66." THE MOST EVOCATIVE SONGS MAY BE RASCAL FLATTS' COVER OF CANADIAN ROCKER TOM COCHRANE'S "LIFE IS A HIGHWAY," AND RANDY NEWMAN'S "OUR TOWN," PERFORMED BY JAMES TAYLOR, WHO ORIGINALLY APPEARED IN *TWO-LANE BLACKTOP* (1971) WITH DENNIS WILSON OF THE BEACH BOYS (PAGE 88).

THE WHITE STRIPES
THE BIG THREE KILLED MY BABY

MARK ARMINSKI

In the parking lot of Amy Jo's Donut Shop, Richie Brigidi slowed but did not stop. "Very depressing," he said, and with the heel of his right hand levered the T-bar Hurst shifter down into second gear. The car gurgled and bubbled power.

Three women—with the slightly tired look of being 35 in their eyes—peered out the windows of their station wagon parked nearby. They nodded at Richie and smiled. Then, an unmistakable leer began to spread across the face of each woman as the long, proud red hood of Richie's car circled the station wagon like an effortlessly swimming shark.

Yes, they knew. The car struck something within them, as if an old '60s hit had been played. But before they could put a finger on just what it was, the big car was gone, rumbling slowly in second gear as Brigidi cranked the wheel, sighed, and said, "Nothing going on here."

Ten years before, 12 years before, 14 years before, the scene at Amy Jo's at Cheltenham and Ogontz Avenues would have been different. Then, Brigidi would have assumed a cocky, decisive manner as he powered his car out of the lot and chirped the tires, heading toward a dark, wide section of Route 309 not far away in Cheltenham Township. Word would spread, and the solid thump of dense American car doors slamming shut would spread it further: a match was set. Amy Jo's would empty as Brigidi's army tagged after him.

What would have followed was simple. Two cars would line up, side by side. A cadence would be called; sometimes a flag would be waved. Then, white-hot pure power would be set loose on the still night air. On the shift from second to third, low in the throat, bass to a tortured, snarling tenor that ripped and tore across the evening, clawing toward a climax, a sound would come:

"Aahhhhwwwaaaarrrr AAAAAAAAARaaaaRRRRRR"

It was the sound of a 1960s muscle car in street-race drag-battle. When you hear it today, as you still do sometimes, it is more than that. It is the sound of our past on the night air, a piece of Americana as important to modern popular culture as the creak of Conestoga wagons was to their time. It stands alongside combat troops, peace marchers, and bull markets as a symbol of what the '60s were all about, of the whole idea of unlimited power, of constantly bigger and better things, of wars on poverty and wars in Asia, of peace and promise and Gross National Products that roared always up, up, up like the madly whirring sound of a muscle car crescendoing through its gears forever.

And in the sense of power lost, and lost so quickly, I think the muscle car is a fitting symbol for the changes that have taken place in this land.

All of which explains something of why I recently rode with Brigidi and learned a little of how he is coming to terms with this era, having been born and raised in another one full of an abundance of American power. In that, he may be like you or me, if you are 25 to 40 years old. Except that Brigidi

MIKE MARTIN/ENGINEHOUSE 13

was a hero of that era, an honest-to-god drag-racing king of a large section of Philadelphia, and his flag-wavin' V8 engine, which will become extinct sometime, played a much larger part in his life than in yours or mine.

Brigidi is 34 now, with charcoal gray flecks in his hair. But when I rode with him in the summer of 1981, the tattoo of crossed racing flags still showed on his right arm, and the good Lord knows his car was still willing and able.

Brigidi's car cost $2,574.18 new in 1966. Off the showroom floor, it was something special—bright red with a white convertible top and the special tiger paw tires with the red-wall stripe. Under the hood, the car was simply awesome. The Oldsmobile 442 had been brought out as an Oldsmobile version of the Pontiac GTO, but it never quite gained the reputation of its sister car. Brigidi's 442 was different, still. While most 442s had a single four-barrel carburetor, his had the L-69 option: three two-barrels sat stop Brigidi's 400-ci engine, giving it awesome power.

But for some other unexplainable reason, the red car was just plain hot. Maybe it was the way the car fell together at the plant. Maybe it was the way Brigidi drove it. Probably it was a combination of the two, and the tri-power, but whatever it was, other fast drivers with cars that should have muscled a 442 ate Brigidi's dust instead. One moment they were bound for glory, the next, they saw the 442's taillights and heard the high tenor chorus the tri-power makes in full-throated cry, UuhhhwaaAAAAA! "That thing would suck in air, birds, and leaves off the trees," Brigidi said.

It was a great sound, and a great car and a great driver. Brigidi was building a rep. On North Broad Street; on the Meadows near Tioga Marine Terminal; down near Pattison Avenue; and on Front Street, too, on any strip where the road was wide, the word spread there was a hot Philly Olds 442. Just the way the great songs forever boasted.

Soon, Brigidi and his buddies did not have to travel far. The boys from South Philly would come north to Amy Jo's, circling the lot in second gear, checking the two 'Vettes and the two 442s that were the stallions in Amy Jo's stable. There was a steady stream of such challengers, a steady stream of processions to the strip on Route 309, and a steady stream of Brigidi victories. The car drew more than challengers, of course. It drew women, providing conquests of a different sort. "It was a good pick-up car," Brigidi said matter-of-factly. "One in five would say yes when you asked them if they wanted to ride."

He sold the 442, then found it years later and bought it back. It was like finding a wooly Mammoth flash-frozen in a glacier. "Want to go back 10 years fast?" Brigidi asked me. The cassette deck switched on and "Jumpin' Jack Flash" filled the car. The engine gurgled power. The Stones' hard-driving rhythm answered back, and we were rolling. We drove to the old strip on

I GOT A SIXTY-NINE CHEVY WITH A 396, FUELIE HEADS AND A HURST ON THE FLOOR

SHE'S WAITING TONIGHT DOWN IN THE PARKING LOT, OUTSIDE THE SEVEN-ELEVEN STORE

ME AND MY PARTNER SONNY BUILT HER STRAIGHT OUT OF SCRATCH, AND HE RIDES WITH ME FROM TOWN TO TOWN

WE ONLY RUN FOR THE MONEY, GOT NO STRINGS ATTACHED, WE SHUT 'EM UP AND THEN WE SHUT 'EM DOWN

TONIGHT, TONIGHT THE STRIP'S JUST RIGHT, I WANNA BLOW 'EM OFF IN MY FIRST HEAT

SUMMER'S HERE AND THE TIME IS RIGHT, FOR RACIN' IN THE STREET

BRUCE SPRINGSTEEN, *RACING IN THE STREET*

ANDY BRIZIO/ANDY'S TEE SHIRTS/SIGNATURES NETWORK

309. "It was something back then," Brigidi said, in a tone of benediction. "My car against yours. Plain and simple. The fastest wins."

Now, once again, but this time alone in the center of a deserted highway, Brigidi smiled and said, "Wanna light 'em up?" The car surged forward and a little to the side as the tires lit up, screamed, shrieked, then grabbed the pavement in earnest. One hand on the wheel, Brigidi rose over the gear shift so that all his weight was behind the flat-out speed shift down into second. The car leaped and again veered to the side. My head snapped like a whip. Then, the shift into third; again the veer, the squeal, the surge; and one more time, a body slam into fourth, and the car, like a mighty racehorse pounding toward the final stripe, reached and found all its power in the finishing gallop.

It had been just a few seconds. We were traveling over 100 miles per hour. But there was no one for the Olds to beat, and there was nowhere else to go, except back to the present and Brigidi's home.

— Bob Frump
Philadelphia Inquirer, 1981

MICHAEL N. MARKS

MITCH RYDER

MITCH RYDER, BORN WILLIAM LEVISE JR. IN THE DETROIT SUBURB OF HAMTRAMCK IN 1945, AND HIS BAND, THE DETROIT WHEELS, REACHED THE TOP 10 ON BILLBOARD'S SINGLES CHART IN EARLY 1966 WITH "JENNY TAKE A RIDE." IT WAS AN INSPIRED, SUPERCHARGED WELDING OF LITTLE RICHARD'S "JENNY, JENNY" AND CHUCK WILLIS' TAKE ON "C.C. RIDER." LATE IN 1966, RYDER AND THE DETROIT WHEELS RELEASED AN EQUALLY INTENSE TOP 5 SINGLE COMBINING "DEVIL WITH A BLUE DRESS ON" AND "GOOD GOLLY MISS MOLLY."

RYDER'S WORK—BRIDGING MOTOWN SOUL AND TAKE-NO-PRISONERS HARD ROCK—HEAVILY INFLUENCED IGGY & THE STOOGES, TED NUGENT, BOB SEGER, AND BRUCE SPRINGSTEEN. *DETROIT*, RYDER'S 1971 REUNION WITH THE WHEELS' DRUMMER JOHN BADANJEK, WAS HIGHLIGHTED BY THEIR FEROCIOUS RENDITION OF LOU REED'S "ROCK AND ROLL" FROM THE 1969 VELVET UNDERGROUND RELEASE *LOADED*. STANLEY MOUSE HANDLED THE COVER ART.

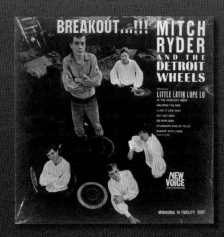

MOTOWN STUDIO A, DETROIT

PAUL GRUSHKIN

MOTOWN STUDIO CONTROL, DETROIT

SESSIONS
3:00
5:00 Supremes
10:30 Tempts

THE FOUR TOPS IN DETROIT

DETROIT PUBLIC LIBRARY/HACKLEY COLLECTION

PAUL GRUSHKIN

MOTORTOWN REVUE

Before he moved on to careers as a jazz shop owner and moonlighting song-writer for Jackie Wilson, Berry Gordy was an auto-assembly worker. Then in 1959 Gordy borrowed $800 from family members to found Detroit's Motown Records in a modest house he called "Hitsville USA." There, he created the legendary "Studio A" pictured above right.

Many African American–owned record labels were created beginning in the 1920s, but none enjoyed the combination of strategic vision, business instincts, and artist-and-repertoire (dance and diction coaching and innova-tive songwriting, all melded to a disciplined studio band known as the Funk Brothers) practices of Gordy. These attributes, along with market timing, defined Motown. Gordy's genius was to envision modern R&B music as a crossover vehicle with the potential to turn on millions of white rock & roll–oriented fans—all of which was to come true.

In the fall of 1962 Gordy decided the best way to market his artists, their songs, and his label was to put the performers on a bus, call it the Motor-town Revue, and take them out on the road for 10 weeks at a time into the Deep South's "chitlin' circuit" of black clubs and theaters, then before semi-integrated audiences in the Midwest and along the Eastern Seaboard, and eventually arrive—in triumph—at the famed Apollo Theater in New York City's Harlem district. One bus tour took the Motown sound across Europe and into Paris.

Gordy was taking a gamble: many of the artists and the accompanying Motown staff would have their first encounters with the segregation their parents had moved to Detroit to escape (restaurants and restrooms were still black or white, and guns were fired at the bus itself). But in fact, no record company before Motown had ever, on its own, packaged its full artist roster as a self-sustaining tour.

So it was that in 1963–1965 (see the exemplary concert poster to left) America discovered Little Stevie Wonder, The Supremes, The Temptations, The Marvelettes, The Four Tops, Gladys Knight & The Pips, Martha Reeves & The Vandellas, Mary Wells, Tammi Terrell and Marvin Gaye, and Smokey Robinson and the Miracles. Later tours in 1968 and 1969 would include the Isley Brothers and the Jackson Five.

It was a family affair at all times. Beyond the endless hours on a poorly heated or barely air-conditioned bus (a far cry from today's luxury liners), there were few private dressing rooms, and every day was marked by a dozen little squabbles (think of all those young women crowding around a mirror trying to get ready). But Mary Wells spoke for all when she remembered the Motortown Revue as their "college days."

Jerry Lee Lewis owned a '58 Cadillac Sixty Special. Isaac Hayes a '72 Eldorado "Superfly" trimmed in gold leaf. Fats Domino cherished his '59 Eldorado Biarritz, painted in two tones of lilac. Chuck Berry drove both a '57 and '64 Eldorado, and was given a red Coupe DeVille onstage for his sixtieth birthday by Keith Richards. The stories of musicians and their Cadillacs are simply endless, and more songs have been written about the marquee than any other brand in history, American or otherwise. Two notable songs were penned about the Cadillac assembly line: one by Wayne Kemp that was recorded by Johnny Cash (see facing page), the other by Albert King.

One of the "three Kings" of the Blues guitar (along with B. B. and Freddie), Albert King was an especially imposing figure, standing 6 foot 4 and weighing 260 pounds. He was born in Indianola, Mississippi, in 1923, and later became a bulldozer driver. His first recordings were released in 1959, and in 1966 he signed with the Stax label, under which he released his legendary LP, *Born Under a Bad Sign*. In 1968, Albert King became the first blues musician to play promoter Bill Graham's Fillmore West, when he opened a show featuring John Mayall and Jimi Hendrix.

King was an "upside-down/backwards" guitarist. He was left-handed but usually played right-handed guitars flipped over upside down. His preference was the Gibson Flying V model, and he was known for his expressive bend-ing of notes. Stevie Ray Vaughan was heavily influenced by King, as were Mike Bloomfield and Eric Clapton.

"Cadillac Assembly Line" was released when King moved to the Tomato label in the mid-1970s. The assembly line process was first incorporated into production at the Ford Motor Company department that built Model T magnetos, which generated electricity for the ignition. Previously, one worker had assembled each magneto from start to finish. Under the new approach, each worker performed a single task as the unit traveled past his station. The savings in time and money were so dramatic that the assembly line approach was extended to virtually every phase of the car-manufacturing process.

By 1914, the Ford factory resembled an immense river system, with subassemblies taking shape along tributaries and feeding into the main channel, where the chassis moved continuously along rails at a speed of 6 feet per minute. The time needed for the final stage of assembly dropped from more than 12 hours to just 93 minutes. Model Ts accounted for half the cars in the world by 1920, and factory life in America would never be the same.

Eventually, a number of Detroit musicians worked in car factories while honing their musical skills, including (briefly) members of the MC5 (page 162) and Bob Seger (page 180).

Cadillac assembly line, Detroit.

TRAVIS BARKER, DRUMMER FOR BLINK 182, BOX CAR RACER, THE AQUABATS, THE SUICIDE MACHINES, SNOT, AND OTHERS, HAS SPENT OVER $30,000 ON HIS BODY ART. "I PURPOSELY DID THAT," HE SAID, "SO I COULDN'T GET A NORMAL JOB AND LIVE A NORMAL LIFE. I DID IT SO I HAD TO PLAY MUSIC." BARKER COLLECTS CADILLACS AND SOME OF HIS TATTOOS SYMBOLIZE HIS LOVE FOR CARS. IN PARTICULAR, TWO RACE FLAGS ON THE SIDE OF HIS NECK WITH THE NUMBER 66 TO COMMEMORATE THE MODEL YEAR OF HIS FAVORITE CADILLAC, AND ON HIS CHEST A CADILLAC EMBLEM SURROUNDED BY MUD-FLAP "TRUCKER LADIES" AND SPARKPLUGS.

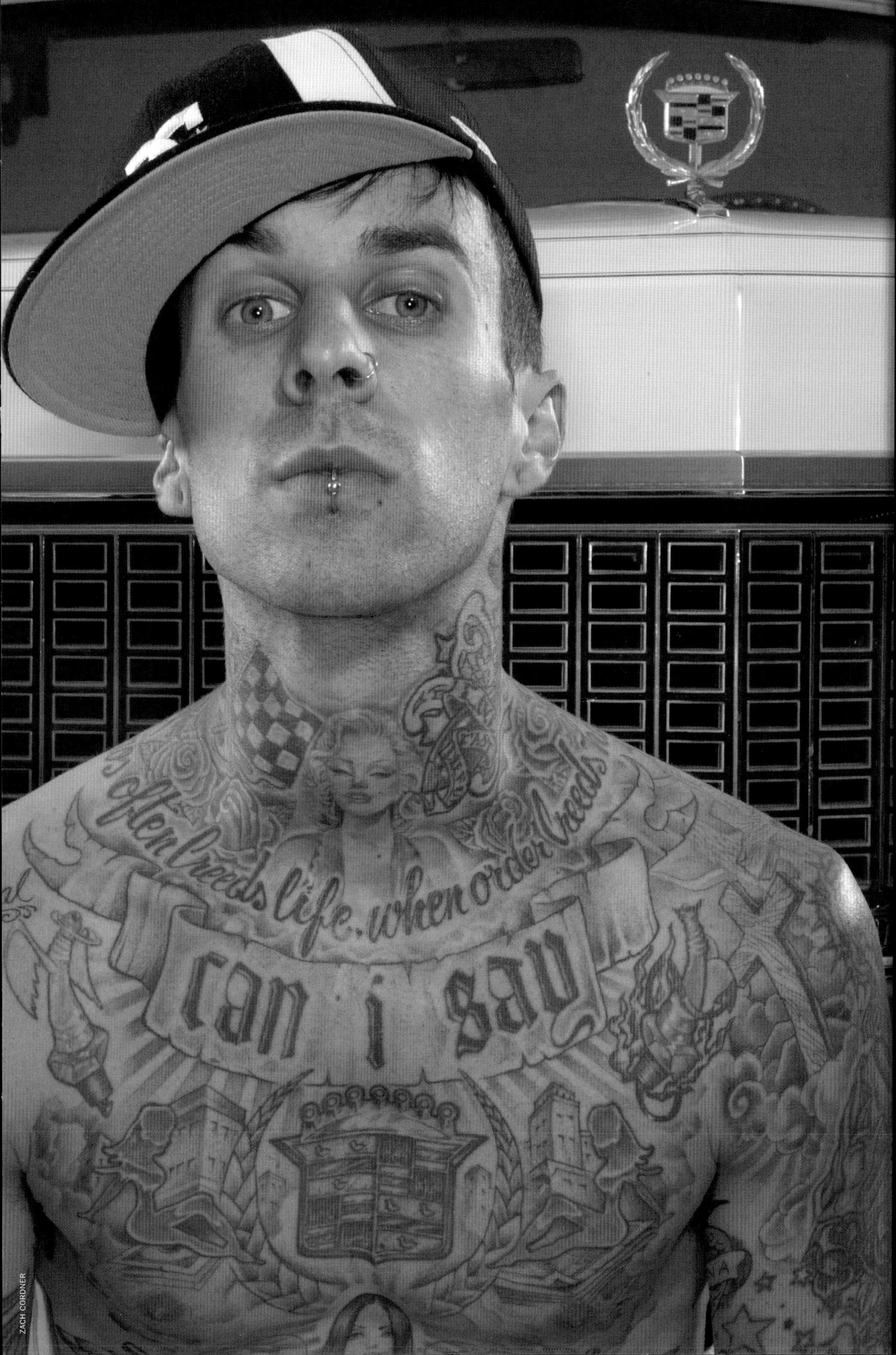

ONE PIECE AT A TIME

JOHNNY CASH'S "ONE PIECE AT A TIME," PENNED BY SONGWRITER WAYNE KEMP, HIT #1 ON BILLBOARD'S COUNTRY SINGLES CHART IN 1976. A COMEDIC DITTY DELIVERED IN CASH'S INIMITABLE STYLE, IT INVOLVES AN AUTOWORKER'S DETAILED PLAN TO BUILD AN IMPROVISED, HODGE-PODGE CADILLAC WORTH "AT LEAST A HUNDRED GRAND," BY SNEAK-ING PARTS OUT OF THE FACTORY "ONE PIECE AT A TIME" IN A BIG LUNCHBOX AND A "BUDDY'S MOBILE HOME." "YOU MIGHT SAY I WENT RIGHT UP TO THE FACTORY AND PICKED IT UP—IT WAS CHEAPER THAT WAY," CASH SANG.

SOME OF THE CAR'S BIZARRE "'49, '50, '51 …" FEATURES INCLUDE:

· HEADLIGHTS—TWO ON THE LEFT, ONE ON THE RIGHT—ALL THREE OF WHICH TURN ON WHEN THE SWITCH IS PULLED
· ONE TAILFIN
· THE OLDEST PARTS WERE FROM 1949, THE LATEST FROM THE EARLY '70S, INCLUDING A 1953 TRANSMISSION AND A 1973 ENGINE. THE CADILLAC'S POWERTRAIN IS FINALLY LINKED ONCE A FANCY "A-DAPTOR" KIT IS INSTALLED.
· THE "PSYCHO-BILLY CADILLAC'S" TITLE WEIGHED 60 POUNDS AND TOOK AN ENTIRE COURTHOUSE STAFF TO TYPE IT UP

CASH HIMSELF HAD A ONE-WEEK STINT AS A PUNCH-PRESS OPERATOR IN A PONTIAC FACTORY IN 1950.

THE TERM "ONE PIECE AT A TIME" IMMEDIATELY ENTERED THE AMERICAN LEXICON. HIGH SCHOOL FOOTBALL FIELDS, CIVIC AUDITORIUMS, AND ALL MANNER OF DREAMED-UP, WORTHY PROJECTS NOW HAD INSPIRATION WRITTEN INTO THEM. QUITE A NUMBER OF COMPOSITE 1949-73 SEDAN DEVILLES WERE CONSTRUCTED IN CASH'S HONOR. SOME SO IMPRESSED THE MAN IN BLACK THAT HE PERFORMED BENEFITS TO RAISE FUNDS NEEDED TO COMPLETE THEM.

Warren G., at home.

GM PRODUCT

The longest continuously manufactured car model in the United States is—believe it or not—the Chevrolet Suburban. That four-door, heavy-duty, beefed-up wagon *cum* truck was introduced in 1935, and GM's been cranking them out ever since. Yet, possibly only one pop or hip-hop song has included a reference to the Suburban: rapper Masta Ace Incorporated, as in, *You're in a 'Burban with ten woofers.*

But nearly 200 songs have otherwise romanticized Chevrolets, from Impalas and Corvettes to the classic mid-'50s Bel Airs (superbly referenced, although in error, by Joni Mitchell in "Raised on Robbery"—i.e., there was no "'57 Biscayne" to put in a ditch). Musicians as varied as Elton John, Iron Maiden, and Nils Lofgren have all sung about Chevys, as have, over the course of time, pop acts like Paul Revere & The Raiders ("SS 396") and Cake (*But when we're driving in my Malibu/It's easy to get right next to you*).

It's America, after all, and Americans love GM brands. Accordingly, there have also been paens to the Oldsmobile Rocket 88 (pages 26–27), the Buick Roadmaster (Steve Earle and Bruce Springsteen), and more recently, the Cadillac Escalade (Fabolous, and many others). Even GM's more recently acquired brand, Hummer, has a considerable number of admirers-in-song.

There's hardly a black American over 50 who doesn't remember their father owning or wanting to own a deuce-and-a-quarter—the 225-ci, four-door, smooth-riding, slab-sided Buick Electra 225 family cruiser—later celebrated in song by the likes of Prince (*In my deuce and a quarter, feelin' funky funky fine*) and Ry Cooder (*Well, I put you behind the wheel of a deuce-and-a-quarter, yes I did*).

In a social context far from Dinah Shore's mid-'50s white bread evocation of the brand (*Drive your Chevrolet through the USA/America's the greatest land of all*), yet with much the same respect for the product, rappers and hip-hoppers have taken particularly affectionately to one brand in the Chevy marque: the Impala. "This is for the ballas, the young shot callas/Nineteen-inch blades on the Impalas," raps E.S.G. More specifically, Lil' Rob defines the actual year of preference, *So watch-a/Jump in my six-three Impa-la.*

The defining circumstance concerning a GM brand being adopted by a rock band involved musicians Dick Wagner, Tony Carlucci, and Lenny Renda, all Brooklyn, New York, high-schoolers in the early '50s who needed a name for their new band. After rejecting dozens of titles, their final tag, *The Impalas*, came the day Lenny's father brought his new Chevrolet home.

ED HAMMEL HE TRAVELS IN A **RED CAVALIER**

PUT A HUNDRED FIFTY THOUSAND MILES ON IT THIS YEAR

DON'T YOU EVER THINK HE WONDERS

"WHAT AM I DOING OUT HERE?"

I SURE KNOW I DO, 'CUZ IT'S LONELY OUT THERE

OL' YELLER, OUT THERE

OUT IN THE BACK SEAT OF MY '60 CHEVY

FRIDAY   SHOW AT 8:30

Aug 5   Hanover's

BROKEN TEETH ☠ The ADDICTIONS ☠ BUTCHERWHITE

POSTER BY PERKINS • PRINT BY SLEEPY GIANT

BILLY PERKINS

THE CYRKLE "CAMARO" PAUL REVERE AND THE RAIDERS "SS 396"

SWINGING CHEVY CIRCLE

CREATED EXCLUSIVELY FOR CHEVROLET DEALERS BY
COLUMBIA SPECIAL PRODUCTS
A Service of Columbia Records
FREE... and available only at Chevrolet dealers

LITHO—U.S.A.

PAUL GRUSHKIN COLLECTION

THE IMPALAS
(I RAN ALL THE WAY HOME)
CONDUCTED by LEROY HOLMES

CUB 8003

CUB HIGH FIDELITY

U.S.A. 102

LET'S HAVE A PARTY

CALIFOR

EB 9811

THE CHEVELLES
MALA-BOO
BLUE CHEVELLE

BANGAR RECORDS

BARRY WICKHAM COLLECTION

SHE SWEAT, WET, GOT IT

GOIN' LIKE A TURBO 'VETTE

SIR MIX-A-LOT, BABY GOT BACK

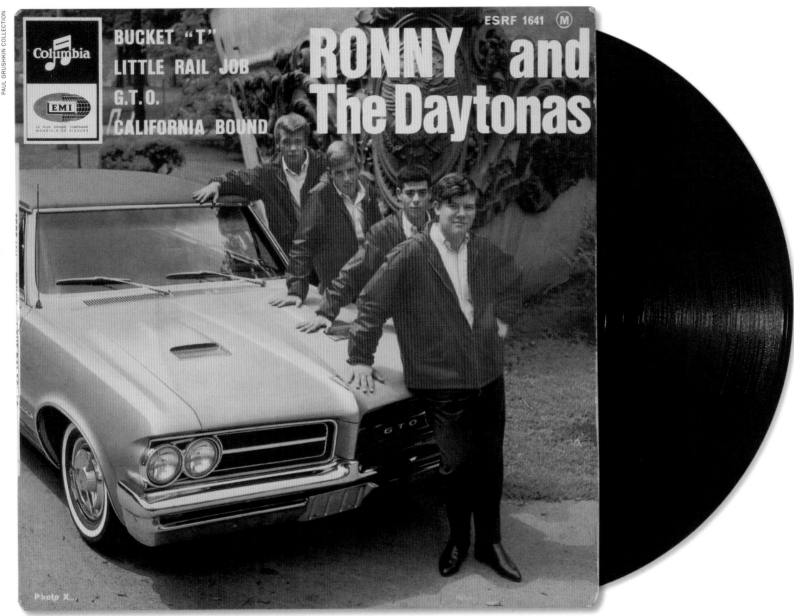

BUCKET "T"
LITTLE RAIL JOB
G.T.O.
CALIFORNIA BOUND

RONNY and The Daytonas

ESRF 1641 Ⓜ

Columbia
EMI
LA PLUS GRANDE COMPAGNIE
MONDIALE DE DISQUES

Photo X...

FRENCH EP

PONTIAC GTO

A muscle car, by the strictest definition, is an intermediate-size, performance-oriented model, powered by a large V8 engine at an affordable price, and in regular production. Examples include Chevrolet's Chevelle SS and Impala SS models; Dodge's Charger RT, Daytona, Super Bee and Demon; Ford's GT, Cobra, and Mustang GT, Mustang Mach 1, and Boss Mustang; Plymouth's 'Cuda, GTX, Road Runner, and Superbird; Oldsmobile's 442; and Pontiac's GTO, Firebird and Trans Am.

The start of the classic "muscle car" era is dated to the moment the 1964 Pontiac GTO went on sale—although the American love affair with V8 engines was already at least 32 years old (back to when the 1932 Ford, with the first affordable V8, was introduced).

What sold the GTO was a completely new attitude—a bigger V8, hood scoops (initially phony ones), the rumble of dual exhausts, a Hurst shifter, racy trim, and a name stolen from Ferrari. Not just any Ferrari either, but that which many consider the greatest front-engined production Ferrari of them all, the 1962 250 GTO. The three letters stood for "Gran Turismo Omologato," which, translated, meant "Grand Touring Homologation." |In other words, the Ferrari GTO was sold as a road car solely to qualify it for GT competition. Homologation referred to the formal process by which a car was accredited by the FIA (Federation Internationale de l'Automobile).

WIND IT UP, BLOW IT OUT, GTO

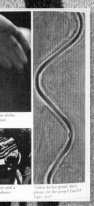

SCORCHED EARTH

IT WAS, SAID JIM WANGERS, THE INVENTOR OF THE PONTIAC GTO (AND THEREBY THE FATHER OF ALL MASS-PRODUCED AND MASS-MARKETED MUSCLE CARS), THE *AGE OF IDOLIZATION*, AN AGE WHEN "WE MADE ABSOLUTE GODS OUT OF OUR YOUNG PEOPLE." WANGERS WAS AN ADVERTISING MAN, NOT AN ENGINEER, AND THEREFORE PERHAPS BETTER ABLE TO SEE SOMETHING OUT THERE MOVING IN THE MARKET BEFORE ANYONE ELSE.

PONTIAC WAS BUILDING CARS THAT RAN STEADILY AND DELIVERED COMFORTABLE FAMILY TRANSPORTATION FOR DICK, JANE, DAD, AND MOM. BUT WANGERS KNEW THE STREETBOYS HAD BEEN FOOLING WITH HOT CARS FOR YEARS, SLAPPING BIG ENGINES IN FORDS AND CHEVYS. IN A MEMO TO JOHN DELOREAN, THEN OF PONTIAC, HE OUTLINED PLANS FOR A CAR THAT WOULD BE "THE FASTEST THING YOU COULD PUT YOUR HANDS ON."

"WE WANTED TO MAKE CERTAIN IT WAS FASTER THAN A CORVETTE," WANGERS RECALLED. PONTIAC'S BIGGEST ENGINE WAS PLUNKED INTO PONTIAC'S LIGHT TEMPEST BODY. TECHNICALLY, IT WAS ILLEGAL UNDER COMPANY GUIDELINES TO BUILD A STREET RACER, SO THE FIRST GTO CAME OUT IN NOVEMBER 1963 AS A 1964 TEMPEST WITH A GTO OPTION, NOT AS A MODEL IN ITSELF.

BUT THE OPTION WAS *INCREDIBLE*. WANGERS' BOYS CREATED AN ENTIRELY NEW MACHINE. IT WENT FROM 0 TO 60 MPH IN A PREPOSTEROUS 4.6 SECONDS AND IT RADICALLY ALTERED ACCESS TO THE ROAD AND THE MARKETING OF AUTOS IN AMERICA FOR THE NEXT 10 YEARS.

ACCORDING TO WANGERS, HE NEXT THOUGHT TO CONTACT AN EMERGING NASHVILLE-BASED GROUP CALLED RONNY & THE DAYTONAS ABOUT A BEACH BOYS–LIKE SONG HE HEARD THEY WERE WORKING ON, ABOUT A GTO. CENTERED AROUND SINGER-GUITARIST-SONGWRITER JOHN "BUCKY" WILKIN, THE DAYTONAS WERE BIRTHED BY NASHVILLE PRODUCER BILL JUSTIS WHO INSTRUCTED BUCKY TO TAKE ON A STAGE NAME (RONNY DAYTON) AND COME UP WITH A GROUP NAME (THE DAYTONAS) TO BEST ADVANCE THE RECORD. WILKIN SEEMS TO HAVE CARED LITTLE ABOUT PLAYING LIVE, AND, AFTER A SHORT TIME FRONTING A THROWN-TOGETHER COMBO FOR A FEW SELECT DATES, SIMPLY PUT TOGETHER A PHANTOM GROUP TO GO OUT AND HONOR TOUR COMMITMENTS.

WANGERS SAYS HE ACTUALLY HELPED TINKER WITH THE SONG, HELPED REWRITE THE LYRICS, AND AFTERWARDS "THOUGHT THE TIME WOULD BE WELL SPENT IF IT GOT PLAYED SOMEWHERE, ANYWHERE, BY ANYONE." HE AND THE DAYTONAS LUCKED OUT. LIKE THE CAR, "G.T.O." WAS AN INSTANT SUCCESS. IT STAYED ON THE CHARTS FOR 31 WEEKS, SELLING 1.2 MILLION COPIES. BETWEEN JUNE 1964 AND THE END OF 1968, THE SONG WAS PLAYED 7 MILLION TIMES ON THE RADIO.

UNWITTINGLY AT FIRST, THEN KNOWINGLY, THE PONTIAC PEOPLE HAD CREATED IN MOVING METALLIC SCULPTURE A PIECE OF THE AMERICAN DREAM. INCARNATE, THE MUSCLE CAR SPIT FIRE, SCORCHED THE EARTH WITH SCREAM OF RUBBER, ROARED IN PUBLIC, AND BESTOWED UPON EVERYMAN UNBELIEVABLE POWER TO PUT THE PEDAL TO HE METAL AND SHOW THE WORLD HIS TAIL.

"WHAT WAS IT THESE CARS PROVIDED?" WANGERS LATER RECALLED. "IT WAS AN OPPORTU-NITY FOR ANYBODY TO BE EQUAL TO ANYBODY ELSE. GET INTO THE CAR, AND THE POWER TO PUT ALMOST ANYONE DOWN WAS RIGHT UNDER YOUR FOOT. THERE WAS AN INCREDIBLE EMOTIONAL INVOLVEMENT WITH THESE CARS, JUST AS THERE WAS WITH ALL THE CAR SONGS. YOU COULD BE WHO YOU WANTED TO BE. YOU GOT TO BE THE REAL COOL GUY, THE GUY IN THE AD, AND WITH THE CHICKS ALL OVER YOU."

BEFORE THE BIG THREE BEGAN PHASING THEM OUT, WHEN POST-1973 GAS PRICES MADE DRIVING A CAR THAT GOT NO BETTER THAN 15 MILES PER GALLON IMPRACTICAL, MUSCLE CARS HAD STALKED THE STREETS FOR A SOLID DECADE. IN ITS 1958 DICK-AND-JANE STAGE, PONTIAC SOLD 245,000 CARS A YEAR. IN 1969, WITH ITS MUSCLE-CAR IMAGE, PONTIAC SOLD 934,000 CARS. IN 1967, YOU COULD BUY FOR STREET USE WHAT WAS PERHAPS THE ULTIMATE MUSCLE CAR—A SHELBY COBRA STUFFED WITH A 500-HORSEPOWER FORD V8. IT COST $7,000, ABOUT THE PRICE THESE DAYS OF A USED TOYOTA WITH A TAPE DECK.

— BOB FRUMP

PHILADELPHIA INQUIRER, 1981

I WENT DOWN 13 HIGHWAY, DRIVIN' A
OH YOU KNOW I WAS DRIVIN' SO FAST, BABY I COULDN'T HARDLY SEE THE ROAD

BRAND NEW V8 FORD

MUDDY WATERS, THIRTEEN HIGHWAY

The '50 FORD!

new...
ner

1955 FORD
with Trigger-Torque
POWER!

MUSTANG!
the zip-codes
Mustang Rumble
WILD, WILD MUSTANG   Red Line ⊕ Dear Henry Ford
THREE-WINDOW COUPE   Classy Lotus Chassis
FANCY FILLY FROM DETROIT CITY   Speed Shift
                           Super Fine 289
RUN, LITTLE MUSTANG   Rally-Pak ⊕ Wild, Wild Woodie

THE CRYSTALS
TWIST UPTOWN

UPTOWN ⊛ THERE'S NO OTHER (LIKE MY BABY)
FRANKENSTEIN TWIST ⊛ GEE WHIZ, LOOK AT HIS EYES (TWIST)
OH YEAH, MAYBE BABY ⊛ PLEASE HURT ME
I LOVE YOU EDDIE ⊛ ANOTHER COUNTRY, ANOTHER WORLD
WHAT A NICE WAY TO TURN SEVENTEEN ⊛ NO ONE EVER TELLS YOU
ON BROADWAY

"Hey Little Cobra"
songwriter Carol
Connors.

CAROL CONNORS AND
CARROLL SHELBY.

HEY LITTLE COBRA

The Rip Chords were primarily a surf-frat studio band in the style of Gary Usher's Four Speeds. They began as the duo of Ernie Bringas and Phil Stewart, who auditioned for Columbia Records' innovative producer, Terry Melcher, the youngest staff producer in the label's history and son of singer Doris Day. Bringas left the group in early 1964 to join a seminary, around the time that Melcher and a young songwriter named Carol Connors were discussing Melcher recording "Hey Little Cobra." To create the sound he had in mind for "Cobra," Melcher decided to complement Stewart and reassemble the Rip Chords with two additional members, Richie Rotkin and Arnie Marcus, as well as the famous Wrecking Crew studio band, but primarily using his own voice and that of his partner, session musician (and future Beach Boy) Bruce Johnston, who had a fantastic Beach Boys–like falsetto. Melcher would be to the Rip Chords what Brian Wilson was to the Beach Boys.

With the success of "Hey Little Cobra" (#4 on Billboard's pop singles chart), Melcher and Johnston now fully took over the lead and key backup harmony reins in the studio. With a top-five single under their belt, naturally an album was called for, this time with Melcher and Johnston dominating the action and with Bringas rejoining the group, although not touring as the Rip Chords (that being the responsibility of Rotkin and Marcus). One of their best but most underrated songs was "The Queen," the lead vocal about a girl given to putting on airs and driving around in a Sting Ray sung by Melcher's girlfriend, Jackie DeShannon.

The LP yielded other singles, including "Trophy Machine" and a follow-up album, this time without Bringas, produced "Three Window Coupe."

What most people remember about the Rip Chords is their classic mid-'60s California sound, never so vibrant as when all four lead voices—Melcher, Stewart, Bringas, and Johnston—were combined. Melcher and Johnston also recorded car songs under the name "Bruce and Terry," and Melcher himself went on to produce records for The Byrds and Paul Revere & The Raiders.

Carol Connors and her brother, Marshall, actually co-wrote "Hey Little Cobra." Connors had just sung her "Yum Yum Yamaha" under the name Carol Connors & The Cycles, and would subsequently sing, with her sister Cheryl, "Go Go G.T.O." Connors is especially proud of her work on "Cobra," telling this author, "It's considered maybe the most important hot rod song ever associated with the Ford Motor Company. Lee Iacocca was head of racing for Ford at the time when Carroll Shelby came up with the Cobra concept. You could say it was the forerunner of the GT40 which went on to win Le Mans.

"I was not at the recording session, but I'd taken the record to Terry Melcher who was the head of A&R for Columbia," Carol continued. "My brother really wasn't much involved, but I wrote it because Carroll asked me to write it. I'd smashed my ex-boyfriend's car in the front—it was a Bristol—and he wanted to see if they could put a Cobra front on a Bristol back. Carroll told me, 'If you write a song about my car and it goes to the Top Ten we'll work something out—you'll go to Le Mans,' which I did. Then I got a Cobra from Carroll. Actually, I had three of them. Each would be worth over half a million dollars today, but I don't own them any more."

THE WICKED PICKETT

It's been written that Wilson Pickett (1941–2006) had a voice of "sheer, unsettling power." Pickett left his home in Prattville, Alabama, in 1955 to live with his father in Detroit. There, he formed a gospel group called the Violinaires that accompanied Sam Cooke, the Soul Stirrers, and the Swan Silvertones on church tours across the country. When Cooke and Aretha Franklin began singing secular music, Pickett was persuaded to do the same. His first major break came when he was invited to join The Falcons in early 1959, where he met Sir Mack Rice.

But not until he was sent off by Atlantic Records to Memphis in 1965 did Pickett find the right situation for creating hits. As part of an agreement between Atlantic and Stax Records, using musicians from the Stax house band, Booker T. & the M.G.'s, Pickett unleashed the incomparable soul classic "In the Midnight Hour."

In early 1966, producer Jerry Wexler and Book T. guitarist Steve Cropper took Pickett to Fame studios in nearby Muscle Shoals, Alabama, where he recorded "Mustang Sally," "Land of 1000 Dances," and "Funky Broadway." That year, the Rice-penned "Mustang Sally" peaked at #23 on the Billboard pop charts. His combination of earthy, gospel urgency and sexual swagger earned him the nickname "the wicked Pickett." As one critic later reflected, "'Mustang Sally' is one of the most urgent singles ever released. Staccato horn parts and the surging bass lines is [*sic*] key to the sound, but it's Pickett's sweaty vocal style that makes the record hot—every note he sings is propulsive and dirty raw, you can hear that even when he was working with session guitarist Duane Allman covering The Beatles' ballad 'Hey Jude.'"

"Style, and timing," Pickett once said to writer Gerri Hirshey, "that's something you have to have inside you. You just *know*, okay? That's how I got to be known as a screamer. And once you get known for doing something special, well, now *that* would be your hood ornament."

Pickett seemingly was never photographed with a Ford Mustang, in 1965 or anytime subsequently. He was, however, extremely proud of his Rolls-Royces.

WILSON PICKETT

WE WERE MAKIN' THUNDERBIRDS

BOB SEGER

JACK VARTOOGIAN/FRONT ROW

MAKING THUNDERBIRDS

Bob Seger was born in 1945 in Detroit, Michigan, where his father was a bandleader who worked in an auto plant to support his wife and two children. When Bob was ten, his father left for California in search of success he never achieved. At night, Seger stayed up late listening to Wilson Pickett, Little Richard, Otis Redding, and other R&B musicians on a transistor radio. His favorite album was James Brown's *Live at the Apollo*.

When Seger discovered rock & roll, he began staying out all night with friends, their cars circled in a farmer's field, listening to music on the car radios. He formed a band in junior high school and by the eleventh grade was playing Michigan bars three nights a week. For nearly 40 years he was among the hardest working musicians in rock. One example: in the early '70s, he and his band drove 25 hours to Florida, played three straight nights with no place to stay, and drove 25 hours back. Seger says he considered himself more a driver than a singer at the time. He has since sold nearly 50 million albums.

"Making Thunderbirds" was a well-regarded song on his 1982 LP, *The Distance*. He had worked at General Motors for half a day, putting rubber around windshield glass, but he cut his hands so he quit. He worked for Ford for three weeks. "I was so poor, I didn't have a car, and I was hitchhiking to work," Seger told journalist Timothy White. "For a long time I had wanted to write a song about the production line in Detroit and make it a blues song, 'cause I remembered how blue I was. I'd become a robot, and nobody would ever talk to me at work because of the plant noise. You couldn't use earplugs because you had to hear bells for when the line would stop.

"I first wrote 'Thunderbirds' around 1978, during the time of my album *Stranger in Town*. I had only the first verse and parts of the second. When I got into it this last time, I wrote the third verse about the plants being closed and people out of work."

Seger's great revenge on Detroit came with the song "Like a Rock," also the title of the LP released in April 1986 that reached #3 on Billboard's Top 200 album chart. Seger spent four months mixing the album, the first time he was in the studio for every part of the creative process. Seger noted that he "honed the limiting on the mix, so it would leap out of the compression of the average car radio, like a monster." Chevrolet's Truck Division picked up "Like a Rock" for years of memorable radio and television ads. Yet the song (which itself charted at #12) is really about a man remembering when he was lean, strong, and unencumbered, said Seger: "It expresses my feeling that the best years of your life are in your late teens when you have no special commitments and no 'career.' It's your last blast of fun before heading into the cruel, real world. I wrote it in 1984, several months after *The Distance* tour ended. It was a reexamination of my unguarded days in this business, when ten years of a $7,000 annual salary and a lifestyle of traveling a hundred thousand miles in a station wagon were something I just enjoyed doing instead of a conventional day gig."

Except for the direct references in "Making Thunderbirds," Seger mostly chose to use cars—as did his friend Bruce Springsteen—as metaphors or transitional elements in songwriting. That would include the '60 Cadillac in "Get Out of Denver" (off the LP *Seven*, released in 1974) and the engine moaning in "Turn the Page" (off the LP *Back in '72*, released in 1973). The latter song was also covered by Metallica on their *Garage Inc.* album. The lyrics are about a rocker's life on the road and Metallica's Lars Ulrich was transfixed by the song one night while driving across the Golden Gate Bridge to San Francisco.

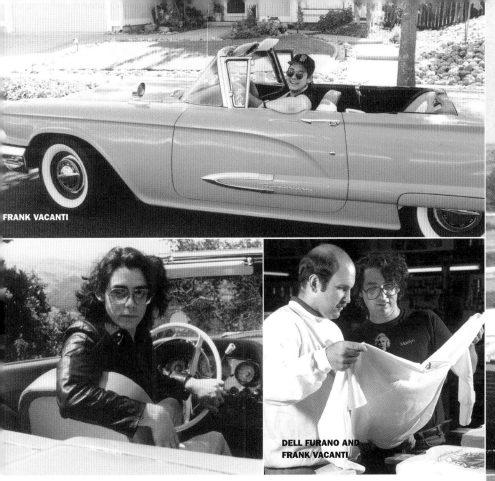

FRANK VACANTI

DELL FURANO AND FRANK VACANTI

DENISE FERRI COLLECTION (BOTH)

HEAD OF PRODUCTION

Frank Vacanti holds nearly all of rock & roll merchandising's prized T-shirt screenprinting records. As head of production for the legendary Winterland Productions (now Signatures Network) based in San Francisco, Vacanti has these marks to his credit:

Most T-shirts printed
- in a day
- in a week
- in a month
- in a year
- for a tour

Vacanti's pictured here with Winterland and Signatures President Dell Furano while the company was working for Springsteen, Madonna, Ozzy, New Kids on the Block, Led Zeppelin, and nearly 100 others. Vacanti bought his prized '59 Thunderbird (known as the second-generation "squarebird") from Boz Scaggs' road manager in 1979. As the photos show, it was re-painted Indian Turquoise early on, but he now has it restored to its factory spec Wimbledon White. For several years Vacanti also had on the console a pre-8-track, early-'60s, upside-down 45-single changer, pictured elsewhere in this book. He used the radio's channel 8 as its amplifier to play tunes from his legendary archive.

PICKIN' UP MY COOL FRIENDS

"BLACK AND WHITE THUNDERBIRD" WAS THE A-SIDE OF "RONNIE IS MY LOVER" (1959), WHICH WAS THE DELICATES' ONLY NATIONAL HIT (#105 ON THE BILLBOARD POP CHART). IT IS, HOWEVER, TO THIS DAY, WELL-REMEMBERED IN THE NEW YORK–NEW JERSEY METROPOLITAN AREA, WHERE LEGENDARY WINS 1010 DJ MURRAY THE K FEATURED THE GROUP ON HIS SWINGIN' SOIREE SHOW.

THE DELICATES WERE THE BELLEVILLE, NEW JERSEY, TRIO OF DENISE FERRI (WHO SANG THE FAMOUS LOW "YEAH'S" ON "THUNDERBIRD"), PEGGY SANTIGLIA, AND ARLEEN LANZOTTI. SANTIGLIA LATER JOINED THE ANGELS, WHO HAD A #1 HIT WITH "MY BOYFRIEND'S BACK" IN 1963. THE GIRLS, FRIENDS SINCE THE AGE OF EIGHT, FORMED THE GROUP WHEN THEY WERE FRESHMEN AT BELLEVILLE HIGH SCHOOL AND TOOK THE NAME "THE DELICATES" FROM A DELICATESSEN OWNED BY ONE OF THE GIRLS' FATHERS. THE IRRESISTIBLY CHEERFUL "BLACK AND WHITE THUNDERBIRD" WAS WRITTEN BY THE GIRLS THEMSELVES AND IS NOW REGARDED AS A CORNERSTONE OF GIRL-GROUP "ATTITUDE," LIKELY HAVING INFLUENCED ANOTHER NEW YORK GIRL GROUP, THE SHANGRI-LAS, WHO SANG "LEADER OF THE PACK."

FERRI AND SANTIGLIA LATER HELPED WRITE AND ARRANGE THE BACKING VOCALS FOR LOU CHRISTIE'S 1965 #1 HIT "LIGHTNING STRIKES," WHICH CHRISTIE FOLLOWED UP WITH "IF MY CAR COULD ONLY TALK."

OH WELL, I RODE AROUND, AROUND THE TOWN

I RODE UP THE STREET AND THEN I CAME DOWN

IN MY BLACK AND WHITE THUNDERBIRD, IT'S GRAND

BLACK AND WHITE THUNDERBIRD, YEAH MAN

BILLY MURE, DENISE FERRI, PEGGY SANTIGLIA & ARLEEN LANZOTTI/ (SAXON MUSIC CORP. (BMI)

BACK IN THE GARAGE WITH MY BULLSHIT DETECTOR
CARBON MONOXIDE MAKING SURE IT'S EFFECTIVE
PEOPLE RINGING UP MAKING OFFERS FOR MY LIFE

BUT I JUST WANNA STAY IN THE GARAGE ALL NIGHT
WE'RE A GARAGE BAND
WE COME FROM GARAGELAND

THE CLASH, GARAGELAND

BLACK FLAG, REDONDO BEACH, CALIFORNIA, 1982

ROAD RUNNER
Rock Re-invention

Punk rock is exemplified by strongly anti-establishment bands emerging in the U.S. and U.K. in the mid- to late-'70s, led by the Ramones, the Sex Pistols, The Clash, X, The Damned, Black Flag, Fear, and hundreds of others. Punk—and by extension later developments in hardcore, alt, indie, and even roots rock—is all about rejecting bloat and excess, and in effect, "living in the modern world," a phrase often associated with proto-punk rocker Jonathan Richman, whose band was the Modern Lovers.

Penelope Spheeris' 1981 movie, *The Decline of Western Civilization* was *the* dead-on portrait of the original raw and physical Los Angeles punk scene. Many feel both the Talking Heads' (led by David Byrne) and Jonathan Richman's often absurdist, reductionist commentary captured the East Coast intellectual side of the scene just as effectively. Wrote "Namgev" in a 2004 Internet post, looking back, "if you've got the memory of being toasted, blasting down Route 128 out by the powerlines in your brother's '70 Nova, then that was you, pounding the dashboard, shouting "Driving by the Stop 'n' Shop with the … RADIO ON!"

Richman's 1973 "Roadrunner" (in a deft association with the Plymouth muscle car) spoke for an original generation X, the first to see a major change in the weather. Punk rock spelled rejection for the post-Woodstock era of sold-out stadiums, pampered rock stars, and swollen bank accounts. Punk (along with the contemporary introduction of the polyurethane wheel) also helped popularize skateboarding, an essential means of personal transport and the basis for street-wise confrontational gamesmanship.

PAUL IMAGINE/INSURGENT ARTS

Punk was necessarily DIY—do it yourself. That meant hauling a band's gear by van, not by a caravan of semi-trucks with two dozen roadies doing the heavy lifting. One of the all-time great rock photographs (facing page) is of Black Flag and their ailing van at a Redondo Beach, California gig in 1982. The photo was taken by Glen E. Friedman, renowned for his documentation of the So-Cal skateboarding scene of the late '70s and early '80s, and hardcore and straightedge punk of the same period. Friedman also created definitive portraits of seminal hip-hop acts like Run-DMC, Public Enemy (page 216), and the Beastie Boys. In his book, *Get in the Van,* Black Flag frontman Henry Rollins later wrote that Friedman "captured the essence of Black Flag, endlessly pushing on one of our broken vans." The pushers, from left, are Chuck Dukowski, Greg Ginn, Chuck Biscuits, Dez Cadena, Rollins, and Davo.

While punk was at its creative peak, artist Shawn Kerri made wickedly incisive flyers for Los Angeles bands like the Circle Jerks and Germs. Her "Skank Kid" archetype illustration appeared everywhere, even as tattoos. She also had a lifelong interest in everything automotive before her untimely death. "Kerri was a major contributor to *CARtoons* magazine, which was kind of like if *MAD* had only been about automobiles, what with all their hot rod, off-roading, drag racing, and Corvette- and muscle-car themed features," said fellow artist Nolen Strals. "I learned so much about cars from Kerri and from her contemporaries like George Trosley (with his "How to Draw [insert car type here]" section). So you can imagine how cool it was a few years later to find out she was so caught up in the punk scene at the same time, especially when I got so heavy into it myself."

FOUND ON ROAD DEAD

MOTORAMA IS (A) AN ITALIAN TWO- AND SOMETIMES THREE-PIECE RIOT GRRRRRL BAND; (B) A TRUE-TO-PUNK NOISE-ROCK BAND FROM VANCOUVER, CANADA; OR (C) A FAMOUS AUTO SHOW STAGED BY GENERAL MOTORS FROM 1949 TO 1961. THE ANSWER … ALL OF THE ABOVE.

NEITHER THE ITALIAN OR CANADIAN MOTORAMA BANDS LIKELY BASED THEIR NAME ON THE AUTO SHOW WHICH DREW OVER TEN MILLION VISITORS DURING ITS RUN. THE SHOW DEBUTED SOME OF GM'S MOST MEMORABLE EXPERIMENTAL AND LIMITED-PRODUCTION CARS.

"OUR MUSIC IS STRIPPED DOWN, INTENSE, AND ENERGETIC, LIKE MOTORHEAD, BLACK FLAG, AND AC/DC," WROTE THE CANADIANS ON THEIR WEBSITE. "WE'VE BEEN COMPARED TO SHELLAC, JESUS LIZARD, THE MELVINS, AND DRIVE LIKE JEHU. AND, WE'RE 100% DIY—WE DO ALL OUR OWN BOOKING, RECORDING, GRAPHIC DESIGN, DRIVING, ROADY-ING . . . EVERYTHING."

MANY COMMENTS ABOUT THE CANADIAN MOTORAMA HAVE AUTOMOTIVE REFERENCES. IN THE 'ZINE *GEORGIA STRAIGHT*, SHAWN CONNER NOTED, "MOTORAMA DELIVERS BUCKETS OF NOISE WITH THE SUBTLETY OF A ROAD-REPAIR CREW." AMANDA AIKMAN, IN *PICCADILLY PUB*, SAID OF THE BAND'S STAGE SHOW, "IT WAS LIKE PUTTING YOUR HEAD IN A CAR-COMPACTOR."

FYI, "FOUND ON THE ROAD DEAD" IS ONE OF MOTORAMA'S BEST-LOVED SONGS. THE LAST LINE IS SUNG, *STAY OUT OF MY WAY/USE YOUR F***IN HEAD/DON'T CUT ME OFF OR YOU'LL BE FOUND ON THE ROAD DEAD.*

"I was a junior in high school, and I went to a buddy's house and this song came on MTV," says Dale Earnhardt, Jr. "We was gittin' ready to go do some shit, and he's like, 'Man, dude, this song is kickass! Let's just sit here and listen to it 'fore we leave.' And I sit down, and man, when it was over I was just fuckin' blown away. It was "Teen Spirit" by Nirvana. It fit my emotions. I was tired of listenin' to my parents. I was tired of livin' at home. I didn't know what I was gonna do, I didn't have any direction. The fact that Kurt Cobain could scream into that mike like that gave me a sense of relief. And the guitar riffs, and the way Dave Grohl played the drums? It was awesome." Dale was, that moment long ago, pulled from the good-ol'-boy path and rebaptized by rock & roll.

He went out and bought Nirvana's *Nevermind*. "I couldn't really get anybody else to dig Nirvana like I dug it," he remembers, "and I never heard nobody else listenin' to it in the high school parking lot the way I did. But I didn't care. I'd just sit there and turn it up." Nirvana led to Pearl Jam, which led to Smash Mouth, Tupac, Third Eye Blind, Moby, Mystikal, Busta Rhymes, and Primus.

"(When I got) my driver's license, I was able to buy music and listen to it on my own and hear the words, and think, 'Man, I never thought about that.' I never really was rebellious against my parents. I never really thought the government was fucked up. I never really paid much attention to the schools suckin'. Up until I was 16, I thought every cop up and down the road was

just happy and glee, and now you hear these songs and you're like, 'Is *that* the case? Is *that* what's goin' on?' You don't learn from anywhere else, until then."

When not working with his NASCAR team or fuckin' off at home, Junior can be found raisin' hell in one of his cars, as in peelin' the tires, every gear *wide-ass open* (read: goin' real fast). He's got a Corvette he won that he almost never drives. He's got a Chevy Impala with a global-positioning system, a VCR, and TV screens in the front and back. He's got a hulking red four-door Chevy pickup truck with a monster stereo system, and if you lift the back seats, on top of where the bass amps are hidden, there's this skull-and-cross-bones design that Skippy from Freeman's Car Stereo etched in there without Junior even askin'. And then there's the breathtaker: a mint-condition, midnight-blue 1969 Camaro with an oversize finger-thin steering wheel and a gearshift shaped like a bridge and a top-of-the-line Alpine stereo. The engine rumbles and gurgles and practically drowns out the music, but the ride is cool, and he turns *Dr. Dre 2001* up way loud. "I like Dr. Dre," Junior says. "He's got attitude. He enjoys success. He's maintained his coolness and not turned into a big jerk."

Then Junior pulls back on the shifter and says, "Check this out." The engine seems to constrict slowly, tightening like a coil, roaring and snarling as if it's angry at us, and then, after three slow seconds of build, the engine growling louder all the time, it reaches 2,500 rpm and there's a loud *pop!* like a gun, and we slingshot off, leaping in a millisecond from 40 miles per hour to 80-plus, and suddenly we're flying past cows and tractors and horses, and the malevolent funk of Dr. Dre is booming out the window. It sounds so alien in Junior's Waltons-ish country town, like music from another planet. But Junior is cool with both.

—Touré
Rolling Stone,
May 11, 2000

Dale Earnhardt Jr.

BIG BLOCK ROCK 'N' ROLL MUSCLE! POWERED BY

NASHVILLE

PUSSY

2005! ON TOUR NOW 2005!

FRI. 2/25 JACKSONVILLE, FL - JACK RABBITS • SAT. 2/26 TAMPA, FL - MASQUERADE • THURS. 3/17 NEW ORLEANS, LA - TWIROPA
SAT. 3/19 AUSTIN, TX - TWO SHOWS! AUSTIN MUSIC HALL ROLLER DERBY (AFTERNOON) & THE CONTINENTAL SXSW
(EVENING SHOW) • TUES. 3/22 HOUSTON, TX - THE CONTINENTAL • WED. 3/23 LITTLE ROCK, AR - STICKY FINGERS
THURS. 3/24 NASHVILLE, TN - MERCY LOUNGE • FRI. 3/25 KNOXVILLE, TN - BLUE CAT'S • SAT. 3/26 RALEIGH, NC - MARTIN ST. MUSIC HALL

STAINBOY (GREG REINEL)

©05-03 ©2005 A STAINBOY VICIOUS IMAGE • WWW.STAINBOYREINEL.COM   WWW.EAGLEROCKENT.COM   PRINTED AT DIESEL FUEL • WWW.DIESELFUELPRINTS.COM

San Pedro, California, is a gritty, blue-collar port south of Los Angeles, known in rock & roll as the home of the Minutemen, a pivotal band in the So-Cal punk scene of the late '70s to mid-'80s. Fronted by singer/guitarist D. Boon (who died in a tour van accident in 1985) and anchored by bassist Mike Watt and drummer George Hurley—three very gifted musicians and famously approachable guys—they destroyed many boundaries during the punk era. It was the Minutemen, along with bands such as SST label mates Black Flag, Hüsker Dü, Sonic Youth, and Dinosaur Jr. that helped establish the nationwide indie rock network of the 1980s and revitalize rock & roll in the process.

Boon, like his bandmates, never fronted and always looked the part of the working-class rocker, but he was confident and assertive in his upper-end-focused lead guitar work. Watt sounded more like Jaco Pastorius than, say, Glen Matlock or Dee Dee Ramone, and Hurley was lauded as one of the tightest drummers in rock. Punk fans loved the Minutemen for their attitude and social commentary, and for their minimalist, one- to three-minute songs (hence their name); progressive rockers loved them for their musicianship and experimentation (incorporating into their work jazz, funk, folk, country, spoken-word poetry, and, naturally, punk, not to mention respectful covers of Creedence Clearwater Revival, Van Halen, Blue Öyster Cult, and even Steely Dan.

The Minutemen's masterpiece was 1984's double album, *Double Nickels on the Dime*, which began with the ignition of a car engine ("D.'s Car Jam"). The title itself stood for "55 mph on I-10" (not to be confused with L.A.'s Harbor Freeway, the I-110 that terminates in San Pedro). Western I-10 begins in Santa Monica and ends southeast of downtown L.A; it's one of the busiest freeways in the world (as one of the southernmost continental traverses, actually winds up in Jacksonville, Florida). The I-10 also defined the world in which the Minutemen traveled, to gig after punk gig in the L.A. Basin.

As with his bass guitar, Mike Watt, the van driver piloted the Minutemen. "With bass you're felt more than you're heard," Watt once told Dan Simon and Paul Rosenberg of *altweeklies.com*. "Guitars are like textures. Bass is the driving force," added Watt, who has literally been driving for the 20-plus years since Boon's death, first with fIREHOSE, then with Porno for Pyros, J Mascis + The Fog, and, most recently, the reformed Stooges.

Watt has had a fondness for the Ford Econoline; hauling his more recent bands' gear, he drove a 1990 E-250 model, nicknamed "the Boat," more than a quarter-million miles before replacing it with a white—always white—2005 E-350. A 2005 film about the Minutemen was entitled *We Jam Econo*, both in acknowledgement of the role the van played in their touring, and because their approach to music was self-described as "jammin' econo," keeping things short and to the point. "Punk teaches you self-reliance, and being in the driver's seat is just that," Watt has been known to say.

In 2000, Watt, as administrator of the Minutemen's publishing, allowed the automaker Volvo to use the D. Boon instrumental, "Love Dance" (from *Double Nickels*), in a television commercial. Watt was motivated by generosity—Boon's royalties were paid to his father who was ill with emphysema. To Watt, D. Boon was simply helping his father from beyond the grave.

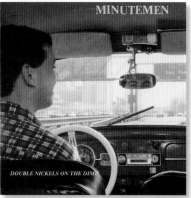

"The Internet is an extension of those old ethics that was early punk," Watt told *Londonist* magazine in 2005, "like being on an indie label, touring in your own van. Punk didn't die, it just changed, manifested into new forms. It's still about empowerment. So yes, that's why I still like driving out into the world, pulling up at the next club. People can see you're real."

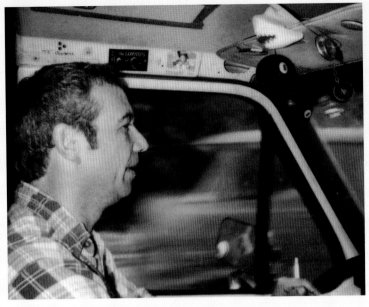

Mike Watt in Econoline

MATT BYLOOS

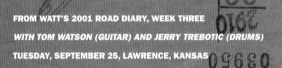

I LET MY GUYS SLEEP IN AS LONG AS THEY WANT, LAWRENCE IS ONLY THREE OR SO HOURS AWAY AND WE BAIL WHEN THEY'RE READY. ACROSS THE MISSOURI RIVER INTO IOWA AND DOWN THE I-29 TOWARDS KANSAS CITY. WE STOP TO GAS/CHOW (SAME THING?) AND I SIT IN THE BOAT TO DOWN A PIMENTO CHEESE SANDWICH AND SOME HARD BOILED EGGS WHILE TOM AND JER SHOVEL AT THE FILLING STATION'S RESTAURANT. FROM THERE, WE TURN THE BOAT STARBOARD AND HEAD WEST ON THE KANSAS TURNPIKE. WE'RE IN LAWRENCE BY THREE. I GO DIRECTLY TO THAT OUTDOORS STORE I FIGURE I CAN GET A SLEEPING BAG AND FIND ONE THAT'S SUPPOSED TO KEEP YOU WARM DOWN TO BELOW FREEZING. I RETURN TO THE CLUB WE'RE PLAYING, THE _BOTTLE-NECK_, AND SAY HI TO BIG AL, WHO HAS A MOHAWK THIS TIME AND JACKIE. I GO UPSTAIRS TO THE HEAVILY, HEAVILY GRAFFITIED DRESSING ROOM AND PLOP DOWN ON THE MOST DISGUSTING FUTON EVER. HOW MANY, MANY STAINS ARE HERE, I WONDER? I CHIMP DIARY INTO THE 'PUTER AND WAIT FOR SOUNDCHECK. AMANDA, TONIGHT'S BOSS, BRINGS CHIPS AND SOME REALLY HOT SALSA. TOM JOINS ME IN HEATING UP THE INSIDES GOOD W/THIS STUFF. AARON, THE SOUNDMAN, DOES A QUICK, ONE SONG SOUNDCHECK. I LIKE IT THAT WAY. I SIGN A CAT NAMED DAVE'S LEFT-HANDED BASS. ANYTHING TO GET CATS WORKING THEIR MACHINES MORE TO GET SOMETHING TO COME FROM THE HEART.

BARGAIN MUSIC IS W/US AGAIN TONIGHT AND IT'S GOOD TO SEE THEM. THERE'S TWO OTHER BANDS TOO: THE URCHIN CATS AND A LOCAL, _FIVE MINUTE FROG_. I GO TO THE BACK OF THE BOAT TO TEST THE NEW BAG OUT AND KONK. I WAKE RIGHT BEFORE SHOWTIME, DAMN IT'S PERT-NEAR MIDNIGHT - THE BAG WORKS GREAT! I TALK TO B-HILL OF THE URCHINS AND ASK THEM TO GIVE US A LITTLE MORE TIME, CLEARING THE STAGE EARLIER TO START ON TIME. ESPECIALLY ON A WORK/SCHOOL NIGHT. I TELL HIM NO DISRESPECT TO THEM, JUST LET'S HELP EACH OTHER OUT HERE W/THIS... . I'M READY TO GO AND WE'RE OFF. THE BAND PLAYS SHARP AND TIGHT - GREAT. ALEX, THE MONITOR CAT, DOES REALLY WELL W/GETTING MY VOICE SO I CAN HEAR IT - THANK YOU, ALEX. WE DO A GOOD SET AND IT'S PROBABLY THE BEST SOUND I'VE HEARD ANY OF MY BANDS ON THIS STAGE - FOR SOME REASON IT CAN BE A TOUGH COOKIE. THE CROWD IS REALLY SWEET AND HAS US BACK FOR AN ENCORE DESPITE THE LATENESS. I'M VERY GRATEFUL, TO MY GUYS TOO. I SHAKE MORE THAN A COUPLE BASS PLAYERS' HANDS. THAT'S A GOOD THING TOO... . WE PACK UP AND I SAY GOODBYE TO ALL THE GOOD PEOPLE AT THE ...NECK AND WE TAKE KEVIN IN THE BOAT W/US TO HIS PAD, WE'RE STAYING THERE TONIGHT ON HIS INVITE.

USUALLY THERE'S LOTS OF FOLKS WAITING FOR US WHEN WE GET THERE BUT THIS TIME THERE'S NO ONE. KEVIN'S GOT SOME OF THAT POTATO AND SAUSAGE STUFFED IN PIG'S STOMACH AND I CHOW A LITTLE OF THAT. JER CHOWS A LOT. I DON'T REALLY LIKE CHOWING MUCH AFTER A GIG, IT CAN BE A BAD HABIT AND ADD TO "BELLING" (GROWING ONE'S SELF SPHERICALLY). [KEVIN] GIVES ME TWO PEARS TOO BUT I'LL WAIT TO DO THESE IN THE MORNING. HARDWARE FLOORS IN THE LIVING ROOM HERE SO I KONK RIGHT ON THE COUCH I'M SITTING ON. THERE'S THIS GREAT, FLUFFY LONGHAIRED CAT THAT HOPS UP ON MY CHEST. TONS AND TONS OF PURRS. I GIVE HER RUBS - SHE LOVES IT - WHAT A GREAT DISPOSITION. EVEN W/THE LIGHTS OFF AND MASK DOWN, THE SENSATION OF FINGERS KNEADING FUR IS CALMING. I THINK OF THE MAN, MY CAT OF SEVENTEEN YEARS THAT PASSED AWAY TWO SUMMERS AGO. THERE, GOOD MEMORIES AND I PASS EASILY INTO A STATE OF KONK AND REST.

WEDNESDAY, SEPTEMBER 26, ST. LOUIS, MO

OFF INTO THE BOAT AND BYE TO KEVIN - THANK YOU, BRO. WE'RE BACK ON THE KANSAS TURNPIKE AND HEADING EAST TOWARDS MISSOURI. INTO KANSAS CITY AND ONTO THE I-70. MAN, MAYBE SEVENTY PERCENT OF THIS ROAD MUST BE UNDER CONSTRUCTION. IT'S PRETTY TEDIOUS BUT WE DRIVE ON. WE'RE TRAVELLING FROM ONE END OF THE STATE TO THE OTHER - FROM THE MISSOURI RIVER TO THE MISSISSIPPI. ON THE WAY, WE PASS "BIFFLE'S" THE PAD THAT POISONED MISTER STEVE REED ALL THE TOURS AGO W/LAME CHOW. WELL, WE SEE THE SIGN BUT NEVER REALLY SEE THE PAD. WE PULL OFF A LITTLE WAY PAST TO GET GAS AND THE STATION HAS THESE FUCKED-UP TEETH YOU PUT IN YOUR MOUTH CALLED "LEE-BOB TEETH." WE ALL RIGHT AWAY THINK OF RIGHTEOUS STICKMAN, MISTER BOB LEE - NOT CUZ OF THE CHOPPERS BUT CUZ OF THE NAME. LATER, BACK IN THE BOAT, WE DECIDE WE SHOULD'VE GOT A PAIR AND FLOWED THEM TO HIM IN THE MAIL. DAMN.

WE GET TONIGHT'S VENUE, THE _BLUEBERY HILL DUCK ROOM_ ... PLAYED THERE LAST WHEN IT WAS HALF THE SIZE AND CALLED CICERO'S, BACK IN THE _FIREHOSE_ DAYS ... I DO AN INTERVIEW RIGHT BEFORE SOUNDCHECK FOR A SKATEBOARD ZINE W/A CAT NAMED GUY WHILE I CHOW A SALAD. HE ASKS GOOD THINGS. I TRY TO WORK MY BASS LIKE I'M RIDING A BOARD, ALWAYS HAVE BEEN INSPIRED BY THOSE CATS EVEN W/THEM BEING MUCH YOUNGER THAN ME. ONE WAY TO BRIDGE THE YEARS W/OUT ANYONE HAVING TO LOOK DOWN ON EACH OTHER. WE DO THE CHECK.... I GO TO THE BACK OF THE BOAT TO KONK. NOT TOO COLD TONIGHT - I ONLY NEED A BUNCH OF THE TOUR SHIRTS TO KEEP ME WARM ON THE PAD BACK THERE. I KONK HARD FOR THREE HOURS.

— MIKE WATT

HOOTPAGE.COM

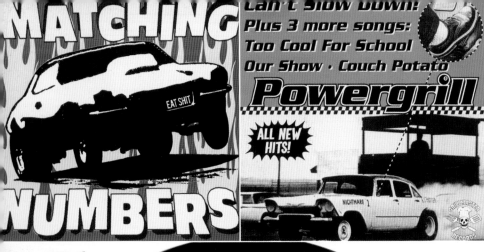

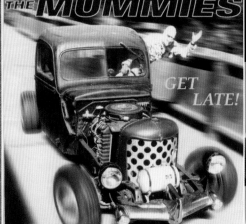

I LIVE IN A CAR . . .

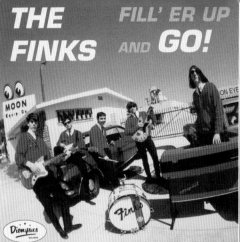

AIN'T GOT NO YARD . . .

MIKE LAVELLA SPEAKS

Gearhead Magazine speaks the same language as punk rockers—and gearheads, naturally—of all persuasions. In each thickly packed issue much love is devoted to muscle cars, tattoos, punk recordings, and the heroes and effluvia of kustom kulture. Its founder (and also founder of the Gearhead Records label), Mike Lavella, now of Oakland, California, but originally from Herminie, Pennsylvania (near Pittsburgh), is a machine gun–talking man of many, great, and related passions, all worn on his sleeve, so to speak, with contagious enthusiasm:

I was a roadie back in the day. The band I worked for most was Government Issue, which was a pain in the ass because I lived in Pittsburgh and they were in D.C., so I had a five-hour drive before I even had them loaded up in the van. I was definitely one of their biggest fans, so I didn't let those miles bug me. I was just glad for all those extra chances to see them. I took them all over the place from '86 through '88. Before I had the van, I used to go out with different bands, like Hüsker Dü and Toxic Reasons, for one or two shows if I could get a ride back to Pittsburgh. I used to help out Samhain, too, which was great because it was better to be onstage than in the pit at one of their shows, especially in New York. I even roadied for Glenn Danzig at their first show, at City Gardens in Trenton.

Yeah, I have some tattoos. There're really only two band tattoos, the Misfits and the Necros. There's also a Dodge Super Bee which the Didjits used as their main logo after it appeared on the cover of their *Hornet Piñata* LP. I got that because I really want a Super Bee, our car club has adopted it as its logo, and yeah, for the Didjits as well, they being the grandfathers of "Drag Punk" and all.

I have Max from *Where the Wild Things Are* because Maurice Sendak drew it in 1964, the year I was born and 'cause I always related to that character. I also have a tattoo of Swampy, which is the official logo of Don "Big Daddy" Garlits, the drag racing legend. I got that not only out of respect for the man, but because I thought it would be cooler than a Rat Fink, which by now everyone's grandmother has. Then, there's the famous Stanley Mouse severed monster hand on an eight-ball gearshift, which is just like a *must have*. Then, there's the smoking wooden match tattoo which I got to symbolize all the bridges I've burned in my life. The most recent one

is also the biggest: the Gearhead tattoo. It has a piston and rod on one side of a banner, or "rocker" as they're sometimes called, that says GEARHEAD, and a sparkplug firing on the other. The whole thing is held together by an elaborate flamejob. At the Mordam (distribution) convention I dared everyone to get a tattoo of their own label or 'zine.

Billy F Gibbons is probably the one guy in the world who totally and completely understands what I'm trying to do with the magazine. He made time to help me with our "Redneck" issue; he flew into San Francisco and made himself available. He's on the level, Billy. One of my favorite spreads was on Mouse, who is to hot rod art what the MC5 were to Detroit rock in the '60s. The Stooges may be more famous, as in some ways Roth was to Mouse, before rock posters, but the way I look at, all these guys rock hard, that's what it's all about, yes?

Okay, you wanna know the bands I like? My top three bands of the moment? PeeChees, Servotron, and the Dragons. The Drags are up there, too. My three favorite punk bands of all time are The Damned, the Misfits, and the Necros. My favorite early-eighties bands are the Flesheaters, The Gun Club, and The Birthday Party. My favorite mid-eighties punk rock bands were Naked Raygun, Government Issue, and either Gray Matter or Honor Roll. My favorite late-eighties bands were Mudhoney, Poison 13, and Halo of Flies. My favorite early-nineties bands were the Didjits, Les Thugs, and The Fastbacks. Mid-nineties bands would be the Devil Dogs, Supersuckers, and Flop. I've also spent a lot of time listening to the Cosmic Psychos and New Bomb Turks (but who hasn't?). My three top live bands are Rocket From the Crypt, Man … Or Astroman?, and, of course, the Smugglers. The band that blew me away most recently was The Lord High Fixers.

I'd have to say the best band outta S.F. is either the Demonics or the Donnas. My favorite garage bands are the Cynics, Thee Headcoats, and the Fall-Outs. My favorite (and only!) metal bands are Kyuss and Prong. The best band that no one talks about anymore is Steel Pole Bath Tub. The most important bands directly relating to Gearhead and "Drag Punk" are Gas Huffer, the Mono Men, and the Untamed Youth. When it's really time to rock, I bust out The Nomads. And, just in case you were wondering, the greatest song to play while driving a car is "Just to Get Away," by Poison Idea. Or any old Motörhead record!

PAUL GRUSHKIN

MIKE LAVELLA

IT ALL STARTED AT GARAGESHOCK '95. FROM THE MOMENT I MET THE NOMADS, MY UNIQUE RELATIONSHIP WITH SWEDES AND SWEDEN BEGAN. SINCE THEN, WE'VE INTERVIEWED THEM, PROMOTED SHOWS FOR THEM ON THE WEST COAST, AND GENERALLY BECOME GREAT FRIENDS. THE THING WAS, OUR LIL' INTERNATIONAL LOVE FEST WAS ALL A ONE-WAY STREET, ALL HAPPENING IN AMERICA, AND THE NOMADS—SWEDEN'S GARAGE-ROCK ROYALTY—WERE DYING TO RETURN THE FAVOR. I KNEW WHEN I FINALLY GOT MY CROATIAN-ITALIAN ASS OUT OF THE U.S. AND OVER TO STOCKHOLM, A "GOOD TIME WOULD BE HAD BY ALL." BUT NOTHING COULD PREPARE ME FOR SVERIGE, NOMADS-STYLE.

MY MAIN REASON FOR GOING WHEN I FINALLY DID, IN JUNE OF '98, WAS BECAUSE LONGTIME NOMADS DRUMMER JOAKIM (JOCKE) ERIKSON ASKED ME TO BE BEST MAN IN HIS WEDDING. UPON ARRIVAL AND SETTLING IN, WE SET OUT FOR GEARFEST, THE PRE-WEDDING EVENT HELD IN OUR HONOR. WE PACKED AS MUCH GEARHEAD MERCH INTO THE TRUNK OF JOCKE'S MINT 1970 SUPER BEE AS WE COULD BEFORE DRIVING OVER TO TANTO GARDENS. TALK ABOUT DEJA VU—THE TANTO GARDENS WAS EXACTLY THE TYPE OF PLACE I GREW UP GOING TO IN WESTERN PENNSYLVANIA. IT WAS A PICNIC GROUNDS, BASICALLY A PAVILION WHERE BANDS PLAY, WITH BOTH AN INDOOR AND OUTDOOR BAR. AROUND NOON, AMERICAN CARS STARTED ROLLING IN ONE BY ONE. "THIS IS THE SURPRISE," JOCKE SAID. "WE ALSO DECIDED TO MAKE THIS AN AMERICAN CAR SHOW FOR YOU." I WAS BLOWN AWAY.

THERE WERE TEN BANDS SCHEDULED TO PLAY, EACH DOING SEVEN SONGS. FIRST OUT WERE THE FLAMING SIDEBURNS FROM FINLAND. THEY LOOKED AND SOUNDED LIKE THEY'D STEPPED OUT OF A TIME MACHINE FROM DETROIT, CIRCA 1968. THE STROLLERS WENT ON NEXT, LOOKIN' STRAIGHT-UP SAN DIEGO, 1985, KIND OF A CROSS BETWEEN THE TELL TALE HEARTS AND GRAVEDIGGER. THERE WAS A PAUSE IN THE ACTION, AND I SOLD GEARHEAD WORKSHIRTS OUT OF THE TRUNK OF JOCKE'S SUPER BEE. IT WAS THERE I MET PELLE FROM THE HIVES, THE PUFFBALL GUYS, AND THOMAS AND MARTIN HILDEBRAND, THE BROTHERS WHO PUT OUT *SAVAGE* MAGAZINE. PEOPLE DROPPED BY ALL DAY TO SAY HELLO AND TELL ME HOW MUCH THEY LOVED *GEARHEAD*.

THE ROBOTS RESUMED THE MUSIC-MAKING, THEN CAME THE TURPENTINES, THEN THE THREE-PIECE SEWERGROOVES. AND WHILE ALL THIS WAS HAPPENING, THE BACKYARD BABIES ARRIVED. THERE WAS A HUGE BUZZ IN SWEDEN ABOUT THEIR GUITARIST, DREGEN, WHO'D RECENTLY LEFT THE HUGELY POPULAR HELLACOPTERS TO RETURN TO HIS ORIGINAL BAND. WHEN THEY HIT THE STAGE, THE JOINT EXPLODED WITH SAVAGE INTENSITY. ONE PART STOOGES, ONE PART HEARTBREAKERS, ONE PART RAMONES, ONE PART SOCIAL DISTORTION, THERE WAS SOMETHING FOR EVERYBODY. IT ROCKED. IT WAS INSANE.

SEEING THE NOMADS IN SWEDEN WAS SORT OF A DREAM COME TRUE. IT WAS SO GREAT WITNESSING THEM ON THEIR OWN TURF, THE CROWD SINGING ALONG WITH EVERY SONG. I PROBABLY HADN'T GONE THAT NUTS SINCE SEEING CHEAP TRICK IN THE EARLY '80S. IT WAS A HUGE TRIUMPH FOR ROCK & ROLLING HOT RODDERS EVERYWHERE.

NORMALLY THAT WOULD BE PLENTY OF SHOW FOR ANYBODY, BUT THIS WAS SWEDEN, DADDY, AND THE MIGHTY HELLACOPTERS WERE UP NEXT! THIS WAS TO BE THEIR FIRST SHOW SINCE DREGEN LEFT AND CHUCK POUNDER FROM THE A-BOMBS WAS BROUGHT IN ON LEAD GUITAR. MY MEMORIES OF THEIR SET ARE JUST LITTLE FRAGMENTS, AS—I GOTTA ADMIT—AFTER A WHOLE DAY OF PEOPLE BUYING BEER FOR "THE SPECIAL GUEST FROM AMERICA," I WAS PRETTY MESSED UP. BUT BEING IN A HELLACOPTERS PIT—IN SWEDEN, WITH A DOZEN AMERICAN MUSCLE CARS LINED UP OUTSIDE THE HALL—AND BEING COMPLETELY SURROUNDED BY FRIENDS OLD AND NEW, I COULD ONLY THINK TO MYSELF, "MAN, THIS IS ONE HELLUVA PLACE TO BE LOADED."

I KNOW MOST AMERICANS NEVER CONSIDER GOING TO SCANDINAVIA LIKE THEY DO OTHER PARTS OF EUROPE, BUT LET ME TELL YA, THE PEOPLE ARE WARM, THE BEER IS COLD, THE FOOD IS GREAT, AND THE PRESERVATION OF SUCH AMERICAN EXPORTS AS ROCK & ROLL AND CAR CULTURE IS EVER PRESENT.

GEARHEAD

— MIKE LAVELLA

GEARHEAD MAGAZINE, ISSUE #9

GEARFEST 2000
PUNK ROCK/HOT ROD SMORGASBORD!

SPRING 2001

#1

HEY, WAKE UP, YOUR EYES WEREN'T OPEN WIDE
FOR THE LAST COUPLE MILES YOU'VE SWERVING SIDE TO SIDE
**YOU'RE GONNA MAKE ME SPILL MY BEER
IF YOU DON'T LEARN HOW TO STEER.**

WILCO, PASSENGER SIDE

the
REVEREND HORTON HEAT
CAIN'S BALLROOM • JANUARY 14, 2005 • DOORS AT 7PM
with throw rag

TIX ARE: $6 ADVANCE AND $17 DAY OF SHOW AND ARE AVAILABLE AT STARTICKETS.COM, STARSHIP RECORDS AND TAPES, ALBERTSON'S, AND CAINS (918.584.2306)

ART BY TODD SLATER AND PRINTING BY DILL SCREENPRINTING

TODD SLATER

Lucinda
Williams

Maj 18 Malmö KB.
Maj 19 Stockholm Cirkus.
Maj 21 Göteborg Trädgår'n.

THE ALT-ROCK-COUNTRY-ROOTS-ROCKABILLY-CAR-LOVIN' SOUND

QUESTION: TO WHICH BAND OR MUSICIAN DO PARTS OF THIS DESCRIPTION BEST FIT?

AN AFFECTIONATE PARODY OF LIBERAL-REARED, LOCAL TRAILER-PARK CULTURE, MELDING A SKEWED—BUT ALWAYS HEADY—GONZO OUTLOOK WITH A WILD, CAREENING BRAND OF HIGHLY INFORMED, RETRO-MINDED ROOTS-ROCK, INCORPORATING A SOUTHERN-FRIED AMALGAM OF PSYCHO-ROCKABILLY, CLASSIC CANNED HEAT-JOHN LEE HOOKER BOOGIE, ALT-COUNTRY-SWAMP-POP AND CHITLIN-CIRCUIT R&B, PLUS A DOSE OF CALIFORNIA SURF GUITAR, A HINT OF PUNK ATTITUDE, A SPLASH OF TONGUE-IN-CHEEK, AND AN ALTOGETHER WISE-ASS PARTY BAND APPROACH DELIVERED WITH RAUNCHY GROOVES, A BLUESY RUMBLE, AND MANIC SHOWMANSHIP?

SOUTHERN CULTURE ON THE SKIDS? DEKE DICKERSON? THE DRIVE-BY TRUCKERS? DAVE AND PHIL ALVIN AND THE BLAST-ERS? LUCINDA WILLIAMS? THE REVEREND HORTON HEAT? THE PALADINS? IGUANAS? BOTTLE ROCKETS? JEFF TWEEDY AND WILCO? KINGS OF LEON?

FAIRLY OR NOT, ALL HAVE AT VARIOUS TIMES IN THEIR CAREERS BEEN DESCRIBED AS EXHIBITING SOME OR ALL OF THE ABOVE ELEMENTS—AND WHAT LINKS ALL OF THEM TO EACH OTHER IS THEIR LOVE FOR CAR, TRUCK, AND ROAD IMAGERY SET AGAINST THEIR OWN, INDIVIDUAL ROAD MAPS ACROSS THE NEW MILLENNIUM.

DEKE DICKERSON: RANDOM SHUFFLE

The music Deke Dickerson and his band, the Eccofonics, make could have been made 50 years ago … or six months ago. A native of Missouri now living in California, and beginning with his indie-surf-garage band, the Untamed Youth, Dickerson has enjoyed a dualistic life: one rooted firmly in the past and squarely in the present. As with friends Dave and Phil Alvin of The Blasters, he's noted for honoring his heroes, such as New Orleans drummer Earl Palmer and R& B vocalist Claude Trenier, by asking them to guest on his albums.

Onstage, playing classics like Johnny Getz's "Hot Rod Queen" amidst a host of double-entendre, genre-jumping showstoppers, Deke slings a '50s-vintage double-neck Mosrite guitar, the kind played by the late Joe Maphis and Larry Collins (of the rockabilly Collins Kids). The name "Eccofonics" comes from a guitar mechanism called an "ecco unit" that dates back to the '50s. Of course, Deke has a '50s Cadillac parked in his garage.

"Car songs are part of all our shows," said Dickerson in an interview with the author. "We do 'em all the time because—guess what?—people just love them. And we sneak in as many truckin' songs as possible, too. The fact is people relate big time to car and truck songs.

"We've been doing 'You're My Cadillac' a lot recently. I wrote it with Lorrie Collins in mind, for the *More Million Sellers* CD (1999), but she was unable to come down and do the session, so I asked Hadda Brooks to help me instead—so sad, she died soon thereafter, but she'd been making music since the '30s, so it was a great honor to work with the Queen of the Boogie.

"We've also put in our recent repertoire Lee Ruth's 'My Car,' which has such great lyrics like 'My car don't run so good/it got no horsepower under the hood/but my car is paid for/and it's my car.' A song like that has all the elements for me: a universal sentiment about a car, a solid, fundamental rockabilly sound—and the song's roots even go back to a Willie Dixon blues.

"My '57 Cadillac Coupe DeVille is a great daily driver, but I've never gotten around to fixing it up like I want—being a musician and all, just don't have those hours to wrench on it properly. It starts on the first go,

though, and I have a ball driving it. I like Cadillacs because I'm a big guy and there's lots of room to stretch and get comfortable.

"All of our U.S. dates are done with a van. A lot of people don't realize … they think you magically appear in their town or think you charter one-way flights. But no, most of us musicians are out there slogging across America in our 15-passenger vans, typically putting 80,000 to 100,000 miles a year on our vehicles. I go through vans about once every two years. Put a hundred thousand on the odometer, sell it, buy another one. And yes, I have two positions: either driving (90 percent of the time) or sleeping (the other 10 percent). I *can't stand* to just be riding along. I just go crazy!

"We play music all the time in our van. The iPod has been a great tool for rediscovering lots of stuff I forgot I had—random shuffle rules! Plus, it's so much better not to be gumming up your CD collection when the guys are spilling taco sauce on everything. As far as driving music goes, any kind of instrumental music is the worst for me because I start falling asleep. I have to have words to focus on in order to stay awake. Staying alive, that's kinda the key thing out on the road!

"I probably drive all the other guys crazy, but to me it's important to set a soundtrack to your life. I like to get a sense of the atmosphere, where songs were recorded. For instance, when we're driving through Texas, I'll listen to nothing but Lefty Frizzell or Bob Wills. A few hours before we pull into Memphis, I'll listen to everything recorded at Sun. In New York City, it's the Ramones—who, by the way, are very, very good for nighttime driving. Punk rock and '60s garage rock are what you want for all-weather, anytime driving—the music keeps pounding you awake over the long stretches, and the songs are short, which keeps it interesting.

"Country music and truckin' music, that also helps eat up good hours on the road. Just like the song says, it's about seein' the world 'fly by me on the right.' You can tell why it's so popular with truck drivers … just set the cruise control to 73 and you git up and *go.*"

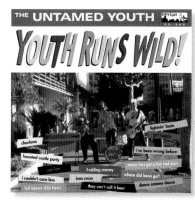

TERMS OF SALE

I called her the "Bad Luck Truck" after two Social Distortion songs, somewhere between "Bad Luck" and "Ball and Chain" ("… as I sit and I pray, in my '57 Chevrolet, I'm singing to myself, Lord, there's got to be another way…"). I'd have painted some hot rod–styled Bad Luck graphics on her, like living dead black cats and 13's, but I never quite had the time. Now me and my partner, Matt, are looking to start up our own tattoo studio and art gallery down in Savannah, and I need to raise as much business collateral as I can, and pretty damn fast. This truck is one of my main assets, and although it breaks my heart to do it, and I desperately hate to see her go, it means I can be my own boss for the first time in 20 years. So, not only will you be scoring yourself the baddest custom pickup in the Northeast, you'll be supporting underground tattoo and rock & roll art at the same time. The title is clear and in my possession, so we can close the transaction as soon as your funds are transferred.

Bottom line: this truck is mean and ugly, just like me, and ready to be a daily driver to anyone who subscribes to *Gearhead* or *Garage* magazines, straight from a *Juxtapoz* lowbrow artist. She really stands out here in North Jersey, where the most people see of custom culture is on the Discovery channel.

Most of the real headaches have been worked out of this truck, if you're looking for that West Coast koolsville style of driver, as opposed to airbags, a Mach 2 front-end clip, power steering, or cushy, pretty-boy nonsense like that. She's solid as fuck, a classic year and make, and holds to her roots. If I was to keep her, I'd take care of the tie rods, the weather stripping, and maybe doll up the empty holes in the dash, give her a 1- or 2-inch rake, maybe a sun visor. Even with all the loot I dumped in her, she's still cheaper than a Harley! And just as loud, too! And if you're looking to turn her into a show truck, or God forbid, some digital trailer queen with VDO gauges and a DVD player, well, she's at a great starting point.

VEHICLE DESCRIPTION

This truck will get you chicks! Here she is, boys, a 1957 Chevrolet stepside pickup truck, based on a farm model, with no frills, like a radio or even door locks. The previous owner (enthusiast Paul Millinchuk of Teaneck, New Jersey) decided to hot rod her out, until he got taken up by other projects and sold her to me in the fall of 2001.

The idea was to fly in the face of those Jersey *primadonnas* who gleaned everything they know about cars from *The Fast and the Furious*. Instead, I had designs on turning her into a mean Left Coast custom. I wanted a truck I could run to bike shows and tow all the never-running rat bikes I usually collect, and at the same time pay tribute to my heroes like Von Dutch.

She's pretty solid with very little rust; the undercarriage could survive a direct nuclear assault. Bodywork is not show condition, but passable. She has coats of flat matte-black utility paint on her, with red pinstriping on the headlights, door jams, glovebox, and tailgate, as well as white stripes across the entire dash over a maroon color, done by North Jersey's favorite pinhead, Anthony White.

This is the only year Chevy did that killer eight-toothed grill, and she has the small rear window (not the configuration of the big five-window cab on previous models). Under the hood is a very clean small-block 350. She's a solid runner with a new alternator, battery, fan, belts, wiring rig, hoses, filters, plugs, distributor cap, ignition, valve covers, *et al*.

The carb is a stocker and could easily be swapped out for a Holley or a Demon. She has Edelbrock intakes, a performance cam, and dual exhaust that gives her a sweet throaty rumble in punk rock style, and although she hasn't been cracked open I'd bet the engine's got less than 10,000 miles on her. She's fast enough to catch rubber in two gears.

Under the frame she has a Posi rear end, a spanking new tranny with less than 100 miles on it, four onna floor, and everything else is stock. Which means, stock steering and suspension (but with new, short springs to drop her 3 inches all around and new shocks), giving it that nice '50s driving feel.

The brakes are the original drums but have all new lines, shoes, and a master cylinder, and are tight as hell. The electricals are all rewired, all the lights work—she's even got highbeams, turn signals, and hazards. Most of the gauges work; I'm not going to even tell you how much they charged me to get the speedo working, but I have to tell you the needle is moving only half the time. But, there's a new gas sender unit, oil and temp gauges to keep things honest, and the original heater box is still mounted under the dash. I took the windshield wipers off, as the motors had already been removed, and I just put on chrome bullets, hot rod style. The rear bumper is brand new, so is the original steering wheel.

The doll-up stuff: We dropped her 3 inches all around. My personal feeling is she could use another 2 inches up front, but *whatever*. I put diamond plate in the flatbed, a nod to my punk roots. Traditionally, maybe you'd like to see oak boards back there, but this truck is bulldog mean and I didn't feel wood would do. She has small steel loops in all four corners for tie-downs. There's a new prefabbed bench seat, with black tuck & roll vinyl, new black carpet, firewall insulation, and leopard-print door panels and roofliner. Diamond kickplates on the floor, with a small one allowing access to the master cylinder. Moon Eyes provided the dummy spots, the Maltese cross peep mirrors, the chrome fire extinguisher, and the 15-inch spun aluminum hubcaps. The steering wheel is new, replacing the racing wheel the truck came with, and goes back to the original size, only now it has a chrome bullet in the center and a pin-up girl suicide knob. The shift knob is a handcrafted skull sculpted and pinstriped by lowbrow artist and Hot Rod Hall of Famer Dennis McPhail. New Coker radials complete the West Coast look with 2 1/2 inch whitewalls. The radials really help the handling, making it actually possible to parallel park the beast.

VEHICLE CONDITIONS

The downsides: The one glitch I haven't gotten to yet, as I dropped $7K into her this year alone, is that her front tie rods are bent. This gives the steering more play than is comfortable at high speeds, but still hasn't stopped me from driving her into NYC for shows or all through the mountains of New Paltz. On the highway, I found myself passing people left and right. And my spring guys told me they could bend 'em straight without having to replace 'em, which I was planning on doing when we lowered her again.

Also, she has original glass, and the weather stripping is shot, which means a loud, shaky ride that sounds like the doors could fall off any minute. New rubber and stripping all around will fix that right up. With no windshield wipers I was reliant on Rain X for bad weather, but I drove her year round, despite the lack of heat. Yes, the dash is spotted with a lot of empty holes where the knobs have been taken out, and there's no accelerator pedal. Oh, and the really hot Goth chick is not included.

One of my clients, Knucklehead Steve, from Indian Larry's garage in Brooklyn, climbed all over and under her and gave me a really fair assessment, so please, serious inquiries only, okay?

YOU GOTTA NASTY DISPOSITION,
NO ONE REALLY KNOWS THE REASON WHY

SOCIAL DISTORTION, BAD LUCK

HEAVY REBEL WEEKENDER

The annual three-day Heavy Rebel Weekender—otherwise known as HRW—held in late June or early July, is one of the great independent car-and-rock festival events in the United States, taking place at the Millennium Center in Winston-Salem, North Carolina's arts district. The name comes from "all the heaviest rebels of rock & roll."

Cofounder Mike Martin: It's come a long way, but we still hope it remains a manageable event. We're now drawing upwards of 2,500 people a day! In 2001, our first year, we organized, promoted, and executed in under six months and for less money than a decent used Honda would cost. *Cheeeeap.* Dave Quick (who promoted the infamous "Elvis Fests" in Chapel Hill) and I pooled our resources and connections and booked 45 bands for three days on three stages. Vendors, tattoo artists, and a custom car show complete with burnouts were parts of the attraction (despite some, uh, illegality involved). That first year we drew 650 people a day, from all over the U.S., and when the smoke had cleared, the stages were silent, and the beer cans swept up, we realized we'd pulled off an amazing party where everyone—most people previously unknown to each other—felt like friends.

HRW was designed to bring together musicians, bands, bikers, hot rodders, custom clubs, and "kool culture" where that mix might not have happened under normal car show circumstances. In my mind, the event is symbolized by the cars themselves—customs, hot rods, beaters, and drivers, but no trailer queens.

At HRW, known and unknown bands trade sets, share stages, and mix it up with newly acquired friends. The nearest thing like it is the Kontinentals' Lone Star Rod & Kustom Round Up, in Austin, Texas (see pages 206–209). Our Crossroads Guitar Contest has blown up into a premiere event to see and be seen in. It features the bravest gunslingers blasting off in front of 1,000-plus crowds, all while playing to previously undisclosed back lines provided by Dave Quick himself.

The 2005 HRW featured a new event: the Upright Bass Slap-Off, featuring 12 or so upright bassists pairing off and strutting their stuff to a live band led by Johnny Knox vamping in the background—actually not so much a cutthroat contest as a rare chance for these musicians to be featured exclusively and for the crowd to see one of the most interesting instruments driving classic rockabilly. Then, there are the perennial crowd-pleasers like rock & roll "mud wraslin."

The whole weekend is unique, fun, funny, and sometimes quite disturbing, if you're not used to so much fun and funny. We say it's based on the old Commander Cody lyric: *There's a whole lotta things I've never done, but I ain't never had too much fun.*

THE ANNUAL HEAVY REBEL WEEKENDERS IN WINSTON-SALEM, NORTH CAROLINA, WERE INSPIRED BY THE ORIGINAL LO-DOWN HO-DOWN, FIRST HELD IN 1999 AT SURFSIDE BEACH, SOUTH CAROLINA. IN 2001, A SECOND HO-DOWN WAS HELD IN COLUMBUS, OHIO (THE HOME OF POSTER ARTIST MIKE MARTIN, NOT TO BE CONFUSED WITH HRW COFOUNDER MIKE MARTIN), ALSO THE YEAR OF THE FIRST HEAVY REBEL. GOT IT?

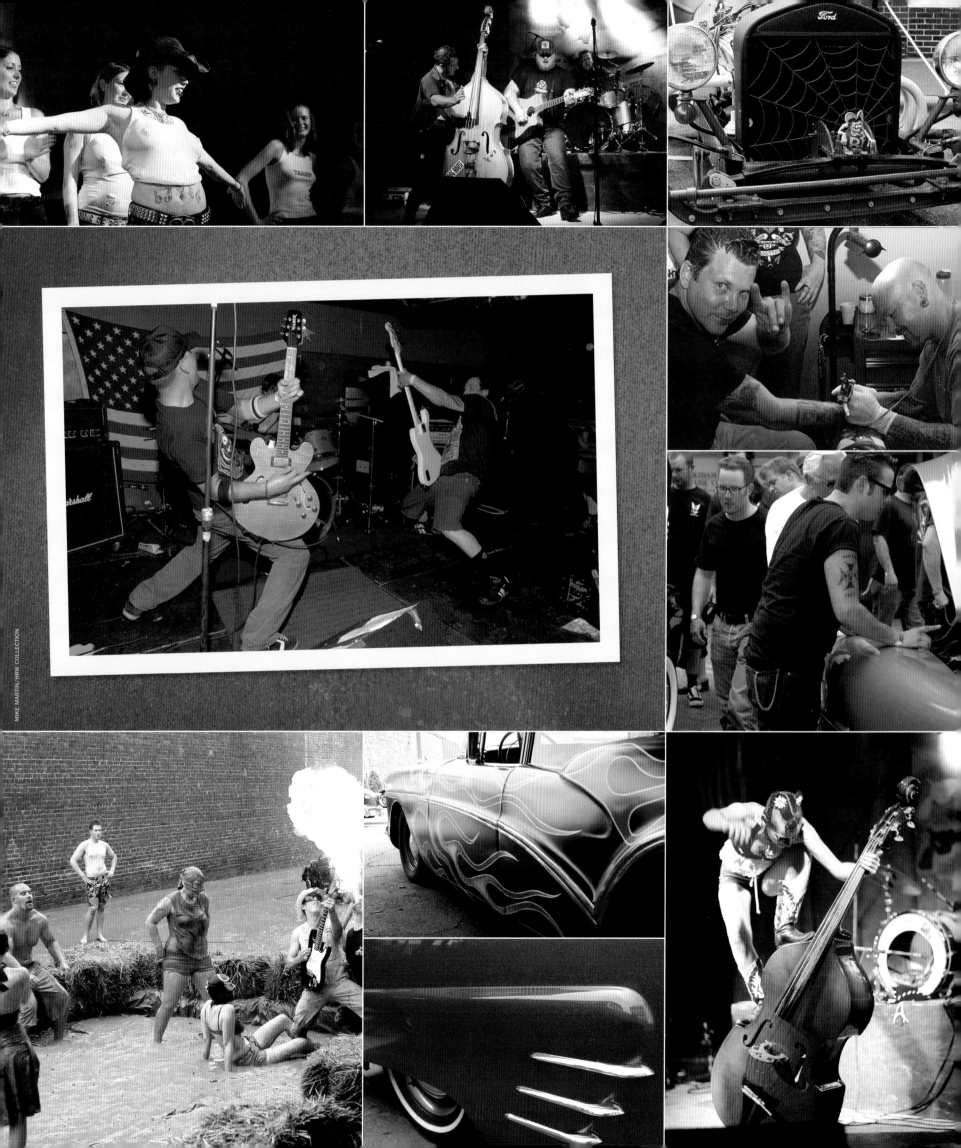

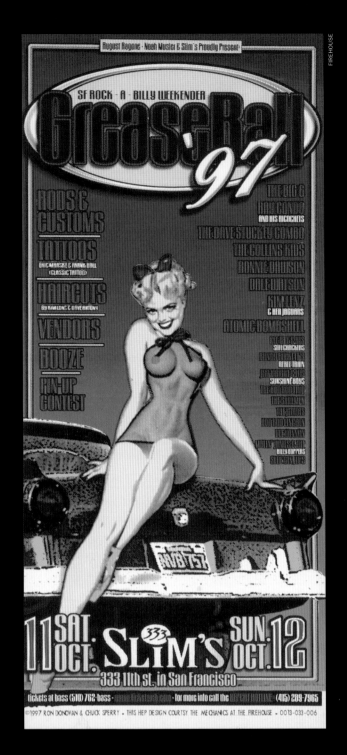

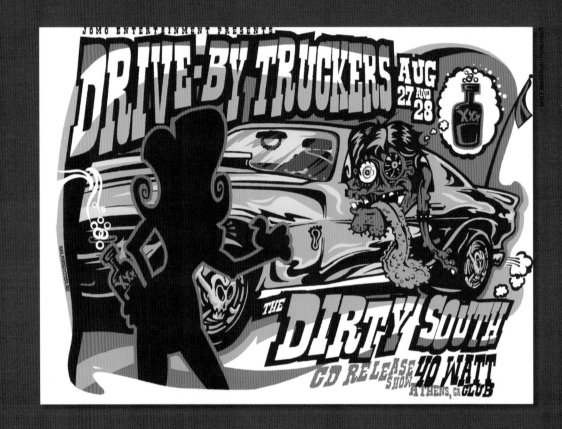

CHUCK SPERRY: TEACHER-MAN

CHUCK SPERRY, PICTURED HERE AT A CUSTOM CAR
SHOW IN GERMANY, TRAVELS THROUGHOUT EUROPE
EACH YEAR TEACHING ROCK & ROLLERS HOW TO
SCREENPRINT. SPERRY'S STUDIO IS THE FIREHOUSE
IN SAN FRANCISCO, WHERE HE PARTNERS WITH
RON DONOVAN, WHO, LIKE SPERRY, IS A MASTER
ILLUSTRATOR, CARTOONIST, AND HANDS-ON TECHNICIAN.
MANY GEARHEAD RECORDS–SPONSORED EVENT
POSTERS WERE PRODUCED AT THE FIREHOUSE.
SPERRY AND DONOVAN'S ROCK CONCERT AND POLITICAL
POSTERS, MANY EXHIBITING LOWBROW, ROCKABILLY,
PUNK, AND CUSTOM CAR ELEMENTS, ARE TREASURED
BY THOSE WHO APPRECIATE FINE-ART-QUALITY,
MULTILAYERED, LIMITED-EDITION SCREENPRINTS.

JERAL TIDWELL

HEADLINERS MUSIC HALL AND PRODUCTION SIMPLE PRESENT:

SEPTEMBER **14TH**

CLUTCH

9PM
18 & over $18/$20

TIDWELL

WITH SPECIAL GUESTS: STINKING LIZAVETA

© 2005 JERAL TIDWELL • WWW.HUMANTREE.COM • HAND PRINTED AT CRACKHEAD PRESS • LOU. ,KY • CAR OWNED & BUILT BY JERRY "PORKCHOP" WALKER

GARY HOUSTON

kathleen
edwards
back to me
tour 2005

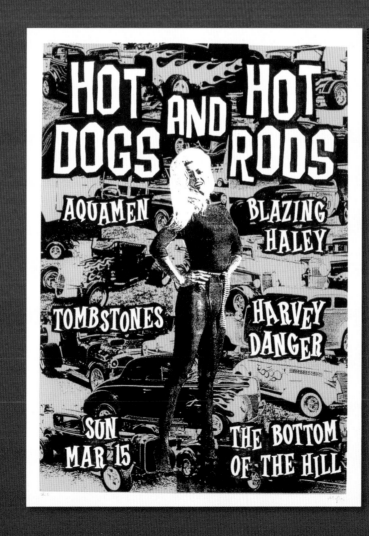

PRINT MAFIA

HOT DOGS **AND** HOT RODS

AQUAMEN

BLAZING HALEY

TOMBSTONES

HARVEY DANGER

SUN MAR 15

THE BOTTOM OF THE HILL

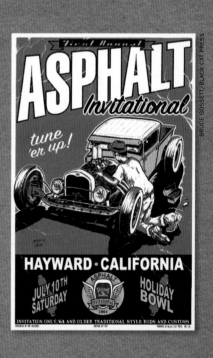

BRUCE GOSSETT/BLACK CAT PRESS

ASPHALT Invitational

tune 'er up!

HAYWARD • CALIFORNIA

JULY 10TH SATURDAY

HOLIDAY BOWL

INVITATION ONLY, '64 AND OLDER TRADITIONAL STYLE RODS AND CUSTOMS

ALAN FORBES

HOT DOGS HOT RODS

ALL YOU CAN EAT B.B.Q!

MARCH 28

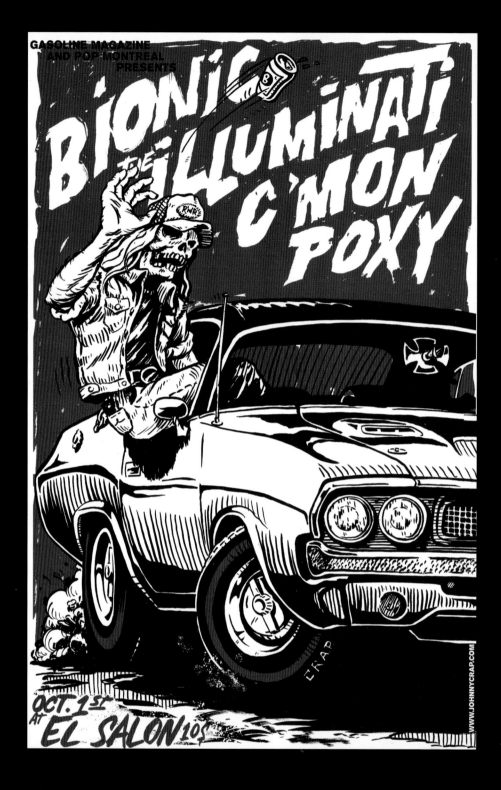

JOHNNY CRAP

YOU GOTTA LOVE THE NAME: JOHNNY CRAP. IT SPRANG FROM AN ATTEMPT AT PLAYING IN A BAND. IT DIDN'T MATTER HE HAD NO INSTRUMENTAL SKILLS, AND HIS FRIENDS FIGURED HE COULD DO THE LEAST DAMAGE ON THE DRUMS. BUT WHILE SCREWING AROUND AT REHEARSAL ONE DAY, ONE OF HIS PALS STATED THE OBVIOUS: "JOHNNY, YOU PLAY LIKE CRAP." THE NAME STUCK. A MONTREAL-BASED LOWBROW PAINTER AND FREELANCE ILLUSTRATOR WITH A SERIOUS HOT ROD JONES, HE STARTED SIGNING HIS PAINTINGS AND ILLUSTRATIONS WITH THAT NAME. HIS ROCK & ROLL CONCERT POSTERS ARE DEVELOPMENTS OF HIS WORK WITH ACRYLICS, OILS, SPRAY PAINT, AND SCREENPRINTS ON CANVAS, WOOD, PLASTIC, AND WALLBOARD.

NEAL PRESTON

BRIAN SETZER: BUILT FOR SPEED

Brian Setzer's no Brit. That may be a shock to some people who think the rockabilly revival stirred up by Setzer's Stray Cats in the early '80s was a U.K. occurrence. Yes, the 'Cats tore up the British singles charts. Yes, they were the tattooed darlings of a madly boppin' social scene. But the commitment to the music itself—*American* rockabilly—has endured with Setzer to this day. And, he's no gearhead poser either, having owned and driven the hot rods of which he sings.

Setzer was born in New York City in 1959. He was influenced early on by late-'70s punk, as well as Led Zeppelin's American blues–based rock. But rockabilly simply sounded the best to him. His first band, with his brother Gary on drums and friend Bob Beecher on bass, was called the Tom Cats. Then, with Massapequa, Long Island, school buddies Slim Jim Phantom (Jim McDonnell) and Lee Rocker (Leon Drucker), he formed the Stray Cats.

Initially establishing themselves in London, they were championed by producer/bandleader Dave Edmunds and recorded their first album in October 1980. The success of their first single, "Runaway Boys," enabled their return to the United States, and with their album *Built for Speed* (1982), the big hits finally followed, including "Stray Cat Strut" and "Rock This Town."

Although the Stray Cats are years in Setzer's past—he's been leading a big band, the Brian Setzer Orchestra, for more than a decade now—the guitarist and songwriter's continued passion for American roots music led him to record *Rockabilly Riot Vol. 1: A Tribute to Sun Records* (2005), which focused on tunes waxed from 1954 to 1957—music that likely set many early hot rodders' hearts beating fast. To recapture the period sound, Setzer rented vintage microphones and tube amps, and brought his legendary collection of

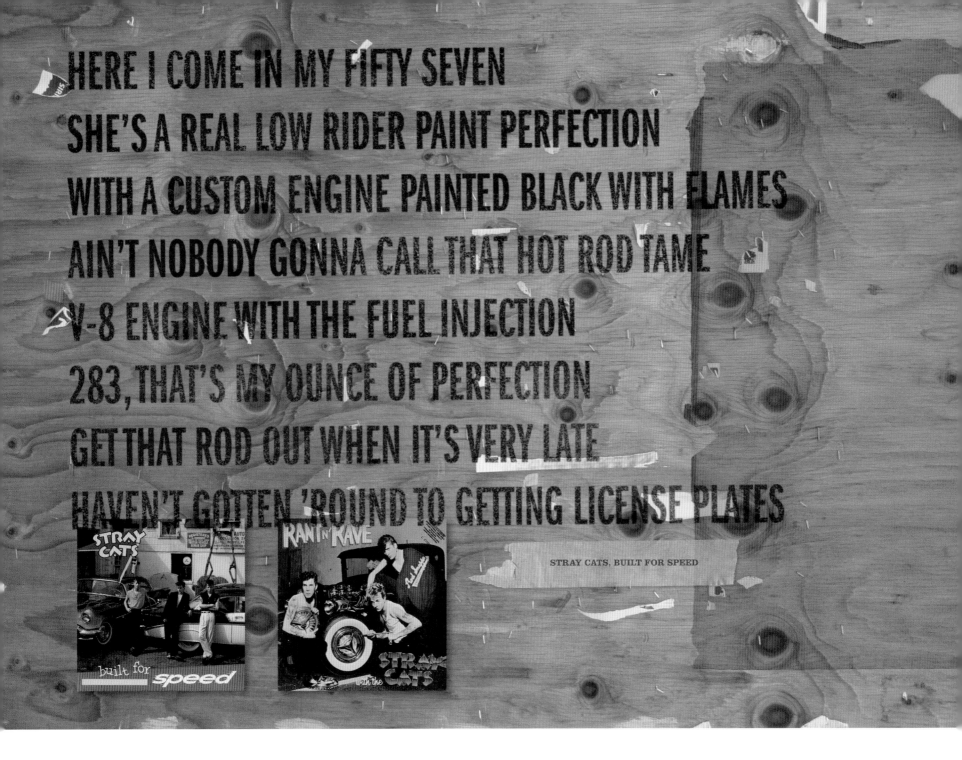

HERE I COME IN MY FIFTY SEVEN
SHE'S A REAL LOW RIDER PAINT PERFECTION
WITH A CUSTOM ENGINE PAINTED BLACK WITH FLAMES
AIN'T NOBODY GONNA CALL THAT HOT ROD TAME
V-8 ENGINE WITH THE FUEL INJECTION
283, THAT'S MY OUNCE OF PERFECTION
GET THAT ROD OUT WHEN IT'S VERY LATE
HAVEN'T GOTTEN 'ROUND TO GETTING LICENSE PLATES

STRAY CATS, BUILT FOR SPEED

late-'50s Gretsch guitars to the sessions. He later told Greg Tutwiler of *Singer & Musician* magazine, "I had a blast. I had a stack of vinyl and I used my turntable. I cranked it up and played original records all day. I went through hundreds of songs—I mean, you could make whole records full of Carl Perkins alone, you know?"

Amid a set by Sun mainstays Roy Orbison and "The Killer" Jerry Lee Lewis, Setzer included two car songs: Warren Smith's "Red Cadillac and a Black Moustache" and Jumpin' Gene Simmons' (not to be confused with the KISS bassist) "Peroxide Blonde in a Hopped Up Model Ford."

Setzer continued: "I also learned the instrumentation in the classic rockabilly era was not a three-piece like the Stray Cats (guitar, bass, drums). It was always an electric guitar playing against a stand-up bass—and they really slapped that bass, which gave the Sun records their unique sound. And while they had drums, they also had either an acoustic guitar or a piano pretty prominent in the mix. In modern-day rockabilly you never hear a piano or acoustic guitar. Then, I had all my musicians play in the same room, like they did back in the '50s. The energy was created by the musicians playing *together*, not in separate alcoves."

THE ROAD DEVILS CC

The Road Devils were brought to life in California in 1946 by soldiers returning from World War II. They wrenched on their "gow jobs" on weeknights and dragged on weekends. Despite initially "spreading like the black plague," as one current chapter president, Patrick Brown, puts it, the car club died off in the middle '60s.

In 1997 a few guys 2,200 miles away in and around Columbus, Ohio, brought the Road Devils back to life. Today, there are chapters in Ohio, New Jersey, Northern and Southern California, Colorado, Texas, Nevada, and Germany.

According to their manifesto, Road Devils are "the people your mother told you to stay away from when you were a kid. We've deep roots in Kustom culture, a tradition of hell raisin', and are trying to keep the old style of true poorboy hot rodding alive. If you've grease under your nails, oil for blood, and music blasting in your skull, you're our kind of man and woman."

Mike Martin, one of the top rock poster artists in the United States (see page 42), is a founding member of the Ohio chapter, pictured here. He and his wife, Cari, drive a '50 Buick. Patrick and his wife, Josie, wheel a '50 Buick Sedanette, Josh Brown a '55 Bel Air, Matt "Face" Miller a '48 Ford, and Big Jon a '40 Ford

PATRICK BROWN, ROAD DEVILS PRESIDENT

POSTER ARTIST MIKE MARTIN AND WIFE CARI

MIKE MARTIN COLLECTION

MIKE MARTIN/ENGINEHOUSE 13 (PAUL GRUSHKIN COLLECTION)

PAT BROWN'S GARAGE, COLUMBUS, OHIO

ALL PHOTOS BY PAUL GRUSHKIN

JOSH BROWN

MIKE MARTIN

BRENT RECTOR (AND REX) AND HIS '59 CADILLAC

JIM LUKE AND HIS '52 CHEVY

JAY GATLIN AND HIS '36 PLYMOUTH

JIM CAMPOS AND HIS '40 CHEVY TRUCK

DRAG LYNX

Brent Rector, this book's designer and art director, was the bassist in the rockabilly band Lonesome Train and is a member of the Sacramento, California, chapter of the Drag Lynx car club. Rector drives a '59 Cadillac, and he and his family (wife Jennifer and son Rex) make an annual pilgrimage to Paso Robles, California, where the great rodders and racers gather (see page 233 and Metallica's James Hetfield showing his just-pieced-together '36).

The Drag Lynx came together in the summer of 1958 in Fort Morgan, Colorado, when six friends, including Harry Blecha (who subsequently moved to Sacramento), decided they should form a car club. They all agreed to build one car together to drag race—a 1928 Model A coupe on a Model T frame with a 1947 Mercury rear end coupled to a 1938 Ford transmission, powered by a 1953 Chrysler Hemi. Blecha raced the car at the Cheyenne and Jewlesburg, Colorado, airport drag strips, turning 118 miles per hour.

Today, the eight-person Sacramento chapter features pre-1963 traditionally styled rods and customs, some of which are shown here.

DRAG LYNX MEMBERS

HARRY BLECHA '51 TAUNUS

RENATO CONSOLINI '49 MERCURY

BRENT REES '54 MERCURY

MIKE GLECKLER '60 CADILLAC

BRENT RECTOR '59 CADILLAC

JIM LUKE '52 CHEVROLET

JIM CAMPOS '31 FORD

PAUL GARLAND '50 FORD, '41 CHEVROLET

JAY GATLIN '36 PLYMOUTH

GEORGE HERNANDEZ '51 FORD VICTORIA

RANDY CANNAROZZI '34 FORD

THE KONTINENTALS' LONE STAR
ROD & KUSTOM ROUND UP

Few car-and-music shows anywhere in America top The Lone Star Rod & Kustom Round Up. A "gen-u-wine throwback to the '50s," it's an annual early-Spring, cannot-miss, weekend-long party in Austin, Texas, featuring traditional hot rods and customs, stomping-hot live music (rock primarily, but also rockabilly, punk and luminaries like Bill Kirchen, and Junior Brown), Texas ribs, and a sea of lowbrow art. The Kontinentals car club hosts the event; their message is, "We understand it's about building 'em and driving 'em, and we try to pack the weekend with events both in the day and at night to give people a chance to wrench and show, then tool around and enjoy themselves in one of the great music capitals of the world."

According to the Round Up's "official" itinerary, the event doesn't really kick off until early afternoon on Friday, but being that Austin is a town full of things to be entertained by, many people show up as early as Wednesday to make a mini-vacation out of it. *Custom Rodder* magazine opined, "The deal is, to do the Round Up right, maybe you should lift weights and train for it. You definitely need to be willing to sacrifice sleep for fun."

The location for the Saturday car show is Festival Beach, a park on the banks of the Colorado River in downtown Austin. Then there are unending musical and gustatory events in and around Steve Wertheimer's famed Continental Club, on one of Austin's main drags, South Congress.

Hop Up magazine had this to say: "We knew some people there and met more, and we're goin' back, son. The vibe is greasers and stone-to-the-bone music but it's really all about … the iron. All kinds. Traditional, turned-out rods are certainly there, but also customs … and kustoms … and scrappers, too. Seems everybody knows one another in a familial way, a *Paso Robles* or *Billetproof* or *Heavy Rebel* kinda feel. You can mingle with Jimmie Vaughan from the Fabulous Thunderbirds and swap lies with his buddy and car builder, Lee Pratt. And at night, most people get their butts over to the Continental Club because Steve is about the coolest club owner and custom cat you're gonna ever meet. Don't wanna sound too groupy about the whole weekend, but *cavrone*!"

Junior Brown in Steve Wertheimer's Golden Rod.

THE Continental CLUB

STEVE WERTHEIMER

JIMMIE VAUGHAN'S IRONIC TWIST

SUGAR RAY ROBINSON, 1950

CHAPTER 8

ROCK DREAMS
Bigger Than a Cadillac

ALL THE KING'S THINGS

"I grew up with 'Rock and Roll' as a car commercial before I had a clue what Led Zeppelin was," wrote "SJB" in an Internet chat. "I finally realized it was a Zeppelin song during a school bus ride, when this dude told me all about the band." Another chatter, Jeannette, wrote back, "My friend's mom was always saying Led Zeppelin was a thoroughly worthless band. Then the 'Rock and Roll' ad started playing in the car one day, and she was totally singing along, and I was . . . like, what??? Then I told her it was a Zeppelin song and she said, 'Hey, that really is a great song.'"

Cadillac used Led Zeppelin's "Rock and Roll" to kick off a new advertising campaign in 2002 with the tagline "Breakthrough." The company was going for a hip, new image, as their traditional customer base was, in effect, slowly dying off. The spots aired for the first time on Super Bowl Sunday and sales rose 16 percent over the next year. It was the first Led Zeppelin song used in a commercial.

Actually, "Rock and Roll" was General Motors' second choice. Offering $15 million up front, they originally tried to obtain a license to use The Doors' "Break on Through (To the Other Side)" but were rejected when drummer John Densmore (who, like each of the surviving bandmembers, had veto power in all decisions affecting the group) refused to agree, citing the late Jim Morrison's unhappiness with an earlier attempt by GM to use "Light My Fire" in a 1969 Buick Opel commercial.

For years, Zeppelin refused to license its songs. They explained their change in tune came about because much of rock radio no longer played their songs in steady rotation. If they wanted to keep their music in front of a large audience, TV commercials were a way to do that and get handsomely paid at the same time. Still, some musicians, like Bruce Springsteen, Neil Young, and the Grateful Dead, have routinely refused these opportunities, invoking time-honored rock & roll ethics. Others, like The Who and Sting, rise to the bait. When Sting released his "Desert Rose" single in 2000, radio

programmers largely refused to play it, citing research that supposedly proved listeners did not want to hear the song. So he went over their heads and licensed "Desert Rose" to Jaguar. The TV ad ran everywhere, radio gave in, and the song became Sting's biggest hit in ten years.

Used to promote Chevy trucks, Bob Seger's "Like a Rock" likely was the most successful car-song choice ever made by an ad agency. But there certainly have been odd pairings, too. Jethro Tull's "Thick as a Brick" was an unlikely choice for Hyundai. David Bowie's "Rebel Rebel" was pressed into service for Mazda. Ozzy Osbourne's "Crazy Train" sold Mitsubishis. Madness and the Status Quo sold Saturns. Incredibly, Nick Drake's "Pink Moon" was chosen to promote the Volkswagen Cabrio in 2000 (as Stereolab did for the new Beetle the year before). Two particularly inspired choices were those made by Toyota: Sly and the Family Stone's "Everyday People" and Right Said Fred's "I'm Too Sexy." As well, artists as varied as Annie Lennox, Moby, Chris Isaak, the Rev. Horton Heat, the Pet Shop Boys, Kansas, and Styx all have profited from the opportunity for their songs to hawk the latest showroom hits.

One extremely hip ad agency audio director assigned to Nissan's Xterra program is well-versed in rock & roll. For 2006, he or she chose The Bellrays' "Revolution Get Down" to sell the SUV. In 2003, it was The Velvet Underground's "Heroin." In 2001, it was Stevie Ray Vaughan's cover of Jimi Hendrix's "Voodoo Child (Slight Return)." In addition, The Smiths, The Cult, Lenny Kravitz, The Who, Stone Temple Pilots, Rush, The Smithereens, Van Halen, War, and the Woody Guthrie estate all have licensed songs to Nissan.

Of course, the car companies also could go with Fu Manchu's "Don't Bother Knockin' (If This Van Is Rockin')" or even The Magnetic Fields, who wrote some of the sweetest lines ever penned about car ownership: *But I'm the luckiest guy on the Lower East Side/'Cause I've got wheels and you want to go for a ride.*

PINK CADILLAC

EVEN IF THE ONLY YEAR A CADILLAC COULD BE ORDERED IN A FACTORY PINK COLOR WAS 1969, THE SPECIAL-ORDERED, PINK-PAINTED CADILLAC OCCUPIES A CELEBRATED NICHE IN AMERICAN AUTOMOTIVE AND ROCK HISTORY.

MANY AMERICANS FROM THE 1950S—PARTICULARLY ENTERTAINERS AND ATHLETES SUCH AS BOXER SUGAR RAY ROBINSON (FACING PAGE)—SAW THE PINK CADILLAC AS ONE OF LIFE'S CROWNING ACHIEVEMENTS. ONE OF ELVIS' FIRST MAJOR GIFTS TO HIS MOTHER WAS A PINK CADILLAC (PAGE 25). A PINK '59 COUPE DEVILLE TO THIS DAY IS A RECOGNIZABLE ROCK & ROLL SYMBOL ALL ITS OWN.

NATALIE COLE GOT MORE MILEAGE—*WAVIN' TO THE GIRLS, PEELIN' OUTTA SIGHT*—OUT OF HER "PINK CADILLAC" THAN DID ITS SONGWRITER, BRUCE SPRINGSTEEN. IN 1988, COLE'S THUMPING DANCE REMAKE HIT #5 ON THE BILLBOARD SINGLES CHART. SPRINGSTEEN HIMSELF HAD RELEASED THE SONG IN 1984 AS THE B-SIDE OF "DANCING IN THE DARK."

"PINK CADILLAC" CAME ABOUT AS A LATE-NIGHT STUDIO INSPIRATION WITH A MEMORABLE VOCAL EMPHASIS ON *"CRUSHED VELVET SEATS,"* BUT IT WAS NOT SEEN BY MOST SPRINGSTEEN FANS AS A LIFE-DEFINING ANTHEM IN THE MODE OF, SAY, "BORN TO RUN." MORE IN THE SPIRIT OF THE ROMPING "SHERRY DARLING" (1980), IT WAS HIS SECOND SONG WITH "CADILLAC" IN THE TITLE, THE FIRST BEING "CADILLAC RANCH" OFF *THE RIVER* (1980). "PINK CADILLAC" DID NOT APPEAR ON ANY SPRINGSTEEN ALBUM UNTIL 1998. THE ONLY SPRINGSTEEN PICTURE DISC WITH A CAR AS ITS MOTIF WAS THE UK-RELEASED "DANCING IN THE DARK" B/W "PINK CADILLAC.

SHE MET ME AT THE STATION
'CAUSE I'M COMING HOME ON LEAVE

I LET HER USE MY XKE SO SHE'D DRIVE AROUND AND THINK OF ME

BABY, I'M HOME, YOU LOOK SURPRISED,

I SEE IT ON YOUR FACE

WHERE'S THE OLD CROWD?

DO THEY STILL HANG OUT AT THE PIZZA PLACE?

A FLASH OF SUSPICION —

YOU LEARNED A NEW WAY OF KISSIN'?

LOU CHRISTIE,
IF MY CAR COULD ONLY TALK

1973 XKE, LINWOOD, NEW JERSEY

ALVIN AND MIKE COHAN COLLECTION

JAZZ, POP, AND THE JAGUAR

Just like their rock & roll counterparts, jazz musicians from Louis Armstrong to Miles Davis have had tremendous fondness for their cars. But it was the renowned Blue Note jazz record label that notably featured cars—mid-'50s Jaguars, in particular—as part of their artwork and designs that sought to exemplify modern music.

What made Blue Note Records so special? It was a combination of elements: Alfred Lion's production, Francis Wolff's photography, Reid Miles' design, and Rudy Van Gelder's engineering. The heyday of the label was from 1957 to 1967, and its stable of newly emergent cool-jazz artists included Sonny Rollins, Cannonball Adderley, Horace Silver, Hank Mobley, Art Blakey, Jackie McLean, Donald Byrd, Jimmy Smith, Lee Morgan, McCoy Tyner, Cecil Taylor, and others.

Blue Note was renowned for its inspired packaging, made possible by the transition from 78s to LPs that required newly sized and formatted record jackets. "Beginning in 1951, Francis Wolff laid the foundation for the Blue Note look," wrote historian Jonathan Schneider. "He photographed musicians soaked in sweat amidst their solos." Then, in 1956 the responsibility for designing all the album covers fell solely on Reid Miles, who produced nearly 500 jackets during his fifteen-year tenure.

Felix Cromey, editor of *Blue Note: The Album Cover Art*, wrote, "Reid Miles made each cover look or 'sound' like it knew what lay in store for the listener. He utilized abstract designs and bold photography—sometimes his own—hinting at the musical innovations."

Both Wolff and Miles liked the look of Jaguars, first the X120 and X140 models of the early '50s, then the XK150 in the later '50s, as can be seen in their photos and album art. In March 1961, a year after Chuck Berry recorded "Jaguar and the Thunderbird"—presumably involving an XK150—Jaguar released the revolutionary XKE model (manufactured through 1975), which in turn inspired songs such as XTC's "She's So Square": *Take her to a disco and screaming Lord Sutch it!/ Everyone must look but nobody must touch/what about her car? E-type is the latest/How about the Yardbirds? Jeff Beck is the greatest!!*

But it was Lou Christie (otherwise notable for "Lightning Strikes") who wrote perhaps the most memorable song ever referencing an XKE. His "If My Car Could Only Talk" (1966) referenced Lou's 1964 Army service, his family's South Heights, Pennsylvania, pizza restaurant, and his own red XKE.

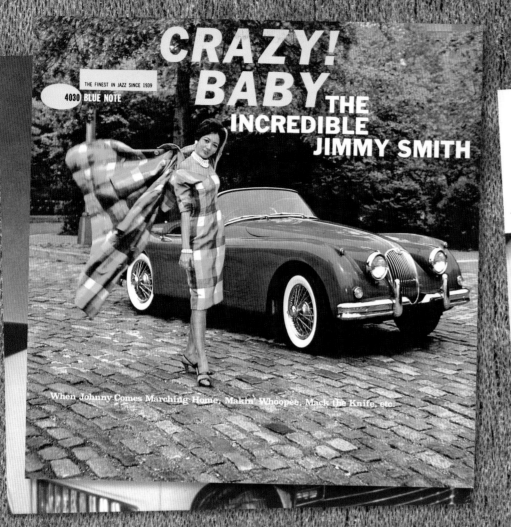

CRAZY!
BABY THE
INCREDIBLE
JIMMY SMITH

4030 BLUE NOTE

THE FINEST IN JAZZ SINCE 1939

When Johnny Comes Marching Home, Makin' Whoopee, Mack the Knife, etc.

STEREO
BST 842

BLP 42
BLUE NOTE

THE
INCREDIBL
JIMM
SMITH

WITH GRANT GREEN & DONALD BAILEY

"I'M MOVIN' ON"

STEREO
THE FINEST IN JAZZ SINCE 1939

84075 BLUE NOTE

Pepper Adams
Duke Pearson
Laymon Jackson
Philly Joe Jones

the
cat
walk
donald
byrd

STEREO
THE FINEST IN JAZZ SINCE 1939

84124 BLUE NOTE

a new perspective
donald byrd band & voices

SWANGIN'

Over the decades, the descriptives separating urban blues from rhythm & blues, old-skool R&B (e.g., Sam Cooke and Aretha Franklin) from modern R&B (e.g., R. Kelly and Beyonce Knowles), R&B itself from hip-hop, and even hip black culture (e.g., rap and crunk) from hip white culture (e.g., alt and metal) have become increasingly blurred. In part, this is due to decades of slang terminology spontaneously arising in song and on the street, then crossing over both ways. If something is cool, it means cool in all languages—same as it ever was.

Just as the pleasures of the flesh are celebrated in the latest wicked terminology, in the playas' lyrics, the latest, hottest rides are *whips* and *slabs*. A stylish car is variously *da shit*, *mint*, *fresh*, *mean*, *tight*, *bitchin'*, *sick*, *dope*, *sweet*, and *phat*—all depending on who's making the case for what, and especially if it's *swangin'* all over the road.

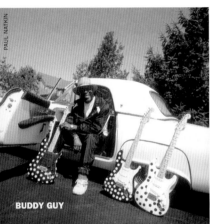

BUDDY GUY

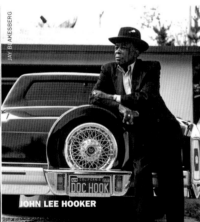

JOHN LEE HOOKER

ALICIA KEYS

THE FIRST TIME I HEARD ONE OF MY SONGS ON THE RADIO, I WAS DRIVING ON THE BROOKLYN-QUEENS EXPRESSWAY IN MY LITTLE MAZDA 626 LATE AT NIGHT. FUNKMASTER FLEX, WHO IS A BIG NEW YORK DJ, WOULD DROP SOUND-EFFECT BOMBS ON THE RECORDS THAT HE LIKED. [THE SONG HE WAS PLAYING] WAS "GIRLFRIEND." I HEARD THE BEGINNING PIANO, BUT I DIDN'T PAY ANY ATTENTION. THEN I REALLY BEGAN TO HEAR IT, AND HE WAS DROPPING BOMBS ON IT!

THEN I HEARD MY VOICE SINGING! I WAS LIKE, *"OH MY GOD!"* I'M ALMOST CRASHING INTO THE ORANGE CONSTRUCTION THINGAMAJIGS, I WAS SO EXCITED.

— ALICIA KEYS

INTERVIEWED IN *PEOPLE*, OCTOBER 17, 2005

LARRY GRAHAM (GRAHAM CENTRAL STATION)

You-are-there cinéma vérité set to an urban beat has been part of television since the '50s. Reality television, beginning in the '90s, simply yanked the script away, replacing it with real-life improv, filmed hand-held and cleverly edited. First was *Cops* in 1989, then MTV's *The Real World* in 1992 (conceived ten years after MTV was born). A decade later, the first reality TV devoted to car customizing was offered up—taking the viewer from concept to fulfillment by way of a million human foibles and led by entertaining (although sometimes overbearing) personalities—starting with Discovery Channel's *Monster Garage* (created by West Cost Choppers motorcycle builder Jesse James), *American Chopper* (featuring Orange County [New York] Choppers' Teutel family), and *Overhaulin'* (starring custom car designer Chip Foose).

But the real breakout was MTV's *Pimp My Ride*. Its first season (2004) was seen by over 72 million viewers worldwide. The plot was inspired: each week, one takes an unfashionable or decrepit "ride" and "pimps" it. The teaming of rapper Xzibit (who began his career with the 1996 album *At the Speed of Life*) and the hip-hop and punk-fueled crew from West Coast Customs updated urban Southern California car-ridin' sensibilities for a multiracial, across-all-musical-genres college- and high school–age audience. The whole effect was deliberately over-the-top.

Pimp My Ride made for highly compelling television. It was, in effect, an extension of twenty years of made-for-TV rock and rap videos, the best of which often included cars. These mini-movies continue to reflect important regional trends, although a basic combination of trick rides, scantily clad girls, boastful talk, and bling flashing always carries the day.

MTV's *Cribs* next opened the front door to the homes and carports of star athletes and musicians. Then, *DUB* and *RIDES* magazines built on the concept by publishing mouthwatering photos and interviews synched to the latest CD releases and couching car culture as the hippest lifestyle imaginable.

"It's interesting how cars are replacing girls in some hip-hop videos," Brian Scotto, senior editor of *RIDES*, told the author. "Girls have been the eye candy forever, but take a look at Comillionaire's 'Riding Dirty.' Look at what people are staring at. The cars are the common culture in music. Hip-hop is the leader in this, but hip-hop wouldn't be doing so fantastically well—as music, as fashion, as lifestyle—if white culture didn't admire what it's all about. But what's also interesting is the reverse, like cruising the strip, new/old aspects that are being rediscovered by the urban crowd.

"Any scene tied to the newest music, by nature, has to constantly reinvent itself. It's freshest when your jaw drops. Like the Bay Area *hyphy*

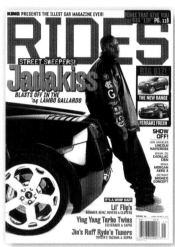

scene with its sideshows and guys 'ghost riding the whip' (controlling a moving car by effectively leashing it in cruise control, getting out, and walking beside it). Crossover in car and music cultures continues to amaze me—like hot rodders admiring the skyscrapin' 24-inch-rim Donk, Box, and Bubbles scene down South. Or this full-on rediscovery of '70s muscle cars—not just by white guys, but by rappers and hip-hoppers, and especially because Funkmaster Flex is so into it."

Funkmaster Flex (born Aston Taylor) may be the music world's top muscle car–lovin' guy . Beginning in the mid-'90s, he got his notoriety issuing hugely successful mix albums. For the past ten years Flex has been the number-one DJ in the country's number-one market; on Hot 97 he reaches more than 2 million listeners a week—that's 10 percent of everyone listening to the radio in New York City.

A cross-promotional genius and a justly celebrated car customizer, Flex also has the Spike TV show *Ride with Funkmaster Flex* that debuted in 2003. Eminem, Queen Latifah, Ludacris, Busta Rhymes, Travis Barker, and Lil' Kim are just a few artists Flex has promoted in the urban crossover car culture. He's also created the touring Funkmaster Flex Custom Car and Bike Show (and International Sneaker Battle), which in 2006 included his tricked-out Mustang, Expedition, Ford F-150 pickup, and cutting-edge Fusion (from his collection of over 30 vehicles)—along with 50 Cent's '68 Impala and LL Cool J's Bentley Continental GT. "I love cars, and I'm a talker," says Flex. "I love to talk to people about cars. At my show there's no VIP area. I'm in the mix."

Like Flex, MTV/VH1 veteran DJ Skribble also wears other related hats, including that of music producer and hometown auto entrepreneur (Skribbles Auto Spa in Queens, New York). "I was an art major in school," he told roadgearmag.com. "I used to go around bombing walls and trains. I was so into hip-hop—every aspect of the culture—I buried my head in the art and the music. But I'm also into classic muscle cars and I continue to build sound systems.

"Being a DJ, I learn about sound every day—still. The most important thing for me in a car is the sound quality. When I come out of the studio—whether we're doing a hip-hop or a dance production—after we remix a record we always go into my truck and listen to it. For me, the car tells the truth. Great sound is about stereo separation and clarity—not about volume and distortion. That works for every kind of music. I ought to know—mine's a diverse crowd, from the all-out ravers to the hip-hoppers to the college kids. My truck packs twelve crates of records wherever I go."

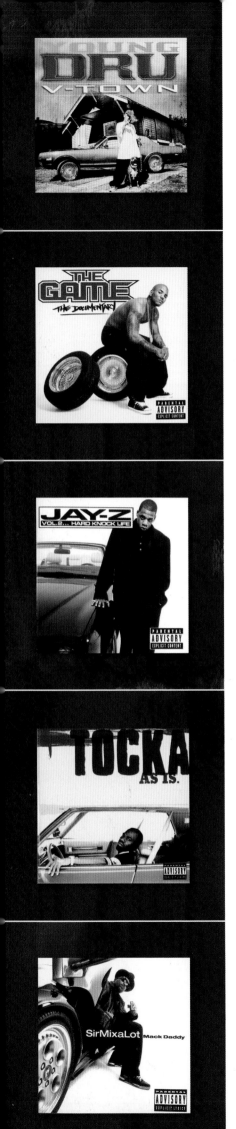

A TRUNK HOLD 6 BODIES IF YOU STACK 'EM RIGHT

ICE-T AND CREW

GLEN E. FRIEDMAN

BUSTA RHYMES

DANNY CLINCH

SUGARHILL GANG

Released in October 1979, the 12-inch single "Rapper's Delight" by the Sugarhill Gang launched hip-hop as a multi-billion-dollar enterprise. The song—the first raps over a beat—had peak sales of 50,000 copies a day; it was a manifestation of live performance music born in the clubs and parties of the South Bronx, a borough of New York.

Sylvia Robinson, whose All Platinum/Sugarhill Studios was headquartered in Englewood, New Jersey, and having heard rap for the first time at a Harlem club, set out to record the first "name" rappers. The group was literally discovered man by man, while Robinson, her son Joey, and Joey's school friend, Warren Moore, cruised Palisade Avenue in Englewood, driving Joey's Oldsmobile 98.

Henry "Hank" Jackson, a sometime rapper, was pulled from his job at Crispy Crust Pizza. Next, Guy O'Brien, part of the nascent One on One crew, climbed into the car. Finally Mike Wright joined the curbside audition. The following week, Robinson transformed them into Big Bank Hank, Master Gee, and Wonder Mike, respectively, and they were given the cross-promotional name the Sugarhill Gang.

They recorded "Rapper's Delight," a fifteen-minute track, in one take; in 1980, it became one of the highest-grossing singles of all time. Grandmaster Flash and the Furious Five were next, and the rest—scratching with records, MCs, influential club DJs, and all the great rap stars—were etched into American history, all due to a fortuitous car ride.

PUBLIC ENEMY

GLEN E. FRIEDMAN

LIL' KIM — GREGORY BOJORQUEZ

MISSY ELLIOTT — RAYON RICHARDS (RAYONRICHARDS.COM)

JADAKISS

LUDACRIS — GREGORY BOJORQUEZ

XZIBIT

SNAP!

ROCK JOURNALISM HAS TO ITS CREDIT GREAT PHOTOGRAPHERS LIKE JIM MARSHALL, NEAL PRESTON, HENRY DILTZ, RICHARD AARON, BOB ALFORD, JOEL BERNSTEIN, MICHAEL MARKS, JAY BLAKESBERG, KEN REGAN, LYNN GOLDSMITH, ROGER RESSMEYER, KENDALL MESSICK, PAUL NATKIN, CHARLES PETERSON, AND PAM SPRINGSTEEN—ALL REPRESENTED IN THIS BOOK. THERE'S ALSO A NEW WAVE OF SHUTTERMASTERS HEADED BY ZACH CORDNER, GLEN E. FRIEDMAN, FRANK OCKENFELS III, GREG BOJORQUEZ, DANNY CLINCH, AND RAYON RICHARDS. MANY HAVE CROSSED OVER, WHICH IS TO SAY THEY'RE EQUALLY COMFORTABLE PORTRAYING RAP AND ROCK STARS. ON A WHIM, CLINCH BROUGHT HIS PHOTOS TO DEF JAM RECORDS; HE BEGAN TO SHOOT PUBLIC ENEMY AND LL COOL J, AND BEFORE LONG RAP MU-SICIANS WERE AMONG THE BIGGEST STARS. HIS PORTFOLIO WAS NEVER THE SAME AGAIN. SPRINGSTEEN TO BUSTA RHYMES AND BACK, SOUL COMES IN ALL COLORS, CLINCH FOUND.

ALL THESE PHOTOGRAPHERS ALSO HAVE SHOWN THEIR AFFINITY FOR COMBINING THE ALLURE—OR STATURE—OF AUTOMOBILES WITH THE QUIXOTIC NATURES OF HUMAN BEINGS. RICHARDS STATES HE ATTEMPTS TO DISPEL MYTH AND STEREOTYPE BY CAPTURING PEOPLE IN THEIR NATURAL STATE, BUT THE ADDED ELEMENT OF CARS HELPS HIM EXPLORE THE NA-TURE OF PERSONALITY. "IT CAN BE THAT THE DETAILS OF AN INANIMATE OBJECT ACTUALLY GIVE ME A MORE COMPLETE VIEW INTO A PERSON'S CHARACTER," HE SAYS.

BOJORQUEZ IS MORE BLUNT. "WE'RE PERFORMERS—WE SHOW UP, WORK OUR MAGIC. YOU JUST HAVE TO BE OPEN TO ANYTHING . . . ABSOLUTELY ANYTHING! YOU'RE EITHER FULL OF SHIT OR THE GUY WHO'S PLAIN, FREAKIN' CRAZY. I'D LIKE TO THINK I'M THE SECOND ONE, 'CAUSE THAT'S THE PLACE WHERE ALL THE GOOD STUFF COMES FROM."

PAUL GRUSHKIN

BIG SLICE

SNOOP 'N' SLICE

MTV's Pimp My Ride, *originally featuring rapper Xzibit and West Coast Customs, whose new shop is out of Corona, California (see page 107), and Spike TV's* Ride with Funkmaster Flex, *along with specialized magazines about hot and hotter cars commissioned by musician celebrities and urban cognoscenti—*Rides *being one of the most jawhanging—has put a mainstream eye on hip-hop and its vibrant cultural scene. The* New York Times *took notice as early as 2004.*

In an era when every cable channel seems to have a show celebrating tricked-out cars, and aftermarket auto accessories have become a multibillion-dollar business, the ultimate celebrity status symbol might be having a guy on retainer who can pimp your ride.

For rap musician Calvin Broadus, known as Snoop Dogg—singer, actor, and cultural trendsetter—that guy is Michel Rich, who at 6 feet 6 inches and 295 pounds is known as Big (or Bigg) Slice. Big Slice does not work only for Snoop. He has built cars for other celebrities and for movies, and he recently lent one of his cars to the rapper Master P for a video. But most of his work is for Snoop.

Some of the cars he has built and rebuilt for his chief patron are crammed into Big Slice's small garage in Montclair, 30 miles east of Los Angeles. They have names. "Huggy Bear" is a 1977 white-on-baby-blue Lincoln Continental that Snoop drove in the movie *Starsky and Hutch* and named for his character. The Lakermobile is a 1967 Pontiac Parisienne convertible redone in the purple and gold of the Los Angeles Lakers. A hydraulic system in the trunk, controlled by dashboard switches encrusted with purple and gold cubic zirconium, "hops" the car up and down.

Snoop and Big Slice also have collaborated to build more than a dozen Snoop DeVilles, a few in a custom-classic green tint, also with sophisticated hydraulics. [Note: Their latest creations include the 1960 Cadillac "Angel Dust" and a navy blue-and-gold "VSOP" DeVille.] One of Big Slice's

proudest creations is the customized school bus for Snoop's youth football team, the Rowland Heights Raiders, who are based in a Los Angeles suburb, coached by the rapper himself, and quarterbacked by his 9-year-old son, Corde Broadus, who is known as Spanky.

The bus is a considerable step up from the used $4,500 clunker it was when Big Slice purchased it on Snoop's behalf and began modifying it. For starters, it has 27 video screens for a team of 27 eight-to-ten-year-olds, and about $90,000 worth of stereo equipment, including 70 speakers (that's 2.6 speakers for each player). Beyond the DVD and VHS players, for the most valuable player of each game, there's an Xbox to play video games on the ride home.

Snoop calls at all hours with an idea, and then Big Slice draws up a plan. He builds the hydraulic systems himself, but farms out parts of the job to specialists in exterior paint detailing or upholstering. "It can go anywhere from 10 grand to $250,000," he said, adding, referring to Snoop, "With him, it's like 12 to 13 grand a month. With my basic customers, it depends how fast they want it and what they want. It's either the 'I need it now' price or the 'take your time' price. People say I'm expensive. I'm not expensive; I'm a luxury."

Snoop Dogg may represent an extreme, but the infatuation with customizing cars is widespread. Spending on aftermarket car parts and accessories has doubled over the last decade to $28.9 billion a year, according to the Specialty Equipment Market Association. Drivers are investing in multicolored taillights, bright xenon headlights, and custom wheels that often sell for thousands of dollars apiece—wheel models with names like "Beyonce" and "B-Diggity." [Note: P-Diddy now owns a controlling interest in a custom wheel company.] Spinners, or wheel rims that revolve independently of the wheel, are also popular.

For a self-described former crack dealer who grew up around the projects in Watts, life has turned out pretty well. Big Slice says, "It's a job that's not a job. Back in Watts, I didn't have a whole lot of options. It was either sell dope, gang bang, or just hang out and do nothing, and I did 'em all. But, I'm glad I did all that when I was young. That's all behind me. I grew up."

In his later teens, Big Slice became a disc jockey for a West Coast gangsta rap group, Above the Law, and began working on cars on the side. He spent part of the 1990s building hydraulic systems for cars overseas. "Low riders are big in Japan," Big Slice explains.

He crossed paths with Snoop after returning home. "We were always in the same circle, but just didn't hang together. Finally, I did one car for him, and I kept it for him while he was out on tour. He liked that, and he was just like, 'OK, I need you to take care of all my cars.'"

Big Slice does not advertise. "A lot of celebrities come and think they can just throw money at you," he says. "The only reason I build so much for Snoop is that he has imagination, you know what I mean? He'll wake up in the middle of the night and think, 'OK, I want this kind of car and I want this on it.' So it's more of a challenge, working with Snoop."

"I tell people I'm not a car builder—I'm an artist," Big Slice concludes. "One thing I learned with Snoop: if people, when they see the car you're driving down the street, if they don't do the neck snap, something is wrong. Every car [of ours] going down the street gets a double take."

— Danny Hakim
New York Times, October 28, 2004

VSOP

ANGEL DUST

ROWLAND HEIGHTS RAIDERS TEAM BUS

VSOP

I'VE GOT ABOUT 23 CARS. I HAVE A '39 CHEVY, A '47 CHRYSLER, A '67 PONTIAC THAT'S YELLOW AND PURPLE, AN ORANGE '77 CHRYSLER NEW YORKER, AND THE STICKY ICKY, A '74 CADDY THAT'S IN THE NEW VIDEO. I LIKE THE 2001 PORSCHE CARRERA I'M DRIVING TODAY. MY *TIA CARRERA*, THAT'S WHAT I CALL IT.

— SNOOP DOGG
BLENDER MAGAZINE, 2003

ALL PHOTOS PAUL GRUSHKIN

BOBBY DIXON

ELVIS' EXOTIC CARS

During the later stages of his career, Elvis owned a number of exotic and luxury cars, including a 1971 Stutz Blackhawk, one of designer Virgil Exner's "Revival Cars." Elvis had ordered a Duesenberg, but the production was never initiated, so instead he went with the Blackhawk. According to longtime Elvis bodyguard Sonny West, the first Stutz dealer, Jules Meyers, showed up at Elvis' home at Hillcrest Drive in Los Angeles with the Blackhawk. Elvis expressed interest. Meyers told him he could sign a contract and that Stutz would build him his Blackhawk during the following months.

Elvis wasn't interested in signing a contract; he was interested in buying the car sitting in front him. Meyers tried to explain that he needed the car to show to potential buyers. Elvis answered with a question, "How do you think you will sell more cars—when *you* drive it, or when people see *me* driving it?"

Elvis also owned a yellow mid-engine De Tomaso Pantera (see fan's photo of him driving it, with girlfriend Linda Thompson). The Pantera was created by Ford as a new niche between European exotics and American muscle cars—an international supercar. The intention was to offer a specialty vehicle that rivaled Ferrari in performance, but with a Ford V8 engine borrowed from the Mustang. With its aggressive cam, the Pantera's sound was legendary, a primeval howl that could wake the dead. Elvis actually bought it for Thompson in 1974, but it was a poor starter. It often frustrated Elvis, who, one morning in a fit of pique, shot off a pistol at it, wounding the steering wheel. Some years later, it was discovered by Rockin' Robin Roseaaen, one of Elvis' greatest fans and keeper of the All the King's Things Archive, at a San Mateo, California, dealership (see photo and ad). Today, it's owned by Robert Petersen, who has it displayed as part of the permanent collection at the Petersen Auto Museum in Los Angeles.

Elvis also owned a Rolls-Royce Mulliner Park-Ward–bodied Phantom V limousine, one of only a few hundred made and similar to one owned by The Beatles. While stationed in Germany with his regiment in 1959, Elvis purchased both a BMW 507 sports car and a Messerschmitt two-seater. It was while he was in Germany that he ordered one of the first 1960 Lincoln Mark V limousines (see photographs), further customized by the firm of Hess and Eisenhardt, which also built the convertible that John F. Kennedy was assassinated in. After arriving home from Germany, Elvis was so excited about the Mark V that one of the first things he did was have his photograph taken with it, still in his Army uniform, in front of Graceland. The Lincoln became one of Elvis' favorite automobiles, and he was often seen driving it around Memphis and in Southern California.

LYNN GOLDSMITH ARCHIVE

BOTH PHOTOS BARRETT-JACKSON AUCTIONS

FORD IMPORTED ROUGHLY 5,500 PANTERAS INTO THE U.S. BETWEEN 1971 AND 1974. THEY WERE SOLD THROUGH LINCOLN-MERCURY DEALERS. ELVIS IS SAID TO HAVE PURCHASED HIS FOR $2,400, ALTHOUGH THE LIST PRICE WAS JUST OVER $10,000. A SAD FOOTNOTE: MÖTLEY CRÜE LEAD SINGER VINCE NEIL WAS DRIVING A PANTERA WHEN HE CAUSED THE INFAMOUS ACCIDENT THAT KILLED HANOI ROCKS DRUMMER RAZZLE (NICHOLAS DINGLEY).

ancisco Chronicle
July 7, 1976

435
SPORTS & IMPORTS

PANTERA   1971.   Beauti-
full(7860)
WAS "ELVIS PRESLEY'S"
Call today 344-7512 Dealer
PEUGEOT   New '76
30 YEARS SAME LOCATION
        PRIOLA MOTORS
4900 Mission, S.F   587-7935
PEUGEOT '71 sunroof, radio,
super car $1450 776-8742

ELVIS, GIRLFRIEND LINDA THOMPSON, AND THE BALKY 1974 DETOMASO PANTERA AS SEEN IN A FAN PHOTO.

ROCKIN' ROBIN ROSEAAEN, TRACKING DOWN ELVIS' PANTERA AT A SAN MATEO, CALIFORNIA, USED-CAR LOT.

ALL THE KING'S THINGS (ALL)

ELVIS AT GRACELAND

DANNY CLINCH

JAMES HETFIELD

MICHAEL N. MARKS

JIM MANGRUM

ROBERT ALFORD

MARK FARNER

AU NATURALE

Some rock stars' cars are farm-worthy pickup trucks and rugged SUVs from back in the day when SUVs were built to stare down the wilderness. Here, we see items from the garages and barns of Jim Dandy (Black Oak Arkansas), Mark Farner (Grand Funk Railroad), James Hetfield (Metallica), and *the* American bow-hunter himself, Ted Nugent.

During downtime from touring and working in the studio, Hetfield is an avid hunter, skateboarder, snowboarder, and jet-skier, so it's not surprising he's particularly proud of his four-wheel-drive Chevy Blazer, known as *The Beast.*

Farner led one of the loudest-ever power trios, formed in 1969 in the working-class, auto-industry city of Flint, Michigan. The band's name was taken from that of a railroad that served the auto industry, the Grand Trunk Western. Largely patterned after Cream, GFR sold more albums than any American band in 1970 and a year later broke The Beatles' record at Shea Stadium in Queens, New York, selling out 50,000 seats in the shortest time ever. Farner, who later became a Christian recording artist, sunk his earnings into his farm, pictured here.

Black Oak Arkansas—formed in 1965 in Black Oak, Arkansas—were long-haired Southern misfits led by Jim "Jim Dandy" Mangrum, who, unable to find work, turned to making party-band rock & roll. Over a span of some ten years they developed into a raunchy, freaky live act known for lewd celebrations of the pleasures of the flesh. BOA was considerably rawer than the Allman Brothers or even Lynyrd Skynyrd, and songs like their "Hot Rod" carried—or shall we say hung—double meanings.

Ted Nugent, another Michigan stalwart, began bow-hunting in 1953 and playing very loud guitar in 1956. Between 1967 and 2006 he sold over 30 million albums worldwide. He's a man of hugely impassioned opinions, but also the three-time winner of The Outdoor Channel's People's Choice Golden Moose Award for Best Hunting Show, and the *New York Times'* best-selling author of *God, Guns & Rock and Roll* (2000) and *Kill It & Grill It* (2002), among much, much more.

Nugent zealously extols the values of responsible parenting and is all about developing passion for the outdoors by way of gun ownership. He never fails to speak his mind, as is evident on tednugent.com: TAKE A YOUNGSTER INTO THE WILD AS SOON AND AS OFTEN AS YOU CAN. GET 'EM SHOOTING, EXPLORING, AND THROBBING. NOW! Not surprisingly, Nugent has in his garage all the automotive equipment necessary to venture afield purposefully and in style.

LYNN GOLDSMITH

TED NUGENT

THE KILLER

YOU SHOOK MY NERVES AND YOU RATTLE MY BRAIN. AS THE STORY'S
TOLD, THAT PO' BOY FROM FERRIDAY, LOUISIANA, JERRY LEE LEWIS, ONCE
SET HIS PIANO ON FIRE AT THE END OF HIS SET TO MAKE IT IMPOSSIBLE
FOR CHUCK BERRY TO FOLLOW HIS ACT. NOBODY MESSED WITH THE
KILLER. *'CAUSE I'M WAITIN, UH HUH, AT THE END OF THE ROAD, YEAH.*

FUN WITH CARS

Pink Floyd drummer Nick Mason's first love was not music, but cars. "The cars came first," he told Andrew Frankel of the *Sunday Times*. "My dad used to race a vintage Bentley and from my earliest memory, cars and racing were part of my life."

Mason is the only member to have remained with the band since its inception in 1965. Pink Floyd has sold over 200 million albums, with the accrued royalties making possible one of the most expensive hobbies imaginable. Mason is indeed one of the great car collectors, but his collection of approximately 40 automobiles—of which 25 to 30 are what he terms "serious racing cars" of the absolute highest quality—is not a static display of wealth. Even the most historic of his cars are active racers. He's been quoted saying, "A stuffed tiger is all well and good, but it doesn't compare to the sight of the animal in the wild." Mason himself has raced in five Le Mans.

He proudly shows visitors a Type 35 Bugatti and a 1961 Lotus 18 (one of the first rear-engined Grand Prix cars), along with D-Type and 1936 B-Type Jaguars. He has both the Maserati 250F and the 1960 "Birdcage" model. He counts among his many Ferrari's a 250GT, a 512S, an F40, a 1972 356 GTB/4 Daytona, an Enzo, and even Canadian hero Gilles Villeneuve's 312T3 Formula One racer. Many are maintained at a remote

aircraft hanger in Gloucestershire, England. His 1901 Panhard B1, which does a sprightly 0–40 in 36.4 seconds, sees active service in the London-Brighton rally every year.

Mason told automotive historian Nick Hall that he will spend whatever it takes to get a car he wants, then go to the ends of the earth to rebuild it from a bare chassis. What he won't do is buy a car unless he feels he'll get good value from it in terms of pleasurable track time.

With *Into the Red: 22 Classic Cars That Shaped a Century of Motor Sport*, a book co-authored by Mason and motorsport journalist Mark Hales, Mason's Bugattis, Alfas, Lotuses, Ferraris, Maseratis, and an awesome 1990 Porsche 962—to name just a few of the marques involved—were put through their paces on England's hallowed Silverstone circuit. The book was enhanced by a bound-in CD that captured the notes of the highly tuned engines.

"While the music is clearly more important . . . I've had great fun in cars. But when you go racing, you find things you don't find in music," Mason told *The Times*. "The people have a more level-headed approach, and tend to be more self-effacing. Also, when you're in the car, how well you do is down to you and you alone—no band, no management, no marketing."

RONI CARLISLE WITH JOHN SEABURY (PSYCHOTIC PINEAPPLE)

BUDDY MILES

CARMINE APPICE

BUN E. CARLOS (CHEAP TRICK)

JOEY KRAMER (AEROSMITH)

NEAR-DEATH BY FERRARI

IN THE SUMMER OF 1998, AEROSMITH DRUMMER JOEY KRAMER NARROWLY ESCAPED DEATH WHEN HIS FERRARI BURST INTO FLAMES AT A GAS STATION IN SCITUATE, MASSACHUSETTS.

"THE AUTOMATIC SHUT-OFF VALVE ON THE HOSE DIDN'T WORK, SO WHILE I WAS CONCENTRATING ON SOMETHING ELSE, GAS BEGAN TO OVERFLOW OUT OF THE CAR TO THE TUNE OF 14 GALLONS. WHEN IT POOLED UP UNDERNEATH THE VERY HOT CATALYTIC CONVERTER, THE FERRARI BASICALLY IGNITED. FLAMES ENGULFED THE CAR'S ENTIRE BODY WHILE I WAS INSIDE. IF I'D SAT THERE FOR ANOTHER EIGHT OR NINE SECONDS, I PROBABLY WOULDN'T BE HERE TALKING TO ANYONE RIGHT NOW."

AEROSMITH GUITARIST BRAD WHITFORD'S FIRST FERRARI

"I went to the Ferrari dealership in snooty Cohasset, Massachusetts, and they showed me a three-year-old Daytona, one of the finest production cars ever made. I said I'd take it. They looked at me, this long-haired hippie, and said, 'Sure, kid, right.'

"I was back the next day with a cashier's check for $22,000, which was a steal considering that for awhile in the '80s that car was worth half a million. It was really an oversize toy, though. You basically had to drive it in a big circle—round and round on the streets without stopping—because it was too valuable to park on the curb or leave in someone's driveway."

L.A. BOYZ

"Diamond Dave," otherwise known as the David Lee Roth, was Van Halen's flamboyant frontman when that So-Cal band knocked Led Zeppelin, Aerosmith, or The Rolling Stones (depending on who you're talking to) out of the top-band-in-the-world spot in the late '70s.

In early 1985, while still a Van Halen bandmember, Roth released a solo EP of offbeat standards, including a remake of The Beach Boys' "California Girls." Roth used the new power of rock & roll video to huge effect, whipping up for this song a potent mix of beautiful, barely-clothed models wrapped around his own larger-than-life personality—all connected to the extensively modified 1951 Mercury shown here on display at the Petersen Automotive Museum in Los Angeles.

Originally a sedan, the car was cut down into a convertible for the video. Other custom features include DeSoto grille teeth, shaved door handles, and a beautifully sculpted recess for the radio antenna. It was the hit of the 1985 MTV Video Music Awards.

"Hot for Teacher" was a Van Halen concert staple in 1984, as well as another memorable video spotlighting Roth. At the close of the video, a number of students jump in the supercharged 1932 Ford phaeton shown here (owned and customized by the late Tom McMullen). Roth, in the driver's seat, tears off down the street. For that scene, "Hot for Teacher" was scrawled on the sides and rear of the car in dripping red paint.

Travis Barker, another rock & roll personality living large on the L.A. stage (drummer for Blink 182 and other post-punk bands), was the co-star of his own MTV reality series, *Meet the Barkers*, with his actress (and 1995 Miss USA and December 2001 Playboy Playmate) wife, Shanna Moakler.

Barker is a lifelong admirer of Cadillacs, with his own fine collection stored in an oversize garage beneath his home. He stays involved with many music genres, including synth-rock, progressive R&B, and hip-hop, having worked on albums for the Black Eyed Peas and Pharrell Williams. He was featured in the opening sequence of the Dem Franchise Boys music video "Ridin' Rims" in 2006.

DAVID LEE ROTH

CALIFORNIA GIRLS MERCURY AT THE PETERSEN AUTOMOTIVE MUSEUM

TRAVIS BARKER AT HOME

HOT FOR TEACHER FORD PHAETON

SO I PUSHED IT UP TO 110,
THAT FLATHEAD MOTOR WAS ABOUT TO GIVE IN,
I CROSSED MY FINGERS AND PRAYED TO THE LORD,
DON'T LET ME DOWN YOU F***ED UP FORD.
REVEREND HORTON HEAT, FIVE-O FORD

REV HO 50

JIM HEATH'S (THE REVEREND HORTON HEAT) '50 FORD

GREGG ALLEN
SEARCHING FOR SIMPLICIT

CHRIS ISAAK'S CHEVY NOVA

JIMMIE VAUGHAN WITH '61 CADILLAC

CAR CUSTOMIZER LEE PRATT

ART YOU CAN DRIVE TO THE STORE

"The Ironic Twist" is both the nickname for Jimmie Vaughan's well-traveled, much-exhibited, and thoroughly acclaimed 1961 Cadillac custom, and a Grammy-nominated instrumental on Vaughan's 1998 album, *Out There*.

The world knows Vaughan as a much-celebrated blues-rock guitarist, the older brother of the late Stevie Ray Vaughan, and the founder, with Kim Wilson, of the Fabulous Thunderbirds, the quintessential Texas blues-rock band.

Vaughan lives *style*. His ethos defines his music-making and is echoed in the sharp vintage threads he wears and the classic cars he owns or has helped create. As he told a Fender guitars website biographer, "I don't play golf. Cars are my hobby. I was into cars as soon as I was old enough to walk. Cars are not just transportation—it's art you can drive to the store."

Vaughan's first custom restoration is a legend on the streets of Austin, Texas: a 1951 Chevy Fleetline that inspired Eric Clapton to take up hot

rodding. Vaughan next added a 1963 Buick Riviera and then the *piece de resistance*: Ironic Twist, his low-slung, pearl-based, lime green 1961 Cadillac Coupe DeVille that took first place at the 1999 Sacramento Autorama and second at the 50th Annual Grand National Roadster Show—the same year *Out There* (which also included a cover of Johnny "Guitar" Watson's "Motor Head Baby") took off.

Customizers Lee Pratt (pictured at his Los Angeles shop) and Texan Gary Howard both played significant roles in the development of Ironic Twist. As Coonan's pointed out in *The Rodder's Journal*, Vaughan envisioned the '61 incorporating performance characteristics of a '46 Cadillac Sedanette alongside the sweet and subtle styling touches borrowed from Italy's Pininfarina—no small endeavor.

THE BEST OF MOTOR CRUISIN'S
JUST THE JOY TO GET THERE

ZZ TOP. CHEVROLET

03950

TONY THACKER

BFG

Billy F Gibbons, frontman for ZZ Top, has one of the country's most eclectic collections of hot rods and customs, including the famous Eliminator, CadZZilla (pages 124–129), the '62 Chevy Slampala, the '50 Ford Kopperhed, the '36 Ford Mambo Coupe, the '48 Pontiac Leapin' Limo, and close to a hundred others in various stages of remake.

There's only one question. Why so many? Gibbons has famously told many an interviewer that hot rodding is limited only by one's imagination. "The creative process brings one's personality to a project" Gibbons told the U.K.'s *Telegraph* newspaper. "It's another way to stand out. It's part of showmanship. That, or lunacy, what with the exorbitant costs involved.

"I enjoy getting involved, but my own driving—and I'm a cruiser—is rather rarefied as an event, unfortunately. We get to spend a lot of time and effort assembling this legion of iron, and then find ourselves, as a band, trapped in either a room with no windows called a recording studio, or a tour bus. And I'm not about to drive *that*."

LOUD AND FAST

Meet Jeff Beck, guitar virtuoso, techno-wizard, and hands-on hot rod collector. Beck's passions are interchangeable. For example, the description of his current main axe, a well-worn, surf-green Jeff Beck–model Fender Stratocaster, reads like an ad for a well-loved ride: "Named *Little Richard*, its body shows signs of having been completely split apart in two places. At times all bashed up. Now, completely broken-in."

Whether we're talking about cars or studio and stage equipment, Beck enjoys modification and reinvention. In one instance, to accommodate his vigorous string bending, an unusual double-roller was devised for the top three strings of his signature guitar. "It stops that extraneous ringing noise you don't want, and helps the intonation as well," Beck explained in the manner of a man quite skilled under the hood. By listening hard to what others—such as car builder Roy Brizio, whose South San Francisco, California, shop is now linked to Beck's notoriety—help him dream up, and then executing on the inspiration, Beck's able to stay at the top of his craft.

BOTH PHOTOS STEVE COONAN / THE RODDER'S JOURNAL

Beck lives in a house built in 1591, approximately 40 miles south of London. On the estate is a carriage house, also centuries old, wherein he stores his car collection. He's been a passionate hot rodder for nearly four decades. As of this writing, he owns ten, six of which include steel '32 Fords, a steel '34 Ford roadster, and three fiberglass-bodied specials. According to *The Rodder's Journal*, "At any given point, Beck seems to have at least two of these vehicles in some stage of disassembly in the main work area of the carriage house, and it's where he spends a good deal of his waking hours."

ITSONLYROCKNROLL.COM

MUSIC HALL FRIDAY, NOV. 8
ONE SHOW - 8:30 P.M.
TICKETS ONLY $3.00 - $4.00 $5.00

From LONDON, ENGLAND !

THE JEFF BECK GROUP

SPECIAL GUEST STARS

THE MOVING SIDEWALKS

AND HOUSTON'S "PENDRAGON"

Beck picked up his first issue of *Rod & Custom* in 1953, and with guidance from an empathetic uncle has never been the same since. He quickly developed a fondness for *loud* and *fast*, as expressed in hot cars and hotter rock & roll. As a gunslinger, he's led world-touring bands and created cutting-edge music with Jimmy Page, Rod Stewart, Mick Jagger, Jimi Hendrix, and dozens of other luminaries. In addition to his fleet of guitars, one significant possession was a Chevy-powered T-bucket that put him in the hospital in 1969, preventing him from playing Woodstock; the car was later sold to John Bonham of Led Zeppelin.

In 1971, Beck attended the second annual Street Rod Nationals in Memphis, Tennessee, which set him on a relentless path to acquiring '32 Fords—roadsters, coupes, and more recently an Orange Crate–style sedan that's the apple of his eye. In 1973 he met Roy Brizio, beginning their decades-long friendship. Around 1974, obsessed with George Lucas' *American Graffiti*, he began a quest to clone the Milner five-window coupe.

Beck, who as a very young man hand-rubbed paint as an apprentice body man, over the decades has become a rather impressive welder, fabricator, and mechanic. As a guitarist, his goal continues to be "to make music of today, and not be too derivative."

THE JEFF BECK COLLECTION

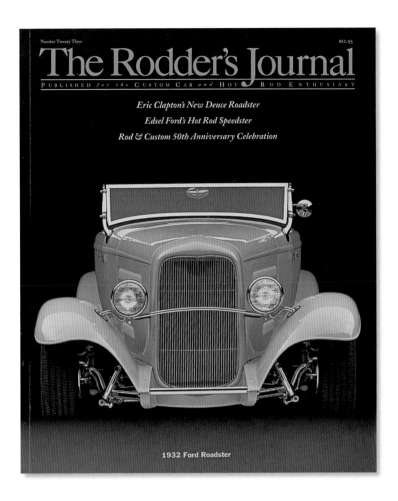

1932 Ford Roadster

ERIC CLAPTON'S '40 FORD

SLOWHAND'S FAST CARS

A surprise guest showed up at the Goodguys then-largest Rod & Custom Nationals event in Columbus, Ohio, on July 11, 2004, when guitarist Eric Clapton arrived with his two Roy Brizio–built hot rods. In a simple twist of fate, Clapton actually drew the 6,000th tag for the event upon entering his baby blue 1932 Ford roadster pictured here (licensed in England and driven on the roads around his home near the beach in the south of France), marking the first time in the event's seven-year history it attracted in excess of 6,000 cars. In Ohio, Clapton even did some treasure-hunting at the swap meet, looking for parts for his next project, a 1932 Ford Victoria coupe.

Clapton also brought his black, Thom Taylor–rendered 1940 Ford coupe—another Brizio creation, and his first hot rod (also shown here), which he uses as a daily driver when living at his part-time Southern California residence. Clapton's M.O., according to *The Rodder's Journal*, is to be true to his boyhood fantasies while squaring them up with his profound adult sense of aesthetics and the annoyingly restrictive realities of street driving.

Clapton is a longtime collector and driver of cars (Ferraris, in particular), and throughout his career has sung and played car-related blues, including "Crossroads," "Key to the Highway," and more recently "Riding with the King" (page 214). He only recently, however, has begun to acquire hot rods. Growing up in post–World War II England, Clapton was fascinated with most things American and was aware of hot rod culture by age nine. Then, as a teen, he became an avid model-kit builder. In the early 1990s, Clapton spent several days in Austin, Texas, driving around with guitarist Jimmie Vaughan of the Fabulous Thunderbirds. He became particularly enamored of Vaughan's Chevy Fleetline and with Vaughan as his guide, visited the 50th Annual Grand National Roadster Show in January 1999, where he began talking with Brizio.

Brizio also created the iridescent finish on Clapton's "Rainbow Rod" guitar, a circa 1996 Fender Stratocaster that realized $220,300 at a 2004 Christie's auction (the same charity-supporting event that moved Clapton's "Blackie"—the black-and-white circa 1956–1957 composite Fender Strat that served as Clapton's sole stage and studio guitar from 1970 to 1985— which sold at $959,500, becoming at the time the most expensive guitar ever sold at auction).

From his first tastes of success with the Yardbirds in 1964 and John Mayall's Bluesbreakers in 1966, through larger acclaim with Cream from 1966 to 1969, Blind Faith in 1969, and his own Derek and the Dominoes in 1970, Clapton has earned sufficiently to become a gentleman hobbyist. In the 1970s he was an enthusiastic supporter of the West Bromwich Albion football club. He took up fly fishing and cricket in the 1980s and has been quoted as saying, "I like to be good at everything I do, whether it's fishing, playing the guitar, or singing. But the only thing cricket has taught me is humility." As Jeff Beck would surely tell ol' Slowhand, maintaining a fleet of hot rods also will teach you patience and wise exercise of the checkbook.

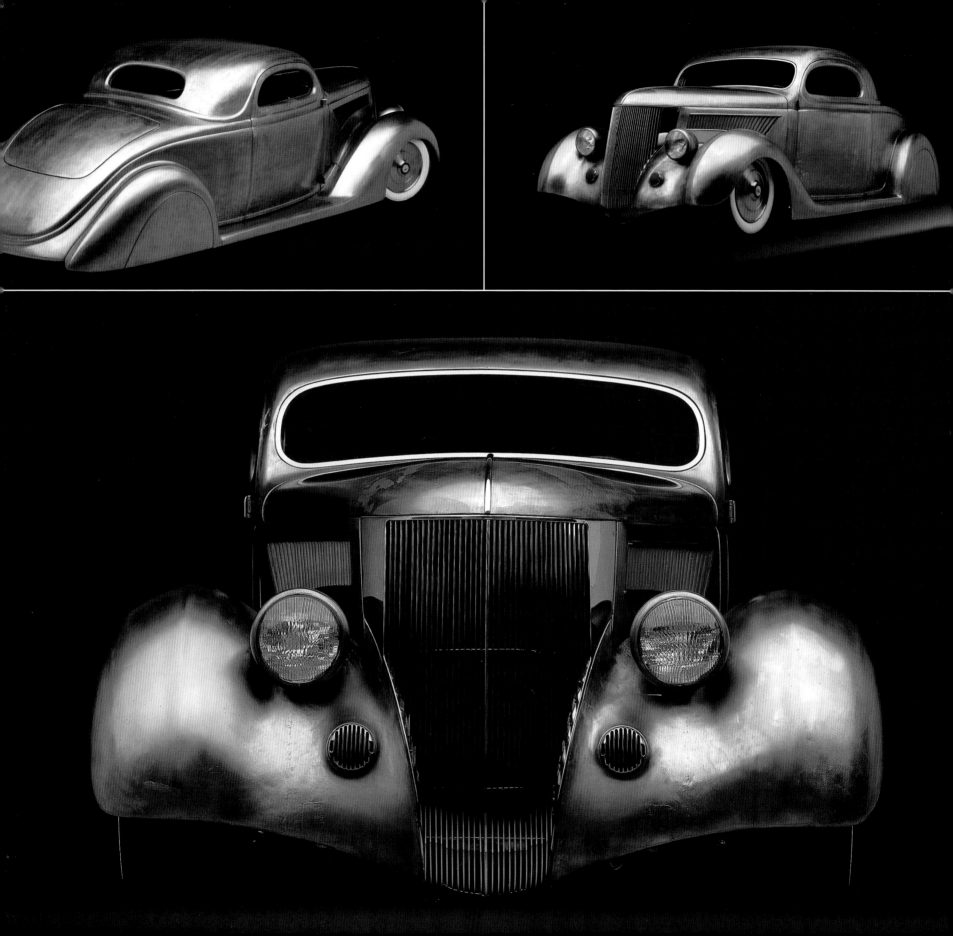

JAMES HETFIELD'S '52 OLDS

JAMES HETFIELD

STONE CUTTING

James Hetfield and Kirk Hammett, the dueling guitarists in Metallica, came to hot rodding relatively recently, with their band's success already well-established. Each had a fortunate encounter with a top car customizer: Robert Roling (Kustoms Royale, of Little Rock, Arkansas), whose shop did the bodywork, paint, and drivetrain assembly on Hetfield's '52 Oldsmobile sedan, and Cole Foster (Salinas Boyz Customs, of Salinas, California), who conceived the extensive design modifications for Hammett's '36 Ford three-window coupe—originally a five-window from Riverside in Southern California—and proceeded to reconstruct it from the ground up.

Hetfield, a member of the Beatniks car club, is a wrencher and the more active gearhead of the two (Hammett, being a San Francisco city kid, did not count driving among his early passions). Hetfield also owns *The Beast* (page 222) and counts as one of his personal accomplishments the restoration of a '55 Chevy Bel Air. Most recently, at the West Coast Kustoms 2006 Cruisin' Nationals in Paso Robles, California, he proudly debuted the rough-cut hot rod pictured here, almost by design the polar opposite of Hammett's elegant, hand-formed '36, with its confident, masculine fenders and triumphantly rolling roofline—a damn-near *musical* composition that has become one of Foster's signature pieces.

Subscribers to *The Rodder's Journal* have watched the three-window's progress with great interest. Publisher/photographer Steve Coonan's capture of the car in its initial bare-metal guise endures as an event unto itself. Foster described the creative process brought to bear on the '36 as "cutting away the stone until you see the statue."

Hammett told Coonan that he liked the sci-fi aspect of the '36 model-year Ford. "I always wanted a car that reminded me of the old Batmobiles—the ones from the comics of the '40s. I have the utmost faith in Cole's work . . . to be able to craft a vehicle that encompasses that mean, evil, art-deco kind of look . . . I'm so into that." Another special touch is the inside trunk enclosure, form-fitted for one of Hammett's black Strats, a '54.

By contrast, Hetfield's '52 Olds, engineered and finished as a daily driver, respects the tradition of the mild custom—albeit one that's super detailed. "For me, this car started a lot like some of my songs do," he told *The Rodder's Journal*. "I found a single element and kind of started from there. With songs, it might be a word or a phrase; with this car, it was the microphone shift knob."

BRENT RECTOR/FUEL CREATIVE GROUP (BOTTOM PHOTOS)

DEMON

TOM MORELLO AND HIS DODGE DEMON

In 1971, a new model was added to the Dodge Dart lineup. Sharing the Plymouth Duster body, Dodge's version was called the Demon and featured a different grille and rear taillight assembly than its Plymouth cousin. Dodge also used a devilish little cartoon character holding a pitchfork as a logo, although some religious groups publicly complained about it. Buyers looking for performance opted for the "Demon 340." Priced at $2,721, it was one of the most affordable muscle cars ever. Exactly 10,098 Dodge Demon 340s were produced in 1971.

The 108-inch wheelbase Demon 340 was powered by Chrysler's 275-horsepower, four-barrel 340 engine. A heavy-duty, three-speed manual transmission with floor shifter was standard. A Rallye suspension package also was included, along with a Rallye instrument cluster featuring a 150-mile-per-hour speedometer. On the outside, buyers had a choice of fourteen standard colors and four extra-cost, "High Impact" colors. Appearance options included dual hood scoops and a blacked-out hood treatment. A 6,000-rpm tachometer was also an option. In April 1971, Road Test *magazine established the following marks: 0–60 in 7.8 seconds; the quarter-mile in 14.56 seconds at 96 miles per hour; and an estimated top speed of 127 miles per hour.*

The 1971 Dodge Demon is an interesting footnote in rock & roll history. It gave the San Francisco Bay Area punk band The Demonics its name (pages 51, 188), and it became the prized ride of Tom Morello, guitarist in Audioslave (and previously Rage Against the Machine). A Harvard graduate committed to social change, Morello was named by Rolling Stone *magazine as one of the 100 greatest guitarists in rock history.*

Tom Morello: I stubbornly held onto the car that I moved to Los Angeles with in 1986, which was a beat-up maroon Chevy Astro van. It was the ride with which I headed west to seek my fortune, the touring vehicle for all of my formative-years rock bands and for Rage Against the Machine in the early days. I held onto it long after my bandmates had bought fancy SUVs and sports cars. Finally, there came a time when I realized the thing was about to disintegrate underneath me. Yet, I never had any desire to get something fancy, like a Mercedes or some high-end BMW.

I wanted a car that felt right. And, in thinking long and hard about it, it became very obvious to me what that was. When I was growing up my family had a six-cylinder, canary-yellow Dodge Demon, and I always loved that car. I wasn't a big fan or historian of muscle cars, but I remember thinking that it just looked *so cool.* And, as a kid, I got to choose the color—my mom let me—and that was great.

So, when the Astro van's days were numbered, I started looking around on the Internet and in trader magazines, and I discovered there was this whole little world of kick-ass muscle cars that were in the same vein as the car of my youth. I had to fly out to Denver to buy the thing, but I found it! A gen-u-wine 1971 Dodge Demon 340, with the essential four-barrel. I bought it for $7,500 cash. I intended to drive it back to California but my plans were thwarted by a snowstorm and I ended up shipping it back—pretty fortunate, actually, because when it arrived I discovered it had a bad fuel leak and I'd have probably made it about seventy miles out of Denver before the thing died and stranded me in one of the biggest white-outs ever.

I show the car often, but there's really nothing quite like the feeling I get driving the Demon through town. It has a factory sunroof, you know. I heard there were only eleven of those made! It's like having a specialty-built factory convertible from a really great and rare year. But the important thing—at least to my ears—is that it has that certain tough *rumbly sound*—a sound that only a '71 Demon made—and for that reason I've kept it pretty stock and true to its factory roots. That is, except for the stereo! 'Cause it's really all about pulling up to a club with AC/DC's "Back in Black" just shaking the foundations of Sunset Boulevard. A uniquely California expression of *This is what's happenin'*, you'd have to say.

Now, I'll tell you a story. As someone who's really more appreciative of form than function, I did have one moment of elemental revelation. It was on a night I was driving out for pancakes with a friend of mine. It probably was somewhere around midnight, in Hollywood. I was stopped at a light. In fact, I was the first car stopped at the light, and, out of nowhere, up pulls a Ford Mustang. Now I've never dragged a car in my life, never had a desire to turn a quarter-mile, never even had a *glimmer* of a thought about the possibility of street-racing a car. But the Mustang driver looked over at me, and I gave him the same look back. A stare down! Then the light turned green and I heard his tires squeal.

It was just basic instinct from that moment. I absolutely *slammed* the gas, and proceeded to kick the guy's ass six ways to Tuesday, for two blocks down. There was this huge adrenaline rush like I've never felt before or since. And I was thinking to myself, this is *so cool.* So *frickin' cool!* I didn't think I had it in me. Me and my Demon were thrust into the fire . . . and we came out on top. For those long, few seconds it beat anything I've ever done on stage. I mean, it was the quintessential American dream moment—you take your car by the balls and you blow somebody away—and I was living it!

— Tom Morello
interviewed by the author

WELL SETTLE DOWN I WON'T HESITATE
TO HIT THE HIGHWAY
BEFORE YOU LAY ME TO WASTE

AUDIOSLAVE, GETAWAY CAR

AUTHOR ACKNOWLEDGMENTS

The bookplate for the Englewood, New Jersey, public library, in my hometown, reads "Books are Friends." This book, too, has brought hundreds of friends together. I apologize if I've left anyone out—I know you're there.

The collaboration among author, editor, and book designer was a joy, even through the hardest parts of the slog. Dennis Pernu—yer one rockin' editor and a fine literary companion. I tip my hat. Brent Rector—on the occasion of your first big book, I'm grateful it's mine. Thank you—and all props to the masking tape! All three of us know rock & roll ain't no easy science—not to mention overlaying it with cars. But we hung in there.

Darrell Mayabb, you took me around my first hot rod shows, and now the cover of Rockin' is yours. Full circle indeed. Coop, the title page is one of your finest inkings. I'm honored by both yours and Darrell's presence.

Stanley Mouse, the fact that you trusted me with your archive speaks to our decades-long friendship. My gratitude is equally unending to these special artists and their inspiration: Mark Arminski, Ken Eberts, Eleanor Grosch, Gary Houston, Kathleen Judge, Mike Martin (Enginehouse 13), Greg Reinel (Stainboy), and Alison Zawacki.

I thank the publisher, MBI/Motorbooks/Voyageur Press, and its staff (Randy Roland, Michael Dregni, Mike Hejny, Dorothy Molstad, Becky Pagel, and Kou Lor) for their commitment, perseverance, delivery, and promotion of a high-quality product. Also, thanks to David Glossner, the book's associate producer, for scoring so many of the key appointments. The thousand-plus digital captures are the work of both photographer Sam Sargent and Kevin Wright (Cantoo Imaging).

Every photographer dug deep for me, and I thank Richard Aaron, Robert Alford, Casey Burns, Matt Byloos, John B. Cooke, James Haefner, David Jensen, Richard Koch, Frank Ockenfels III, Michael Marks, Tom Medley, Kendall Messick, Paul Natkin, Charles Peterson, Roger Ressmeyer, Rayon Richards, Tony Thacker, and Jack Vartoogian.

I also want to particularly cite the help given by these photographers: Joel Bernstein, Jay Blakesberg, Greg Bojorquez, Danny Clinch, Steve Coonan (The Rodder's Journal), Henry Diltz, Glen E. Friedman, Lynn Goldsmith, Zane Kesey, Jim Marshall, David Perry, Neal Preston, Jennifer Rector (FUEL Creative Group), Ken Regan, Pamela Springsteen, and Bruce Steinberg.

Big thanks go to the concert poster artists: Marco Almera; Courtney Callahan (Lucky Mule); Connie Collingsworth, Jim Madison (Print Mafia); Johnny Crap; Johnny "Thief" DiDonna; Ron Donovan, Chuck Sperry (Firehouse); Emek; Alan Forbes; Judy Gex, Jeff Wood (Drowning Creek Studios); Bruce Gossett (Black Cat Press); Grego; Justin Hampton; Matt Lane Harris (Standard Deluxe); Paul Imagine (Insurgent Arts); Frank Kozik; Lindsey Kuhn (Swamp); Dave Leamon; Matt Mastrud (Punchgut Studios); Billy Perkins (Penhead Studios); Dan Quarnstrom; Nick Rhodes; Jay Ryan (The Bird Machine); Todd Slater; and Jeral Tidwell. And, as well, to three heroes—Andy Brizio, Ed "Big Daddy" Roth, and Robert Williams—and to the everlasting memory of Rick Griffin.

Special thanks go to Ray and Sunny Anderson (Grooves); George and Joji Barris (Barris Kustom City); Big Slice (Snoop Dogg Productions); Bill Blackwell (Kid Rock); Roy Brizio; Pat Brown (Road Devils CC); Barbara Carr, Tammy Comstock (Bruce Springsteen/Jon Landau Management); Jack Chisenhall (Vintage Air); Lisa Connelly (Danny Clinch Photography); Lauren Crew, Ben Harris, Brian

Scotto, Datwon Thomas (RIDES magazine); Phil Cushway (Art Rock); Larry Erickson (CadZZilla archives, Ford Motor Company); ESPRIT/e.i.l.com; Ryan Friedlinghaus (West Coast Customs); Dell Furano (Signatures Network); Scott Glascoe, John McCord, Opal Nations (Downhome Music); John Goddard (Village Music); Jim Henke (Rock & Roll Hall of Fame and Museum); Debi Jacobson (L'Imagerie); Judy Johnson (Flipside Records); Paul Johnson (The Bel-Airs); Leslie Kendall (Petersen Automotive Museum); Paul Knotts, Jake Jundef (Funkmaster Flex); Michael Lederman (Crystal Enterprises); Sheryl Louis, Stacie Surabian (Chris Isaak/HKM); Virginia Lohle and Bill May (Starfile Agency); Larry Marion (ItsOnlyRockNRoll.com); Mike Martin (Heavy Rebel Weekender); Chris McCreary (The Rodder's Journal); Gary Meadors, Marc Meadors (Good Guys); Donald Miller (Jackson Browne); Melissa Moore (Corbis); Dennis Newhall (Sacramento Radio Museum); Michael Ochs (Michael Ochs Archives); Gregg Perloff (Another Planet); Niels Schroeter, Anita Strine (Brian Setzer/Surfdog); Stephen Schwartz (Getty); Susan Sherwood (Elvis Presley Enterprises, Inc.); Chris Strachwitz (Arhoolie Records vault); Marc Suroff (Hip Hop Immortals); Steve Tihanyi (General Motors Corporation); Shane Trulin (Mike Ness/Rebel Waltz); Joann Voss (Voss Transcriptions); Peggy Vezina (General Motors archive); Steve Wertheimer (Continental Club); and Ginger Wilbur (Barrett-Jackson Auctions).

Hundreds of books helped feed my fevered brain, but I wish to thank these authors in particular: John Blair and Stephen J. McPartland (The Illustrated Discography of Hot Rod Music); Jim Dawson and Steve Propes (What Was the First Rock 'N' Roll Record?); and Peter Guralnick and Ernst Jorgensen (Elvis Day By Day).

These friends helped keep me rockin': David Addington; Barry Ament and Coby Schultz (Phantom Shirts, Ames. Bros. Design); Hans Bennewitz, Steve Worth (FUEL Creative Group); Stephen Braitman; Jeff Chang; Lyle Ferbrache; Steve Gerstman; Paul Getchell; Elaina Gustat (NGI); Barry Herman; Alton Kelley; Andy Levison; Roger McNamee; Norman Ruth; Rick Steinberg (Quantum Color); Mike Taylor (Headline Entertainment); Tom Vickers; Kenny Wardell (SFPR); Scott Wolfman (Wolfman Productions)

Some of us never stop rockin', so let me thank, above and beyond: Curt Catallo (Catallo family archives); Brian Chidester and Domenic Priore (Dumb Angel Gazette archive); Dean Jeffries; Dennis King (Art of Modern Rock archive; D. King Gallery); Mike LaVella (Gearhead Magazine); Mickey McGowan (The Unknown Museum); Robin Roseaaen (All The King's Things); Steve Routhier; Chris and Paul Scharfman (Chic-a-Boom); Joel Selvin (Selvin Library); and Barry Wickham (GoldenGateRecords.com). Also, special acknowledgements to Herb Fishel for insight and access, and Frank Vacanti, my friend and compatriot in all things rock & roll.

My mom, librarian Jean Grushkin, and my dad, book designer Philip Grushkin, gave me the fire within to keep producing art books. My brother, Jonas, and my sister, Dena, both photographers, have been hugely encouraging. My kids, Jessica and Jordan, know what it's like to have a dad often driven by art and process.

Jane Eskilson, my wife, deserves all the credit for helping this book achieve its purpose. When we sit in front of the tube and watch the documentary, then, together, we'll lift a glass and smile.

— Paul Grushkin
Pinole, California

PERMISSION THANKS

The author and publisher wish to thank the following writers and publications for kindly sharing their talents in granting permission to reprint the following works:

"Driver Speaks Out About Singer Hank Williams' Last Ride," by Jim Tharpe, Milwaukee Journal Sentinel January 5, 2003; reprinted on page 70 by permission.

Selection from "How the Buffalo Springfield Met in Los Angeles," Joel Bernstein, from the liner notes to Buffalo Springfield: The Box Set, Rhino Records, 2003; reprinted on page 97 by permission of the author.

"Ker-chuuukk," from an internet blog by Kellum Johnson, 2006; reprinted on page 105 by permission.

"Levon Helm," interviewed by Robyn Flans, Modern Drummer, August 1984; reprinted on page 36 by permission of the author.

Selection from The Heart of Rock & Soul: The 1001 Greatest Singles Ever Made, by Dave Marsh, DaCapo Press (New York), 1989; reprinted on page 141 by permission of the author.

"25 For the Road," by Sheryl Crow, Vanity Fair; November 2005; reprinted on page 154 by permission of the author.

"APPRECIATIONS: Born to Run," by Helene Cooper, New York Times, November 18, 2005; reprinted on page 158 by permission.

"A Requiem for Real Wheels," by Robert R. Frump, Philadelphia Inquirer, 1981; reprinted on pages 164–165 and 175 by permission.

"Mustang Sally: The Man Behind the Song Provides a Ride Down Memory Lane," by Sally Tato, Detroit Free Press, August 16, 2002; reprinted on page 178 by permission.

"Kurt Is My Co-Pilot," by Touré, Rolling Stone, May 11, 2000; reprinted on page 184 by permission.

Selection from "Hootpage.com," by Mike Watt; reprinted on page 186 by permission.

"Spinning the Wheels of Snoop Dogg's Fleet," by Danny Hakim, New York Times, October 28, 2004; reprinted on page 218 by permission.

The author and publisher also wish to thank: Aimee Schecter (Wennermedia.com); Dan Short (Copyright Clearance Center); Robert Frump (author); Susan Dilanni (Philadelphia Inquirer); David Seitz (New York Times); Pam Wertheimer (W Management); Dave Marsh (author); Sally Tato and Jody Williams (Detroit Free Press); Kellum Johnson, RMT (author); and Robyn Flans (author).

Thanks also to: Sharon Agnello (Steel Toe Artist Management); Terry Bozzio; Lacey Chemsak (Sony/ATV Publishing); Larry Collins; Jay Farrar; Denise Ferri; Bryan Garofalo; Jim Heath; James Kirkhuff (Southern Crescent Publishing); Rich Mattson (SMA Records and Sparta Sound Studio); Tom Morello; Dave Newgarden (Manage This!); Rob Pollard; Alan Trist (Ice Nine Publishing); Tex Rubinowitz; Scott Weiss (Atomic Music Group).

Finally, special thanks to these individuals for providing the 78s, 45s, LPs, and CDs used throughout this book: Lyle Ferbrache; Mike LaVella (Gearhead Records); Mickey McGowan (The Unknown Museum); Joel Selvin (Selvin Library); Chris Strachwitz (Arhoolie Records); Frank Vacanti; and Barry Wickham (GoldenGateRecords.com).

INDEX

JOE BERNSTEIN

NEIL YOUNG DEPARTS THE SUNSET MARQUIS HOTEL GARAGE,

WEST HOLLYWOOD, CALIFORNIA, 1973.